EUROPE
IN FLAMES

The Stackpole Military History Series

**THE AMERICAN
CIVIL WAR**
Cavalry Raids of the Civil War
Ghost, Thunderbolt, and Wizard
Pickett's Charge
Witness to Gettysburg

WORLD WAR I
Doughboy War

WORLD WAR II
After D-Day
Airborne Combat
Armor Battles of the
    Waffen-SS, 1943–45
Armoured Guardsmen
Army of the West
Arnhem 1944
Australian Commandos
The B-24 in China
Backwater War
The Battle of Sicily
Battle of the Bulge, Vol. 1
Battle of the Bulge, Vol. 2
Beyond the Beachhead
Beyond Stalingrad
Blitzkrieg Unleashed
Blossoming Silk against the
    Rising Sun
Bodenplatte
The Brandenburger Commandos
The Brigade
Bringing the Thunder
The Canadian Army and the
    Normandy Campaign
Coast Watching in World War II
Colossal Cracks
Condor
A Dangerous Assignment
D-Day Bombers
D-Day Deception
D-Day to Berlin
Destination Normandy
Dive Bomber!
A Drop Too Many
Eagles of the Third Reich
The Early Battles of Eighth Army
Eastern Front Combat
Europe in Flames
Exit Rommel
Fist from the Sky
Flying American Combat Aircraft
    of World War II
For Europe
Forging the Thunderbolt
For the Homeland

Fortress France
The German Defeat in the East,
    1944–45
German Order of Battle, Vol. 1
German Order of Battle, Vol. 2
German Order of Battle, Vol. 3
The Germans in Normandy
Germany's Panzer Arm in
    World War II
GI Ingenuity
Goodwood
The Great Ships
Grenadiers
Hitler's Nemesis
Infantry Aces
In the Fire of the Eastern Front
Iron Arm
Iron Knights
Kampfgruppe Peiper at the Battle
    of the Bulge
The Key to the Bulge
Knight's Cross Panzers
Kursk
Luftwaffe Aces
Luftwaffe Fighter Ace
Luftwaffe Fighter-Bombers
    over Britain
Luftwaffe Fighters and Bombers
Massacre at Tobruk
Mechanized Juggernaut or
    Military Anachronism?
Messerschmitts over Sicily
Michael Wittmann, Vol. 1
Michael Wittmann, Vol. 2
Mountain Warriors
The Nazi Rocketeers
Night Flyer / Mosquito
    Pathfinder
No Holding Back
On the Canal
Operation Mercury
Packs On!
Panzer Aces
Panzer Aces II
Panzer Aces III
Panzer Commanders of the
    Western Front
Panzergrenadier Aces
Panzer Gunner
The Panzer Legions
Panzers in Normandy
Panzers in Winter
The Path to Blitzkrieg
Penalty Strike
Poland Betrayed
Red Road from Stalingrad

Red Star under the Baltic
Retreat to the Reich
Rommel's Desert Commanders
Rommel's Desert War
Rommel's Lieutenants
The Savage Sky
Ship-Busters
Siege of Küstrin, 1945
The Siegfried Line
A Soldier in the Cockpit
Soviet Blitzkrieg
Stalin's Keys to Victory
Surviving Bataan and Beyond
T-34 in Action
Tank Tactics
Tigers in the Mud
Triumphant Fox
The 12th SS, Vol. 1
The 12th SS, Vol. 2
Twilight of the Gods
Typhoon Attack
The War against Rommel's
    Supply Lines
War in the Aegean
Wolfpack Warriors
Zhukov at the Oder

**THE COLD WAR /
VIETNAM**
Cyclops in the Jungle
Expendable Warriors
Fighting in Vietnam
Flying American Combat
    Aircraft: The Cold War
Here There Are Tigers
Land with No Sun
MiGs over North Vietnam
Phantom Reflections
Street without Joy
Through the Valley

**WARS OF AFRICA AND
THE MIDDLE EAST**
Never-Ending Conflict
The Rhodesian War

**GENERAL MILITARY
HISTORY**
Carriers in Combat
Cavalry from Hoof to Track
Desert Battles
Guerrilla Warfare
Ranger Dawn
Sieges

EUROPE IN FLAMES

Understanding World War II

Edited by Harold J. Goldberg

STACKPOLE
BOOKS

Published in paperback in 2011 by
STACKPOLE BOOKS
5067 Ritter Road
Mechanicsburg, PA 17055
www.stackpolebooks.com

Originally published in hard cover as *Competing Voices from World War II in Europe: Fighting Words* by Greenwood Press, an imprint of ABC-CLIO, LLC, Santa Barbara, CA. Copyright © 2010 by Harold J. Goldberg. Paperback edition by arrangement with ABC-CLIO, LLC, Santa Barbara, CA. All rights reserved.

Cover design by Tracy Patterson

Printed in the United States of America

10 9 8 7 6 5 4 3 2 1

ISBN: 978-0-8117-0873-9 (paperback)

The Library of Congress has cataloged the hardcover edition as follows:

Competing voices from World War II in Europe: Fighting Words / Harold J. Goldberg, editor.
    p. cm. — (Fighting words)
  Includes bibliographical references and index.
  ISBN 978-1-84645-033-4 (hard copy : alk. paper)—ISBN 978-0-313-38514-8 (ebook)
 1. World War, 1939–1945—Sources. 2. World War, 1939–1945—Personal narratives.
I. Goldberg, Harold J.
  D735.C59 2010
  940.53—dc22   2009050073

For my family with love and pride:
Nancy, Alex, Emily, Jake, Simon, Zack, Alena

Contents

Preface

Competing Voices from World War II in Europe focuses on major
controversies and different national and ideological perspectives
intrinsic to the bitterness of that conflict. The editor has made several
decisions about the presentation of material to illuminate for the reader
the impact of the war on participants as well as bystanders. First, the
book is organized chronologically to replicate the way that people
experience historical events in real time. Each chapter therefore deals
with one year in the war. Within each chapter, however, a thematic
organization juxtaposes competing voices to clarify the arguments and
conflicts that persisted at that time. Second, the editor intentionally
avoids information from previously published texts or well-known
narratives. Although a few essential treaties or speeches have been
included where necessary, long excerpts from the speeches of wartime
leaders mostly have been omitted. The reader who wants to find all of
Franklin D. Roosevelt's or Winston Churchill's famous orations should
not look here, as that material is readily available elsewhere. Instead,
the editor presents individual and personal stories—of soldiers,
civilians, victims, and survivors. These testimonies are kept relatively
brief to allow the inclusion of a variety of perspectives from different
sides in the struggle. Many of these accounts cannot be found in any
other source on World War II. Finally, the editor includes newspaper
headlines from many of the European belligerent nations—allowing
those headlines to play the role of "fighting words," telling the reader
how various events, battles, and conflicts were viewed within each
country and from different perspectives.

The theme of competing voices runs throughout this book. In
Chapter One, dealing with the Munich Pact, we see that Adolf Hitler
considered the Treaty of Versailles a humiliation that had to be
challenged and reversed. Despite the Munich Pact's twenty-first-
century reputation as a surrender to aggression and encouragement of
dictatorship, western leaders at the time were willing to accommodate
Hitler's demands to prevent war. Those western leaders were hailed at
home for having saved the peace. Dissonant voices existed in the
Union of Soviet Socialist Republics (U.S.S.R.) and in Czechoslovakia
(and in a few western countries), but they were overwhelmed by
general praise for the Munich Pact.

In Chapter Two, we view the rush to war in 1939 and the ensuing
arguments about assigning blame. Angered by the Munich agreement,
Stalin accepted Hitler's offer of a nonaggression pact that allowed the
Soviet Union to avoid the approaching war. Western voices blamed
Stalin for his deal with Germany, while Stalin accused them of ignoring

his search for allies and security. Germany blamed England and Poland for refusing to sanction the transfer of Danzig and the Corridor to German control. Hitler continually mentioned the English guarantee to Poland as a cause of war, whereas England viewed that action as necessary to stop German aggression. Finally, when war did break out, each leader spoke to his people or legislature explaining and excusing his own actions—competing voices that assigned responsibility to the other in every case.

In Chapter Three, on 1940, German voices claimed self-defense against English and French aggression, while all western leaders again agreed that Germany was the aggressor. While the argument continued, the military situation quickly clarified with a series of decisive German victories. German diplomacy had been successful in neutralizing the U.S.S.R. and avoiding a two-front war, and as a result, German victories on the battlefield followed each other from Poland in 1939 to Scandinavia, Western Europe, and finally to France in 1940. Even among allies, explanations for the debacle on the western front produced competing interpretations: England saw the collapse of French morale, the French complained about British abandonment, and everyone noted betrayal by the king of Belgium. On the Axis side, what was accepted in the west as a tragedy was celebrated in Germany as evidence of Hitler's genius.

Chapter Four, covering 1941, includes two of the most important military events of the war—the German invasion of the U.S.S.R. and the Japanese attack on the United States. Fortunately for the west (in the long run), German ambition and greed led Hitler to abandon his policy of fighting on one front. In June, he sent the German army into the Soviet Union, and at the end of the year, he declared war on the United States. Hitler created the conditions for failure that he previously had avoided. He hoped to redress the balance somewhat by involving Spain in the war, but Franco continued to profess loyalty to fascism while evading any military commitment. This discordant voice remained frustrating for both Hitler and Benito Mussolini until the end of the war.

For the west, 1941 was also a crucial year, as a new alliance—Britain, the U.S.S.R., and the United States—came into existence. Although this alliance worked well militarily, competing voices among the Allies periodically threatened their delicate unity. They disagreed frequently over the timing of a second front in France. In addition, they never resolved their differing interpretations of the postwar fate of Poland. Nevertheless, they remained allies as long as Germany posed a threat to them—the common enemy provided the glue for their relationship. As soon as the Axis powers had been defeated, the competing voices of the Allies overwhelmed their cooperative voices and the alliance fell apart.

Chapter Five, covering 1942, explores at greater length the internal Allied struggle concerning the second-front issue. Stalin and his representatives pressed for a rapid invasion of France, while the United States and Britain argued that they were militarily unprepared for that commitment. While Stalin complained that the Soviet Union was fighting alone and needed German forces pulled away from the eastern front, the western allies tried to convince him that other actions—sending aid or fighting in North Africa—compensated for the lack of a second front in France. The alliance survived this disagreement, but the bitter feelings continued until June 1944.

Chapter Six reveals competing views and interpretations of events that continued into 1943. Hitler and Mussolini insisted again that Franco owed them military assistance to repay their help during the Spanish Civil War. Franco cited the same event, his civil war, to argue that Spain was not prepared for another military adventure. At the same time, the western powers celebrated the victory of the Battle of Stalingrad but still disagreed on the second-front issue. To placate Stalin on this demand, the United States and England focused attention on their battles in North Africa and Italy. In the propaganda war, Germany responded to Allied victories by warning all European countries of the threat of communism and claimed to be the continent's best hope against the Bolshevik danger.

Although most readers would expect unanimous support for the Allied invasion of France in June 1944, in Chapter Seven, we explore a variety of views—British, American, French, and German. The most positive voices were British and American, with French expression divided between the dwindling number of supporters of the collaborationist Vichy regime and supporters of General de Gaulle and the resistance. This chapter includes extensive testimony by French civilians in Normandy to provide perspectives on living through an invasion of that magnitude. Many German soldiers voiced a sense of nationalism, often pro-Germany, but also sometimes pro-Nazi, which explains the depth of German military resistance.

Chapter Eight, on 1945, again produces competing voices—even among the victorious Allies. Despite the Yalta Conference that included understandings on the future of Poland, Stalin on one side and Roosevelt and Churchill on the other argued about the meaning and implementation of those agreements even as they cooperated militarily. While the Allies congratulated each other on victory in May, they realized that their areas of competition would soon destroy the alliance that had defeated the Axis powers. The Cold War replaced the Grand Alliance.

Every chapter in this book deals with the German occupation. The Nazi racist agenda and the intentional war against civilians was a major

theme throughout the period and separated this war from previous
conflicts. The implementation of Nazi genocidal ideology was unique—
in the most horrific sense. Nevertheless, modern readers may be
surprised to discover German perspectives that defended the so-called
final solution, such as Heydrich establishing genocidal guidelines at the
Wannsee Conference or General Stroop describing the destruction of
the Warsaw Ghetto. The testimony of concentration camp survivors,
also included here, provides a stark "competing voice" to that of the
Nazi regime.

Many of these themes are tied together by the extensive use of
newspaper headlines from most of the major countries involved in the
war. Although often censored or controlled in wartime, headlines
conveyed news as well as the government's perspective on a battle or
developing situation. The political and military reality in every
European country determined the presentation of the news. In
countries with strong propaganda ministries, headlines reflected an
official position rather than objective reporting. Occasionally, a
newspaper that had been following a battle would drop all coverage
when military defeat contradicted official propaganda (Italian papers on
North Africa or German papers on the eastern front, for example). The
situation was somewhat different in the west, but again the reader had
to be alert to the specific historical moment and context. Belgian,
French, and Norwegian newspapers generally were anti-German until
1940 (with some exceptions); some of these papers ceased publication
after German occupation and some became collaborationist and
supported puppet regimes. Several of the collaborationist newspapers
stopped publishing in June 1944 and were reborn as pro-western after
the Allied invasion (occasionally with a new name). The modern reader
should pay attention to the headlines themselves and to the situation of
publication—whether a newspaper existed under the occupation, was
openly collaborationist, or had changed sides. These headlines and
their ideological perspectives are important historical documents. For
these reasons, this book integrates newspaper headlines with the
presentation of documents or testimonies—to examine different views
from a variety of countries and to encourage discussion of the
competing voices that continue to make World War II a fascinating
historical subject.

Acknowledgments

It is impossible to thank all of the people who assisted with this project, but many individuals deserve special mention. I would like to thank Simon Igel, a Holocaust survivor, who shared his story with me as well as with schools and groups around the world as part of his education mission. His remarkable journey from Poland to France and in and out of concentration camps is told too briefly in this book. Peter Reichmuth, whose family was involved in resistance to the Nazis, not only told me his family history but also gave me letters and other materials he had gathered over the years. He has been a caring and generous friend who continues to dedicate his work to uncovering the truth about the Nazi regime.

I am grateful for the warm reception I have received in France and especially in Cherbourg, primarily thanks to the efforts of my wife, Dr. Nancy Sloan Goldberg, a professor of French literature at Middle Tennessee State University. It is through her network of friends and colleagues that I have been able to accumulate extensive French contacts and sources. While in Cherbourg, I worked in the archives of the newspaper *La Presse de la Manche*, and the staff there opened their records on the Normandy invasion to me. Frédéric Patard, editor and publisher of special editions of *La Presse de la Manche* issued in 2004 for the sixtieth anniversary of D-Day, kindly granted permission for me to use their materials. In Cherbourg in 2006, I heard Madame Agnès Lelion speak about the testimonies she had collected about the war years, and after her presentation, she kindly gave me a copy of her book and permission to use it for my work. While in the area, I spent time in the departmental archives at St.-Lô and was treated with great courtesy.

Several local friends and connections have contributed to this work. Professor Scott Bates, who taught French and Film Studies at the University of the South for many years, sat down with me for five hours and told me much of his life story related to the war. I am only sorry that I was not able to include more of his fascinating perspective. Another colleague, Professor Scott Torreano, informed me that his father served in the war in Italy and elsewhere, and John Torreano graciously consented to an interview for this book. One of my former students, Michael Lelchitski, questioned his grandparents on my behalf about their experiences in Leningrad during the war. A good friend, Irina Willis, born and raised in the Soviet Union, interviewed her father and established a connection with her Russian friends for this book as well.

The inclusion of numerous newspaper headlines from many parts of
Europe is a unique feature of this book that allows the reader to
confront "competing voices" from various countries. The assistance
and expertise needed to translate the many languages included here
came from relatives, colleagues, friends, and even generous strangers.
When my own French or Russian quickly reached its limits, Professors
Nancy Sloan Goldberg (French) and Mark Preslar (Russian) helped
complete those translations. Another friend and colleague, Professor
Thomas Spaccarelli, as well as Sewanee student Erin Smyth, worked
on the Italian newspapers. Still another colleague, Professor Karen Yu,
volunteered her friend Ulf Ahlstrom, who translated a newspaper from
Helsinki that was printed in old Swedish. Joseph Farber, a student at
the School of Theology in Sewanee, also assisted with that newspaper.
My son Zachary Goldberg and his wife Alena Švejdová translated both
German and Czech sources. Dr. Paul Glenn, who teaches in the
Department of Business Administration at Stord/Haugesund University
College in Norway, kindly agreed to translate the Norwegian
newspaper. Elzbieta Bule volunteered to translate the Polish headlines
and suffered through my handwritten copies without complaint. For all
of these kind volunteers and helpers, I again express my gratitude and
thanks.

Many other individuals gave me permission to use the testimonies
included here: Elena Zvereva who has collected many of her family
stories and is the great granddaughter of Feodor Ivanov, Catherine
Cilfone McCarthy who allowed me to use the oral history of her father
Charles J. Cilfone, Robert Chow for the testimony of his father
Raymond Chow, Warren Hirt and his daughter Joan Hirt, Carol
Snyder for her father Keith Campbell, Cindy Brashler for her father
John Misa, Cynthia Blaine for her father Oliver Stork, Patrick
Donoghue for his father Michael John Donoghue, Willard Reese, Eric
Strauss, LeRoy "Whitey" Schaller, Hubert Berkhout of the Nederlands
Instituut voor Oorlogsdocumentatie, Michlean Amir at the U.S.
Holocaust Memorial Museum, and David Bell at the Imperial War
Museum.

Oral history collections on various Web sites have been an important
source for this book. I especially want to thank the creators of two
excellent Web sites: Artem Drabkin, whose site I Remember provided
several Russian testimonies, and Derrick Marczynski, whose site the
Electronic Museum is a source for Polish testimony. For accounts
related to the Holocaust, I thank John Menszer, creator of Holocaust
Survivors, and Edward Serotta of Centropa/The Central Europe
Center for Research and Documentation. Other Web sites that were
extremely useful and allowed me to use their material include the
following: William Fray at the Avalon Project of Yale University Law

School, Shaun Illingworth at the Rutgers Oral History Project, Paul Vyšný from the University of St. Andrews for his Crisis over Czechoslovakia Web site, and Maria Sutherland for permission to use her Web site on the Dutch Underground.

I have worked at various libraries collecting testimonies and thank all of the staff members and professional archivists who assisted me. These locations include the Library of Congress (the Veterans History Project, the European Reading Room, and the Newspaper and Current Periodical Reading Room), the National Archives, and the U.S. Holocaust Museum, Washington, D.C.; the Bibliothèque de Documentation Internationale Contemporaine, Nanterre; Bibliothèque Nationale, Paris; Bibliothèque Royale, Brussels; Imperial War Museum, London; and the Nederlands Instituut voor Oorlogsdocumentatie (Netherlands Institute for War Documentation), Amsterdam.

In addition, I express my gratitude to Professor G. Kurt Piehler of the Center for the Study of War and Society (Veterans Oral History Project) at the University of Tennessee–Knoxville for his advice, the Appalachian College Association, and the Sabbatical Leaves Committee and the Research Grants Committee of Sewanee: The University of the South.

I also thank the editor of this series on competing voices, J. Michael Francis, in the Department of History at the University of North Florida. My working relationship with him has been entirely pleasant and productive.

Introduction

This study of *Fighting Words: Competing Voices from World War II in Europe* demonstrates that there were almost as many perspectives on that war as there were countries involved in fighting it. Inhabitants of Britain, Czechoslovakia, France, and Poland viewed Germany as the aggressor; eventually the Soviet Union and the United States (both neutral at first) would share that view. Germany perceived the war in a completely different light—first as necessary to redress the injustices imposed by the Treaty of Versailles and then as a war of self-defense in response to aggression perpetrated by all of the nations that viewed Germany as the aggressor. Where the west saw German aggression, Germany claimed Czech, English, French, or Polish aggression. Using this perspective and official propaganda, the Nazi government launched preemptive strikes against enemies who supposedly were mistreating German civilians and planning offensive action against Germany. Objective study rejects the German government's arguments and sees them as part of Adolf Hitler's long-held plan to avenge the Great War, to establish Germany as the dominant power in the world, and to fulfill his racist agenda.

For the Axis (Germany, Italy, and others) and the Allies (Britain, France, and others), a strategic issue that dominated all military planning was the question of fighting a one- or two-front war. In terms of the most important Axis nation, German leaders believed that they could win any contest if their army fought on one front at a time. The German military had accepted this concept at least since the Franco-Prussian War (1870–1871) when Germany won a decisive victory over France. The French too learned the lesson, but in reverse. France knew that it had to force Germany to fight on two fronts simultaneously, and the French government moved in the 1890s to create an alliance with Russia to compel Germany to split its forces in the future.

When war broke out in 1914, the Germans hoped to achieve a quick victory over France (a one-front war) and then deal with Russia alone. Facing a possible repeat of the 1870 debacle, the French appealed to the Russian government for immediate relief, and poorly prepared Russian forces sacrificed tens of thousands of men in an attack in East Prussia that nevertheless achieved the goal of relieving pressure on the western front. When neither side was able to move forward or push the other back in Belgium and northern France, the only choice was to turn temporary defenses into long-term shelters and prepare for a prolonged engagement. The result was trench warfare. Most important, the Franco-Russian alliance forced Germany into the two-front engagement that saved France in the short-term, prolonged the war, and wore down the German military in the long-term.

Hitler understood the lessons of World War I, as did the French. Although he believed that Germany lost World War I because of betrayal, he also was convinced that his country could defeat any single enemy it faced. Hitler's diplomacy of the 1930s and early 1940s applied the principle well—he isolated his opponents and was able to fight them individually in 1939 and 1940. Throughout the early years of the war, this strategic concept allowed Germany to mass its armed forces on a single front and made the Nazi state unstoppable. Wherever Germany committed its military to one front at a time, it enjoyed success and victory. Nevertheless, in 1941 Hitler's success, ambition, and racial theories led him to ignore the military principle that had been the basis of his triumphs; he ordered an invasion of the Union of Soviet Socialist Republics (U.S.S.R.), and the result was disastrous for Germany.

The Allies were aware of this principle both before and during the war, and their application of this same strategic concept was intended to force Germany to fight simultaneously on two fronts. Nevertheless, as war approached in 1938 and 1939, western diplomacy failed the test and allowed the U.S.S.R. to succumb to German enticements. The result was devastating for the Allied powers—Czechoslovakia was betrayed, Poland was overrun, and finally all of continental Western Europe was defeated and occupied. Only after 1941, when Germany abandoned its guiding principle of the previous two years and the western allies were able to engage Germany in a two-front war, did the military situation change dramatically; as a result, Germany ultimately was crushed.

Hitler's desire for another war was clear even before he attained power in 1933. In *Mein Kampf*, as well as in his speeches, he outlined his plan to repudiate the provisions of the Treaty of Versailles. Rather than negotiating revisions to the treaty, he demonstrated his contempt and nonrecognition of the treaty by intentionally and unilaterally violating its articles. Throughout the 1930s, he moved methodically toward achieving his goal in a series of diplomatic and military actions that included rearmament, reoccupation of the Rhineland, and Anschluss with Austria.

In 1935, Hitler undertook the first significant challenge to the treaty system and announced that Germany would rearm and build an air force. Hitler was not the only European leader who understood the lessons of the Great War, and unilateral German rearmament forced a diplomatic response by France and the U.S.S.R. The French government moved to recreate its pre-1914 alliance with Russia to force the German army to plan for a two-front war. But times had changed, and while France and Russia understood the military principle essential to their mutual survival, neither nation trusted the other. By 1935, Russia had become the Soviet Union, a less trustworthy ally than the Russia of 1914. For a variety of reasons, including Communist ideology and the purges of the Soviet officer corps in 1937, the French government and military did not trust Joseph Stalin. At the same time, France was divided politically and was governed by a series of weak coalition governments. The Franco-Soviet alliance was born out of necessity but without any genuine enthusiasm or trust. Nevertheless, the alliance gave each side a needed ally, not with the goal of actually fighting Germany together but rather with the hope of frightening Hitler—a Franco-Soviet bluff intended to warn Germany that it might have to fight simultaneously France and the U.S.S.R.

Hitler understood the stakes, and he systematically outmaneuvered his political counterparts on the continent as he led Europe toward its disastrous fate. He followed his rearmament announcement with other challenges—in the Rhineland and in Austria, and in all cases, weak or inept western diplomacy allowed him to achieve his goals. By 1938, an even more confident German leader escalated his demands to include the Sudetenland in Czechoslovakia, and the subsequent negotiations played right into his hands. Despite the treaty relationship that tied Czechoslovakia, France, and Russia together, the French government did not attempt to include Soviet (or Czech) representatives in the talks at Munich. In September 1938, Hitler won two victories. He was awarded the Sudetenland by England, France, and Italy in their attempt to avoid war; more important, the Franco-Soviet alliance was shattered.

When British Prime Minister Neville Chamberlain announced "peace for our time" on September 30, 1938, he did not realize that Europe was exactly eleven months from general war. Historians have judged his policy of appeasement, intended to reach accommodation through reasonable concessions to Hitler, as surrender to aggression. Well-intentioned as he was, Chamberlain believed that Hitler had limited goals that could be satisfied through negotiation and compromise. The Sudetenland seemed a small price to pay for a general European peace.

Chamberlain and the French leader Premier Edouard Daladier misunderstood the larger and long-term consequences of their expedient bargain that traded a part of Czechoslovakia for Hitler's promise of good behavior. Leaving aside the moral question of four major powers (Britain, France, Germany, Italy) deciding the fate of a smaller nation against the wishes of that country's government, Chamberlain, Daladier, Hitler, and Benito Mussolini set into motion an inevitable rush to war. Of the four, only Hitler looked forward to the test of wills and, from his perspective, a contest that primarily would be a racial war demonstrating the superiority of the Aryan people of Germany. And only Hitler understood definitively that Stalin held the key to German victory and western defeat.

Once Stalin had been detached from his alliance with France, Hitler recognized the opportunity and moved to turn Russia's isolation to his strategic advantage. If Hitler could win Stalin to his side, the German dictator would have his one-front war with France and almost certain victory. Stalin played along for his own reasons. Angered by the snub at Munich and suspecting that war was on the horizon, the Soviet ruler signaled his willingness to talk with Germany by firing his Foreign Minister M. Litvinov, associated with the French alliance and the policy of collective security, and replaced him with V. Molotov. From that moment on, it was relatively easy for Hitler to neutralize the willing Stalin. Unlike his rivals, Hitler could offer incentives that would allow the Soviet dictator to watch the coming war from the sidelines. Visiting Moscow in August 1939 for just this purpose, German Foreign Minister Ribbentrop offered Stalin and Molotov territory in Eastern Europe in exchange for Soviet neutrality in the impending conflict. A pact was signed, and both dictators happily assessed their diplomatic and military triumph. Stalin could stay out of the war as the capitalist states destroyed each other. Hitler would have his one-front war and victory first in Poland and then in the west.

The situation unfolded exactly as planned by the aggressors. At the end of August, Germany claimed that Polish forces were mistreating German citizens and attacking along the border. The German army invaded Poland in supposed self-defense, moving quickly against the outgunned Polish military. Despite their inability to prevent or thwart the German invasion, the western powers presented Germany with an ultimatum for cessation of hostilities that Germany ignored, thereby triggering the official state of war between Germany and the west. War was declared on September 3, but it was too late for Poland. Without a contiguous border with Poland and still in the process of rearming, England and France were powerless to stop the inevitable German conquest. Poland was overrun while the Russians, under the terms of their nonaggression pact signed only weeks earlier, moved in and occupied eastern Poland. Having neutralized Russia, Hitler won his expected victory—fighting on one front against one country without the need to divide his forces.

After Poland's defeat and occupation first by German and then Soviet forces, the ensuing winter months of late 1939 and early 1940 saw all sides preparing for an expected spring confrontation; only the Soviet Union engaged in combat from November through February in a difficult but ultimately successful war against Finland. The Finns, like the Poles a few months earlier, fought bravely against a much larger adversary. As in Poland, the outcome in Finland was inevitable, and eventually the Finnish government had to accept a peace treaty that adjusted the border in Russia's favor. This so-called Winter War was a sideshow for most of Europe, as the major powers armed and mobilized for the anticipated battles ahead.

Once again, Hitler prepared well. With Russia committed to noninvolvement, the German army could mass its forces on one front. The spring offensive of 1940 remains one of the most impressive military campaigns in history. In April, the German army moved through Denmark and into Norway. On May 10, the German attack drove through the Ardennes Forest, taking French forces by surprise and outflanking the forts along the Maginot Line. Within a few days, German panzer units crossed the Meuse River and broke through French defenses at the city of Sedan. Only five days after the German attack started, a despondent French Premier Paul Reynaud told British Prime Minister Winston Churchill, "We have been defeated. We are beaten; we have lost the battle."[1] Reynaud shuffled his cabinet, bringing World War I hero Marshal Pétain into the government. A politically divided nation that relied on an aging and ineffective military establishment, France collapsed more quickly than either friends or enemies had expected.

Coordinated with successful attacks against the Benelux countries, the German army won a series of brilliant victories. Toward the end of May, the military situation had deteriorated further: Belgium surrendered, and British General Lord Gort gave the order for the Allied evacuation at Dunkirk (Operation Dynamo). While Belgian, British, French, and other troops scrambled to escape the continent, Churchill vowed to fight on: "we shall fight on the beaches, we shall fight on the landing grounds, we shall fight in the fields and in the streets, we shall fight in the hills; we shall never surrender."[2]

Despite Churchill's promise to resist, Germany's success continued unabated. Norway fell by June 10, the same day that Italy entered the war against England and France as Mussolini calculated the opportunity to share in the spoils of certain Axis victory. By the middle of the month, the French government abandoned Paris, and a week later, on the anniversary of the signing of the Treaty of Versailles, France formally surrendered to Germany. The eighty-four year old Marshal Pétain took control of a compliant, authoritarian, and truncated French state with its capital at Vichy. Pétain's slogan for transforming France into a stable and disciplined ally had a Germanic resonance: "Work, Family, Fatherland." By mid-1940, only two leaders offered any hope in this otherwise bleak picture: British Prime

Minister Churchill refused to consider a deal with Hitler and French
General Charles de Gaulle rejected Pétain's leadership of France. The
Vichy government declared de Gaulle an enemy of the state and
sentenced him to death in absentia.

Hitler's plan had succeeded. By neutralizing Russia and
fighting a one-front war in the west, the German army had achieved
the spectacular victory that had eluded it in the Great War. Only
England remained unconquered, and Churchill's rhetorical skills
played a major role in shoring up public confidence in Britain's ability
to continue the struggle alone. Throughout the summer and fall of
1940, the German air force, the Luftwaffe, carried out a bombing
campaign against its only remaining adversary. While Hitler intended
to spread terror and fear throughout the United Kingdom, this Battle
of Britain strengthened England's determination to fight. On August 20,
1940, the prime minister thanked members of the Royal
Air Force for their contributions to the defense of the nation:
"Never in the field of human conflict was so much owed by
so many to so few."[3]

Despite England's refusal to surrender, the military situation had
resolved itself in Germany's favor. Now Europe faced a new menace—
German domination. Nazi racial ideology meant that this would not be
a normal occupation, concerned with the annexation of enemy territory
or the collection of monetary compensation in exchange for
withdrawal. Rather, this occupation concerned itself with the collection
of souls—supposed enemies of the Aryan race—primarily Jews but
eventually including many Slavs, gypsies, intellectuals, Communists,
and others deemed a threat to racial purity or German hegemony.
Germany's war against civilians started immediately after the conquest
of Poland and eventually engulfed all of Europe.

For the Nazis, the inhabitants of occupied countries did not have to
commit any crime or hold any particular political belief or live on any
valuable territory—they had only to be born a member of an ethnic or
national or religious group on the target list. While civilians had always
suffered as casualties of wars and the world had witnessed atrocities
before, the Germans perpetrated a war against civilians on an
unprecedented scale in both the quantity and the quality of its cruelty.
Later, the Germans introduced industrial age horrors and used
technologically advanced techniques that included concentration camps
and assembly-line gassing to speed up their war against
noncombatants. After the war, survivors from every country testified to
the sadistic nature of the German camp system—the killing of civilians
elevated to a new level of intentionality and scale. The extermination of
millions of ordinary people was carried out with an intensity and level
of brutality not seen before—and provided World War II with one of

its unique features, introducing the concepts of "war crimes" and "crimes against humanity" into international law. The so-called final solution revealed this war's most singular theme—the deliberate war against civilians.

For military, ideological, and racial reasons, Hitler broke his pact with Stalin and ordered his army to turn east in the summer of 1941. Although England remained in the war, it did not possess the military capability to invade the continent or threaten German control of Western Europe. Fighting in North Africa was important for strategic reasons but not considered a major front, and the United States still remained officially neutral. By attacking the Soviet Union in June 1941, Hitler could synthesize the major themes of the war: (1) the military principle of fighting a one-front war against the U.S.S.R. combined with the war on civilians and (2) the capture and destruction of inferior races and peoples—all as part of one operation. In addition to these objectives, Hitler would control the rest of Europe and destroy the Communist state. His plan almost succeeded.

Preparations for Operation Barbarossa continued throughout the spring of 1941. Hitler knew that the Soviet Union had a huge army and occupied the world's largest territory. In anticipation of what would be his crowning achievement, Hitler accumulated the biggest invasion force in history—more than 3 million men—and planned a three-pronged invasion of the Soviet Union. Divided into Army Group North, Center, and South, German units moved on June 22, 1941. In general, targets included Leningrad in the north, Moscow in the center, and food and oil in the south. At first, German troops advanced quickly, destroying or capturing Soviet forces in large numbers. Stalin issued unrealistic orders that seemed divorced from the situation at the front—he opposed any strategic retreats and even ordered Red Army attacks in impossible military situations. The results were disastrous for the U.S.S.R. during the first months of the invasion.

Despite losing most of the early battles and the apparent catastrophe suffered by Soviet forces, several elements worked in Stalin's favor. Soviet attacks as well as defensive stances wore down German units, depleted German equipment, and in some cases meant the loss of the best front-line German forces. Second, Soviet resistance slowed the German advance and delayed the anticipated German victory until the colder months when Soviet forces would have the advantage. Finally, as it lost tanks and other supplies, the German army began to feel the effects of the logistical nightmare that came with occupying such a vast country. Although a quick victory remained Hitler's best hope, drawing out the conflict played to the advantage of the U.S.S.R.

The Soviet population suffered horribly from direct military engagement as well as Nazi policies that included mass murder and starvation of the local inhabitants. The invasion placed millions of Jews and other targeted groups under German control. At first, the Germans used killing squads (*Einsatzgruppen*) attached to their armed forces as they moved into occupied territory to eliminate the civilian enemy. Massacres occurred throughout Soviet territory, including the infamous slaughter of more than 30,000 Jews at Babi Yar near Kiev in September 1941. The Nazis targeted other social, ethnic, and religious groups as well, including (but not limited to) Communists, intellectuals, and much of the Slavic population in general. One of the three invading German armies raced toward Leningrad, and while the Nazis never occupied the city, the city's inhabitants endured a cruel fate that included siege and starvation. The Soviet army turned the tide against the Germans only after terrible sacrifice—late in 1941 at Moscow, in 1943 at Stalingrad, and finally in 1944 with the liberation of Leningrad.

By October 1941, the Germans were approaching the Soviet capital, but Red Army resistance and bad weather slowed the German offensive. In November, the Germans moved closer to their target, and in early December, they were only fifteen miles from the Kremlin. Nevertheless, the advantage shifted to the Soviet side, as temperatures plummeted and rain turned to snow. At about the same time, Soviet intelligence reported that Japan would continue its aggression toward the south, not against the U.S.S.R., and Stalin was able to mobilize Siberian reserves for the defense of Moscow. The Germans never captured the city, and the battle for Moscow was the first time since 1939 that the German army had not achieved its goal.

Soviet intelligence was accurate—Japan attacked the United States on December 7. At this point Hitler committed another blunder (attacking the U.S.S.R. was his most serious) by declaring war on the United States. His long and rambling speech to the *Reichstag* on this subject provided insight into Hitler's mental perspective—he verbally attacked President Franklin Roosevelt as a man of "limited intelligence," a hypocrite as a Christian, and as part of an "Anglo-Saxon-Jewish-Capitalist World" in alliance with the Bolsheviks. Hitler did not respect the United States, as it represented the values of racial (despite segregation) and religious and political tolerance he rejected.

Hitler's invasion of the U.S.S.R. in June and his declaration of war against the United States in December violated the military principle that had taken Germany to the brink of victory in Europe. His unlimited ambition led him to abandon the rule that had been so successful—to fight on one front at a time. The new American-British-Soviet alliance created multiple fronts for Germany and doomed Germany to defeat. In the long run, the Axis powers could not compete with the combined productive capacity and military potential of the Allies. Germany and Italy could not sustain simultaneous military fronts in North Africa, Italy, France, and the U.S.S.R.

Beginning in June 1941 and continuing throughout 1942 and 1943, the subject of the timing for opening a second front in France dominated Allied conversations. The U.S.S.R. anticipated a quick American-British commitment to an invasion of Western Europe to relieve pressure on the Red Army. In other words, England and the United States were supposed to improvise an invasion of France to save the U.S.S.R.—applying the same principle (in reverse) that Russia employed in 1914 to assist France in World War I. The Soviet Union and its diplomats insisted that this military action take place sooner rather than later, with Foreign Minister Molotov visiting London and Washington during 1942 to persuade the Allies that they should invade the continent immediately. At one point, Molotov thought that he had received a promise to this effect, only to be told later that the Allies were not ready for a military offensive on the scale necessary to succeed. The argument continued into 1943, with Stalin showing his displeasure with Anglo-American inaction by removing Litvinov as Soviet ambassador to Washington, ironically the foreign minister who had been fired in 1939 to indicate Stalin's disgust with the Munich Pact and the collapse of collective security.

Despite his impatience with the lack of a second front in Europe, Stalin was more complimentary toward the Allies throughout 1943. The reasons were varied: an increasing flow of supplies from the United States to the U.S.S.R., the invasion of North Africa at the end of 1942 and Allied victories there, and finally the invasion of Sicily and Italy in 1943. The latter event led to the overthrow of the Mussolini government and a formal change for Italy from enemy to ally. Despite this positive sign, the fighting in Italy continued and ranked among the most difficult in the entire war. The German army committed itself to Italy's defense and made the Allies pay for every foot of territory they liberated.

In addition to the defeat of Italy, the Allies enjoyed several diplomatic and military successes in 1943. At the beginning of the year, Roosevelt and Churchill met at Casablanca and issued the famous pronouncement calling for Germany's "unconditional surrender." In February, the Battle of Stalingrad ended with a decisive victory for the U.S.S.R. Not only were thousands of German soldiers killed or captured, but also, to Hitler's rage, German generals surrendered to the Russians in the final debacle. This battle has been called the turning point in the war in Europe for good reasons (although the Battle of Moscow has been underrated in this area)—from February 1943 onward, German forces in the U.S.S.R. were on the defensive rather than moving forward. Terrible battles remained—at Kursk in the summer of 1943 and subsequently throughout the Ukraine and Belorussia—but the ultimate fate of the German army in the Soviet Union had been decided in Stalin's favor. At the end of the year, Stalin agreed to meet in Iran's capital to discuss the timing of a second front in France. The Tehran Conference brought Stalin, Roosevelt, and Churchill together for the first time. The "big three" made a firm commitment to the invasion of Normandy in the spring of 1944.

The question of the second front in France remains one of the controversial subjects in discussions of the war—especially from a Soviet perspective that asked whether the western powers were content to allow Soviet forces to bear the brunt of the German onslaught and suffer enormous casualties, whether the western powers were hoping that the German invasion would weaken the Communist regime in the U.S.S.R., and finally whether the western powers could have invaded sooner.

In 1942, as Soviet pressure for a second front increased, the British and Americans realized that much preliminary work was needed to ensure success and, furthermore, that a premature invasion with the risk of failure could set back the Allied cause indefinitely. While careful not to offend Stalin, the Allies had many reasons for postponing the invasion of France until 1944.

In early 1942, the United States had just entered the war and was immediately concerned with Japan. With the apparent crippling of its fleet at Pearl Harbor, the United States had to focus on the retooling of factories, building of ships, and training of recruits before it would be prepared to confront the German army. American troops were not battle tested and were not ready for a massive military action such as the invasion of France. Their early difficulties in North Africa suggest that a hurried or improvised invasion of France might have been a disaster. American forces learned important lessons in North Africa, in Sicily, and in Italy. They were much better prepared militarily by the spring of 1944.

In addition, the logistical problems involved in moving huge numbers of men and supplies from the United States to England had not been solved at the time that Molotov, speaking for Stalin, insisted on an invasion in 1942. Only toward the end of 1943 could the western powers claim victory in the Battle of the Atlantic—depleting the German submarine force and thereby allowing Allied convoys a high success rate in the transfer of equipment from American factories to British territory. The victory over German U-boats was a prerequisite for a second front.

One other factor can be considered, and again it indicates that precipitous action would have been a mistake. By 1944, Allied bombing of Germany helped create the necessary precondition for a successful amphibious landing—total air superiority—a dominance that did not exist earlier in the war. With the *Luftwaffe* at full force, any Allied convoy crossing the English Channel would have been vulnerable to a devastating counterattack. Instead, as the Allies crossed the Channel in June 1944, they anticipated armed resistance and other obstacles on land, but they no longer had to worry about the German air force.

For all of these reasons, the military decision to wait until 1944 was the right one. In any alliance, there are political considerations as well, and arguably, a commitment of American and British forces before 1944 might have gained Stalin's confidence for the postwar period. Given the disagreements that split the Allies regarding Poland and other Eastern European countries before the end of the war, and Stalin's clear determination to dominate that part of Europe, the possibility of a protracted alliance after Germany's defeat was highly unlikely in any case. A landing in France could have been a disaster if attempted before 1944; it would have harmed Allied relations if postponed beyond 1944. Despite the arguments and debates, the alliance's timing was optimal for military and diplomatic impact.

The successful opening of the second front in June 1944 excited all Allied leaders and their populations as well. A vast armada of ships carried American, British, Canadian, Free French, and other Allied troops across a stormy Channel to meet German troops, well entrenched in concrete bunkers. The Canadians and British landed on the eastern beaches, while the Americans assaulted Utah and Omaha Beaches. The latter landing was particularly difficult, but in all cases, Allied forces succeeded in obtaining control of their target areas and began to move forward. It is easy to forget now just how dangerous and precarious this landing was at the time; General Eisenhower prepared two press releases in anticipation of the invasion—one announcing a success and one apologizing for a failure.

On the first day of the landing, the Allies put approximately 150,000 men on the French beaches. While American forces attempted to cut the Cotentin peninsula and capture the port city of Cherbourg, British troops under General Montgomery moved toward Caen. At the same time, French resistance fighters blew up railway lines and took other measures to harass and prevent the Germans from moving reinforcements to Normandy. Germans took revenge for resistance actions, including the brutal destruction of the buildings and inhabitants of the town of Oradour-sur-Glane. In Paris and elsewhere, German army officials killed their prisoners before retreating ahead of the Allied onslaught. The Nazi war against civilians continued despite deteriorating military conditions at the front lines.

Rome was liberated in June, Paris in August, and Brussels in September. By the end of the summer, the Allies were moving through France toward the German border. Seeing an opportunity to race into German territory, Montgomery commanded an assault in Holland in mid-September, code-named Operation Market Garden. This Allied push proved premature and ultimately unsuccessful; British and American forces suffered heavy casualties as the Germans held the bridges over the Rhine.

Following this failure, Allied forces maintained their formation close to the German border as winter approached. Hard pressed from both east and west, Hitler attempted a daring attack against the American-British line similar to his successful offensive in 1940. The plan even copied the three-pronged formation of the 1940 (France) and 1941 (U.S.S.R.) campaigns. The offensive started on December 16, and despite frigid weather, the Germans moved through the Ardennes and broke into American positions at key points. This "bulge" in Allied lines gave its name to the ensuing bloody battle.

At first, Hitler's plan seemed to be working, but several factors doomed German military prospects. German tanks began to run out of fuel at about the same time that the weather cleared sufficiently for Allied planes, previously grounded because of cloud cover, to resume attacks on enemy positions. General Eisenhower was able to regroup his forces, ordering Generals Montgomery and Patton into action—predictably each one claimed individual credit for the ultimate victory. Although the German offensive eventually was stopped, the Bulge was the costliest battle that Americans fought during the war, with an estimated 80,000 casualties (20,000 killed).

In addition to the carnage, the battle provided several famous moments—German soldiers who spoke English disguised in American uniforms infiltrating Allied lines to create chaos and confusion, and American soldiers responding by setting up checkpoints to quiz each other on details of American sports and culture. In the town of Bastogne, surrounded and asked to surrender by the German commander, General Anthony McAuliffe became a military legend with his one word response—"nuts!" General Patton added to his own myth by telling Eisenhower that he could move divisions of his Third Army into action within forty-eight hours, leaving out the detail that his units were already under way as he made that boast. Finally, German *Schutzstaffel* (SS) troops shot and killed approximately 100 captured American soldiers at Malmédy, an action that shocked even battle-hardened veterans.

When the battle ended in January 1945, the Germans had depleted their last forces available for the defense of the western front. The Rhine and western Germany lay open for the Allied advance. American, British, French, and Canadian forces crossed the river in February and deployed across Germany in March. At the same time, the Red Army continued to roll across Eastern Europe and took Warsaw (January), Budapest (February), Berlin (April), and Prague (May). In the process of crossing Eastern Europe, the Soviet army liberated concentration camps in Poland and Czechoslovakia. The horrific discoveries, combined with the cruel treatment that German troops had visited upon Soviet civilians, fueled anger and rage that some Soviet soldiers took out on German civilians. This book includes ample testimony from the Nuremberg Trials as well as eyewitness accounts from concentration camp survivors to demonstrate the deliberate war against civilians that was implemented by the Axis and specifically the racist Nazi regime.

With military victory in sight, the Allied leaders met at Yalta in the Crimea in February 1945. Roosevelt, Churchill, and Stalin agreed on zones of occupation in Germany, the punishment of Nazi leaders, the collection of reparations, the creation of a United Nations, and a timetable for a Soviet declaration of war on Japan. The three leaders were unable to resolve their differing understanding of the postwar disposition of Poland—although they called for the creation of a democratic Poland, Stalin made it clear that he insisted on a pro-Soviet state on his western border. This argument continued throughout 1945 and beyond and became a major issue in the developing Cold War. The status of Poland remained central to both World War II and the Cold War.

April brought the brutal but ultimately successful siege of the German capital city by the Soviet army. President Roosevelt did not live to see the fall of Berlin, having died on April 12. Before the end of the month, Italian partisans killed Mussolini, and Hitler committed suicide. The German state collapsed in early May, with several leading perpetrators of the terror committed by the Nazi regime captured to stand trial for their crimes against humanity; others followed Hitler's example and committed suicide, and still others disappeared or escaped. Victory in Europe was celebrated on May 8 in the west and on May 9 in the U.S.S.R.

CHAPTER 1

Appeasement in Munich, 1938

Introduction to 1938

After coming to power in January 1933, Hitler pursued two goals simultaneously: domestically, he moved quickly to destroy the fragile and flawed democracy of the Weimar Republic, while in foreign policy, he sought to undo and undermine the provisions of the Treaty of Versailles.[1] In 1935, Hitler announced the rearmament of Germany, an action that included both conscription and the creation of an air force. The following year Hitler ordered the German army to reoccupy the Rhineland, and early in 1938, Germany violated Versailles again with unification (*Anschluss*) with Austria.[2] In all of these areas Hitler acted unilaterally to flaunt his disdain for the Versailles settlement.

European powers reacted in a variety of ways to Germany's rearmament in 1935. The United Kingdom basically accepted Hitler's actions by signing a naval agreement that ensured British supremacy on the seas. As traditional continental powers, the French and Russians countered the German resurgence by negotiating a mutual assistance pact in which they promised to defend each other in case of attack; their hope was the containment of Germany with the threat of a two-front war. In a further attempt to surround Germany and restrain Hitler, they included Czechoslovakia in the pact with a provision that mandated Soviet aid for the Czechs as long as the French provided assistance as well. Despite the superficial resemblance to the French-Russian alliance that prevented Germany from winning World War I, this agreement did not lead to military collaboration between France and the Union of Soviet Socialist Republic (U.S.S.R.).

By the summer of 1938, Hitler had enjoyed complete success in terms of his domestic and foreign policy objectives. The Weimar Republic had been replaced by the Nazi dictatorship and the provisions of the Treaty of Versailles were in tatters as well. His next target—Czechoslovakia—involved greater risk and necessarily elicited a general European response. Hitler raised the stakes for all of Europe by insisting that the Sudetenland, a part of Czechoslovakia that bordered on Germany, be turned over to German control.[3] As fall approached, Hitler escalated his demands, each time bringing Europe closer to the brink of war. German newspapers whipped up war hysteria, claiming that Czechs were slaughtering innocent Germans at the behest of Communists.

Western leaders, all of whom remembered the previous war and feared a return to the horrors of the trenches, sought a way to avoid confrontation. The British and French decided that they would not fight to defend Czechoslovakia and pressured Czech President Beneš[4] to surrender the territory in question. Nevertheless, when an impatient Hitler insisted on the immediate transfer of the Sudetenland with a deadline of October 1, war again seemed imminent. With time running out, British Prime Minister Chamberlain, French Premier Daladier, and Italian Premier Mussolini,[5] agreed to meet with Hitler in Munich to resolve the crisis. A settlement could be achieved only by capitulation to Hitler's ultimatum, and the infamous Munich Pact gave Hitler all that he had demanded. Chamberlain and Hitler then signed a supplemental accord expressing "the desire of our two peoples never to go to war with one another again."[6] The British prime minister and the French premier returned to their capitals as heroes, acclaimed for having prevented another war. Italian newspapers praised Mussolini for saving the peace of Europe. Despite appearances in London, Paris, and Rome, Hitler had his victory. And ominously, Stalin,[7] who had not been invited to Munich, saw that his mutual assistance pact with France would not provide protection from German aggression or the security his country needed.

The German press celebrated Hitler's victory at Munich. They called the Munich Pact the most important international agreement since World War I, as it brought together the four major powers of Europe to resolve a territorial dispute in Germany's favor. Over the next few days, German propaganda intensified its fawning praise for Hitler, and in early October, Hitler himself visited the scene of his latest triumph. In November, the Nazis sponsored attacks on Jewish shops and religious establishments in Germany, leaving broken glass in the streets—*Kristallnacht*—but more ominously foreshadowing what Nazi occupation would mean for all of Europe during the war.[8]

Despite its treaties with France and the U.S.S.R., Czechoslovakia had not been invited to the Munich meeting. Rather, the great powers dictated the settlement to Czechoslovakia, and in losing the Sudetenland, Czechoslovakia also lost its best defensive fortifications, opening the country to further German aggression. Europe did not have long to wait for that action, as the German army occupied the rest of Czechoslovakia in early 1939. That military occupation was disappointing news for the British and French governments; they realized that Hitler did not intend to keep the assurances he had given in Munich. As Germany took over Czech and Slovak populations, Hitler could not use his usual excuse about uniting all German-speaking peoples into the Reich. German aggression demanded a wider European response, although Hitler had already set his sights on his next target. The following year brought war—a war that Hitler wanted—and it came on Hitler's terms.

THE SOURCES

German Accusations Before the Munich Pact

Press accounts of the events leading up to the Munich Pact reflect the different voices, the competing perspectives, and the opposing world views of each of the major European powers. German newspapers fomented anti-Czech war frenzy by claiming that Czechs were attacking German towns and shooting German civilians. These accusations blamed Czech Communists, operating on orders from Moscow, for these supposed atrocities. Hitler stepped up his demands and set an October 1 deadline for war.

In the Headlines

Völkischer Beobachter, Berlin, September 21, 1938[9]
OPEN ATTACK ON GERMAN BORDER TOWNS
MANY CRITICALLY INJURED BY CZECH BULLETS

Völkischer Beobachter, Berlin, September 22, 1938
DOWN WITH THE BENEŠ STATE

Völkischer Beobachter, Berlin, September 24, 1938
BLOODBATH ON MOSCOW'S ORDERS
COMMUNISTS SPILL INNOCENT GERMAN BLOOD

Völkischer Beobachter, Berlin, September 27, 1938
WORDING OF ULTIMATUM—SUDETENLAND MUST BE
   SURRENDERED ON OCTOBER 1
GERMANY'S LAST WARNING—PRAGUE HAS RESPONSIBILITY FOR
   WAR OR PEACE

Soviet Reaction to German Threats

The primary response to these threats came from the Soviet Union, based on its treaty of mutual assistance with France and Czechoslovakia and its own propaganda needs. The Soviet government proclaimed solidarity with the struggle of the Czech people and condemned German aggression as a threat to peace.

In the Headlines

Izvestiia, Moscow, September 23, 1938
CZECHOSLOVAKIAN GOVERNMENT REJECTS HITLER'S MEMORANDUM
GERMAN ARMY PREPARES TO ATTACK

Pravda, Moscow, September 29, 1938
CZECHOSLOVAKIAN PEOPLE PREPARE TO PROTECT THEIR LAND

Izvestiia, Moscow, September 30, 1938
GERMAN FASCISTS CONTINUE PROVOCATIVE "INCIDENTS"
CZECHOSLOVAKIA PREPARES FOR THE BATTLE FOR INDEPENDENCE
SOLIDARITY WITH THE CZECH PEOPLE

Czech Reaction to German Threats

The rather lonely voice in this situation belonged to the Czech press, which hoped for French intervention and still expected to be included in any talks on the Sudetenland.

In the Headlines

České Slovo, Prague, September 6, 1938[10]
FRANCE IS STRENGTHENING ITS BORDER DEFENSES

České Slovo, Prague, September 19, 1938
ENGLAND AND FRANCE TO DECIDE ABOUT CZECHOSLOVAKIA
   TODAY
IT IS NOT POSSIBLE TO NEGOTIATE WITHOUT CZECHOSLOVAKIA

České Slovo, Prague, September 25, 1938
HITLER STILL INCREASING HIS DEMANDS

Večerní České Slovo, Prague, September 27, 1938[11]
HITLER'S NEW DEMANDS
HITLER SETS DEADLINE FOR SATURDAY!

České Slovo, Prague, September 27, 1938
PRAGUE REJECTS NEW DEMANDS

České Slovo, Prague, September 29, 1938
CONFERENCE OF FOUR IN MUNICH TODAY—WHO WILL SPEAK FOR US?

The Munich Pact Is Signed

With Europe seemingly on the brink of war, Mussolini helped to organize and mediate a conference in Munich that resulted in Hitler receiving exactly what he wanted. The outcome was the Munich Pact that surrendered the Sudetenland to Germany.

The Munich Agreement, September 29, 1938

Germany, the United Kingdom, France and Italy, taking into consideration the agreement, which has been already reached in principle for the cession to

Germany of the Sudeten German territory, have agreed on the following terms and conditions governing the said cession and the measures consequent thereon, and by this agreement they each hold themselves responsible for the steps necessary to secure its fulfillment:

(1) The evacuation will begin on 1st October.

(2) The United Kingdom, France and Italy agree that the evacuation of the territory shall be completed by the 10th October, without any existing installations having been destroyed, and that the Czechoslovak Government will be held responsible for carrying out the evacuation without damage to the said installations.

Munich, September 29, 1938
Adolf Hitler, Neville Chamberlain, Edouard Daladier, Benito Mussolini

Hitler-Chamberlain Declaration, September 30, 1938

We, the German Führer and Chancellor and the British Prime Minister, have had a further meeting today and are agreed in recognizing that the question of Anglo-German relations is of the first importance for the two countries and for Europe.

We regard the agreement signed last night and the Anglo-German Naval Agreement as symbolic of the desire of our two peoples never to go to war with one another again.

We are resolved that the method of consultation shall be the method adopted to deal with any other questions that may concern our two countries, and we are determined to continue our efforts to remove possible sources of difference and thus to contribute to assure the peace of Europe.

European Reaction to the Munich Pact

French and British newspapers hailed the signing for saving peace in Europe. Premier Daladier and Prime Minister Chamberlain were viewed as heroes in their own countries. Neutral Switzerland credited Chamberlain for the settlement, while Italy trumpeted the role of Mussolini as the savior of the day. The only negative notes came from Soviet and Czech newspapers that lamented the capitulation of democratic Britain and France to German dictatorship. The Czech president was forced to resign and early the next year Czechoslovakia ceased to exist as an independent country.

In the Headlines

Cherbourg-Éclair, Cherbourg, September 30, 1938
PEACE IS SAVED!
MR. DALADIER, CHAMBERLAIN, HITLER AND MUSSOLINI HAVE
    SIGNED THIS NIGHT THE HISTORIC MUNICH ACCORD, SETTLING
    THE GERMAN-CZECH CONFLICT

The Times, London, September 30, 1938
AGREEMENT REACHED AT MUNICH TODAY
PLAN FOR TRANSFER OF TERRITORIES
ENTHUSIASTIC WELCOME FOR MR. CHAMBERLAIN

Journal de Genève, Geneva, October 1, 1938
AGREEMENT ON THE MEANS FOR TRANSFERRING THE
    SUDETENLAND
CREDIT TO M. CHAMBERLAIN

Corriere Della Sera, Milan, September 30, 1938[12]
IL DUCE HAS SAVED THE PEACE
GRATITUDE FROM THE ENTIRE WORLD FOR THE INCOMPARABLE
    LEADER WHO, WITH HIS GENIUS AND PRESTIGE, HAS OPENED THE
    WAY FOR RECONCILIATION AMONG PEOPLES

Il Popolo D'Italia, Milan, October 1, 1938
HONORS FOR THE TRIUMPH OF IL DUCE

Pravda, Moscow, October 1, 1938
WORRIED DAYS IN PRAGUE

Pravda, Moscow, October 2, 1938 [dateline Prague]
UNDER THE FASCIST BAYONET

Izvestiia, Moscow, October 16, 1938
THE DISMEMBERMENT OF CZECHOSLOVAKIA CONTINUES

Večerní České Slovo, Prague, October 2, 1938
DICTATORSHIP AND DEMOCRACY SHAKING HANDS

České Slovo, Prague, October 6, 1938
PRESIDENT DR. E. BENEŠ FORCED ASIDE

Testimony of Czech Citizens

Ladislav Homola and Bohuslav Krajíček were young when the war started, but they both had memories of the effect of the war on their lives. Their views of Hitler, Stalin, and Americans provide interesting insight into local reactions to these events.

Testimony of Ladislav Homola[13]

Q: Do you remember what you or your parents thought about the Munich Pact?

A: I didn't care about the Sudetenland issue. I was young; I didn't take it seriously.

Q: About the Nazi-Soviet Non-aggression Pact?

A: That was something for politicians and not for normal people.

Q: About the start of the war?

A: I was young, and we made jokes about the war. I didn't take it seriously . . . I didn't care about the war.

Q: About Hitler as a leader?

A: Hitler was a maniac, a crazy person; he was able to hypnotize people. Everybody in Czechoslovakia at the time believed that he couldn't win the war.

Q: About Stalin as a leader?

A: Russia needed a strong hand and leader. Russia would have ended really badly without Stalin's strong hand.

Q: How did the start of the war affect you?

A: I had to go to Germany for forced labor in a factory in 1942. They needed me because I was a locksmith. I worked in a factory that worked with aluminum. I got a telegram that my mother had gotten sick after almost one year (spring 1943). I was allowed to go home for a 14-day leave. My mother got worse and the doctor negotiated another 14 days. A guy from my town saw that I was back home and turned me in. I got arrested although I was at home legally. They brought me to the Gestapo. I got slapped around first and then they cross-examined me for one hour. I didn't know why I had been arrested. They kept cross-examining me. They probably thought that I didn't want to work in the forced labor unit in Germany. They sent me to "Terezín"[14] after two months. I stayed there for almost one year. We had to go to the "Appelplatz" where they did the roll call. They yelled at us "Hats off!" If somebody's hat fell on the ground, they beat him up. We got cooked blood for dinner. We heard that it was from the executed prisoners. The whole time I thought that I was going to die. I didn't drink it. They were throwing Jewish children from a dam and then they were shooting at them. From there I could see where there were prisoners to be executed. Once I saw how the Nazis killed a prisoner. They put him against a wall and shot him from the tower. Some prisoners pulled him away. We also had to load up dead bodies—these were Jews from the ghettos—with bare hands into boxes for the incinerator every day at 7:30 in the morning.

Q: Do you hate the Germans?

A: Whose fault was it that they started the war? A lot of Germans died. It was war. How can you hate anybody?

Testimony of Bohuslav Krajíček[15]

Q: Do you remember what you or your parents thought about the Munich Pact?

A: The people were upset. They lost their homes and the people were scared that the Germans would take over all of Czechoslovakia. Czechs and Germans had gotten along in the Sudeten area; they married each other. Hitler frightened them, and a lot of Czechs left the Sudetenland. The Germans who lived there had to go to war.

Q: About the start of the war?
A: The Czechs didn't have to fight because the Germans didn't trust them to do so. The Slovaks had to fight, and they had their own country. The Germans trusted them; they were their allies.
Q: About whose fault the war was?
A: People knew that it was Germany's fault.
Q: How did the war affect civilians in your country?
A: There were hidden partisans in my village in 1943. One of the farmers in the village was giving them food. Nobody knew about it; it only came out after the war.
Q: If you remember, please describe food conditions?
A: People had to give their food to the Nazis, so they had to hide it from them to keep some for themselves. When the Nazis came to people's houses the people had to give them food and allow them to eat their food. They couldn't say no . . .
Q: What were your views of Germans?
A: The Germans were intelligent people, but Hitler controlled them. The Germans tortured us for six years but the Russians did it for forty years!
Q: What were your views of Americans?
A: Americans saved us three times: in 1918, in WWII—although they weren't allowed to go to Prague because the Russians didn't allow them to cross the line of demarcation. The Americans liberated us the third time from the Communists. The American nation saved us!
Q: What were your views of Russians?
A: People welcomed them as liberators. They were nice at first, but then they started to bother women; the women had to dress up as old grandmothers to avoid being raped. The Germans were well behaved but the Russians were pigs.
Q: Do you think Emil Hácha[16] could have done more?
A: Hácha had to do what the Germans told him and he couldn't have done anything more.
Q: Could Beneš have done more?
A: He did all that he could.
Q: What did you think of the assassination of Heydrich?[17]
A: A lot of people died for nothing. Normal people just wanted the war to end and they didn't care about assassinating Heydrich. The normal people knew that a lot of people would die for it and it wouldn't really help. Nothing changed after the assassination for average people.

German Reaction to Munich

German newspapers celebrated the Munich Pact for what it was in reality—complete victory for Hitler's bellicose foreign policy. He claimed territory that belonged to a sovereign state, he threatened war to achieve his goals, and the western powers capitulated to his demands. This triumph was one of several that Hitler would celebrate over the next couple of years.

In the Headlines

Völkischer Beobachter, Berlin, October 1, 1938
AFTER THE ACCEPTANCE OF THE MUNICH AGREEMENT BY
　　PRAGUE, GERMAN TROOPS ENTER THE SUDETENLAND TODAY
ADOLF HITLER-CHAMBERLAIN: NEVER AGAIN WAR BETWEEN
　　GERMANY AND ENGLAND

Völkischer Beobachter, Berlin, October 2, 1938
THE REICH'S CAPITAL PAYS HOMAGE TO THE LIBERATOR OF THE
　　SUDETENLAND
BERLIN THANKS ADOLF HITLER IN THE NAME OF 80 MILLION
　　PEOPLE

Völkischer Beobachter, Berlin, October 4, 1938
THE FÜHRER IN THE SUDETENLAND

CHAPTER 2

War Is Declared, 1939

Introduction to 1939

In March 1939, in direct violation of the promises he made to Prime Minister Chamberlain in Munich the previous September, Hitler ordered the German army to occupy all of Czechoslovakia. This time he made no pretense that German nationals were being reunited into the Reich; this was a clear act of aggression. Nevertheless, the western allies took no action to defend the only democracy in Eastern Europe. Instead, Chamberlain responded to German expansion by offering a guarantee for the security of Poland. If Hitler forced the issue of Danzig and the Polish Corridor[1]—and if the western powers did not back down as they had on the Sudeten crisis—Britain's promise, echoed by France, made war inevitable.

In a speech to Parliament, Chamberlain indicated his hope that the German-Polish issue could still be settled through negotiations. Nevertheless, he stated that the British and French governments had given "assurances" to the Polish government that they would provide "all support in their power" in response to any German threat to Polish independence. Later in the year, Hitler frequently cited this British "guarantee" to Poland as one of the reasons for Polish intransigence and the need for subsequent German military action.

The diplomatic situation grew more threatening as the year went on. Hitler's direct response to Chamberlain came at the end of April. As always, he played the victim, blaming the Treaty of Versailles for the crisis in Poland. He insisted that Danzig was a German city and had to be returned to the Reich. At the same time, he offered Poland guaranteed economic rights in the port city in exchange for Polish capitulation.

The Polish foreign minister firmly rejected Hitler's demand that Danzig be turned over to Germany.[2] Arguing the position of his government, he delineated the reasons why Germany's conditions were unreasonable and unacceptable. He called Hitler's offer insincere and observed that Germany's ultimate objectives were more aggressive than Hitler admitted. In conclusion, he defended Poland's inability to compromise further:

Peace is a valuable and desirable thing. Our generation, which has shed its blood in several wars, surely deserves a period of peace. But peace, like almost everything in this world, has its price, high but definable. We in Poland do not recognize the conception of "peace at any price." There is only one thing in the life of men, nations and States which is without price, and that is honor.[3]

Poland would fight for its honor.

Throughout the summer, European governments focused their attention on the crisis in Danzig and the Polish Corridor. As the possibility of war grew, the major powers realized that the diplomatic and military position of the Soviet Union was crucial to the balance of power. After Munich, Stalin calculated the prospects for war, weighed the Soviet Union's best options, and considered how he would repay the perceived betrayal by the west at Munich. The U.S.S.R. sent diplomatic signals to the Germans, suggesting that some accommodation was possible. One such hint was the replacement of Foreign Minister M. Litvinov, whose policy of collective security was associated with anti-Fascism and attempts to form alliances with the west. The appointment of V. Molotov as foreign minister indicated a new start for Soviet policy.[4] The western allies soon learned that angering Stalin had important negative consequences.

In August, Germany increased pressure on Poland, and Chamberlain realized that Europe was on the brink of war. As a result, the British prime minister sent a letter to Hitler appealing for a peaceful resolution of the crisis. He alluded to the misunderstanding of 1914 and with that example suggested that once war broke out it would be difficult to stop. Chamberlain proposed further talks between Germany and Poland to try to resolve their differences, and he offered Britain as a possible guarantor of any solution that might be reached.

Hitler had no incentive to negotiate with England. He was not afraid of war; indeed, he welcomed it. Not surprisingly his response to Chamberlain left little hope for a peaceful resolution of the crisis. The German leader made it clear that he would not compromise on the principle of control of Danzig and the Corridor. Hitler knew that he was on the verge of achieving all his goals without talking to England or Poland. At that moment, Germany and the U.S.S.R. were moving to formalize a realignment in Eastern Europe that would give Germany what it needed—a neutral Soviet Union and a free hand in Poland.

In the third week of August 1939, German Foreign Minister Ribbentrop[5] traveled to Moscow to sign a nonaggression pact with Stalin and Molotov. The pact also included a protocol, not published at the time, dividing territory in Eastern Europe between Germany and the U.S.S.R.; in addition to Poland, the Baltic States and Romania were also affected.

The pact freed Germany to fight on one front, and the major powers knew that this agreement meant imminent war. A variety of European leaders made appeals for continued negotiations. Speaking for six different countries, the so-called Oslo Group of States, King Leopold III of Belgium appealed to the larger powers to attempt to reconcile their differences. He observed that a war among the great powers inevitably would affect the smaller and even neutral nations as well.[6]

President Roosevelt, citing the large Italian-American population as a factor that brought the United States and Italy together, asked King Victor Emmanuel III to intervene to maintain peace in Europe. Roosevelt suggested that the major powers take a pledge not to invade weaker countries and, at the same time, open talks on reducing armaments. He indicated that the United States would participate in such discussions, but he hoped that Italy might take the lead in proposing such peace-saving measures.

Roosevelt also wrote to the president of Poland in an effort to prevent war. The Polish response balanced a hard line against Germany with a promise to negotiate if possible. While insisting that Poland was not the instigator of this threat to world peace and that it was German demands that were leading Europe to war, the Polish president asserted that his country remained amenable to resolving the dispute with Germany.

Pope Pius XII entered the conversation on preserving peace in Europe. Appealing in the name of God, the pope affirmed the universal desire for justice and freedom and beseeched those in power to seek peaceful resolution of their differences. Taking the request a step further, he encouraged the people of Europe to work with their own leaders to insist on solutions that did not involve the use of violence.

Coulondre, the French ambassador in Berlin,[7] kept the government in Paris apprised of the situation in Germany. Coulondre spoke at length with Hitler about the crisis and sent a summary of Hitler's remarks to the French government. In their conversation, Hitler expressed his regret that a conflict with Poland might lead to war with France. The German leader insisted that he had made a fair proposal to the Polish government regarding Danzig but that the government in Warsaw had rejected his ideas and had subjected Germans living in Poland to unjust treatment. Hitler made exaggerated claims of Germans being castrated and placed in Polish camps; he also stated that Poles were firing on German forces and airplanes without provocation. As he often did to intimidate visitors, he began to shout at the French ambassador, this time to say that no country could tolerate such behavior from another. Alluding to possible war with France, Hitler suggested that his nonaggression pact with the Soviet Union gave Germany a clear advantage, and he was certain of victory. If war between Germany and France were to occur, Hitler argued that it would be the fault of England and France for giving Poland a "blank check," an allusion to Germany's unconditional support for Austria before the start of World War I.

In the continuing diplomatic exchange, Premier Daladier rejected
Hitler's claim that France would be responsible for war and instead
argued that, "the fate of peace still rests solely in your [Hitler's]
hands." Daladier not only pointed out that his own political career
proved his commitment to French-German friendship, but also
asserted that French honor bound his country to support Poland if the
situation deteriorated further. Daladier declared that France and its
allies, including Poland, viewed the issues dealing with Danzig as
negotiable and remained open to talks that could resolve the current
crisis in a fair way. The French premier evoked the memories and
horrors of the previous war and insisted that German honor would be
preserved in any process that maintained peace in Europe.[8]

Following Daladier's lead, the French ambassador in Berlin again
spoke at length with Hitler about the horrors of war and urged him to
try once more for a peaceful solution to the Danzig crisis. Coulondre
begged the German leader to try to avoid war, suggesting that Hitler's
prestige would be enhanced if he saved Europe at the last minute.
Hitler stated that it was too late. He asserted that the English
guarantee to Poland made Poland unwilling to compromise. He
blamed England and France for creating the conditions by which
Poland was "committing suicide." Hitler claimed that the situation
had "gone too far" and that German honor was at stake. Despite
Daladier's best intentions, which Hitler maintained he did not doubt,
compromise with Warsaw was no longer possible. Again Coulondre
appealed for direct talks between Germany and Poland, but Hitler
stated that such actions would be "useless."[9]

Hitler soon made it clear that war could not be avoided unless
Poland capitulated. He told the British government that Poland had
rejected his attempts at a peaceful solution of the Danzig issue by
using the last several months to strengthen its military capacity at the
expense of Germany. He returned to the theme of the mistreatment of
German civilians under Polish administration and called the situation
"unbearable."[10] Nevertheless, Hitler claimed that he would accept a
Polish representative to try to settle the problem—as long as the
settlement included the immediate transfer of Danzig and the Polish
Corridor to German control. Hitler knew that his demands were
unacceptable to Poland and that war was imminent. For Hitler,
everything was coming together exactly as he had anticipated—he had
neutralized Stalin at the same time that he knew the western powers
were unprepared to intervene militarily. Rather than send aid to
Poland, logistically impossible at that time, western leaders spent the
next few days assigning blame and rationalizing their own role in the
events leading to war.

As German troops moved into Poland, Chamberlain explained to members of parliament the efforts that his government had made over the previous several days to preserve peace by encouraging direct talks between Poland and Germany. Chamberlain indicated that Poland had agreed to cooperate in this process but that Hitler rejected every attempt to resolve the problem. Although a state of war did not formally exist between Britain and Germany, Chamberlain asserted that his government was in the process of mobilizing all of its military forces for the struggle ahead. The British people, he declared, had no quarrel with the German people, but only with the Nazi government whose very existence meant that peace was impossible.

The next day, the British prime minister further excused his own actions in the sequence of events that led to war. Like Daladier, Chamberlain insisted that his government had done everything possible to avoid war; he had given Germany an ultimatum demanding that Germany cease all aggressive acts against Poland by 11:00 A.M. on September 3 or face war with England and France. As the deadline passed without a German response, Britain considered itself at war with Germany. On a personal note, Chamberlain admitted that his life's work, the attempt to preserve the peace in Europe by appeasing Hitler, was in ruins.

Joining in the process of excusing his own actions, Premier Daladier reviewed the reasons why France had to join the war against Germany. He reminded the representatives in his legislature that he was a strong proponent of peace and that he had tried to satisfy Hitler's demands on several occasions. At the last minute, France and England attempted to restart talks between Germany and Poland on the Danzig issue, but Hitler's foreign minister had refused further negotiations. Daladier indicated that all French soldiers were in the process of joining their units and that morale was high. Appealing more directly to French interests, he declared that Germany's actions proved that the guarantees for France's eastern border, for the territories of Alsace and Lorraine, were no longer valid in light of Hitler's behavior toward Austria, Czechoslovakia, and now Poland. He called on all French citizens to unite behind the military effort.

Finally, with the German invasion of Poland under way, Hitler continued to perpetrate the fiction of Polish responsibility. He called on all German soldiers to fight for "the honor" of their country. In response to Britain's state of war with Germany, Hitler told the German people that fault lay with England, a nation that always had attempted to dominate the world and Europe. He claimed that British hostility began as soon as Germany started to recover from the ravages of World War I. Hitler asserted that the same British liars and war instigators that had forced World War I on the German nation were

blocking his peaceful intentions at this time. Although the primary
field of battle was in Poland, Hitler warned his soldiers in the west to
be prepared to defend Germany's border against possible British or
French attack. He returned to the example of World War I, claiming
that the western wall was not breached then and would hold against
the English and French aggressors once again.

The day after Britain and France formally entered into a state of
war against Germany, the British prime minister again attempted to
justify his country's position, this time in a broadcast directed to the
German people. Indicating no animosity between the British and
the Germans, Chamberlain instead placed all blame on Hitler and
argued that Hitler's leadership had been discredited as a result of his
perpetual perfidy.

With war already certain, Italy joined the conversation. In an attempt
to remain on good terms with both Germany and the Allies, Mussolini
offered a last-minute appeal for another Munich-type meeting. On
August 31 he floated a plan for a conference on September 5. Mussolini
contacted the British and French governments to gauge their willingness
to meet, and he sent their terms to Hitler. By then it was too late for
such mediation. It is likely that Mussolini was aware in advance that his
efforts were meaningless, but he hoped that his role as an honest broker
would earn him credibility with the eventual winner.

Despite the diplomatic maneuvering and posturing by politicians
trying to preserve their reputations, the German invasion made rapid
progress toward Warsaw. Some Poles were surprised by the outbreak of
war. They believed that there would be a last-minute settlement, or that
the Polish army would deter a German invasion. The overwhelmed
Polish military resisted against impossible odds. Within weeks, Nazi
occupation was in place. Polish Jews found themselves in a difficult
situation. Caught between the Germans and the Russians, they had no
place to go and no escape from a terrible fate. At first many were
drafted into the Polish army, but they often were mistreated despite
their willingness to fight alongside other Poles. Most Poles had no place
to run or hide—some lived in the part of Poland that was first overrun
by the German invasion and, in accord with the Nazi-Soviet
nonaggression pact and supplementary agreements, then was occupied
by the U.S.S.R. after about two weeks. For almost all Poles, their
wartime stories would be agonizing and tragic.

While Britain and France and Germany prepared for future battles,
Stalin occupied eastern Poland. In the fall, he demanded that Finland
push its border back from Leningrad—he wanted Finnish territory
transferred to Soviet control. When the Finnish government refused
the demand, Soviet troops invaded Finland. The Finns, outnumbered
and outgunned, fought bravely and tried to use the cold and winter in

their favor. The Finnish newspaper *Hufvudstadsbladet* reported these events, from Soviet intransigence on negotiations to the break in diplomatic relations and finally the Soviet bombing of civilian targets in Finland. While the Soviet army suffered some setbacks, it eventually won the war and acquired the disputed territory. At the same time, the Soviet high command learned some lessons from its lackluster performance in Finland and initiated reforms in the Red Army that would prove to be beneficial in 1941.

In a futile and largely symbolic gesture, the moribund League of Nations expelled the U.S.S.R.

THE SOURCES

European Leaders Discuss Poland

Following the German occupation of Czechoslovakia, England, joined
by France, promised to defend Poland against foreign aggression.
While Prime Minister Chamberlain considered this assurance of
support both logical and necessary after Hitler had broken his Munich
pledge, Hitler viewed this English intervention as provocative.
Throughout the rest of the year, Hitler argued that English backing
made Poland less amenable to negotiation.

Chamberlain Guarantee to Poland, March 31, 1939

As the House is aware, certain consultations are now proceeding with other
Governments. In order to make perfectly clear the position of His Majesty's
Government in the meantime before those consultations are concluded, I
now have to inform the House that during that period, in the event of any
action which clearly threatened Polish independence, and which the Polish
Government accordingly considered it vital to resist with their national
forces, His Majesty's Government would feel themselves bound at once to
lend the Polish Government all support in their power. They have given the
Polish Government an assurance to this effect.

I may add that the French Government have authorised me to make it
plain that they stand in the same position in this matter as do His Majesty's
Government.

Hitler's Speech to Reichstag on Poland, April 28, 1939

There is little to be said as regards German-Polish relations. Here, too, the
Peace Treaty of Versailles—of course intentionally—inflicted a most severe
wound on Germany. The strange way in which the Corridor giving Poland
access to the sea was marked out was meant, above all, to prevent for all
time the establishment of an understanding between Poland and Germany.
This problem is—as I have already stressed—perhaps the most painful of all
problems for Germany. Nevertheless, I have never ceased to uphold the view
that the necessity of a free access to the sea for the Polish State cannot be
ignored, and that as a general principle, valid for this case, too, nations which
Providence has destined or, if you like, condemned to live side by side would
be well advised not to make life still harder for each other artificially and
unnecessarily . . .

Nevertheless, there remained one open question between Germany
and Poland, which sooner or later quite naturally had to be solved—the
question of the German city of Danzig. Danzig is a German city and wishes

to belong to Germany. On the other hand, this city has contracts with Poland, which were admittedly forced upon it by the dictators of the Peace of Versailles ... I am no democratic statesman, but a National Socialist and a realist.

I considered it, however, necessary to make it clear to the Government in Warsaw that just as they desire access to the sea, so Germany needs access to her province in the east. Now these are all difficult problems. It is not Germany who is responsible for them, however, but rather the jugglers of Versailles ...

The Polish Government have rejected my offer ...

I have regretted greatly this incomprehensible attitude of the Polish Government, but that alone is not the decisive fact, the worst is that now Poland, like Czechoslovakia a year ago, believes, under the pressure of a lying international campaign, that it must call up troops, although Germany on her part has not called up a single man and had not thought of proceeding in any way against Poland.

Beck's Speech to Polish Parliament, May 5, 1939

The Polish-British Agreement has been employed by the Chancellor of the German Reich as the pretext for unilaterally declaring non-existent the agreement which the Chancellor of the Reich concluded with us in 1934 ...

The population of Danzig is today predominantly German, but its livelihood and prosperity depend on the economic potential of Poland ...

Peace is certainly the object of the difficult and intensive work of Polish diplomacy. Two conditions are necessary for this word to be of real value: (1) peaceful intentions, (2) peaceful methods of procedure. If the Government of the Reich is really guided by those two pre-conditions in relation to this country, then all conversations, provided, of course, that they respect the principles I have already enumerated, are possible ...

Peace is a valuable and desirable thing. Our generation, which has shed its blood in several wars, surely deserves a period of peace. But peace, like almost everything in this world, has its price, high but definable. We in Poland do not recognize the conception of "peace at any price." There is only one thing in the life of men, nations and States which is without price, and that is honor.

Chamberlain to Hitler, August 22, 1939

Whatever may prove to be the nature of the German-Soviet Agreement, it cannot alter Great Britain's obligation to Poland which His Majesty's Government have stated in public repeatedly and plainly, and which they are determined to fulfill ...

If the case should arise, they are resolved, and prepared, to employ without delay all the forces at their command, and it is impossible to foresee the end of hostilities once engaged. It would be a dangerous illusion to think that, if war once starts, it will come to an early end even if a success on any one of the several fronts on which it will be engaged should have been secured.

Having thus made our position perfectly clear, I wish to repeat to you my conviction that war between our two peoples would be the greatest calamity that could occur.

. . . it is reasonable to hope that suitable conditions might have been established for direct negotiations between Germany and Poland upon the issues between them.

Hitler to Chamberlain, August 23, 1939

The German Reich, however, like every other State possesses certain definite interests which it is impossible to renounce. These do not extend beyond the limits of the necessities laid down by former German history and deriving from vital economic pre-requisites. Some of these questions held and still hold a significance both of a national-political and a psychological character which no German Government is able to ignore.

To these questions belong the German City of Danzig, and the connected problem of the Corridor . . .

The unconditional assurance given by England to Poland that she would render assistance to that country in all circumstances regardless of the causes from which a conflict might spring, could only be interpreted in that country as an encouragement thenceforward to unloosen, under cover of such a charter, a wave of appalling terrorism against the one and a half million German inhabitants living in Poland. The atrocities which since then have been taking place in that country are terrible for the victims, but intolerable for a Great Power such as the German Reich which is expected to remain a passive onlooker during these happenings. Poland has been guilty of numerous breaches of her legal obligations towards the Free City of Danzig, has made demands in the character of ultimata, and has initiated a process of economic strangulation . . .

Your Excellency informs me in the name of the British Government that you will be obliged to render assistance to Poland in any such case of intervention on the part of Germany. I take note of this statement of yours and assure you that it can make no change in the determination of the Reich Government to safeguard the interests of the Reich.

Nazi-Soviet Nonaggression Pact

The arguments between Germany and England regarding Poland led to Hitler's decision to seek accommodation with the Soviet Union. The goal for Germany was neutralizing the U.S.S.R.—allowing Germany to fight a one-front war. German, Italian, and Soviet newspapers praised the agreement; western powers viewed the pact as a travesty of justice and an obvious step toward war. England, France, and Poland all condemned the Hitler-Stalin alliance, and other countries also understood the implications of a neutral U.S.S.R. The agreement allowed Germany to increase its verbal attacks on Poland to provide a rationale for war.

In the Headlines

Völkischer Beobachter, Berlin, August 23, 1939
POLAND CONCENTRATES TROOPS ON BORDER
WORLD SURPRISED BY BERLIN-MOSCOW PACT

Gazeta Polska, Warsaw, August 23, 1939
STRONG REACTION OF ENGLAND IN RESPONSE TO GERMAN-SOVIET
   ALLIANCE [article refers to English opposition to Nazi-Soviet Pact]

Il Popolo D'Italia, Milan, August 23, 1939
THE PACT OF NON-AGGRESSION BETWEEN BERLIN AND MOSCOW
   INFLICTS A MORTAL BLOW TO THE POLITICS OF ENCIRCLEMENT

Tübinger Chronik, Tübingen, August 24, 1939
MOSCOW PACT SIGNED
TWELVE HOURS AFTER ARRIVAL OF FOREIGN MINISTER IN MOSCOW
   EVERYTHING WAS COMPLETED

Völkischer Beobachter, Berlin, August 24, 1939
POLAND'S GUILT GROWS

Pravda, Moscow, August 24, 1939
SOVIET-GERMAN TREATY OF NONAGGRESSION [with photo of smiling
   Ribbentrop, Stalin, and Molotov]

Nazi-Soviet Nonaggression Pact, August 23, 1939

   1. The two Contracting Parties bind themselves to refrain from any act of force, any aggressive action and any attack on one another, both singly and also jointly with other Powers.

   2. In the event of one of the Contracting Parties becoming the object of warlike action on the part of a third Power, the other Contracting Party shall in no manner support this third Power.

   3. The Governments of the two Contracting Parties shall in future remain continuously in touch with one another, by way of consultation, in order to inform one another on questions touching their joint interests.

   4. Neither of the two Contracting Parties shall participate in any grouping of Powers which is directed directly or indirectly against the other Party.

5. In the event of disputes or disagreements arising between the Contracting Parties on questions of this or that kind, both Parties would clarify these disputes or disagreements exclusively by means of friendly exchange of opinion or, if necessary, by arbitration committees.

6. The present Agreement shall be concluded for a period of ten years on the understanding that, in so far as one of the Contracting Parties does not give notice of termination one year before the end of this period, the period of validity of this Agreement shall automatically be regarded as prolonged for a further period of five years . . .

Secret Protocol [Not Published in 1939], August 23, 1939

Article I. In the event of a territorial and political rearrangement in the areas belonging to the Baltic States (Finland, Estonia, Latvia, Lithuania), the northern boundary of Lithuania shall represent the boundary of the spheres of influence of Germany and U.S.S.R. In this connection the interest of Lithuania in the Vilna area is recognized by each party.

Article II. In the event of a territorial and political rearrangement of the areas belonging to the Polish State, the spheres of influence of Germany and the U.S.S.R. shall be bounded approximately by the line of the rivers Narev, Vistula and San.

The question of whether the interests of both parties make desirable the maintenance of an independent Polish State and how such a state should be bounded can only be definitely determined in the course of further political developments.

In any event both Governments will resolve this question by means of a friendly agreement.

Article III. With regard to Southeastern Europe attention is called by the Soviet side to its interest in Bessarabia. The German side declares its complete political disinterest in these areas.

Article IV. This Protocol shall be treated by both parties as strictly secret.

Calls for Peace

Following the Nazi-Soviet Nonaggression Pact, western leaders realized that war was imminent. Various world leaders appealed for peace, including the King of Belgium, President Roosevelt, and Pope Pius XII.

In the Headlines

L'Indépendance Belge, Brussels, August 24, 1939
KING LEOPOLD INVITES THE GREAT POWERS TO SUBMIT THEIR
   CLAIMS TO OPEN ARBITRATION

L'Indépendance Belge, Brussels, August 25, 1939
M. ROOSEVELT ASKS THE KING OF ITALY TO FIND A FORMULA TO
SETTLE THE CRISIS PEACEFULLY

Appeal of King of Belgium, August 23, 1939

The world is living through a period of tension such that there is a risk that
all normal collaboration between States will become impossible. The Great
Powers are taking measures almost equivalent to the mobilization of their
armed forces. Have not the small Powers reason to fear that they will be victims in a subsequent conflict into which they will be dragged against their will
in spite of their policy of indisputable independence and of their firm desire
for neutrality? Are they not liable to become the subject of arrangements
reached without their having been consulted?

 . . . Is our continent to commit suicide in a terrifying war at the end of
which no nation could call itself victor or vanquished, but in which the spiritual and material values created by centuries of civilization would founder?

Roosevelt to King of Italy, August 23, 1939

Any general war would cause to suffer all the nations, whether belligerent or
neutral, whether victors or vanquished, and would clearly bring devastation
to the peoples and perhaps the Governments of some nations most directly
concerned . . .

 Were it possible for your Majesty's Government to formulate proposals
for a pacific solution of the present crisis along these lines, you are assured
of the earnest sympathy of the United States.

Pope's Appeal for Peace, August 24, 1939[11]

Once again a critical hour strikes for the great human family; an hour of
tremendous deliberations, towards which our heart cannot be indifferent
and from which our spiritual authority, which comes to us from God to lead
souls in the ways of justice and of peace must not hold itself aloof . . .

 Today, notwithstanding our repeated exhortations and our very particular
interest, the fear of bloody international conflict becomes more excruciating;
today, when the tension of minds seems to have arrived at such a pass as to
make the outbreak of the awful scourge of war appear imminent, we direct
with paternal feeling a new and more heartfelt appeal to those in power and
to their peoples: to the former that, laying aside accusations, threats, causes of
mutual distrust, they may attempt to resolve their present differences with the
sole means suitable thereto, namely, by reciprocal and trusting agreements;
to the latter that in calm tranquility, without disordered agitation they may
encourage the peaceful efforts of those who govern them . . .

The danger is imminent but there is yet time.

Nothing is lost with peace; all may be with war. Let men return to mutual understanding. Let them begin negotiations anew.

European Leaders Debate Responsibility for Crisis

In the week following the Nazi-Soviet Pact, German and Polish newspapers traded accusations about border incidents and provocations. In addition, Hitler and French Premier Daladier engaged in a debate on the prospects for peace and the threat of war. Hitler blamed England and France for supporting Poland and encouraging Poland to resist diplomatic solutions. Poland and its western allies saw Germany as the aggressor, intent on expansion and war.

In the Headlines

Czas, Warsaw, August 25, 1939[12]
HISTORICAL DELIBERATIONS IN LONDON AND PARIS
EUROPEAN FATE BEING DECIDED
HITLER DOES NOT ACKNOWLEDGE LONDON'S WARNING

Völkischer Beobachter, Berlin, August 25, 1939
POLAND MOBILIZES—CLOSES BORDER AROUND DANZIG

Gazeta Polska, Warsaw, August 25, 1939[13]
GERMAN TERROR TOWARD POLISH PEOPLE IS ACCELERATING HOUR
    BY HOUR

Czas, Warsaw, August 26, 1939
LASTING ALLIANCE BETWEEN POLAND AND GREAT BRITAIN

Völkischer Beobachter, Berlin, August 26, 1939
POLISH ANTIAIRCRAFT FIRE SHOOTS AT GERMAN STATE SECRETARY

Völkischer Beobachter, Berlin, August 27, 1939
ALL OF POLAND IN WAR FEVER

Gazeta Polska, Warsaw, August 28, 1939
INTENSE ANXIETY FOR POLISH PEOPLE IN GERMANY

Tübinger Chronik, Tübingen, August 28, 1939
DANZIG AND THE CORRIDOR MUST COME BACK!
THIS WAS REQUESTED IN A LETTER BY THE FÜHRER TO DALADIER

Le Temps, Paris, August 29, 1939
M. DALADIER PROPOSES TO M. HITLER A LAST ATTEMPT
    AT PEACE BETWEEN GERMANY AND POLAND—THE FÜHRER
    REFUSES

Czas, Warsaw, August 29, 1939
HITLER REJECTS DALADIER'S PROPOSAL FOR PEACEFUL RESOLUTION
OF POLISH-GERMAN CONFLICT

Völkischer Beobachter, Berlin, August 29, 1939
POLISH TERROR ORGANIZATIONS DISCOVERED IN DANZIG
FÜHRER TO DALADIER—DANZIG AND CORRIDOR MUST BE
RETURNED TO GERMANY

Tübinger Chronik, Tübingen, August 29, 1939
ENGLAND'S RESPONSIBILITY
WHOEVER DOES NOT LISTEN TO GERMANY'S
REQUEST TO RECTIFY THE WRONGS OF VERSAILLES IS PROVING
THAT THEY WANT WAR

Czas, Warsaw, August 30, 1939
ENGLAND STANDS STRONGLY WITH POLAND

Tübinger Chronik, Tübingen, August 30, 1939
POLAND OPPOSES EVERYTHING GERMAN—FIRES ON FLEEING
WOMEN AND CHILDREN

Tübinger Chronik, Tübingen, August 31, 1939
POLAND PROVOKES: MOBILIZES

Evening Standard, London, September 1, 1939
GERMANS INVADE AND BOMB POLAND—BRITAIN MOBILISES

Völkischer Beobachter, Berlin, September 1, 1939
GERMANY'S NEW OFFER—POLAND REJECTS NEGOTIATIONS

Polish President's Note, August 25, 1939[14]

I should like to emphasize that the Polish Government have ever considered direct talks between Governments to be the most suitable method of resolving difficulties which may arise between States. We consider that this method is all the more suitable where neighboring States are concerned. On the basis of these principles Poland concluded non-aggression pacts with Germany and Russia. We consider also that the method of conciliation through the intermediary of a disinterested and impartial third party is a just method of resolving differences which have been created between nations.

Although I clearly wish to avoid even the appearance of desiring to profit by this occasion to raise points of litigation, I deem it my duty, nevertheless, to make clear that in the present crisis it is not Poland which is formulating demands and demanding concessions of any other State. It is, therefore, perfectly natural that Poland should hold aloof from any action of this kind, direct or indirect.

Hitler Remarks to French Ambassador in Berlin, August 25, 1939[15]

I bear no enmity whatever towards France. I have personally renounced all claims to Alsace-Lorraine and recognized the Franco-German frontier. I do not want war with your country; my one desire is to maintain good relations with it. I find indeed the idea that I might have to fight France on account of Poland a very painful one. The Polish provocation, however, has placed the Reich in a position which cannot be allowed to continue.

. . . But the guarantee given by the British Government has encouraged the Poles to be obstinate. Not only has the Warsaw Government rejected my proposals, but it has subjected the German minority, our blood-brothers, to the worst possible treatment, and has begun mobilization . . .

No nation worthy of the name can put up with such unbearable insults. France would not tolerate it any more than Germany. These things have gone on long enough, and I will reply by force to any further provocations. I want to state once again: I wish to avoid war with your country. I will not attack France, but if she joins in the conflict, I will see it through to the bitter end. As you are aware, I have just concluded a pact with Moscow that is not only theoretical, but, I may say, practical. I believe I shall win, and you believe you will win: what is certain is that above all French and German blood will flow, the blood of two equally courageous peoples.

Daladier Appeal to Hitler, August 26, 1939

I can vouch not only for the good will of France, but also for that of all her allies. I can personally guarantee the readiness which Poland has always shown to have recourse to methods of free conciliation. . . . In all sincerity I can assure you that there is not one of the grievances invoked by Germany against Poland in connection with the Danzig question which might not be submitted to decision by such methods with a view to a friendly and equitable settlement . . .

In so serious an hour I sincerely believe that no man endowed with human feelings could understand that a war of destruction should be allowed to break out without a last attempt at a pacific adjustment between Germany and Poland. Your will for peace may be exercised in all confidence in this direction without the slightest derogation from your sense of German honor . . .

If the blood of France and that of Germany flow again, as they did twenty-five years ago, each of the two peoples will fight with confidence in its own victory, but the most certain victors will be the forces of destruction and barbarism.

Hitler's Response to Daladier, August 27, 1939

[E]ver since Poland had had the English guarantee, it had become vain to seek to lead her to a sound comprehension of the situation. Poland's mind was set in morbid resistance. Poland knew that she was committing suicide, but was doing so telling herself that, thanks to the support of France and England, she would rise once more.

Besides . . . things have now gone too far. No country having any regard for its honor could tolerate the Polish provocations. France, in Germany's place, would have already gone to war. No doubt there were some reasonable men in Warsaw, but the soldiery of that barbarous country had now broken loose. The central Government no longer had the situation in hand . . .

Moreover, if Poland showed any willingness to talk matters over, it would, doubtless, be in order to gain time for her mobilization . . .

It is useless—Poland would not give up Danzig; and it is my will [Hitler] that Danzig, as one of the ports of the Reich, should return to Germany.

Hitler to British Government, August 29, 1939

To this [Polish rejection of German proposal] were added barbaric actions of maltreatment which cry to Heaven, and other kinds of persecution of the large German national group in Poland which extended even to the killing of many resident Germans or to their forcible removal under the most cruel conditions. This state of affairs is unbearable for a Great Power. It has now forced Germany, after remaining a passive onlooker for many months, in her turn to take the necessary steps for the safeguarding of justified German interests. And indeed the German Government can but assure the British Government in the most solemn manner that a condition of affairs has now been reached which can no longer be accepted or observed with indifference.

European Nations Debate Causes of the War

Following Germany's invasion of Poland, newspapers and politicians in Germany and the west presented dramatically different views of the causes of war and prospects for peace. England and France emphasized German aggression, German atrocities, and German intransigence. German voices focused on English treachery and Polish inflexibility as causes for the war. Both sides promised to fight to victory. A western deadline did nothing to deter Germany from completing its takeover of Poland.

In the Headlines

Cherbourg-Éclair, Cherbourg, September 2, 1939
GENERAL MOBILIZATION IN FRANCE AND IN GREAT BRITAIN
WITHOUT DECLARATION OF WAR, GERMANY ATTACKS POLAND
    AND HER SQUADRONS BOMB WARSAW, CRACOW AND OTHER
    CITIES

The Times, London, September 2, 1939
INVASION OF POLAND—GERMANS ATTACK ACROSS ALL FRONTIERS
WARSAW AND OTHER CITIES BOMBED
BRITISH OBLIGATIONS WILL BE FULFILLED

Völkischer Beobachter, Berlin, September 2, 1939
THE FÜHRER BEGINS THE STRUGGLE FOR SECURITY AND RIGHTS
    OF REICH

Tübinger Chronik, Tübingen, September 2, 1939
"I KNOW NO SURRENDER" THE FÜHRER TELLS THE GERMAN PEOPLE
    AND THE WORLD
SUCCESSFUL BATTLES OF THE GERMAN TROOPS ALONG THE ENTIRE
    FRONT

Daily Mail, London, September 3, 1939
WAR

Völkischer Beobachter, Berlin, September 3, 1939
GERMAN MARCH ON ALL FRONTS IS SUCCESSFUL

Völkischer Beobachter, Berlin, September 4, 1939
GERMAN ANSWER TO ENGLISH HYPOCRISY AND CHALLENGE
THE FÜHRER IS ON THE WAY TO THE FRONT

Tübinger Chronik, Tübingen, September 4, 1939
ENGLISH ROBBER BARON POLITICIANS ON SUNDAY DECLARED WAR
    BETWEEN ENGLAND AND GERMANY AND A FEW HOURS LATER
    FRANCE TOOK THE SAME ACTION

Völkischer Beobachter, Berlin, September 5, 1939
FÜHRER AT THE FRONT
DUTCH AND DANISH NEUTRALITY VIOLATED BY BRITISH BOMBERS

Tübinger Chronik, Tübingen, September 5, 1939
WORLD CRIMINAL ENGLAND VIOLATES NEUTRALITY OF HOLLAND
    AND DENMARK THREE TIMES IN 24 HOURS

Chamberlain's Speech to House of Commons, September 1, 1939

German troops crossed the Polish frontier this morning at dawn and are
since reported to be bombing open towns. In these circumstances there is
only one course open to us. His Majesty's Ambassador in Berlin and the
French Ambassador have been instructed to hand to the German Government the following document:

    "Early this morning the German Chancellor issued a proclamation to the
German Army which indicated clearly that he was about to attack Poland.

Information which has reached His Majesty's Government in the United Kingdom and the French Government indicates that German troops have crossed the Polish frontier and that attacks upon Polish towns are proceeding. In these circumstances it appears to the Governments of the United Kingdom and France that by their action the German Government have created conditions, namely, an aggressive act of force against Poland threatening the independence of Poland, which call for the implementation by the Governments of the United Kingdom and France of the undertaking to Poland to come to her assistance. I am accordingly to inform your Excellency that unless the German Government are prepared to give His Majesty's Government satisfactory assurances that the German Government have suspended all aggressive action against Poland and are prepared promptly to withdraw their forces from Polish territory, His Majesty's Government in the United Kingdom will without hesitation fulfil their obligations to Poland."

. . . We have no quarrel with the German people, except that they allow themselves to be governed by a Nazi Government. As long as that Government exists and pursues the methods it has so persistently followed during the last two years, there will be no peace in Europe.

Hitler to German Army, September 1, 1939

The Polish State has refused the peaceful settlement of relations which I desired, and has appealed to arms. Germans in Poland are persecuted with bloody terror and driven from their houses. A series of violations of the frontier, intolerable to a great Power, prove that Poland is no longer willing to respect the frontier of the Reich.

In order to put an end to this lunacy, I have no other choice than to meet force with force from now on. The German Army will fight the battle for the honor and the vital rights of reborn Germany with hard determination. I expect that every soldier, mindful of the great traditions of eternal German soldiery, will ever remain conscious that he is a representative of the National-Socialist Greater Germany. Long live our people and our Reich!

Hitler Addresses Reichstag, September 1, 1939

Danzig was and is a German city. The Corridor was and is German. Both these territories owe their cultural development exclusively to the German people. Danzig was separated from us, the Corridor was annexed by Poland. As in other German territories of the East, all German minorities living there have been ill-treated in the most distressing manner. More than 1,000,000 people of German blood had in the years 1919–20 to leave their homeland.

As always, I attempted to bring about, by the peaceful method of making proposals for revision, an alteration of this intolerable position. It is a lie when the outside world says that we only tried to carry through our revisions by pressure . . .

[T]he Versailles Diktat is not law to us. A signature was forced out of us with pistols at our head and with the threat of hunger for millions of people. And then this document, with our signature, obtained by force, was proclaimed as a solemn law . . .

Poland has directed its attacks against the Free City of Danzig. Moreover, Poland was not prepared to settle the Corridor question in a reasonable way which would be equitable to both parties, and she did not think of keeping her obligations to minorities.

I must here state something definitely; Germany has kept these obligations; the minorities who live in Germany are not persecuted. No Frenchman can stand up and say that any Frenchman living in the Saar territory is oppressed, tortured, or deprived of his rights. Nobody can say this . . .

An attempt was made to justify the oppression of the Germans by claiming that they had committed acts of provocation. I do not know in what these provocations on the part of women and children consist, if they themselves are maltreated, in some cases killed. One thing I do know—that no great Power can with honor long stand by passively and watch such events . . .

I will not war against women and children. I have ordered my air force to restrict itself to attacks on military objectives. If, however, the enemy thinks he can from that draw carte blanche on his side to fight by the other methods he will receive an answer that will deprive him of hearing and sight. . . .

[F]rom now on bombs will be met with bombs. Whoever fights with poison gas will be fought with poison gas. Whoever departs from the rules of humane warfare can only expect that we shall do the same. I will continue this struggle, no matter against whom, until the safety of the Reich and its rights are secured . . .

As a National Socialist and as German soldier I enter upon this struggle with a stout heart. My whole life has been nothing but one long struggle for my people, for its restoration, and for Germany. There was only one watchword for that struggle: faith in this people. One word I have never learned: that is, surrender.

Daladier to Chamber of Deputies, September 2, 1939

The Government yesterday decreed general mobilization . . .

Thus has the Government put France into a position to act in accordance with our vital interests and with national honor . . .

And at dawn on September 1 the Führer gave his troops the order to attack. Never was aggression more unmistakable and less warranted; nor for its justification could more lies and cynicism have been brought into play.

Indeed, are we only dealing with the German-Polish conflict? We are not, Gentlemen; what we have to deal with is a new stage in the advance of the Hitler dictatorship towards the domination of Europe and the world. How, indeed, are we to forget that the German claim to the Polish territories had been long marked on the map of Greater Germany, and that it was only concealed for some years to facilitate other conquests . . .

And indeed, Gentlemen, it is not only the honor of our country: it is also the protection of its vital interests that is at stake.

Thus, our honor is but the pledge of our own society . . .

Forfeiting our honor would purchase nothing more than a precious peace liable to rescission, and when, tomorrow, we should have to fight after losing the respect of our allies and the other nations, we should no longer be anything more than a wretched people doomed to defeat and bondage . . .

If we were not to keep our pledges, if we were to allow Germany to crush Poland, within a few months, perhaps within a few weeks, what could we say to France, if we had to face aggressors once more? . . .

Gentlemen, in these hours when the fate of Europe is in the balance, France is speaking to us through the voice of her sons, through the voice of all those who have already accepted, if need be, the greatest sacrifice of all. Let us recapture, as they have done, that spirit which fired all the heroes of our history. France rises with such impetuous impulses only when she feels in her heart that she is fighting for her life and for her independence.

Gentlemen, today France is in command.

Daladier to People of France, September 3, 1939

Since daybreak on September 1, Poland has been the victim of the most brutal and most cynical of aggression. Her frontiers have been violated. Her cities are being bombed. Her army is heroically resisting the invader.

The responsibility for the blood that is being shed falls entirely upon the Hitler Government. The fate of peace is in Hitler's hands. He chose war . . .

We are waging war because it has been thrust on us. Every one of us is at his post, on the soil of France, on that land of liberty where respect of human dignity finds one of its last refuges. You will all cooperate, with a profound feeling of union and brotherhood, for the salvation of the country.

Vive la France!

Chamberlain to House of Commons, September 3, 1939

This is a sad day for all of us, and to none is it sadder than to me. Everything that I have worked for, everything that I have hoped for, everything that I have believed in during my public life, has crashed into ruins. There is only one thing left for me to do; that is, to devote what strength and powers I have to forwarding the victory of the cause for which we have to sacrifice so much. I cannot tell what part I may be allowed to play myself; I trust I may live to see the day when Hitlerism has been destroyed and a liberated Europe has been re-established.

Hitler to German People, September 3, 1939

We ourselves have been witnesses of the policy of encirclement which has been carried on by Great Britain against Germany since before the war. Just as the German nation had begun, under its National Socialist leadership, to recover from the frightful consequences of the Diktat of Versailles, and threatened to survive the crisis, the British encirclement immediately began once more.

The British war inciters . . . oppressed the German people under the Versailles Diktat the faithful fulfillment of which would have sooner or later exterminated 20 million Germans.

. . . I am more firmly determined than ever to beat back this attack. Germany shall not again capitulate. There is no sense in sacrificing one life after another and submitting to an even worse Versailles Diktat. We have never been a nation of slaves and will not be one in the future. Whatever Germans in the past had to sacrifice for the existence of our realm, they shall not be greater than those which we are today prepared to make.

Hitler to German Army on the Western Front, September 3, 1939

The British Government, driven on by those warmongers whom we knew in the last War, have resolved to let fall their mask and to proclaim war on a threadbare pretext.

The German people and your comrades in the East now expect from you, soldiers of the Western Front, that you shall protect the frontiers of the Reich, unshakable as a wall of steel and iron, against every attack, in an array of fortifications which is a hundred times stronger than that western front of the Great War, which was never conquered.

If you do your duty, the battle in the East will have reached its successful conclusion in a few months, and then the power of the whole National Socialist State stands behind you. As an old soldier of the World War, and as your Supreme Commander, I am going, with confidence in you, to the Army on the East. Our plutocratic enemies will realize that they are now dealing with a different Germany from that of the year 1914.

Chamberlain's Broadcast to German People, September 4, 1939

You may ask why Great Britain is concerned. We are concerned because we gave our word of honour to defend Poland against aggression. Why did we feel it necessary to pledge ourselves to defend this Eastern Power when our interests lie in the West, and when your Leader has said he has no interest to the West? The answer is—and I regret to have to say it—that nobody in this country any longer places any trust in your Leader's word . . .

Your Leader is now sacrificing you, the German people, to the still more monstrous gamble of a war to extricate himself from the impossible position into which he has led himself and you.

In this war we are not fighting against you, the German people, for whom we have no bitter feeling, but against a tyrannous and forsworn regime which has betrayed not only its own people but the whole of Western civilisation and all that you and we hold dear.

Mussolini's Call for Peace, September 4, 1939

Duce, while realizing exceptional difficulties which then made pacific solution extremely problematic, wished to make final attempt to save European peace. With this object English and French Governments were informed that Duce, if he could have previous certainty of Franco-British adhesion and Polish participation assured by action in London and Paris, would have been able to summon an international conference for 5th September with object of reviewing clauses of Treaty of Versailles which are cause of present disturbance in life of Europe . . . In the meantime, in night between 31st August and 1st September frontier incidents occurred which led Führer to initiate military operations against Poland. Replies reaching Italian Government being favorable in principle both on French and English side and great interest having been shown on French side despite military clash which had already taken place between Germany and Poland in a possible development of initiative of Duce, Italian Government on morning of 2nd September at 10 o'clock informed Chancellor Hitler . . . that there was still possibility of summoning conference, preceded by armistice conference, which would have been designed to solve German-Polish conflict by peaceful means.

Results of Invasion of Poland

By the middle of September, the Polish government had been forced to evacuate its own country. The Soviet Union and Germany then signed supplemental agreements dividing Poland and allowing the U.S.S.R. to occupy what had been Polish territory—that is, western Ukraine and western Belorussia. Soviet voices proclaimed these actions as liberations, just as the German press referred to the triumphant entry of German forces into Danzig. The German invasion also led to the implementation of measures against the Jewish population of Poland as expressed in the testimonies of Shep Zitler and Eva Galler.

In the Headlines

Journal de Genève, Geneva, September 18, 1939
THE SOVIET ARMY ENTERS POLAND
SOVIET AGGRESSION AGAINST POLAND

L'Indépendance Belge, Brussels, September 18, 1939
THE POLISH PRESIDENT AND GOVERNMENT SEEK EXILE IN ROMANIA

Izvestiia, Moscow, September 18, 1939
PEOPLE OF THE SOVIET UNION WITH GREAT ENTHUSIASM GREET THE
    GOVERNMENT'S DECISION TO RENDER BROTHERLY AID TO THE
    POPULATION OF WESTERN UKRAINE AND WESTERN BELORUSSIA

Pravda, Moscow, September 19, 1939
POPULATION OF WESTERN UKRAINE AND WESTERN BELORUSSIA
    ENTHUSIASTICALLY WELCOME VALIANT RED ARMY

Völkischer Beobachter, Berlin, September 19, 1939
AGREEMENT BETWEEN BERLIN AND MOSCOW ON POLAND

Völkischer Beobachter, Berlin, September 20, 1939
TRIUMPHAL ENTRY OF FÜHRER INTO DANZIG
HITLER SPEAKS TO FREED GERMAN CITY
DANZIG—HAPPY CITY

Izvestiia, Moscow, September 29, 1939
CONCLUSION OF GERMAN-SOVIET TREATY OF FRIENDSHIP AND
    BORDERS BETWEEN THE U.S.S.R. AND GERMANY

L'Indépendance Belge, Brussels, September 30, 1939
THE REICH AND THE U.S.S.R. OFFER PEACE BASED ON FAIT
    ACCOMPLI IN POLAND

Testimony of Shep Zitler—Polish Holocaust Survivor

My private hell started six months before the war began. In February 1939, I
was drafted into the Polish army. The army was the first time that I associated with Poles. In Vilna, the Jews lived on one side of the street and the
Poles lived on the other side. We spoke Yiddish and Russian. My Polish
accent was not that great. The Polish soldiers laughed at me.

In the Polish army we had a lieutenant. . . . On his office he had a sign
which read: ENTRY IS FORBIDDEN TO JEWS AND DOGS. We, Jews, were
told, "First we are going to take care of the Germans, then we are going to
take care of you." How did I feel going against my enemy, the Germans, fighting with my second enemy, the Poles?

On September 1, 1939, the war started when Germany invaded
Poland. Poland lost the war in sixteen days. I was with the 77th Infantry

Regiment. Our unit was captured. . . . We were sent to a prisoner-of-war camp . . . I remember that the Jews had already been separated from the Polish soldiers. The Germans could not tell the Jews apart from the other Polish soldiers. They depended on the Poles to tell them that.

I was forced to work on the Autobahn. . . . As Jews we were singled out for special treatment . . . the Jews had to clean excrement out of the slit latrines with our hands. The Jews were always given the dirtiest and most dangerous jobs. Our lives were threatened and we were beaten. We were always hungry, and many of us did not survive.

Testimony of Eva Galler—Polish Holocaust Survivor

Somehow we did not believe Hitler would come to Poland. Until the last minute people did not believe that the Germans would invade us. The Polish soldiers used to sing patriotic songs. They would not give up an inch of our Polish soil to the last drop of their blood. They sang songs about fighting for the port of Danzig.

People did not believe that the Germans would come until they saw the airplanes. It was so sudden. In a couple of days the Germans occupied the whole of Poland . . . the German-Soviet Pact divided Poland . . . Because our town was on the Russian side, the Germans occupied our part of Poland for just two weeks. Then, according to the Treaty, the Russians came in. Until 1941 the Russians were in charge.

The Winter War in Finland

In the fall, the Soviet government demanded border adjustments with Finland to the north of Leningrad. When the Finnish government refused these demands, Soviet forces invaded Finland. The western powers condemned this Winter War, while Soviet voices blamed the war on Finnish attacks against the U.S.S.R. The press in Finland, as well as most of Europe, saw the Russians as aggressors. On the Soviet side, soldiers such as Nikolai Shishkin described the Winter War as necessary training for the battles to come.

In the Headlines

Hufvudstadsbladet, Helsinki, November 4, 1939[16]
MOSCOW—NEGOTIATIONS CONTINUE

Hufvudstadsbladet, Helsinki, November 27, 1939
RUSSIAN CLAIM OF BORDER VIOLATION REJECTED BY FINNISH GOVERNMENT

L'Indépendance Belge, Brussels, November 27, 1939
RUSSIANS DEMAND THAT FINLAND MOVE ITS ARMY 25 KM. FROM
   THE BORDER

Hufvudstadsbladet, Helsinki, November 28, 1939
FINLAND READY TO NEGOTIATE ON TROOP MOVEMENTS

Hufvudstadsbladet, Helsinki, November 29, 1939
RUSSIA CANCELS NONAGGRESSION PACT
BLAMES FINLAND FOR SYSTEMATIC VIOLATIONS OF THE
   AGREEMENT

Hufvudstadsbladet, Helsinki, November 30, 1939
RUSSIA BREAKS DIPLOMATIC RELATIONS WITH FINLAND

Izvestiia, Moscow, December 1, 1939
THE BAND OF MILITARIST PROVOCATEURS WILL BE DESTROYED!
FINNISH WORKERS AND PEASANTS ARE OUR FRIENDS

L'Indépendance Belge, Brussels, December 1, 1939
SOVIET AIR FORCE BOMBS HELSINKI

Journal de Genève, Geneva, December 1, 1939
SOVIET AGGRESSION AGAINST FINLAND
RESISTANCE IS VIGOROUS

The Times, London, December 1, 1939
FINLAND INVADED
RUSSIAN AGGRESSION ON THE NAZI MODEL

Hufvudstadsbladet, Helsinki, December 1, 1939
SOVIETS LAUNCH BRUTAL ATTACK
BRUTAL BOMBINGS OF CIVILIANS

Cherbourg-Éclair, Cherbourg, December 1, 1939
RUSSIAN TROOPS ATTACK FINLAND BY LAND, AIR, AND SEA

Journal de Genève, Geneva, December 3, 1939
HEROIC FINNISH RESISTANCE

L'Indépendance Belge, Brussels, December 5, 1939
MOSCOW REJECTS PEACE OVERTURES FROM HELSINKI

Hufvudstadsbladet, Helsinki, December 27, 1939
BOMBINGS TARGETING OUR CIVILIANS CONTINUES

Testimony of Nikolai Konstantinovich Shishkin—Soviet Soldier in Winter War

I went through the Finnish War . . .

I ended up going to the Vyborg sector. Heavy battles raged there. In the month of December the snow was waist deep. It was true for us that Siberia had prepared and equipped us well. We were dressed in sheepskin coats, hats that covered our ears, and mittens to our elbows. I can't say that 40 degrees below zero was nothing to us, but we didn't feel it so severely. We could and did lie in the snow for several days. They taught it to us in Siberia, and they also taught us to run in the snow . . .

The command underestimated the enemy. I think the soldiers are not to blame. They fulfilled the task that they were given. The defense of the Finns was competent, with concrete bunkers, flanking fire, and if you advanced into this defense without reconnaissance, without preparation, and without reliable suppression of enemy weapons emplacement—this happened more than once—then losses would be great and unjustified. The war was very hard, but if it had not been for it—the Great Patriotic War would have been even worse for us than it was. The Finnish War—it was the schooling that came with much blood.

CHAPTER 3

Germany Conquers Western Europe, 1940

Introduction to 1940

During the winter of 1939–1940, Europe experienced a lull in the fighting (except in Finland), while all sides anticipated a spring offensive. The German army prepared to turn west. The first step was an attack on Scandinavia—specifically Denmark and Norway. On April 20, 1940, German newspapers congratulated Hitler on his birthday; at the same time the army and air force prepared a daring invasion of Western Europe. Again Germany played the victim, with the government and its newspapers claiming that England intended to invade several countries in Europe, including the Reich. German military action was presented as defensive, necessary to save Belgium, Holland, and Germany itself from English and French aggression.

The German attack started on May 10, with panzer units smashing through the Ardennes Forest and breaching the Maginot Line at Sedan.[1] With the Soviet Union neutralized, Hitler had his one-front war, and the German army rolled through Western Europe—across Luxemburg, Holland, and Belgium, and then into France. The western defeat was unprecedented in speed and scale; German newspapers celebrated their rapid victory. The headlines were accurate in their boastful reporting; this time they did not have to exaggerate the extent of German success.

Using rapid offensive tactics, German forces often caught opposing armies unprepared. By the middle of May, Holland surrendered, followed by Belgium at the end of the month. The sudden surrender of Belgium by King Leopold III left British and French forces in a precarious defensive position. The British government decided to abandon the continent and fight another day. British and some French units retreated to Dunkirk on the northern coast, and British ships of all types and sizes carried out a rescue effort of the beleaguered Allied troops. This defeat was transformed into a morale-boosting moment as the British government emphasized the rescue rather than the humiliation of the forced escape. At the same time German newspapers triumphantly focused on the heroics of the *Luftwaffe* (German air force) and the disarray among British and French army units.

Calculating that the fighting was almost over, the cautious Mussolini declared war on the Allies. Claiming that his conscience was clear because he had attempted to mediate and prevent war, Mussolini now argued that Italy had to solve "the problem of our borders"—an attempt to take advantage of the imminent French defeat. He stated that "fascist morality" bound him to stand by his friend (Hitler) at this crucial time. Later that fall, Mussolini tried to enhance his reputation and territory by invading Greece; within one month, the Greeks inflicted an embarrassing defeat on Italy.

Commenting only briefly on Italy's entry into the war, German
headlines focused primarily on the approaching French collapse. These
newspapers celebrated both the military and psychological aspects of
victory, with each German advance and each French defeat followed
closely and hailed loudly within Germany. These overwhelming
victories were proclaimed as the restoration of justice and pride for the
German people. For Hitler, the successful invasion of France was not
just a military victory—it was revenge for the hated armistice of 1918
and humiliation of Versailles in 1919. Compared with World War I
when France fought valiantly for four years, the fall of Paris after only
six weeks in 1940 signaled a moment of dishonor for France and
exuberant boasting for Germany. The victory was a triumphant
moment for the Reich and for Hitler personally.

Perhaps the highlight of Hitler's life came on June 22, 1940. France
surrendered to Germany, and Hitler insisted that the capitulation
ceremony be held at Compiègne, in the same clearing where Germany
had signed the armistice ending World War I. Hitler celebrated by
dancing a jig and posing in front of the Eiffel Tower.[2] The surrender
agreement ordered all French forces to cease fighting, to turn over
their weapons, and to deliver to Nazi authorities any German citizen
who had taken refuge in France and was wanted by the German
government. The latter order meant torture or death for thousands of
refugees caught between Nazi-dominated France and Fascist Spain.
For their part, the victorious Germans occupied northern and western
France, particularly the coasts for defensive reasons, but left the rest of
France nominally independent under a compliant French government.

Only England remained undefeated, and the new prime minister,
Winston Churchill, vowed that the struggle was not yet over.
Throughout the summer and fall, the German air force, the *Luftwaffe*,
bombed England in the Battle of Britain. The notorious destruction of
much of Coventry, including the cathedral, occurred in
mid-November, yet Churchill again promised to fight on.[3] Despite
England's refusal to surrender, there was no way to minimize the
disaster that had devastated nearly all of Western Europe.

The fate of various newspapers also reveals the depth of this
catastrophe. Following Belgium's surrender at the end of May, the
newspaper *L'Indépendance Belge* ceased to publish; similarly the
Norwegian paper *Arbeiderbladet* went out of existence several weeks later.
By the end of June, the independent French press was suppressed,
replaced by collaborationist newspapers such as *Paris Soir*. The repression
and gloom seemed to echo Sir Edward Grey's comment on the outbreak
of World War I: "The lamps are going out all over Europe."[4]

One country that is often neglected in discussions of World War II
is Spain, yet the Axis powers spent considerable effort over the next

few years trying to convince Spain to join the struggle. Francisco Franco, the cautious Spanish ruler, attempted to take advantage of the fall of France without committing his country to the war itself. He explained to Mussolini that while he could not enter the war because of continued hardships resulting from Spain's civil war, he nevertheless wanted to remind Italy of Spain's historic claims to parts of North Africa—especially Morocco. Franco wanted to ensure that Spain received a share of the spoils if the French Empire were to be divided among the Axis powers. Not surprisingly, he expressed anti-English views because of the issue of Gibraltar.

Mussolini tried a hard line approach to pull Franco into the war on the Axis side. The Italian leader assured Franco that the Axis would win the war, but he warned that if Spain were not part of the victorious alliance, it would "alienate" itself from European history and from the future. Mussolini added that if Spain did not join Germany and Italy soon, Franco would not have any "moral justification" for his claims in Africa.

After Mussolini's attempt, Hitler himself tried to convince Franco to enter the war. In a meeting between Franco and Hitler near the Spanish border, Franco explained his position: Spain remained grateful to Germany and Italy for assistance during the civil war, but Spain needed time to recover from that turmoil and wanted economic aide from Germany. For his part, Hitler spoke of the great German victories that had been achieved, his concerns about General de Gaulle, and his hopes that the war would end soon.[5] He felt that Spanish participation in the broad coalition of Fascist nations fighting together would ensure triumph for the Axis. Both dictators expressed their pleasure in meeting the other, but no military alliance resulted from this conference.

While these diplomatic efforts went forward, German success brought new hardships for the people of Western Europe. Many French citizens dreaded the moment when German troops entered their country; they did not know what to expect from the group they derisively called "boches" [krauts]. Several comments by French civilians are included in this section and subsequent chapters on the subject of the occupation. Indeed, fear was an appropriate emotion, as Germany imposed a new type of occupation regime throughout Europe—harsh, brutal, racist.

As a result of their rapid victory, the German army captured many prisoners of war, including the French soldier Paul Roser. Roser with some of his fellow prisoners tried to escape from German custody many times. Held for several years and moved from one camp to another, Roser witnessed a variety of crimes and atrocities carried out by regular German soldiers as well as the *Schutzstaffel* (SS). The German guards repeatedly violated treaties on the treatment of prisoners of war. German soldiers would shoot prisoners with the excuse that they were just following orders. After the war members of the army—the *Wehrmacht*—claimed that all atrocities were the work of the SS, but prisoners like Roser knew the truth.

Hitler's one-front war had succeeded and allowed the Nazi racial agenda to be implemented throughout much of Europe.

THE SOURCES

Winter War in Finland

Because of the lack of fighting between Germany and the western powers, the winter of 1939–1940 was called the "phony war." Both sides used the time to prepare for expected offensives in the spring. The only significant battles took place in Finland, where western voices supported the "heroic" struggle of the outnumbered Finnish divisions against Soviet territorial demands and invasion. The headlines of the time reflected these competing voices, as Swiss and French papers praised Finnish resistance; in March, Finland was forced to give in to Soviet aggression.

In the Headlines

Le Petit Parisien, Paris, January 2, 1940
VICTORIOUS RESISTANCE OF FINLAND—RUSSIAN ATTACKS REPULSED

Le Petit Parisien, Paris, January 4, 1940
BRUTAL RUSSIAN INFANTRY OFFENSIVE STOPPED WITH HEAVY LOSSES

Le Petit Parisien, Paris, January 18, 1940
WE MUST INCREASE ASSISTANCE TO THE VALIANT FINNISH ARMY

Le Petit Parisien, Paris, February 6, 1940
IMPRESSIVE FINNISH RESISTANCE AGAINST MASSIVE ATTACK BY
    20 RUSSIAN DIVISIONS

Journal de Genève, Geneva, February 14, 1940
SOVIET VICIOUSNESS IN FINLAND—HEROISM OF FINNS

Le Temps, Paris, March 5, 1940
THE FINNS DEFEND VYBORG STREET BY STREET

Journal de Genève, Geneva, March 8, 1940
PEACE TALKS TAKE PLACE BETWEEN FINLAND AND THE SOVIETS

Le Temps, Paris, March 14, 1940
AN ACCORD THAT PUTS IN PLACE AN END TO THE CONFLICT
    BETWEEN U.S.S.R. AND FINLAND WAS SIGNED IN MOSCOW

Le Petit Parisien, Paris, March 14, 1940
HELSINKI IN MOURNING
ALL THE FLAGS ON PUBLIC BUILDINGS FLYING AT HALF-MAST

Journal de Genève, Geneva, March 14, 1940
PEACE IMPOSED ON FINLAND

Invasion of Norway

Germany launched the opening battle for Western Europe with an assault on Norway in April. This attack occurred twenty days before the German invasion of the Benelux countries and France, but it diverted British and French forces northward to defend Norway. At first, Allied newspapers claimed victories over the Germans, but by early May, the tide turned in Germany's favor. These events served as a prelude to the massive invasion of Western Europe that started on May 10, 1940.

In the Headlines

Le Petit Parisien, Paris, April 10, 1940
GERMANY OCCUPIES DENMARK AND INVADES NORWAY
FRANCE AND GREAT BRITAIN WILL IMMEDIATELY SEND AID TO
    NORWAY

Le Temps, Paris, April 20, 1940
ALLIED TROOPS CONTINUE TO LAND AT DIFFERENT POINTS ON
    THE COAST OF NORWAY

Tübinger Chronik, Tübingen, April 20, 1940
HITLER AND THE PEOPLE—UNITED
RUDOLF HESS DELIVERS HEARTFELT THANK YOU [for Hitler's birthday]

Arbeiderbladet, Oslo, April 29, 1940[6]
GERMANY'S FOREIGN MINISTER EXPLAINS THE EVENTS THAT LED TO
    THE OCCUPATION OF NORWAY

Boston Daily Globe, Boston, May 1, 1940
ALLIES FACE NORWAY DISASTER

Boston Daily Globe, Boston, May 2, 1940
BRITISH EVACUATE CENTRAL NORWAY

Boston Daily Globe, Boston, May 3, 1940
REICH WINS BULK OF NORWAY

L'Indépendance Belge, Brussels, May 4, 1940
VIOLENT COMBAT AT NARVIK [Norway]

War in Western Europe

On May 10, 1940, because of defeats suffered in Norway, the British government was reorganized with Winston Churchill replacing Neville Chamberlain as prime minister. On that same day, Germany launched a daring invasion of Belgium, France, Holland, and Luxemburg.

German voices claimed that this attack was an act of self-defense against English threats, while the western powers clearly saw German actions as aggressive and unprovoked. Within a few weeks, it was clear that western defenses had broken down, partly resulting from lack of preparation, lack of coordination, and subsequent charges of lack of morale.

In the Headlines

Völkischer Beobachter, Berlin, May 8, 1940
PLANS OF AGGRESSION ARE BECOMING CLEAR [refers to England]

Tübinger Chronik, Tübingen, May 10, 1940
WESTERN POWERS WANT TO INVADE BELGIUM AND HOLLAND
GOAL: RUHR REGION

Arbeiderbladet, Oslo, May 10, 1940 [now collaborationist]
GERMAN TROOPS HAVE MOVED INTO THE NETHERLANDS, BELGIUM,
    AND LUXEMBURG THIS MORNING TO PROTECT THE NEUTRALITY
    OF THESE COUNTRIES AGAINST IMMINENT BRITISH-FRENCH
    ATTACK
VON RIBBENTROP: THE GERMAN ARMY IS NOW TALKING WITH
    ENGLAND AND FRANCE IN THE ONLY LANGUAGE THEY
    UNDERSTAND
CHAMBERLAIN STEPS DOWN—EUROPE FACING TOTAL WAR

Tübinger Chronik, Tübingen, May 11, 1940
GERMAN ATTACK IN WEST

Völkischer Beobachter, Berlin, May 11, 1940
FÜHRER AT THE WESTERN FRONT
ENGLISH-FRENCH ATTACK ON RUHR STOPPED

Le Petit Parisien, Paris, May 11, 1940
GERMAN INVASION CONTAINED BY BELGIAN AND DUTCH ARMIES
M. WINSTON CHURCHILL SUCCEEDS M. CHAMBERLAIN

Le Temps, Paris, May 12, 1940
GERMAN AGGRESSION AGAINST THE LOW COUNTRIES, BELGIUM
    AND LUXEMBURG

Le Temps, Paris, May 13, 1940
BELGIAN AND DUTCH ARMIES WITH GROWING HELP OF ALLIED
    FORCES STUBBORNLY RESIST ENEMY PRESSURE

Tübinger Chronik, Tübingen, May 13, 1940
GERMAN ATTACK MOVES FORWARD QUICKLY

Boston Daily Globe, Boston, May 14, 1940
NAZIS ADVANCE ON ALL FRONTS—
CUT HOLLAND ALMOST IN TWO AND PIERCE BELGIUM DEFENSES

Völkischer Beobachter, Berlin, May 16, 1940
MAGINOT LINE BREACHED AT SEDAN

Tübinger Chronik, Tübingen, May 18, 1940
BRUSSELS IN GERMAN HANDS

Boston Daily Globe, Boston, May 21, 1940
'DISASTER,' SAYS REYNAUD—NAZIS NEAR CHANNEL

Dunkirk and Evacuation

After King Leopold of Belgium surrendered his forces without
warning England and France, the Allied defense plan (already in
trouble) was destroyed. British and French troops close to the
Channel moved toward Dunkirk as the British government mobilized
its ships, naval and private, to rescue the remnants of the Allied
armies.[7] Several Royal Air Force (RAF) pilots remembered the long
lines of soldiers waiting to be rescued. In the end, more than 300,000
Allied troops were saved. For the Allies, the evacuation was a success
and helped boost morale; for the Germans, the Allied withdrawal from
the continent was an Axis victory and Allied humiliation.

In the Headlines

Tübinger Chronik, Tübingen, May 24, 1940
THE ENEMY IS RETREATING EVERYWHERE

Tübinger Chronik, Tübingen, May 27, 1940
CALAIS IN GERMAN HANDS—LUFTWAFFE ATTACKS ENGLISH
   AIRBASES

Völkischer Beobachter, Berlin, May 29, 1940
BELGIUM SURRENDERS UNCONDITIONALLY

Le Temps, Paris, May 29, 1940
KING LEOPOLD III ORDERS THE BELGIAN ARMY TO PUT
   DOWN ITS ARMS

Le Petit Parisien, Paris, May 29, 1940
BELGIANS CONDEMN TREASON OF THEIR KING—
EVENT WITHOUT HISTORICAL PRECEDENT

Le Temps, Paris, May 31, 1940
FRANCO-BRITISH ARMIES, FACING MORE HARD COMBAT,
   WITHDRAW TO DIG IN AT DUNKIRK

Tübinger Chronik, Tübingen, June 1, 1940
NORTHERN FRENCH ARMY DESTROYED

Tübinger Chronik, Tübingen, June 3, 1940
67 SHIPS BOMBED AT DUNKIRK

Tübinger Chronik, Tübingen, June 4, 1940
330,000 ENGLISH AND FRENCH TROOPS TAKEN PRISONER
   AT BATTLE OF FLANDERS—ATTACK ON DUNKIRK CONTINUES

Le Petit Parisien, Paris, June 5, 1940
335,000 MEN OF THE ARMY OF FLANDERS SAVED

Testimony of Group Captain C. Brian Kingcome

Q: Can you describe the view of the beaches [at Dunkirk] that you would have?

A: Yes, one saw the beaches; one saw them packed with soldiers. One saw dozens of these small boats, steaming in and out of the beaches, like a peacetime flotilla of pleasure boats. A lot of them would just heave to just off the beach in wading depth for the soldiers. And there would be a constant stream of soldiers wading out in the water. Every so often, a German fighter would come down, and strafe the beach. And chased hopefully by a Hurricane or a Spitfire. And then you'd chase something up into the clouds. And it was that sort of operation.

    The army was rolling back towards the beaches for some little time. And so the news was full of it. And so one was prepared. Perhaps one didn't quite realize the enormity of the task of getting them all off. Because they were there in their thousands.

Testimony of Air Vice Marshal Harold A. C. Bird-Wilson

As Dunkirk was approaching, our daily trips to France were reduced and we then stood by for the evacuation of our troops from Dunkirk. And I have in my log book the recording that our first patrol over Dunkirk was on the 26th of May. And we were up about twice a day over Dunkirk. Thus everybody had a crack at it and likewise he had a continuous flow of fighters over Dunkirk. I know that the army, when they returned from Dunkirk having had a very rough time of being bombed and strafed, et cetera by the Germans, accused the fighter squadrons and the RAF . . . the point about the army who returned from Dunkirk, they made the accusation that they never saw the RAF fighters over Dunkirk. This did surprise us greatly because as I've said, we had two patrols over Dunkirk, per squadron per day from dawn till dusk. . . . And we protected the beaches quite considerably. In fact, it was a continuous patrol throughout the whole of the daylight hours. . . . When one flew low over Dunkirk, you saw all the soldiers heading for the nearest ship which was going to bring them back to England. . . . We were greatly shocked to see the number of troops that were coming through Dunkirk. And we knew that it was their last exit out of France on the northern part of France and we did our utmost to protect them and even protect the ships that were coming back.

Testimony of Group Captain Denys Edgar Gillam

Q: Did you get much of a sight of the beaches at Dunkirk?

A: Yes, we were generally patrolling about 2,000 feet and we went up and down . . . Helluva mess. Lot of smoke, you could see the smoke from Southend. When you got close you could see all the men standing in the water and all the boats ferrying. Trouble was that one first knew there were enemy aircraft about when bombs suddenly started dropping. . . . But Dunkirk was difficult in that we were fighting so far away at our extreme range and the problem was that one was always very conscious that one had to get back.

Defeat in Norway and Italy Joins the War

Following the surrender of Belgium and the withdrawal of Anglo-French forces from the continent, the Allies were forced to abandon Norway—another success celebrated in German headlines. With German victory imminent everywhere in Western Europe, Italy joined the war. The French army and government suffered a military defeat followed by a harsh occupation.

In the Headlines

Tübinger Chronik, Tübingen, June 10, 1940
THE FRENCH ARE RETREATING

Arbeiderbladet, Oslo, June 10, 1940
FIGHT IN NORTHERN NORWAY ABANDONED AT MIDNIGHT LAST NIGHT

Völkischer Beobachter, Berlin, June 11, 1940
TOTAL VICTORY OF HEROES IN NARVIK—NORWEGIAN TROOPS SURRENDER

Tübinger Chronik, Tübingen, June 11, 1940
ITALY ON GERMANY'S SIDE IN WAR AGAINST WESTERN POWERS

Corriere Della Sera, Milan, June 11, 1940
ITALY AT WAR WITH ENGLAND AND FRANCE—
THE MONARCH ENTRUSTS COMMAND OF OPERATIONS TO IL DUCE

Il Popolo D'Italia, Milan, June12, 1940
IL DUCE ASSUMES COMMAND OF TROOP OPERATIONS ON ALL
  FRONTS

Le Temps, Paris, June 12, 1940
ITALY DECLARES WAR ON FRANCE AND ENGLAND

Mussolini Declares War on Allies, June 10, 1940

Listen—the hour marked out by destiny is sounding for our country. This is
the hour of irrevocable decision. The declaration of war has already been
handed to the Ambassadors of Britain and France.

We are going to war against the plutocratic and reactionary democracies
of the West, who have hindered the advance and often threatened the very
existence of the Italian people.

. . . Today we have decided to face all the risks and sacrifices of war. A
nation is not really great if it does not regard its undertakings as sacred, and
if it recoils from those supreme trials that decide the course of history . . .

This gigantic struggle is only a phase in the logical development of our
revolution. It is the struggle of peoples who are poor, but rich in workers
against the exploiters who fiercely hold on to all the wealth and all the gold
of the earth. It is the struggle of the fruitful and young peoples against the
sterile peoples on the threshold of their decline. It is the struggle between
two centuries and two ideas.

Collapse of France

By mid-June, the situation in France had become hopeless. Desperate
French leaders brought World War I hero Marshal Pétain[8] into the
government, but instead of resistance, he envisioned French-German
cooperation and collaboration as the path to salvation for France.
French surrender and the occupation of Paris led German voices to
proclaim the reversal of the "humiliation" of Versailles. The
testimonies of captured French soldiers as well as Polish soldiers
fighting with the French tell of the disarray on the western front. In
the midst of these events, the U.S.S.R. took advantage of chaos in the
west and occupied the Baltic States.

In the Headlines

Tübinger Chronik, Tübingen, June 12, 1940
FRANCE'S LAST FIFTEEN MINUTES—REYNAUD FLEES TO TOURS

Tübinger Chronik, Tübingen, June 14, 1940
FRENCH NORTHERN FRONT DESTROYED

Tübinger Chronik, Tübingen, June 15, 1940
FRANCE FACES TOTAL COLLAPSE

Völkischer Beobachter, Berlin, June 15, 1940
PARIS IN GERMAN HANDS—COMPLETE COLLAPSE OF
    FRENCH ARMY

Journal de Genève, Geneva, June 15, 1940
THE GERMANS ENTER PARIS

Völkischer Beobachter, Berlin, June 16, 1940
VERSAILLES UNDER THE SWASTIKA

Tübinger Chronik, Tübingen, June 17, 1940
MEETING BETWEEN FÜHRER-DUCE
"FRANCE MUST LAY DOWN WEAPONS" SAYS MARSHAL PÉTAIN

Washington Post, Washington, D.C., June 17, 1940
REYNAUD QUITS—FRANCE DEBATES WAR OR PEACE
MAGINOT LINE ABANDONED—BRITAIN TO FIGHT ON
LATVIA AND ESTONIA BOW TO SOVIET ULTIMATUM

Le Temps, Paris, June 18, 1940
THE CABINET OF PAUL REYNAUD DISSOLVES—
MARSHAL PÉTAIN FORMS A NEW CABINET

Corriere Della Sera, Milan, June 18, 1940
IL DUCE AND THE FÜHRER MEET TO AGREE UPON THE POSITIONS
    OF THE TWO COUNTRIES IN REGARDS TO THE FRENCH OFFER OF
    SURRENDER

Tübinger Chronik, Tübingen, June 18, 1940
FRANCE AT THE END—TOTAL COLLAPSE—REQUESTS CEASE FIRE

Völkischer Beobachter, Berlin, June 18, 1940
FRANCE SURRENDERS—PÉTAIN ANNOUNCES COLLAPSE
AGREEMENT BETWEEN FÜHRER AND MUSSOLINI

Tübinger Chronik, Tübingen, June 19, 1940
FÜHRER AND DUCE IN TOTAL AGREEMENT ON FRENCH REQUEST
    FOR CEASE FIRE

Der Angriff, Berlin, June 19, 1940[9]
AFTER 22 YEARS, ONE MAN DESTROYS CLEMENCEAU'S VICTORY
MOST COMPLETE VICTORY SINCE NAPOLEON

Völkischer Beobachter, Berlin, June 21, 1940
RETALIATION BEGINS AGAINST ENGLAND

Pravda, Moscow, June 20, 1940
ENTRY OF SOVIET FORCES ACROSS BORDERS OF LITHUANIA, LATVIA
   AND ESTONIA

Pravda, Moscow, June 22, 1940
ESTONIAN PEOPLE DEMONSTRATE THEIR FRIENDSHIP WITH THE
   SOVIET UNION—LITHUANIAN PEOPLE REJOICE
PUBLIC DEMONSTRATIONS IN RIGA [article is pro-Soviet]

Der Angriff, Berlin, June 22, 1940
THE STAIN OF SHAME IS ERASED [article refers to shame of
   World War I]

Tübinger Chronik, Tübingen, June 22, 1940
OLD HUMILIATION ERASED IN FOREST OF COMPIÈGNE

Der Angriff, Berlin, June 24, 1940
THE SURRENDER OF THE INVINCIBLE MAGINOT LINE IS THE
   GREATEST VICTORY OF ALL
NOW BEGINS THE NEW PHASE OF THE WAR: AFTER COMPIÈGNE,
   ENGLAND STANDS ALONE

The Times, London, June 24, 1940
HITLER'S TERMS FOR AN ARMISTICE ACCEPTED
HALF FRANCE TO REMAIN OCCUPIED
GENERAL DE GAULLE'S CALL FOR RESISTANCE

Tübinger Chronik, Tübingen, June 25, 1940
THE MOST GLORIOUS VICTORY OF ALL TIME—WAR IN WEST IS OVER

Le Temps, Paris, June 29, 1940
AN ULTIMATUM FROM THE U.S.S.R. TO ROMANIA

Le Temps, Paris, June 30, 1940
ROMANIA CEDES BESSARABIA AND NORTHERN BUKOVINA TO THE
   U.S.S.R.

Armistice Agreement between Germany and France, Compiègne, June 22, 1940

I. The French Government directs a cessation of fighting against the German Reich in France as well as in French possessions, colonies, protectorate territories, mandates as well as on the seas.

It [the French Government] directs the immediate laying down of arms of French units already encircled by German troops.

II. To safeguard the interests of the German Reich, French State territory north and west of the line drawn on the attached map will be occupied by German troops . . .

III. In the occupied parts of France the German Reich exercises all rights of an occupying power. The French Government obligates itself to support with every means the regulations resulting from the exercise of these rights and to carry them out with the aid of French administration . . .

IV. French armed forces on land, on the sea, and in the air are to be demobilized and disarmed in a period still to be set . . .

V. The French Government is obligated to forbid any portion of its remaining armed forces to undertake hostilities against Germany in any manner.

Testimony of Marcel Tison[10]—French Prisoner of War

I was just an ordinary solder in the 11th Cherbourg Artillery Regiment when war broke out. I was captured on June 5, 1940 near Calais.

Within a few days, we were transferred to Germany, traveling on foot and by train, and I ended up in Stalag 8C in Sagan, Poland. I spent almost the whole of the war around that area, in working groups on farms or building sites.

Testimony of Henri Hervieu[11]—French Prisoner of War

When war was declared, I was 25 and had already done two years of national service. But I was recalled. The Germans took me prisoner on June 23, 1940 in the Mayenne region.[12] I stayed in a camp set up on the Le Mans racing circuit until January 1941, and then I was transferred to a prison camp in Trier near the German frontier with Luxemburg. I worked in a quarry, then in a factory that made wooden huts.

Testimony of Karol Wierzbicki[13]—Polish Soldier

On April 23 [1940] the Brigade embarked on transport ships in the port of Brest [France]. For the Brigade this was the beginning of the Norwegian Campaign. Sailing to Norway under wartime conditions took about two weeks. To their amazement and amusement, during the voyage the soldiers heard a German radio announcement about their own supposed sinking. Among the soldiers, as well as the officers, there was a general feeling that the next phase, after pushing the Germans out of Norway, would be the liberation of Poland.

Paradoxically, the tragic defeat of France by Germany in 1940, the sight of organizational chaos, and low morale in the French Army helped thousands of Polish soldiers, who took part in the French Campaign, to regain some emotional balance after the September 1939 defeat of Poland. It also helped them to shake off all unfounded feelings of guilt from the defeat, as well as to regain confidence and the will to fight on.

Testimony of Jozef Franciszek Nowak[14]—Polish Soldier

Officer Cadet Jozef Nowak still "managed" to take part in the French Campaign of 1940. The French military establishment did not have much trust in the Poles—"what kind of soldiers are you, that in 1939 you defended yourselves for only a few weeks." The French Campaign made a very negative impression on Nowak: poor morale, disorganization, obsolete, much worse than Polish, materiel. While struggling against the enemy in the vicinity of Lyon, almost by a miracle he escaped death during a bombing raid. The evacuation from a defeated France was on a coal-transport ship and that was why, when disembarking in the English port of Liverpool, the coal-dust covered soldiers looked more like coal miners than an army.

Testimony of Tadeuz "Wicher" Wichrowski[15]—Polish Soldier

There he joined the then forming 2nd Rifle Division, with which he went through the French campaign of 1940. During defensive operations in the vicinity of Belfort,[16] close to the Swiss border, he and his Fifth Heavy Machine-Gun Platoon were captured by the Germans.

He remembers that time most of all as an unprecedented picture of disintegration of the French Army and overwhelming, defeatist attitude of the French. For Polish military units, trying to hold the defense lines no matter the cost, the French population had, on many occasions, only insults ("those damned Poles"). When nearing one country town, where Wichrowski's detachment was preparing defensive positions in haste, there came a very worried delegation from the town headed by its mayor. They demanded that Poles relinquish all defensive measures immediately. However, what the Poles did immediately was to inflict well-deserved corporal punishment on the mayor for his defeatism, after which, without any further delay, they employed their whole detachment to dig trenches.

Occupation of Western Europe

German victory led to the division of France into one zone of direct German occupation and another region under the collaborationist Vichy government. The arrest and deportation of enemies started immediately, and testimonies from Luxemburg and France suggest some of the early characteristics of German control. The situation worsened as the war continued.

Testimony of Emil Reuter[17]—Luxemburg

Q: Can you tell us whether it is correct that the German authorities
   obliged members of . . . the police to take an oath of allegiance to the
   Chancellor of the Reich?
A: Yes. This was forced . . . with very serious threats and punishments.
   Recalcitrants were usually deported, if I remember rightly, to
   Sachsenhausen,[18] and on the approach of the Russian Army all or a part
   of the recalcitrants who were in the camp were shot (about 150) . . .
Q: In addition to these transplantations, were there deportations to
   concentration camps?
A: Yes, there were deportations to concentration camps which everyone
   knew about. The number of such deportations in the Grand Duchy may
   be approximately four thousand.
       First of all, the young people . . . were pursued and hunted by the police
   and by the Gestapo. Then they were brought before various types of
   Tribunals. . . . Their families were deported; the family fortune was generally
   confiscated. The penalties pronounced by the Tribunals against these young
   people were likewise very severe. The death penalty was general, or else
   imprisonment, forced labor, or deportation to concentration camps . . .
       I believe that it is hardly possible that such a situation could have been
   unknown to the members of the Reich and the Supreme Military Authority. My opinion is based on the following facts: First of all, our young people, when mobilized by force, frequently protested, at the time of their
   arrival in Germany, by invoking the fact that they were all of Luxembourg
   nationality, and that they were the victims of force, so that the military
   authorities must have been informed of the situation in the Grand Duchy.

Testimony of Charles Couppey, June 1940—French Civilian

I asked myself what the "boches" [krauts] would look like? What form would
they have? For me they were like Martians. One assumed they could only be
bad news.
    When they arrived, I left school and we stood on the side of the road.
Soon there appeared two motorcycles with side-cars, carrying armed soldiers. These were the boches! These were the boches!

Testimony of Marie Dubost, June 1940—French Civilian

We had an insane fear of the Germans who we called "boches." Our parents
told us that they would kill us. In reality, no harm was done to us.
    There were a lot of them, in trucks and cars that we saw for the first
time, but we soon got used to it. The hunters hid their rifles in the woods

and buried them in the ground. The Germans requisitioned rooms especially in nicer homes for the officers.

Testimony of Paul Roser—French Prisoner of War

Q. You were born of French parents?

A. I was born of French parents.

Q: You were a prisoner of war?

A: Yes. The Germans, our guards, having recaptured one of us, attempted to make him reveal who the others were who also had sought to escape. The man remained silent. The guards hurled themselves upon him, beating him with the butts of their pistols in the face, and with bayonets—with the butts of their rifles. At that moment, not wishing to let our comrade be killed, several of us stepped forward and revealed that we had been trying to escape. I then received a beating with bayonets on my head and fell into a swoon. When I recovered consciousness, one of the Germans was kneeling on my leg and was still striking me. Another one, raising his gun, was about to strike my head. I was saved on that occasion through the intervention of my comrades, who threw themselves between the Germans and myself. That night we were beaten for exactly three hours with rifle butts, with bayonet blows, and with pistol butts in the face. I lost consciousness three times.

The following morning we were taken to work, nevertheless. We were digging trenches for the draining of the marshes. It was very heavy work, which started at 6:30 in the morning and finished at 6 o'clock at night. We had two breaks, each of half an hour. We had nothing to eat during the day. Soup was given to us when we came back at night with a piece of bread and a small piece of sausage or two cubic centimeters of margarine and that was all.

. . . A French prisoner, Lieutenant Robin, who with some of his comrades had prepared an escape and for that purpose had dug a tunnel, was killed in the following manner. The Germans having had information that the tunnel had been prepared watched with a few German guards for the exit of the would-be escapees. Lieutenant Robin, who was first to emerge, was killed with one shot while obviously he could in no manner attack anyone or defend himself.

At that time there were about twelve to thirteen thousand in that camp. There was for that total number one single faucet which supplied, for several hours a day, undrinkable water. . . . The small rooms contained as many as six hundred men in one room. We were stacked in tiers along the walls, three rows of them, thirty to forty centimeters for each of us.

. . . One of the Frenchmen succeeded in escaping. Without waiting, the German non-commissioned officer selected two men and shot them on the spot. Incidents of this type occurred in other circumstances.

. . . One night, in July 1942, we heard machine gun fire throughout the entire night, and the moans of women and children. The following morning, bands of German soldiers were going through the rye fields on the very edge of our camp, their bayonets pointed downward, seeking people hiding in the fields. Those of our comrades who went out that day to go to their tasks told us that they saw corpses everywhere in the town, in the gutters, in the barns, in the houses. Later some of our guards, who had participated in this operation, quite good-humoredly explained to us that 2,000 Jews had been killed that night under the pretext that two SS had been murdered in the region.

Axis Tries to Bring Spain into the War

While Germany prepared to invade England, the Axis powers tried to convince Spain to join the struggle. These talks between the Axis powers and Franco continued for the next couple of years, but they always ended in a stalemate. Franco hesitated to commit to military action, claiming that Spain was still recovering from its civil war. Some historians judge Franco as cagey and smart in avoiding the conflict, whereas others see him as indecisive and unable to decide how to proceed under wartime conditions.

Franco to Mussolini, August 15, 1940

The consequences, which the conquest of France is to have for the reorganization of the North African territories have made it advisable for me, now that the time has come, to charge my Ambassador in Rome with transmitting to Your Excellency the Spanish aspirations and claims traditionally maintained throughout our history in the foreign policy of Spain, today more alive than ever in our consciousness; to territories, whose present administration is a consequence of that Franco-English policy of domination and exploitation, of which Italy also bears so many scars. To the legitimate Spanish aspirations are added in this case the requirements for security necessitating the elimination of a weak and thinly protected frontier.

Mussolini to Franco, August 25, 1940

Ever since the outbreak of the war I have been constantly of the opinion that "your" Spain . . . could not remain neutral until the end of the war, but at the right moment would change to non-belligerency and finally to intervention.

Should that not happen, Spain would alienate herself from European history, especially the history of the future, which the two victorious Axis powers will determine . . .

There is no doubt that after France, Great Britain will be defeated; the British regime exists only on one single element: the lie.

I certainly do not need to tell you that you, in your aspirations, can count on the full solidarity of Fascist Italy.

Franco to Hitler, September 22, 1940

1. [C]oncerning the political and economic effects of the present struggle, I can only say to you that I have agreed from the first day on with your opinion expressed there. Only our isolation and the lack of resources most indispensable for our national existence made our operation impossible.

I am in agreement with you that driving the English out of the Mediterranean Sea will improve the condition of our transports . . .
2. I am likewise of the opinion that the first act in our attack must consist in the occupation of Gibraltar . . .
3. The possibility of a surprise attack on the Canary Islands by the English in order to create a naval base for themselves to protect overseas connections has always been a worry of mine . . .

I would like to thank you, dear Führer, once again for the offer of solidarity. I reply with the assurance of my unchangeable and sincere adherence to you personally, to the German people, and to the cause for which you fight.

Conversation between Franco and Hitler, October 23, 1940

Spain has always been allied with the German people spiritually without any reservation and in complete loyalty. In the same sense, Spain has in every moment felt herself at one with the Axis . . .

In the present war as well, Spain would gladly fight at Germany's side. . . . A war would necessitate preparations in the economic, military, and political spheres. . . . Therefore, Spain must mark time . . .

The Führer replied that he was glad to see the Caudillo[19] personally for the first time in his life. . . . He knew precisely how difficult the struggle in Spain had been, since he himself since 1918–19 had had to go through similar grave conflicts. . . . The struggle which was raging in Europe today would be decisive for the fate of the Continent and the world for a long time to come. Militarily, this struggle in itself was decided . . .

In the attempt to bring about the end of the war as soon as possible and to render the entry of the United States into the war more difficult, Germany had concluded the Tripartite Pact. This Pact was compelling the United States to keep its Navy in the Pacific Ocean and to prepare herself for a Japanese attack from that direction. In Europe as well, Germany was attempting to expand her base.

Battle of Britain

Following the defeat of France, Hitler began preparations for the invasion of Britain (Operation Sealion). Realizing that they did not have the naval capacity to launch a successful attack, Hitler and Göring planned to use the German air force, the *Luftwaffe*, to destroy English defenses and will to resist.[20] The so-called blitz rallied the English people behind Churchill; England fought on alone.

In the Headlines

Il Popolo D'Italia, Milan, June 26, 1940
THE WAR CONTINUES AGAINST GREAT BRITAIN AND WILL
  CONTINUE UNTIL FINAL VICTORY

Tübinger Chronik, Tübingen, June 27, 1940
LOOKING IN THE DIRECTION OF ENGLAND

Le Petit Parisien, Paris, July 20, 1940 [collaborationist]
FÜHRER ISSUES MAJOR WARNING TO ENGLAND

Le Petit Parisien, Paris, August 17, 1940
MASSIVE ATTACK BY GERMAN PLANES ON LONDON REGION

Le Petit Parisien, Paris, August 26, 1940
GERMAN COMMUNIQUE ANNOUNCES THAT METHODICAL
  DESTRUCTION OF ENGLAND WILL FOLLOW

Testimony of Group Captain C. Brian Kingcome

I'm always surprised at the number of aircraft which took part. One hears now that four hundred and sixty something pilots were killed, or whatever it was, in the Battle of Britain. But the reason we were outnumbered I suppose was because the Germans came over in two or three waves a day. And each wave consisted of as many aircraft as they could get together.

I don't think one feared any German fighter. Certainly in those days, the only German fighters there were the 109s. The German 109 could out-dive you. And could out-climb you. And I think it was faster straight and level. But it didn't have the manoeuvrability. And all in all, there's no Spitfire pilot who'd have swapped for a 109.

Testimony of Group Captain Denys Edgar Gillam

Well we got warned when they were leaving the French coast and we started, we came to readiness and we scrambled, and we started to climb immediately and we generally got to their height about . . . well underneath them about Canterbury. And they came in waves and we tended to go for the bombers, especially towards the end. Our instructions were to ignore the fighters and concentrate on the bombers. It was a running battle from Canterbury inland . . . I hated the Boche [*Krauts*] for what he was doing. I blame the lot of them. In other words I had no time for the Germans and still haven't. I consider that though they were a professional force that they'd allowed themselves to be conned into a situation which they shouldn't have been.

Testimony of Wing Commander Eustace Holden

Q: In the Battle of Britain was there any sense on your part of taking part in a great historical event?

A: No, none whatever, absolutely none. All we knew was that the enemy were attacking, and if we didn't shoot them down, we should be taken over by the Germans, which didn't appeal to us. But that fact that it was a great historical event never occurred to us, or whether it's an historical occasion or not really was not for us to even think about, never occurred to us.

SA stormtroopers parade past Adolf Hitler in Nuremberg, Germany, September 1935. By this time, Hitler had purged the SA in the Night of the Long Knives.

Prisoners at the Sachsenhausen concentration camp, December 1938.

The results of a German air raid during the invasion of Poland, September 1939.

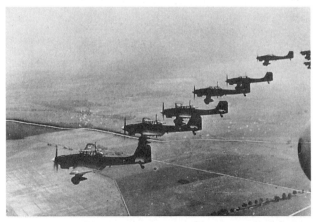

A squadron of Junkers Ju 87 dive-bombers over Poland, September 1939. The Ju 87, or Stuka, was an important component of the German blitzkrieg that swept Europe in the early years of the war.

Hitler and Benito Mussolini in Munich, Germany, June 1940. Germany and Italy had signed the Pact of Steel allying the two countries about a year earlier.

British soldiers at Dunkirk, June 1940. The British and French were able to evacuate more than 300,000 troops from the continent.

French civilians look on as French Army troops leave France for colonies
in Africa, where they will be organized as Free French Forces, 1940.
NATIONAL ARCHIVES

A still from the U.S.
Army propaganda film
Divide and Conquer
shows British troops
escaping from Dunkirk.
NATIONAL ARCHIVES

During the Battle of Britain (July–October 1940), an air observer keeps watch for attacking German aircraft. St. Paul's Cathedral stands in the background.

NATIONAL ARCHIVES

A German SS recruiting poster from the Netherlands, which reads: "Netherlanders, for your honor and conscience, rise up against Bolshevism. The Waffen SS calls you!" During its occupation of Europe, the Waffen SS recruited volunteers from not only the Netherlands, but also France, Belgium, Sweden, and other countries.

NEDERLANDERS

VOOR UW EER EN GEWETEN OP ! - TEGEN HET BOLSJEWISME DE WAFFEN ⚡⚡ ROEPT U !

Two British women walk through the ruins of the almshouse that was their home until leveled by the Germans. NATIONAL ARCHIVES

British prime minister Winston Churchill tours the ruins of Coventry Cathedral, destroyed by the Luftwaffe in November 1940. LIBRARY OF CONGRESS

From a tank turret, Gen. Bernard Law Montgomery watches his forces move up, North Africa, November 1942. One of the war's most effective and controversial leaders, Montgomery had already turned the tide in Africa at El Alamein and would go on to command in Sicily and Italy and in the campaign for France and Germany. NATIONAL ARCHIVES

German grenadiers of the Waffen SS take a break on the Eastern Front in 1942, a year during which the Germans continued their advance against the Soviet Union until halted at Stalingrad. BUNDESARCHIV, BILD 146-1973-115-12 / CC-BY-SA

An Air Transport Command plane flies over the pyramids in Egypt, carrying American supplies to strategic battle zones around the world. NATIONAL ARCHIVES

Joseph Stalin, Franklin Roosevelt, and Winston Churchill at the Tehran Conference in late 1943. The first of only two meetings of the three leaders, this gathering focused largely on the opening of a second front in France (Operation Overlord), long demanded by Stalin. NATIONAL ARCHIVES

Wearing the unit's trademark fez, men of the 13th Waffen Mountain Division of the SS "Handschar" read a pamphlet on "Islam and Judaism," June 1943. Primarily Bosnian Muslims and Croatian Catholics, the division saw action against Communist partisans in Yugoslavia and stood as ironic testimony to the mixed composition of Heinrich Himmler's "pure" SS.

At the Battle of Kursk in the summer of 1943, German and Soviet tanks clashed in one of the largest armored engagements in history. Here German soldiers show the strains of combat, with a Tiger I in the background.

A German soldier inspects a Russian T-34 tank, disabled at Kursk. Of less complicated design than most German tanks, the T-34 proved itself one of the top tanks of the war.

Gen. George S. Patton confers with Lt. Col. Lyle Bernard, commander of the 30th Infantry Regiment, on Sicily, where Patton slapped a soldier and was relieved of duty. He returned to command the Third Army in France in 1944. NATIONAL ARCHIVES

American B-24s, part of the U.S. Fifteenth Air Force, fly over Axis oil refineries in Ploesti, Romania, August 1943. The bombing, code-named Operation Tidal Wave, cost the U.S. more than 600 men killed, captured, and missing and more than fifty planes but did not significantly reduce oil output. U.S. AIR FORCE

The 872-day siege of Leningrad is lifted in January 1944, and its citizens rejoice, removing a sign that warned of artillery barrages.

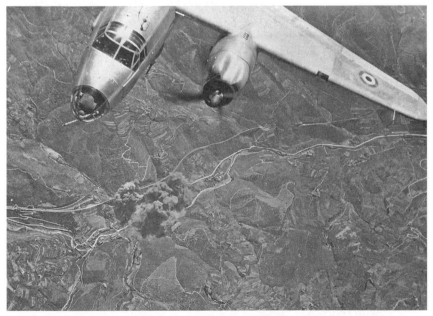

A French B-26 bombs targets in Italy as part of Operation Strangle, an Allied attempt in 1943 and 1944 to cut German supply lines north of Rome.

Men of the 1st Special Service Force are briefed near Anzio, Italy, April 1944. Nicknamed the Devil's Brigade, the 1st was an elite commando unit with members from Canada and the United States. NATIONAL ARCHIVES CANADA / PA 128986

German soldiers confer in the southern Soviet Union, 1944.
BUNDESARCHIV, BILD 101L-024-3535-32 / VORPAHL / CC-BY-SA

An Italian propaganda poster portraying the Allies in a different light.

American troops in a landing craft approach Omaha Beach on D-Day, June 6, 1944. Delayed several times, the Normandy invasion took place on five beaches and involved American, British, and Canadians troops. NATIONAL ARCHIVES

Field Marshal Erwin Rommel inspects troops of the 21st Panzer Division in France before the Allies invaded. After gaining fame as the Desert Fox in Africa, Rommel was placed in command of the Germans' defense of the French coast.

Paratroopers of the 101st Airborne and French civilians in Sainte-Marie-du-Mont, June 7, 1944. NATIONAL ARCHIVES

An American A-20 makes a bomb run in France on D-Day. Though far from perfect, the bombing campaign that took place before and on D-Day helped prevent German reinforcements and supplies from reaching the front lines quickly. NATIONAL ARCHIVES

Gen. Henry D. G. Crerar, commander of the First Canadian Army, which he led
through the end of the war. NATIONAL ARCHIVES CANADA

French children salute Canadian
troops, June 19, 1944. NATIONAL
ARCHIVES CANADA / PA 132807 / BELL

Gen. Dwight Eisenhower with Gen. Ira T. Wyche, July 1944. As Supreme Commander of Allied forces in Europe, Eisenhower displayed his ability to manage subordinates and maintain good relations with alliance partners.
NATIONAL ARCHIVES

German prisoners captured by Canadians south of Caen, France, during Operation Totalize in August 1944.
NATIONAL ARCHIVES CANADA

CHAPTER 4

Invasion of Soviet Union, 1941

Introduction to 1941

Early in 1941, Hitler again tried to convince General Franco of Spain
to join the Axis powers in the war. After winning a difficult civil war,
Franco remained cautious and concerned about involving Spain in a
conflict that could lead to further destruction of his country. Hitler
reminded Franco of oppression by England, the United States, and
"Jewish-international democracy." Hitler also mentioned the issue of
Gibraltar, controlled by England but desired by Spain, as an incentive
for Spanish military action. Furthermore, Hitler offered extensive
economic aid to Spain to help the country recover and prepare for war.
In the end, Hitler appealed to the vision that united Germany, Italy,
and Spain:

I believe that we three men, the Duce, you, and I, are bound to one another
by the most rigorous compulsion of history that is possible, and that thus we
in this historical analysis ought to obey as the supreme commandment the
realization that in such difficult times, not so much an apparently wise cau-
tion as the bold heart, rather, can save nations.[1]

Franco responded with complements but without a commitment.
The Spanish ruler affirmed his support for the Fascist cause: "I
consider as you yourself do that the destiny of history has united you
with myself and with the Duce in an indissoluble way." Nevertheless,
the guarded Franco reiterated the difficulties that his country faced, the
need for more grain, and other economic problems that kept him out
of the war. Without agreeing to any concrete actions, Franco made his
pro-Fascist political leanings clear:

I stand ready at your side, entirely and decidedly at your disposal, united in a
common historical destiny, desertion from which would mean my suicide and
that of the Cause which I have led and represent in Spain. I need no confirmation of my faith in the triumph of your Cause and I repeat that I shall
always be a loyal follower of it.[2]

Mussolini also joined the Axis pressure to compel Franco to enter
the war. In a rambling speech in February, Mussolini referred to the
ideological affinity and obligation that led him to send military
assistance to Franco in the 1930s; it was Franco's duty to return the
favor. The Italian leader went on to justify Italy's participation in the
current war and insisted that victory was inevitable. Perhaps mindful of
Italy's mediocre performance in the battle for Greece, he claimed that
Italy was tired from continuous war (since 1922) against the evil forces
of democracy and capitalism. Despite the reality of Italian defeats, he

saluted the valiant efforts of his military in Albania and Greece.
Mussolini also provided a long list of reasons why Italy and Germany
could not lose—based on the weak character and Jewish control of the
British and American governments.

While Germany and Italy pressured Spain to join their cause, the
still-neutral United States edged closer to the Allied side. Roosevelt
tried to assist Britain as much as possible within the legal constraints of
American law. His actions were cautious yet politically risky, for he was
aware that American public opinion opposed involvement in the war.
Nevertheless, the recently reelected president was able to convince
Congress to pass the Lend-Lease bill in March, providing military
equipment and other assistance to England on a credit basis that
relieved the hard-pressed British budget. In August, Roosevelt met
with Churchill near Newfoundland and joined the British prime
minister in a statement of principles, or war aims, that included the
destruction of "Nazi tyranny." This Atlantic Charter served as the
basic program for the western alliance and eventually for the United
Nations. Unlike World War I, when western war aims were articulated
late in the war (not until 1918), the western allies went on record early
in World War II to establish their reasons for fighting.

Militarily, 1941 was one of the most important years of the war. In
June and December, the entire nature of the war was transformed.
Because of two military errors, Axis prospects turned from inevitable
victory to inevitable disaster. Both Germany and Japan played fatal
roles in this reversal of fortune: Hitler's determination to attack the
Soviet Union and Japan's surprise bombing of Pearl Harbor created a
new balance of power that favored the Allied side. These acts of Axis
aggression forged the Allied coalition that would be victorious four
years later.

The first major military event occurred in June 1941, when Hitler
broke the nonaggression pact that he signed with the U.S.S.R. in 1939.
That agreement had allowed him to fight a one-front war and to
prevail in the west in the spring and summer of 1940. With only
England left in the war, but not considered by military experts as a
threat to Nazi control of the continent, Germany felt emboldened to
fight another one-front war—this time in the east. Amassing one of the
largest land armies in world history for Operation Barbarossa, Hitler
audaciously moved millions of men toward the Soviet border while
denying any aggressive intentions. In one of the continuing mysteries of
the war, Stalin ignored Germany's mobilization as well as the warnings
sent to him by Britain and the United States. Once the invasion
started, German armies made rapid progress, and German newspapers
celebrated the series of victories over retreating Soviet forces.

The Germans invaded with three armies, and one of them targeted Leningrad. While the Nazis never occupied the city, the city's population suffered a cruel fate. Except for access by Lake Ladoga, Leningrad was surrounded and under siege for nearly three years. Probably a million people died in the city, many from starvation or disease. The other German armies targeted Moscow and southern Russia (Ukraine). The Germans made rapid progress in the south, but they were slowed in the center by tenacious Soviet resistance and poor military decisions by Hitler. As a result, German forces finally approached Moscow in the fall. The weather as well as Soviet tactics stalled the German army. Moscow did not fall—the defense of Moscow occurred at the very moment when Japan was taking action to change the balance of power in the Pacific.

The Japanese attack was the second transformative military event of 1941. It occurred at the end of the year on December 7, when Japan's aggression brought the United States into the war. In the days immediately following Pearl Harbor, the government of Germany announced a break in diplomatic relations with the United States and that a state of war existed between the two countries. The German declaration justified the act as defensive, blaming President Roosevelt for siding with Britain and for allowing the U.S. Navy to participate in aggressive actions against German ships. Germany claimed that it had followed international rules governing proper neutral behavior but that the American government had violated those understandings.

On December 11, Hitler explained to the Reichstag and the German people the reasons why he was declaring war against the United States. In a lengthy speech that provides insight into his thinking about the war, Hitler blamed Roosevelt for a series of crimes and transgressions against the German population and ultimately against civilization. He linked Roosevelt and the United States with a variety of entities, including the Soviet Union, Bolshevism, Jewish conspiracies, and military aggression against Germany. At the same time he identified himself with the poor and downtrodden, and saw God's hand guiding his actions to save the world. The German press celebrated the Japanese attack on Pearl Harbor by repeating all of the most optimistic Japanese claims about victory over the Americans. As it had blamed Czechs, Poles, French, and Russians for aggressive actions, the German government now accused the Americans of forcing the Japanese attack. Hitler believed that he eventually would have to fight the United States and that this was a favorable moment given the devastating defeat that the American navy had suffered on December 7. Furthermore, Hitler had little respect for a racially and religiously diverse American society.

On the same day that Germany declared war on the United States, Mussolini issued a statement placing Italy on the side of Japan and Germany against the United States. Like Germany, Italy publicly blamed Roosevelt for provoking the conflict. As he had in previous speeches, Mussolini predicted victory for the Axis nations.

After declaring war against the United States, the Axis powers agreed among themselves not to pursue separate or individual peace treaties with the Allies. Germany, Italy, and Japan pledged to remain in the war and assist each other until victory and to cooperate in the creation of their new world order.

With the battlefield transformed by the new alliance system that placed Britain, the United States, and the U.S.S.R. on the same side, the Polish government in exile (in London) wanted to be certain that it would be included in any discussions about the postwar period. The Polish government assured the United States and Britain of its commitment to the Allied cause and insisted that it had earned special diplomatic status as an ally of England's since 1939, as the first country to resist Germany militarily, as a country that continued to offer resistance to the Germans, and as a country that had good relations with all the Allied nations. Unfortunately for Poland, Stalin viewed the Polish government in London as too pro-western, and he had his own agenda for that country. Despite being allies, the west and the Soviet Union disagreed about the status and future of Poland throughout the war.

In the meantime, further misfortune was plaguing Poland and all the countries of Eastern Europe. German occupation meant new levels of barbarism against the civilian population. At the moment when the Japanese were bombing Pearl Harbor and the Russians were defending Moscow, Hitler issued the Night and Fog Decree to ensure that enemies of the Reich disappeared into the night. *Einsatzgruppen* (killing squads) moved across Eastern Europe looking for Jews, Slavs, Gypsies, and other unacceptable peoples who were to be eliminated. The story of the war against civilians is told by some of the survivors who witnessed these atrocities.

THE SOURCES

Consolidating the Axis Alliance

At the beginning of the year, Hitler and Mussolini increased their pressure on Franco to bring Spain into the war. As they had previously, the Axis leaders argued that their support for Fascist forces in Spain during its civil war had earned Franco's engagement on their side, but Franco continued to avoid making a firm commitment.

Hitler Seeks Spanish Participation, February 6, 1941

For centuries, Spain has been persecuted by the same enemies against whom today Germany and Italy are forced to fight. In addition to the earlier imperial strivings inimical to our three nations there now arose, moreover, antitheses conditioned by world-outlook: The Jewish-international democracy, which reigns in these states, will not excuse any of us for having followed a course which seeks to secure the future of our peoples in accordance with fundamental principles determined by the people and not those imposed by capital. . . . It is my most heartfelt conviction that the battle which Germany and Italy are now fighting out is thus determining the future destiny of Spain as well. Only in the case of our victory will the present regime continue to exist. Should Germany and Italy lose this war, however, then any future for a really national and independent Spain would be impossible . . .

Mussolini Speech in Rome, February 23, 1941[3]

Britain unleashed the conflagration with a criminal and premeditated will . . .

We are not like the English. We boast that we are not like them. We haven't elevated lying into a government art nor into a narcotic for the people the way the London government has done . . .

[W]e continue to follow the cult of truth and repudiate all falsification. . . .

Great Britain cannot win the war . . . the alliance between Italy and Germany is not only between two States or two armies or two diplomacies but between two peoples and two revolutions and is destined to give its imprint upon the century . . . [T]he morale of the Axis people is infinitely superior to the morale of the British people. . . . It is highly ridiculous to count on the eventual moral breakdown of the Italian people. This will never happen. To speak of a separate peace is idiotic.

Churchill has not the least idea of the spiritual forces of the Italian people or of what Fascism can do . . . to beat the Axis, Great Britain's armies would have to land on the Continent, invade Germany and Italy and defeat their armies, and this no Englishman, no matter how insane and delirious by the use and abuse of drugs and alcohol, can even dream of. . . .

Illusion and lying are the basis of American interventionism—illusion that the United States is still a democracy, when instead it is a political and financial oligarchy dominated by Jews, through a personal form of dictatorship . . .

The Italian people, the Fascist people deserve and will have victory. The hardships, suffering and sacrifices that are faced with exemplary courage and dignity by the Italian people will have their day of compensation when all the enemy forces are crushed on the battlefields by the heroism of our soldiers.

Franco Answers Hitler on War, February 26, 1941

You must have no doubt about my absolute loyalty to this political concept and to the realization of the union of our national destinies with those of Germany and Italy. . . . I want to dispel with them all shadow of doubt and declare that I stand ready at your side, entirely and decidedly at your disposal, united in a common historical destiny, desertion from which would mean my suicide and that of the Cause which I have led and represent in Spain. I need no confirmation of my faith in the triumph of your Cause and I repeat that I shall always be a loyal follower of it.

Germany Invades the U.S.S.R.

The most important military events of 1941 were Germany's invasion of the Soviet Union and Japan's attack on the United States. Before moving its forces into the U.S.S.R., Germany was forced to consolidate control in the Balkans by invading Yugoslavia and Greece. The invasion of the U.S.S.R. started in the third week of June, when German and Italian newspapers trumpeted Axis victories and Soviet newspapers urged resistance against the enemy. The testimony of Soviet fighters speaks to the intensity of the struggle, while diplomatically the United States, Britain, and the Polish government in exile pledged support for the U.S.S.R. In August the western powers signed the Atlantic Charter,[4] establishing war aims and promising a more democratic world after victory. Eventually all Allied nations signed the charter.

In the Headlines

Paris-Soir, Paris, April 7, 1941 [collaborationist]
GERMAN TROOPS ENTERED YUGOSLAVIA AND GREECE AT DAWN

Paris-Soir, Paris, April 15, 1941
BELGRADE FALLS

Corriere Della Sera, Milan, June 23, 1941
THE AXIS AT WAR WITH SOVIET RUSSIA
GERMAN TROOPS IN COLLABORATION WITH ROMANIANS AND
FINNS ADVANCE RESOLUTELY INTO ENEMY TERRITORY

Völkischer Beobachter, Berlin, June 23, 1941
MIGHTY GERMANY'S ARMY TAKES ITS PLACE IN THE EAST
CONSPIRACY BETWEEN LONDON AND MOSCOW OPENLY
ADMITTED—
BOTH ACCOMPLICES UNITED IN WANTING TO DESTROY GERMANY
AND EUROPE

Völkischer Beobachter, Berlin, June 24, 1941
CHURCHILL ADMITS CONSPIRACY WITH STALIN

Der Angriff, Berlin, June 24, 1941
SUCCESSFUL PROGRESS OF THE FIGHT AGAINST THE RED ARMY IN
THE EAST

Le Journal de Genève, Geneva, June 24, 1941
THE REICH DECLARES WAR ON RUSSIA
FINLAND AND ROMANIA SIDE WITH GERMANY

Le Journal de Genève, Geneva, June 26, 1941
THE LIGHTNING OFFENSIVE OF THE GERMAN ARMY

Völkischer Beobachter, Berlin, June 26, 1941
ROOSEVELT GIVES HIS BLESSING TO THE WEDDING BETWEEN
LONDON AND MOSCOW
THE HEAD OF THE INTERNATIONAL PLUTOCRACY GIVES HIS
SUPPORT TO BOLSHEVISM [reference to and attack on FDR]

Der Angriff, Berlin, June 28, 1941
GERMAN TROOPS ARE SUCCESSFUL ON ALL FRONTS IN THE EAST
CRUSADE AGAINST THE SOVIETS: ALL OF EUROPE HAS JOINED US

Völkischer Beobachter, Berlin, June 28, 1941
FINLAND AND HUNGARY JOIN THE WAR AGAINST THE SOVIET
UNION
THE FIGHT OF THE PEOPLES OF EUROPE AGAINST BOLSHEVISM
MOSCOW'S OPPRESSION OF FINLAND AN EXAMPLE OF THE
BOLSHEVIK MURDEROUS ATTACK ON EUROPE

Völkischer Beobachter, Berlin, June 30, 1941
SOVIET INVASION BEATEN BACK
THE FÜHRER SAVES EUROPE FROM THE BOLSHEVIK INVASION

Pravda, Moscow, July 3, 1941
ALL OF OUR FORCES—SUPPORTING OUR HEROIC RED ARMY, OUR
GLORIOUS RED ARMY, OUR GLORIOUS RED FLEET!

ALL THE FORCES OF THE PEOPLE—TO THE CRUSHING DEFEAT OF
THE ENEMY!—FORWARD TO OUR VICTORY!

Izvestiia, Moscow, July 4, 1941
ALL POWER TO THE PEOPLE—CRUSH THE ENEMY!

Testimony of Ivan Ivanovich Konovalov[5]—Soviet Pilot

Our training continued right up to the 22nd June 1941. The next morning
the rumor suddenly went round that war had broken out. The air-raid siren
sounded. We grabbed our overcoat rolls and gasmasks, dropped the tent
flaps and threw a couple of branches over them to camouflage them somewhat. And you know, it never occurred to anyone to disperse the planes!
They were standing in the middle of the airfield wing to wing. As I now
recall, there were seventeen superb Tupolev SB high-speed bombers and facing them as many R-5s. That afternoon we went to the mess tent and had
lunch. . . . Suddenly some Heinkel-111 bombers approached; I managed to
count twenty-four of them. Word went round: they're ours. So we were
standing around discussing this when there came the screech of falling
bombs. This terrifying howling smothered all other sounds. Someone nearby
yelled, "Get down!" I scrambled underneath a wing. It felt like the bombs
were falling right on my head. The screech and then the explosions! It was
really dreadful. A bomb hit the opposite wing of the plane under which I was
lying. The Germans completed their bombing run and began to turn away,
but at the same time their rear gunners started machine-gunning us. I
remember my greatcoat roll getting a round through it but I escaped being
hit. They turned about and made for home. What a sight! The whole aircraft
park was ablaze. Of the seventeen SBs only one remained untouched. Not
one R-5. All over were the bodies of colleagues, the screams and groans of
the wounded. It was a shock. That day we buried forty-eight in the bomb
craters. The most seriously wounded were loaded onto trucks and taken to
the field hospital.

Testimony of Naum Kravets[6]

On 22nd June 1941 Molotov held a speech regarding the outbreak of war. All
schoolchildren who were in Moscow rushed to school. We were taught how to
quench fire bombs. We took part in fighting battalions. When Moscow was
bombed, peoples' volunteer corps' were on the roofs of the houses equipped
with boxes with sand. . . . Metro trains weren't operating, the rails were covered
with wooden cover and people slept on them. In the morning, people went back
home. . . . The Germans were close by! It was glowing on the horizon. It seemed
to us that it was the front-line, burning Smolensk, the city where our soldiers
were fighting desperately trying to break through the siege. Many died. Wounded

children were crying from the horror and pain. There were neither doctors, nor nurses. We tore our clothes to make bandages for the wounded. I vaguely remember those things as I was in shock. Dozens of thousands or even hundreds of thousands of schoolchildren and students were working on that defense line. In early October at night the cavalry regiment came to our construction site. Then I found out that it was the cavalry regiment of the regular army that was to take up position here. In the morning I decided to go to the train station. The cars with shells were exploding and I wanted to look at that. I was standing there and watching cars blast and burn.

Treaty between Britain and U.S.S.R., July 12, 1941[7]

(1) The two Governments mutually undertake to render each other assistance and support of all kinds in the present war against Hitlerite Germany.

(2) They further undertake that during this war they will neither negotiate nor conclude an armistice or treaty of peace except by mutual agreement.

Treaty between U.S.S.R. and Polish Government in Exile, July 30, 1941[8]

1. The Government of the U.S.S.R. recognizes the Soviet-German treaties of 1939 as to territorial changes in Poland as having lost their validity. The Polish Government declares Poland is not bound by any agreement with any third power which is directed against the U.S.S.R.

2. Diplomatic relations will be restored between the two governments upon the signing of this agreement, and an immediate exchange of Ambassadors will be arranged.

3. The two governments mutually agree to render one to another aid and support of all kinds in the present war against Hitlerite Germany.

The Atlantic Charter, August 14, 1941

First, their countries seek no aggrandizement, territorial or other;

Second, they desire to see no territorial changes that do not accord with the freely expressed wishes of the peoples concerned;

Third, they respect the right of all peoples to choose the form of government under which they will live; and they wish to see sovereign rights and self-government restored to those who have been forcibly deprived of them;

Fourth, they will endeavor, with due respect for their existing obligations, to further the enjoyment by all States, great or small, victor or vanquished, of access, on equal terms, to the trade and to the raw materials of the world which are needed for their economic prosperity;

Fifth, they desire to bring about the fullest collaboration between all nations in the economic field with the object of securing, for all, improved labor standards, economic advancement and social security;

Sixth, after the final destruction of the Nazi tyranny, they hope to see established a peace which will afford to all nations the means of dwelling in safety within their own boundaries, and which will afford assurance that all the men in all lands may live out their lives in freedom from fear and want;

Seventh, such a peace should enable all men to traverse the high seas and oceans without hindrance;

Eighth, they believe that all of the nations of the world, for realistic as well as spiritual reasons must come to the abandonment of the use of force. Since no future peace can be maintained if land, sea or air armaments continue to be employed by nations which threaten, or may threaten, aggression outside of their frontiers, they believe, pending the establishment of a wider and permanent system of general security, that the disarmament of such nations is essential. They will likewise aid and encourage all other practicable measure which will lighten for peace-loving peoples the crushing burden of armaments.

Battle of Moscow

One of the decisive battles of the war occurred at the end of 1941, as German forces moved toward the Soviet capital city. While German newspapers urged their troops on toward victory, Soviet voices called for sacrifice and defense of the motherland. The outcome remained in doubt until December, when Soviet resistance as well as bitterly cold weather halted the German offensive.

In the Headlines

Völkischer Beobachter, Berlin, October 10, 1941
THE GREAT HOUR HAS ARRIVED: CAMPAIGN IN THE EAST DECIDED

Pravda, Moscow, December 3, 1941
WE WILL FIGHT WITH SELF-SACRIFICE AND HEROICALLY FOR
    MOSCOW, FOR LENINGRAD, FOR OUR MOTHERLAND, FOR THE
    TOTAL CRUSHING DEFEAT AND DESTRUCTION OF EVERY LAST
    ONE OF THE GERMAN OCCUPIERS!

Pravda, Moscow, December 6, 1941
VALIANT DEFENDERS OF THE MOTHERLAND: STRIKE MORE
    POWERFULLY AGAINST THE ENEMY—
DESTROY MERCILESSLY THE FASCIST OCCUPIERS WHO HAVE FORCED
    THEIR WAY ONTO THE TERRITORY OF OUR NATIVE LAND

Pravda, Moscow, December 9, 1941
THE GERMAN FASCIST INVADERS HAVE CRAWLED INTO THE DEPTHS
   OF OUR COUNTRY—FROM HERE THEY SHALL NOT LEAVE ALIVE!—
RED ARMY WARRIORS! DESTROY THE HATED OCCUPIERS—
HE WHO RAISES THE SWORD AGAINST OUR MOTHERLAND SHALL
   DIE BY THE SWORD

The Times, London, December 13, 1941
HUGE GERMAN LOSSES IN MOSCOW BATTLE
85,000 KILLED AND 1,400 TANKS DESTROYED

Testimony of Naum Kravets

By mid-October Moscow became a front-line city, and on 6th October we
were declared besieged. All plants and enterprises were evacuated to the
rear. The government moved to Kuibyshev. The city was taken by anarchy
and panic. Stores were plundered. Military patrols shot the plunderers on
the spot. There were our anti-aircraft guns near the store and a shell pierced
my grandmother's head. She died at once. We came to the train station. It
was crowded with people. We could hear lamentation and wailing. Then, the
sirens were screeching—the warning of a coming air raid.

   In late 1941 we received a notification that my father Solomon Kravets
was reported missing. Only after the war some of my father's front-line fellows came to my mother and told her the details of how my father died.
Their unarmed battalion left Moscow. . . . On their way German spies on
motorcycles chased them down and killed almost everybody, including my father. Few survivors came back to Moscow. So, that was the way my father
died. I had a reason to hate the fascists, so I decided to go to the front as a
volunteer. In July 1942 together with my fellow students I went to the
headquarters of the Ural military circle requesting to be drafted into the
lines.

Siege of Leningrad

The siege of Leningrad, lasting nearly three years, remains one of the
most notorious events of the war. German forces surrounded most of
the city and allowed hundreds of thousands of inhabitants to starve to
death. Two members of the Lelchitski family who survived described
life inside the blockaded city.

In the Headlines

Pravda, Moscow, August 22, 1941
BLOOD FOR BLOOD AND DEATH FOR DEATH!

Izvestiia, Moscow, August 22, 1941
THE WORKERS OF LENINGRAD RISE UP LIKE AN INDESTRUCTIBLE
   WALL FOR THE DEFENSE OF THE CITY—
THE FASCISTS MUST NOT BE ALLOWED IN THE CITY OF LENIN!

Testimony of Samouil Borisovich Lelchitski[9]

The morning of the 22nd, we saw the first reconnaissance planes of the Germans.

We heard Molotov's speech on the radio around noon . . . we were ordered to start preparing trenches.

We only heard good things about the government and Stalin. We believed that he would defend us; we had faith . . .

On the 8 September 1941, the blockade of the city started.

We had heard of the occupation of Belarus and how terrible it was. We knew of Hitler, but didn't understand anything about his ideology, etc. We did know about the German army, and when they attacked the U.S.S.R. the thought of such a mobilized force was terrifying.

My division was mobilized for active duty. We were moved to the outskirts of Leningrad. It was a special unit for reconnaissance. My job was to alert the people in the city and also other soldiers of any bombing raids and shelling. At the end of the war, I ended up receiving a prestigious medal for this.

As the war progressed, we learned to fight. Before that, we knew nothing about combat, weapons, etc. We were unprepared, but we had the duty of protecting Leningrad and its people.

With time came experience, knowledge, and also fulfillment of military operations. Some of my comrades were moved to the east side of Leningrad to defend the Road of Life [Lake Ladoga and supply routes]. It was a terrible time for Leningraders and its defenders. We had rations and, honestly speaking, we were always very hungry.

We took turns sleeping: 8 hours work at the radio alert, 4 hours sleep, then 8 hours of miscellaneous work, chopping wood, etc., then 4 hours sleep again.

Some parts of our division were dispersed throughout the city. On November 28, 1941, a 500 kg bomb destroyed the school where they were stationed. Eighteen of my close friends were killed as the bomb went through all 5 stories of the school to the basement, leaving a circular hole.

As far as food, there was always soup. It was disgusting. They would add rotten parsley to it for flavor! We would have porridge. Also, we were given 100g of vodka to keep warm, especially in the winter. This was called the "Frontovoi 100 gram" [the 100 grams of the front]. Some soldiers did not drink the vodka. Instead, they poured it into a bottle and collected it. Later, some would give it away or trade it to other soldiers, or wait until they had enough to get drunk. As far as the living conditions, these were also terrible. We slept in the trenches. We had no barracks. Most of the time, we slept without a roof over our heads, in the snow, in the rain. Many got sick each day.

We were fighting for peace between countries, for my countrymen, for my Motherland. We fought for the righteous cause.

Germans were very strong. We hated them, but we respected their military power. But towards the later part of the war, their morale was visibly terrible.

We never had any contact with Americans. However, it was the biggest celebration when America joined the war and the second front was opened. We knew how much they had helped us.

When the blockade around Leningrad was ended, my division was sent into the Baltic States to push Germans back. I was there when the war ended. We were surrounding the remaining Nazi troops there and taking many prisoners. Knowing they were defeated, the Germans hung their underwear and long johns up because they were white . . . while in the Baltic States, I was awarded two Red Army Medals for bravery in combat. I'm very proud of my brave comrades and friends who gave their lives for their countrymen.

Testimony of Polina Gregoryevna Lelchitski[10]

At the beginning of the war, we were told to dig trenches and dugouts. Within the first days of the war, we would wait out the air raids in these trenches and bomb shelters. It was absolutely terrifying.

During the first week of German bombing of the city, we watched from the trench as a bomb destroyed our apartment building. We were left with absolutely nothing—only the things we had with us.

We were taken in by a family in the next apartment building over from ours. The apartment was very small and we had to live in the kitchen, but still we were very grateful for the accommodations.

Within the first week, the Germans targeted the warehouses, where food was being stored. With the food destroyed, the city experienced mass hunger and starvation.

Our food ration was 125 grams of bread per day. We had ration cards that were given out to us once per month. Every day we would stand in line and get our bread. To get water, citizens of Leningrad went to the Neva River.

We would break all of the furniture and burn it in the stove to keep warm.

At the beginning, I was in the Komsomol [Young Communist League]. My job was to serve the city of Leningrad by throwing bombs off of the rooftops. The bombs were dropped from planes and had timers. It was a terrifying ordeal to pick these bombs up because they were capable of exploding at any second. I got a medal for my bravery.

During the second year of the blockade, I met a very nice pilot who referred me to work at an airfield where Russian planes were taken to be worked on. This airfield was bombed daily. It was very far away from where we lived, but this job allowed for a higher ration card for me and my brother. To go to the airfield, I had to cross the Kirov Bridge, which was very long. I had to present a special pass to cross the bridge, as well as being out at night, as everyone had a curfew. I was walking through parts of the city that the Germans constantly bombed; it was extremely dangerous. There were signs that read: "citizens, this side of the street is under constant threat from shelling and airplane fire."

Many bodies lay in the street, abandoned. Most, however, were wrapped and taken to the Piskarovskoye Cemetery. Death followed you everywhere, around every corner. Constant warnings played over the loudspeakers: "Citizens! Air Raid warning! Air Raid warning! Please go to bomb shelters." The whining of airplanes still rings in my ears. It was a terrible sound.

One day I heard the whistle of a plane. It had a Nazi symbol and it flew by very close to the ground. I could see the pilot's face perfectly. He made a fly by, turned around, and as he came back he started shooting at us. I was able to hide behind a toilet booth, but there were about ten of us and some did not make it to cover and were killed. Bodies were wrapped in cloth and taken to the cemetery. In the winter, they were taken there on sleds.

At the end, they would bring the Nazi prisoners through the city. Of course, we hated them. But they looked terrible, and it was hard to hate them. They were on the verge of death. People gave them scarves and hats. They were humans after all. Later, they worked in factories.

We first heard about Nazi treatment of Jews during the takeover of Minsk. As they approached Leningrad this was the most terrifying thing about the Nazis, which is why the victory in the war is so meaningful. They were evil.

Testimony of Naum Kravets

I came back to Leningrad, where the main regiment forces were positioned.... But the course of war, especially the Leningrad siege, turned things upside down: aviation, not the battle ships, was the striking force of the Baltic Fleet. Part of the Baltic Fleet was locked in Leningrad and most of the battle ships were stuck in Kronstadt due to severe frosts. The exits to the sea were barred with antisubmarine nets and mine fields. Neither fleet nor submarines could put to sea.... Some submarines were able to break through antisubmarine nets, put to sea and take part in battles. Aviation took up most of the load: reconnaissance, sinking adversary ships, attacking land troops. Aviation was supposed to find antisubmarine nets, and spare navigating channels in 1944...

My first and biggest award was the Medal for the Liberation of Leningrad. It is the most precious medal for me. I think all Baltic marines take pride in the Medal for the Liberation of Leningrad because it was very hard to get it. Then I received a Medal for Military Merits, and then the Order of the Red Star. There were more awards afterwards . . .

I cannot say that my first battle was the hardest. It was scary all the time. But the feeling of fear was momentous during the first seconds of flight. There was a brutal fear when leaving the aerodrome: it gave you the creeps and you had a lump in the throat. When the work is done, you don't fear, just get focused on things to be done. You are to be responsible. Then you calm down. Later on, when you return to your aerodrome, having a meal at the canteen, taking some rest in the cubicle, you are as if in the battle for the second time, analyzing your mistakes, [thinking about] bombers and have an understanding how to escape them. Another thing: you shouldn't think over wrongdoings, perils, or remember the perished comrades before going into battle. I noticed many times, if somebody had such thoughts he was embraced with fear and that person died. . . .

Navy aviation was considered to be among the elite troops. We were supplied very well. The pilots were fed the best way. Every day we had wheat bread, meat, 20 grams of butter and 20 grams of sugar. They must have taken into account that during a two-hour flight each member of the crew lost about three to four kilograms of weight due to high energy consumption. We lived where we were told to—be it a dug out or a non-demolished house, and sometimes right in the open land. We made a fire in the center, covered the ground with pine branches and spent the night in a sleeping-bag.

War against the United States

With the German army on the offensive in Russia, the Japanese military moved southward to seize control of natural resources in Southeast Asia and beyond. Roosevelt responded with economic sanctions against Japan, and the Japanese cabinet under General Tōjō decided on war with the United States.[11] Hitler and Mussolini blamed Roosevelt for provoking the Japanese attack on December 7; the Axis leaders then declared war on the United States. German and Italian newspapers celebrated the great Japanese victory. The Polish government in exile reiterated its commitment to the Allied cause.

In the Headlines

Völkischer Beobachter, Berlin, November 8, 1941
ALL GUILT LAYS WITH ROOSEVELT: THE DANGEROUS GAME OF
ARMING AMERICAN TRADE SHIPS

Völkischer Beobachter, Berlin, December 9, 1941
THE FIRST PUNCHES FELL: JAPAN'S WEAPONS ANSWER ROOSEVELT

Völkischer Beobachter, Berlin, December 12, 1941
JAPANESE SANK U.S.'S BIGGEST AIRCRAFT CARRIER

Corriere Della Sera, Milan, December 12, 1941
THE AXIS AT WAR AGAINST THE UNITED STATES
POWERFUL SPEECH BY MUSSOLINI
THE TRIPARTITE ALLIANCE IS A SURE GUARANTEE OF VICTORY

Völkischer Beobachter, Berlin, December 13, 1941
ROOSEVELT'S GUILT FOR THE NEW WORLD WAR EXPLAINED

Völkischer Beobachter, Berlin, December 15, 1941
THE COUNTRIES OF THE 'THREE POWER PACT' DECLARE THEIR
    SOLIDARITY
FIVE MORE DECLARATIONS OF WAR ON THE USA [the countries listed
    in the article are Bulgaria, Croatia, Slovakia, Romania, and Hungary; the
    article was about Europe uniting to fight against the United States]

Völkischer Beobachter, Berlin, December 19, 1941
THE JAPANESE IMPERIAL HEADQUARTERS ANNOUNCED: USA-PACIFIC
    FLEET PRACTICALLY ANNIHILATED

Germany Declares War on the United States, December 11, 1941

Although Germany on her part has strictly adhered to the rules of international law in her relations with the United States during every period of the present war, the Government of the United States from initial violations of neutrality has finally proceeded to open acts of war against Germany. The Government of the United States has thereby virtually created a state of war.

The German Government, consequently, discontinues diplomatic relations with the United States of America and declares that under these circumstances brought about by President Roosevelt Germany too, as from today, considers herself as being in a state of war with the United States of America.

Hitler Speech to Reichstag, December 11, 1941

Only in obedience to bitter necessity did I decide in my heart in 1939, to make the attempt, at least, to create the pre-requisites for a lasting peace in Europe by eliminating the causes of German-Russian tension. This was psychologically difficult owing to the general attitude of the German people, and above all, of the Party, towards Bolshevism. . . . Add to this the military realization that in case of war, which British diplomacy was to force on the German people a two front war would ensue and call for very great sacrifice. . . .

The lightning conclusion of the Western campaign, however, robbed the Moscow overlords of their hope of an early flagging of German power. This did not alter their intentions—it merely led to a postponement of the date on which they intended to strike. In the summer of 1941 they thought the time was ripe. A new Mongolian storm was now to sweep Europe . . .

And everything which America has not drawn from Europe may well appear worthy of admiration to a judaized, mixed race; Europe, on the other hand, sees in it a sign of cultural decay. . . .

Germany is fighting today, not for herself, but for the entire Continent . . .

I sought no war. On the contrary I did everything to avoid it. But I would have been forgetful of my duty and responsibility if, in spite of realizing the inevitability of a fight by force of arms, I had failed to draw the only possible conclusions. In view of the mortal danger from Soviet Russia, not only to the German Reich, but to all Europe, I decided, if possible a few days before the outbreak of this struggle, to give the signal to attack myself. . . .

The powers behind Roosevelt were those powers I had fought at home. The Brain Trust was composed of people such as we have fought against in Germany as parasites and removed from public life. . . .

All this is not surprising if one bears in mind that the men he had called to support him, or rather, the men who had called him, belonged to the Jewish element, whose interests are all for disintegration and never for order. While speculation was being fought in National Socialist Germany, it thrived astoundingly under the Roosevelt regime. . . .

He guessed that the only salvation for him lay in diverting public attention from home to foreign policy. . . . He was strengthened in this resolve by the Jews around him. . . . The full diabolical meanness of Jewry rallied round this man, and he stretched out his hands.

Thus began the increasing efforts of the American President to create conflicts, to do everything to prevent conflicts from being peacefully solved. For years this man harbored one desire—that a conflict should break out somewhere in the world. . . .

First he incites war then falsifies the causes, then odiously wraps himself in a cloak of Christian hypocrisy and slowly but surely leads mankind to war, not without calling God to witness the honesty of his attack—in the approved manner of an old Freemason. . . .

The President of the U.S.A. ought finally to understand—I say this only because of his limited intellect—that we know that the aim of this struggle is to destroy one State after another. . . . Germany and Italy have enough insight and strength to comprehend that, in these historic times, the existence or non-existence of the nations, is being decided perhaps for ever.

As a consequence of the further extension of President Roosevelt's policy, which is aimed at unrestricted world domination and dictatorship the U.S.A. together with England have not hesitated from using any means to dispute the rights of the German, Italian and Japanese nations to the basis of

their natural existence . . . the sincere efforts of Germany and Italy to prevent an extension of the war and to maintain relations with the U.S.A. in
spite of the unbearable provocations which have been carried on for years
by President Roosevelt, have been frustrated . . .

That the Anglo-Saxon-Jewish-Capitalist World finds itself now in one and
the same Front with Bolshevism does not surprise us National Socialists . . .

You, my fellow party members, know my unalterable determination to
carry a fight once begun to its successful conclusion. You know my determination in such a struggle to be deterred by nothing, to break every resistance
which must be broken.

Italy Declares War on the United States, December 11, 1941

The powers of the steel pact, Fascist Italy and Nationalist Socialist Germany,
ever closely linked, participate from today on the side of heroic Japan against
the United States of America . . .

Neither the Axis nor Japan wanted an extension of the conflict.

One man, one man only, a real tyrannical democrat, through a series of
infinite provocations, betraying with a supreme fraud the population of his
country, wanted the war and had prepared for it day by day with diabolical
obstinacy. [reference to Roosevelt]

The formidable blows that on the immense Pacific expanse have been already inflicted on American forces show how prepared are the soldiers of
the Empire of the Rising Sun. . . .

We shall win.

Axis Pact on War, December 11, 1941

I. Italy, Germany and Japan will henceforth conduct in common and jointly
a war which has been imposed on them by the United States of America and
England, by all means at their disposal and until the end of hostilities.

II. Italy, Germany and Japan undertake each for himself that none of the
parties to the present accord will conclude either armistice or peace, be it
with the United States or with England without complete and reciprocal
agreement [of the three signatories to this pact].

III. Italy, Germany and Japan, even after the victorious conclusion of this
war, will collaborate closely in the spirit of the Tripartite Pact, concluded Sept.
21, 1940, in order to realize and establish an equitable new order in the world.

Poland's Commitment to Allies, December 22, 1941[12]

Poland was the first country to offer armed resistance against the German
aggression of September 1, 1939, and since that time her national army, her
navy, her air force as well as her mercantile fleet have never ceased to fight

on land, on sea and in the air for the defeat of Hitlerism throughout the world. . . .

The Polish Nation in Poland unanimously resists the invader both actively and passively, regardless of terrorism and inhuman oppression which have never succeeded in breaking its spirit of resistance. The subversive warfare conducted by Polish organizations has been continuous and is becoming ever more effective. . . .

The Polish-Soviet declaration of Friendship and Mutual Assistance . . . establishes the principles of full active military collaboration between them during the war and the existence of good neighborly collaboration and friendship and mutual observance of undertakings assumed after the war. . . .

Through its fighting spirit and resistance and the subversive warfare which it carries on, the Polish Nation in Poland has been and continues to be, an important active factor of the joint war effort . . .

The full participation of Poland as a co-belligerent in the partnership about to be established between the United States and the other Democracies fighting in this war, appears therefore of primary importance to all concerned.

Occupation of Europe

In 1940, Germany invaded and occupied most of Western Europe, and in the summer of 1941, Germany turned east and drove deeply into Soviet territory. As a result, almost all of Europe came under German occupation. Unlike previous wars, this one brought a racist ideology and subsequent genocide. Europeans from almost all countries suffered privation, oppression, torture, and often death.

Testimony of Marie Dubost[13]—French Civilian

I did not suffer from hunger; we ate a lot of potatoes. The Germans gave us black bread: it was not great but it was something to eat all the same. We did not eat much meat. Access to the beach was forbidden by the Germans who were everywhere and who we feared. Therefore we could not go looking for any seafood.

Getting clothes was difficult so we repaired our own clothing. We made our own soap. We saved the ashes from the chimney to make a kind of lye to wash the clothes inside a metal pail. We also had trouble getting shoes. We wore a kind of clogs made of leather with a wooden sole. They did not last long, especially the sole. We went barefoot inside the house.

Testimony of Pierre Lecostey—French Civilian

My parents bought a used radio during the Occupation though the connections of my Uncle Charles who lived in Cherbourg. We kept it in the kitchen;

it was not hidden. It was necessary to give the radio to the Germans toward the end of the Occupation. We listened to London but we missed the Appeal of General de Gaulle on 18 June 1940.

We listened each day to the coded messages in French that lasted for a half an hour each night.

Testimony of Charles Couppey—French Civilian

During the Occupation, there were regular forced transports of goods: the Mayor had to requisition the inhabitants on the demand of the Germans to go and search for coal in Cherbourg. Whenever my father was chosen, I went with him or replaced him if possible. We were about half a dozen, accompanied by a guard with his rifle. It took the entire day. The older ones took care of me because I was only 12 years old. The Germans took one of my father's mares. The same year they also requisitioned a horse from my grandfather.

Testimony of Marie Madeleine Leneveu—French Civilian

There was a long period of the construction of the "Atlantic Wall" on the coast by the Todt organization.[14] The workers were dressed in different colors with different names for each group. These workers were from Poland or Alsace where they had been requisitioned and were lodged in a camp on the road to Landemer. The Germans had their own barracks.

In the Headlines

Völkischer Beobachter, Berlin, July 10, 1941
BOLSHEVISM SHOWS ITS JEWISH FACE [this article was a supposed exposé rather than a report on a specific event]

Testimony of Fania Brantovskaya—Lithuanian Holocaust Survivor

On 22nd June the bombings started . . .
    The occupation began . . .
    A few days later pogroms took place in our town. Fascists tortured religious Jews making them shave their beards and forcing them to dance. Every day new orders were issued . . . Jews weren't allowed to walk on pavements, go to the market or stores or use public transportation. There were two small food stores where we could receive food products for cards. The circulating currency was Marks. The curfew started two hours earlier for Jews than for other citizens. Fascists came to Jewish houses taking away valuables and making inventory of the furniture. They also took away more expensive pieces of furniture . . .

Every day men were taken away. At first they explained they were taken to work and men were ordered to take towels and soap with them. But people said they were taken to shooting grounds . . . the victims were forced to dig graves before they were shot themselves. The Jewish population was to pay the contribution of 5 million Marks and we, just like everyone else, gave away all our money and valuables . . .

The ghetto was fenced. In narrower streets wooden or brick walls were installed. . . . On the first days of our imprisonment various actions began. It seemed the fascists enjoyed changing the ways of selecting Jews for killing. Young people were taken to work in the peat bog and one day they were told to go to the sauna. The young people were locked in a shed and burnt . . .

We had hardly any food. These cards were for little rations of gray bread with sawdust.

Testimony of Otto Ohlendorf[15]—Nazi Officer

Every army group was to have an *Einsatzgruppe* [Mobile Killing Unit] attached to it. The army group in its turn would then attach the Einsatzkommandos to the armies of the army group. . . . From June 1941 to the death of Heydrich in June 1942, I led Einsatzgruppe D . . .

The instructions were that in the Russian operational areas of the Einsatzgruppen the Jews, as well as the Soviet political commissars, were to be liquidated. I mean "killed." . . .

Himmler told me that before the beginning of the Russian campaign Hitler had spoken of this mission to a conference of the army groups and the army chiefs—no, not the army chiefs but the commanding generals—and had instructed the commanding generals to provide the necessary support. . . . Himmler assembled the leaders and men of the Einsatzkommandos, repeated to them the liquidation order, and pointed out that the leaders and men who were taking part in the liquidation bore no personal responsibility for the execution of this order. The responsibility was his, alone, and the Führer's . . .

A local Einsatzkommando attempted to collect all the Jews in its area by registering them. . . . After the registration the Jews were collected at one place; and from there they were later transported to the place of execution, which was, as a rule an antitank ditch or a natural excavation. The executions were carried out in a military manner, by firing squads under command. . . . The bodies were buried in the antitank ditch or excavation. . . .

Some of the unit leaders did not carry out the liquidation in the military manner, but killed the victims singly by shooting them in the back of the neck. . . . Then an order came from Himmler that in the future women and children were to be killed only in gas vans. . . . The actual purpose of these vans could not be seen from the outside. They looked like closed trucks, and

were so constructed that at the start of the motor, gas was conducted into
the van causing death in 10 to 15 minutes. . . . The vans were loaded with
the victims and driven to the place of burial, which was usually the same as
that used for the mass executions. The time needed for transportation was
sufficient to insure the death of the victims . . .

Col. Amen: How many persons could be killed simultaneously in one such van?
Ohlendorf: About 15 to 25 persons. The vans varied in size . . .
The Tribunal (Major General I. T. Nikitchenko): And in what category did
    you consider the children? For what reason were the children massacred?
Ohlendorf: The order was that the Jewish population should be totally
    exterminated.
The Tribunal (Gen. Nikitchenko): Including the children?
Ohlendorf: Yes.
The Tribunal (Gen. Nikitchenko): Were all the Jewish children murdered?
Ohlendorf: Yes. . . . One must distinguish here: The order for the liquidation
    [of the Soviet people] came from the Führer of the Reich, and it was to be
    carried out by the Reichsführer SS Himmler.

Testimony of Eva Galler[16]—Polish Holocaust Survivor

When we arrived at the city square, we saw a fire in the middle of it. The
whole inventory from the synagogue was burning, the prayer books, the
torah scrolls, everything was burning. The German soldiers pushed the young
girls up to the old men and made them dance around the bonfire. When we
looked up we saw that each of our town's three synagogues was on fire.

All around us our neighbors and friends were watching and laughing at
us like they were at a show. This hurt us more that what the Germans did.
After the fire burned down they told us to line up and parade through the
whole town so everyone could see us. This I will never forget.

We were living in conditions of hunger and fear, but we were still in our
own homes. People made hiding places in their houses to hide from the
Germans. Our hiding place was in the attic behind a double wall. Whenever
we saw the Germans, we would run to the attic and hide. Even the little
children understood that if they made noise it was a matter of life and death.

Testimony of Hans Cappelen[17]—Norwegian Prison Survivor

I was arrested 29 November 1941 and taken to the Gestapo prison in
Oslo. After ten days I was interrogated by two Norwegian Nazi police
agents.

Then, suddenly, they all started to run at me and beat me with rubber
bludgeons and iron wires. It hurt me very badly and I fainted. But I was brought

back to life again by their pouring ice-cold water over me. I vomited, naturally, because I was feeling very sick. But that only made them angry, and they said, "Clean up, you dirty dog" and I had to make an attempt to clean up with my bare hands . . .

Then they started in another way: they started to screw and break my arms and legs. My right arm was dislocated. I felt that awful pain, and fainted again. Then the same happened as last time: They poured water on me and I recovered consciousness.

Then they placed a sort of homemade—it looked to me homemade— wooden thing, with a screw arrangement, on my left leg, and they started to screw so that all the flesh loosened from the bones. I felt an awful pain and fainted away, but I came back to consciousness again, and I have still big marks here on my leg from the screw arrangement, now, four years afterwards . . .

Well, they dragged me out of the cell . . . four or five Gestapo agents, and they started to trample on me, and kick me. . . . He took my left hand like this and put some pins under my nails and started to break them up. It hurt me badly, and everything went round and round, the double vision came again but the pain was so intense that I drew my hand back. I should not have done that, because that made them absolutely furious. I fainted away, collapsed, I do not know for how long, but I came back to life again, to the smell of burned flesh or burned meat. One of the Gestapo agents was standing with a little lamp burning me under my feet. It did not hurt me too much, because I was so feeble that I did not care, and I was so paralyzed that I could not speak, I only groaned a bit, crying, naturally, always . . .

I heard people screaming and groaning nearly every night . . . I learned afterwards that we were called "Nacht und Nebel" prisoners, "Night and Fog" prisoners.

Testimony of Nisim Navon[18]—Serbian Holocaust Survivor

The first Germans arrived in April 1941. . . . Right after the Germans came, the Jews were ordered to wear a yellow band with the word "Jude," and form a brigade of 200 adults from Kosovo to work at the stone pit. When the Nazis first rounded up the Jews, they came with a truck to our house and took away everything from us. . . . They made our father carry all of the family's belongings out of the house onto trucks, the whole time beating him on the spine. His back never recovered from these beatings and he never regained his strength.

We thought that the Germans wouldn't take my grandfather as he was old, so we gave him everything we had. But my grandfather was taken to prison immediately and killed. My two uncles and I were put in labor camp where we worked at the stone-pit 12 hours a day.

Testimony of Alois Hollriegel[19]—Nazi Camp Guard

Col. Amen: What were your duties at the Mauthausen Concentration Camp?

Hollriegel: From 1942 until the end of the war I was detailed to the inner service of the concentration camp.

Col. Amen: And you therefore had occasion to witness the extermination of inmates of that camp by shooting, gassing, and so forth?

Hollriegel: Yes, I saw that . . . I remember, it was in 1941. At that time I was with a guard company on the tower . . . I was able to observe in the morning about six to eight prisoners who came with two SS men . . . I saw that they were approaching the precipice near the quarry. I saw from my watchtower that these two SS men were beating the prisoners and I realized immediately that they intended to force them to throw themselves over the precipice or else to push them over. I noticed how one of the prisoners was kicked while lying on the ground, and the gestures showed that he was supposed to throw himself down the precipice. This the prisoner promptly did under the pressure of the blows—presumably in despair.

Col. Amen: How steep was the precipice?

Hollriegel: I estimate it to be 30 to 40 meters. . . . These incidents happened frequently.

Testimony of Abram Suzkever[20]—Lithuanian Holocaust Survivor

When the Germans seized my city, Vilna, about 80,000 Jews lived in the town. . . . The man-hunters of the Sonderkommandos broke into the Jewish houses at any time of day or night, dragged away the men, instructing them to take a piece of soap and a towel, and herded them into certain buildings. . . . When the Jews found out that their kin were not coming back, a large part of the population went into hiding. However, the Germans tracked them with police dogs. Many were found, and any who were averse to going with them were shot on the spot . . .

When we reached the old synagogue on this street I saw that wood was piled up there in the shape of a pyramid. A German drew out his revolver and told us to take off our clothes. When we were naked, he lit a match and set fire to this stack of wood. Then another German brought out of the synagogue three scrolls of the Torah, gave them to us, and told us to dance around this bonfire and sing Russian songs. Behind us stood the three Germans; with their bayonets they forced us toward the fire and laughed . . .

[T]housands of Germans . . . surrounded the whole town, broke into the Jewish houses, and told the inhabitants to take only that which they could carry off in their hands and get out into the street. Then they were driven off to the ghetto. I saw the Germans had brought sick Jews from the hospitals. They were all in blue hospital gowns. . . .

About half the Jewish population of Vilna never reached the ghetto; they were shot on the way. . . .

At the end of December 1941 an order was issued in the ghetto which stated that the Jewish women must not bear children . . . if the Germans found out that a Jewish woman had given birth, the child would be exterminated.

Towards the end of December in the ghetto my wife gave birth to a child, a boy. . . . But I saw the hospital surrounded by Germans and a black car standing before the door . . .

In the evening when the Germans had left, I went to the hospital and found my wife in tears. It seems that when she had her baby, the Jewish doctors of the hospital had already received the order that Jewish women must not give birth; and they had hidden the baby, together with other newborn children, in one of the rooms. . . . She saw one German holding the baby and smearing something under its nose. Afterwards he threw it on the bed and laughed. When my wife picked up the child, there was something black under his nose. When I arrived at the hospital, I saw that my baby was dead. He was still warm.

Night and Fog [Nacht und Nebel] Decree, December 7, 1941[21]

Within the occupied territories, communistic elements and other circles hostile to Germany have increased their efforts against the German State and the occupying powers since the Russian campaign started. The amount and the danger of these machinations oblige us to take severe measures as a determent. First of all the following directives are to be applied:

I. Within the occupied territories, the adequate punishment for offences committed against the German State or the occupying power which endanger their security or a state of readiness is on principle the death penalty.

II. The offences listed in paragraph I as a rule are to be dealt with in the occupied countries only if it is probable that sentence of death will be passed upon the offender, at least the principal offender, and if the trial and the execution can be completed in a very short time. Otherwise the offenders, at least the principal offenders, are to be taken to Germany.

III. Prisoners taken to Germany are subjected to military procedure only if particular military interests require this. In case German or foreign authorities inquire about such prisoners, they are to be told that they were arrested, but that the proceedings do not allow any further information.

CHAPTER 5

Occupation and Terror in Europe, 1942

Introduction to 1942

In 1942, the western allies, now calling themselves the United Nations, reaffirmed the principles of the Atlantic Charter and their determination to continue their struggle together until Germany had been completely defeated. Twenty-six nations adhered to this pledge. Concerned that Stalin might quit the war and sign another neutrality or nonaggression pact with Germany, Britain and the United States were relieved when the U.S.S.R. signed the promise to fight to the end as well.

Publicly Stalin affirmed his commitment to the defeat of Germany. Speaking on May 1, an official holiday in the Soviet Union, Stalin first praised his own military for its heroic efforts and then named Britain and the United States as friends and allies of his country. He acknowledged the economic aid that the U.S.S.R. was receiving as a result of rapidly expanding American productivity combined with improved convoy techniques. Despite Stalin's commitment to the anti-Fascist cause, both the United States and Britain remained concerned and believed that extensive military support was necessary to keep the Soviet Union in the war and to prevent a possible separate peace between Stalin and Hitler.

This fear of a Soviet-German rapprochement forced the western allies to accommodate some of Stalin's demands. When Soviet Foreign Minister Molotov visited Washington at the end of May 1942, he engaged in wide-ranging talks with President Roosevelt. Molotov's demand for the opening of a second front in Europe was a crucial agenda items from the Soviet perspective. He urged an Allied landing in Western Europe during 1942 to take pressure off the eastern front. Raising a theme that Stalin and Molotov would often repeat, the foreign minister warned that the price of delaying an invasion of France could be German victory. Having concluded his talks with Roosevelt, Molotov sent the American president a thank you note that claimed that their countries had reached "a full understanding concerning the urgent tasks connected with the creation of a second front in Europe in 1942."[1] In reality, the American government had indicated only its hope that this military action might be possible. This difference in understanding remained an issue of contention for the next two years. Stalin's goal of saving his own country demanded the rapid deployment of Allied forces in Europe to confront Germany with a two-front war. While Britain and the United States agreed with the long-term objective, they knew that their military forces were not yet prepared for an invasion of France.

On the one-year anniversary of the German invasion of the U.S.S.R., the Soviet ambassador to the United States spoke at

Madison Square Garden in New York City. Litvinov reviewed the
reasons why Hitler had invaded his country with reference to
Germany's desire to dominate the world. Hitler "set himself the aim of
European and then of world domination, [and he] could never have
reconciled himself to the independent existence of any great country."[2]
At a time when the outcome of the struggle on the eastern front
remained uncertain, Litvinov asserted that Germany had seriously
miscalculated and underestimated Soviet strength. Furthermore, he
pointed out that the productive capacity of the three allies, the
U.S.S.R., the United States, and Britain, ensured an Allied victory and
the ultimate destruction of the Nazi regime.

In August, Churchill visited Stalin in Moscow, and their discussions
centered on the issue of a second front in Europe. As Molotov and
Litvinov had done previously, Stalin insisted on an Allied invasion of
France in 1942. Churchill attempted to deflect Stalin's demand by
pointing out the other military actions that the United States and Britain
were engaged in against Germany. The prime minister referred to the
bombing of Germany, which was steadily increasing, as well as the
invasion of North Africa (Operation Torch) planned for November.[3]
While both leaders held to their positions, they agreed that they needed
each other and would continue to work together despite their differences.

In the end, Churchill did not convince Stalin that other forms of
military action against Germany were as effective as a landing in
France. While Churchill and Stalin parted amicably, the Soviet leader
remained dissatisfied on the second-front issue. As soon as the British
prime minister left Moscow, Stalin sent a message to Churchill and
Roosevelt pressing again for an invasion of France. He pointed out that
the logistical problems of launching a second front in 1942 would be
eased by the heavy concentration of German troops in the east, and
that there was no guarantee that this favorable balance of forces would
persist into 1943. In addition, Stalin insisted that a commitment to a
second front had been made earlier in the year when Molotov visited
Washington and London, and therefore Stalin was asking only that
the promise be fulfilled.

The question of the timing of a second front continued to cause
tension for the Allies despite one Allied probe of German defenses in
France. In August a force of about 6,000 troops (mostly Canadian)
landed in Northern France at Dieppe. The raid failed, with half of the
attackers becoming casualties. The British and Americans realized that
an invasion of the continent would require much more planning and new
equipment to have any chance of success. Stalin remained unconvinced
and believed that the western powers should try again with a larger force.

Militarily, the western powers enjoyed their greatest achievement at
the end of 1942 in Africa. During the summer, German Field Marshal

Rommel moved toward Egypt, threatening the Suez Canal and the oil fields in the Middle East. In July, the British stopped Rommel at the First Battle of El Alamein, but the Desert Fox (Rommel) regrouped and drove eastward again.[4] For two weeks at the end of October and early November, the Second Battle of El Alamein raged, culminating in a major British victory and fame for General Bernard Montgomery.[5] At almost the same time in November, American troops landed in Western Africa for Operation Torch and engaged in their first significant battle experiences. The Axis forces still won a few battles in Africa after the American landing (for example, Kasserine Pass in early 1943),[6] but the German-Italian forces were caught between the British and American armies and were forced out of Africa by the summer of 1943.

In celebration of the anniversary of the Bolshevik Revolution on November 7, 1942, virtually coinciding with the start of Operation Torch in Africa, Stalin spoke at length about the war and the second-front issue. He attributed continuing German advances to the absence of a second front, allowing Germany to concentrate all its resources on the eastern front. Referring to Germany's inability to win World War I because of the two-front war, the Soviet leader insisted that a second front would drain German forces and place Germany in a "deplorable" situation. After registering his complaint on the timing of the second front, he acknowledged that an invasion of France was inevitable because the Allies realized that France could not be ignored, militarily or politically, in any future victory. Stalin praised Britain and the United States for a variety of reasons. He contrasted the ideologies of the Italian-German Fascists with the British-American-Soviet alliance. He admitted that the U.S.S.R. and its allies did not agree on all principles, but he affirmed that the strength of their partnership had been tested and proven in the course of the past year. Stalin claimed that he had no doubts about the ultimate victory of the Allied cause.

Despite Stalin's expressed optimism, Eastern Europe and large parts of the U.S.S.R. remained under German occupation. The Nazis had control of millions of people designated for destruction. Early in 1942 in the Berlin suburb of Wannsee, a meeting of high-ranking Nazi officials discussed and planned the "liquidation" (killing) of the Jewish population in the occupied territories in Eastern Europe and finally in all of Europe. With Reinhard Heydrich in charge, the conference settled on what was called the "final solution to the Jewish problem." This so-called solution involved the forced movement of up to eleven million Jews away from their homes and into ghettoes as a first step in controlling this population. The goal of the meeting was made clear by the language used in the protocol: expulsion, cleanse, living space, and final solution.

The possible final remnant will, since it will undoubtedly consist of the most resistant portion, have to be treated accordingly, because it is the product of natural selection and would, if released, act as the seed of a new Jewish revival (see the experience of history.) In the course of the practical execution of the final solution, Europe will be combed through from west to east.[7]

The governments forced into exile by the German invasion understood the implications of Wannsee and the oppressive nature of Nazi occupation. Nine of those governments began to press the Allied powers for a pledge that Germany would be held accountable for war crimes and that leading members of the German government would be treated as war criminals. A note from these governments was presented to the Soviet and American governments.

With the reality of German occupation policies becoming clearer, Roosevelt issued two statements on the subject of war crimes and the punishment of war criminals. In his first declaration, the president remarked on the barbaric nature of the occupation in Europe, the severity of which could "even lead to the extermination of certain populations." He indicated that the American government was monitoring the situation in the occupied nations, and he warned the perpetrators that they would have to stand in court and be accountable for their behavior following Allied victory. In his second declaration on this subject, Roosevelt announced the creation of a United Nations Commission for the Investigation of War Crimes. While he assured the civilian populations of the Fascist countries that mass reprisals against them were not anticipated, he again asserted that the leaders responsible for atrocities would have to face justice.

The Soviet government joined the declaration by Roosevelt and promised punishment and retribution against the perpetrators of atrocities in the occupied nations of Europe. Molotov stated that German actions within the Soviet Union gave his government a sense of solidarity and sympathy for the sufferings experienced throughout Europe, where Nazi leaders attempted to annihilate entire ethnic groups. Molotov praised the actions of guerrilla, partisan, and resistance fighters who were working to sabotage the German war machine.

Heydrich, the architect of the Wannsee Conference, was assassinated in a daring attack in Prague in the summer of 1942. German retaliation included the killing or deportation of the civilian population of the village of Lidice, about fifteen miles from the Czech capital. Without Heydrich, the chain of command for the final solution included Heinrich Himmler and Adolf Eichmann.[8] At about the time of Heydrich's assassination, the camps at Auschwitz and Treblinka began to use poison gas to speed the killing of groups targeted for elimination.[9] In testimony given at the Nuremberg Trial in 1946, defendants provided details of the implementation of the final solution. SS official Dieter Wisliceny presented evidence on the killing of Jews in Greece, Slovakia, and Salonika.[10]

THE SOURCES

War in North Africa

While the fighting in the U.S.S.R. and the attack on Pearl Harbor were
the major military stories of 1941, the struggle between Italian and
British forces in North Africa raged on and continued into 1942. With
control of the Suez Canal and oil resources at stake, the Allies had to
hold the line in Egypt. Italy hoped for victory, but the British
reinforced the front and stopped the Axis advance. Germany was
forced to send troops under Rommel to intervene on the side of Italy.
The key battle was at El Alamein, but the issue was not resolved until
later in 1942 and definitively in 1943.

In the Headlines

Corriere Della Sera, Milan, June 22, 1942 [pro-Fascist]
TOBRUK STORMED! MORE THAN 25 THOUSAND PRISONERS AND
   IMPRESSIVE BOOTY
TWO DAYS OF VIOLENT ATTACKS AND THE ENEMY RAISES THE
   WHITE FLAG—SEVERAL ENGLISH GENERALS CAPTURED

Le Journal de Genève, Geneva, July 1, 1942
ROMMEL LESS THAN 140 KILOMETERS FROM ALEXANDRIA

Le Journal de Genève, Geneva, July 6, 1942
ROMMEL NOT SUCCESSFUL IN BREAKING THROUGH BRITISH
   POSITIONS AT EL-ALAMEIN

Le Figaro, Paris, July 10, 1942 [collaborationist]
ATTACKS AND COUNTERATTACKS FOLLOW EACH OTHER IN THE
   AREA OF EL ALAMEIN—INTENSE AIR ACTIVITY ON BOTH PARTS

Le Figaro, Paris, July 14–15, 1942
BERLIN SAYS BRITISH ATTACKS ARE REPULSED IN EL ALAMEIN AREA

The Times, London, October 29, 1942
BIG TANK BATTLE IN THE DESERT—AXIS FORCES HURLED BACK

The Times, London, November 5, 1942
ROMMEL'S ARMY IN FULL RETREAT—9,000 PRISONERS TAKEN

Corriere Della Sera, Milan, November 5, 1942
VIOLENT FIGHTING ON THE EGYPTIAN FRONT
ATTACK OF THE ENEMY CUT SHORT BY THE INDOMITABLE
   COURAGE OF THE AXIS TROOPS

Le Figaro, Paris, November 9, 1942 [Vichy perspective]
AMERICANS AND ENGLISH ATTACK OUR NORTH AFRICA
THE MARSHAL [reference to Pétain] DENOUNCES THIS AGGRESSION
  AND GIVES THE ORDER TO RESIST

Le Figaro, Paris, November 10, 1942
FRENCH RESISTANCE CONTINUES IN MOROCCO [reference to Vichy
  forces resisting Allied landing]

Testimony of Warren G. Hirt[11]—American Seabees

I joined the Seabees and we spent time serving in North Africa.
    . . . When we landed in Africa, the Allies were still trying to drive Rommel back from the western part of Africa all the way up to Tunisia and Bizerte where they finally overcame his forces. So there was a lot of action going on. Most of the action that we saw took the form of air raids. And at that point Germans had enough, and the Italians both had enough aircraft and supplies to be able to make sorties on a fairly regular basis. . . . So we traveled as they pushed Rommel back along the north coast of Africa toward Egypt, we would be traveling along, kind of following the action. But we were working all the time. But most of our equipment was moved up by the LSTs [Landing Ship, Tank], but hard stuff, that couldn't get on board ship, I moved up with a truck convoy. And that was an interesting experience. We traveled from Oran, which is kind of in the northwest corner of Africa along the Mediterranean coast all the way through Mostaganem and Algiers to Tunisia up to Bizerte. . . . We landed outside of Oran. And we started our training there. Also right down here interestingly is the town of Sidi Bel Abbès, which the home of the French Foreign Legion.[12]
    . . . When we were in North Africa—it was during the time when the Italian armed forces just fell apart and they were surrendering by the thousands and thousands. So we had all kinds of Italian prisoners of war around to do our chores for us and everything else.

Allied Agreements and Disagreements—The Second
Front Controversy

Although Britain, the United States, and the U.S.S.R. reaffirmed their alliance in the United Nations Declaration, they disagreed on several important subjects. The most serious and potentially damaging issue was Stalin's demand that the west invade France as soon as possible to relieve pressure on the eastern front, and the American-British position that argued for postponement of the invasion until military conditions were more promising. The west offered generous aid to the U.S.S.R. to keep Stalin from possibly dropping out of the war and even improvised an attack in northern France at Dieppe to probe

German defenses. This invasion led by Canadian forces failed and provided the west with further arguments against a premature invasion. Nevertheless, Stalin, Molotov, and other Soviet diplomats pressed the subject at every opportunity.

Declaration by United Nations, January 1, 1942[13]

Being convinced that complete victory over their enemies is essential to defend life, liberty, independence and religious freedom, and to preserve human rights and justice in their own lands as well as in other lands, and that they are now engaged in a common struggle against savage and brutal forces seeking to subjugate the world, Declare:

(1) Each Government pledges itself to employ its full resources, military or economic, against those members of the Tripartite Pact and its adherents with which such government is at war.

(2) Each Government pledges itself to cooperate with the Governments signatory hereto and not to make a separate armistice or peace with the enemies.

The foregoing declaration may be adhered to by other nations which are, or which may be, rendering material assistance and contributions in the struggle for victory over Hitlerism.

Memorandum of Conference at White House, May 30, 1942

Mr. Molotov thereupon remarked that, though the problem of the second front was both military and political, it was predominantly political. There was an essential difference between the situation in 1942 and what it might be in 1943. In 1942 Hitler was the master of all Europe save a few minor countries. He was the chief enemy of everyone. To be sure, as was devoutly to be hoped, the Russians might hold and fight on all through 1942. But it was only right to look at the darker side of the picture. On the basis of his continental dominance, Hitler might throw in such reinforcements in manpower and material that the Red Army might not be able to hold out against the Nazis. Such a development would produce a serious situation which we must face. The Soviet front would become secondary, the Red Army would be weakened, and Hitler's strength would be correspondingly greater, since he would have at his disposal not only more troops, but also the foodstuffs and raw materials of the Ukraine and the oil-wells of the Caucasus. In such circumstances the outlook would be much less favorable for all hands, and he would not pretend that such developments were all outside the range of possibility. The war would thus become tougher and longer. The merit of a new front in 1942 depended on the prospects of Hitler's further advantage, hence the establishment of such a front should not be postponed. The decisive element in the whole problem lay in the question, when are the prospects better for the United Nations: in 1942 or in 1943.

. . . If, then, Great Britain and the United States, as allies, were to create a new front and to draw off 40 German divisions from the Soviet front, the ratio of strength would be so altered that the Soviets could either beat Hitler this year or insure beyond question his ultimate defeat.

. . . The President then put to General Marshall[14] the query whether developments were clear enough so that we could say to Mr. Stalin that we are preparing a second front. "Yes," replied the General. The President then authorized Mr. Molotov to inform Mr. Stalin that we expect the formation of a second front this year.

Mutual Aid Agreement between U.S. and U.S.S.R., June 11, 1942

The agreement signed today is an additional link in the chain of solidarity being forged by the United Nations in their two-fold task of prosecuting the war against aggression to a successful conclusion and of creating a new and better world.

The agreement reaffirms this country's determination to continue to supply in ever-increasing amounts aid to the Soviet Union in the war against the common enemy. The agreement also provides for such reciprocal aid as the Soviet Union may be in a position to supply. But no matter how great this aid may prove to be, it will be small in comparison with the magnificent contribution of the Soviet Union's armed forces to the defeat of the common enemy.

The agreement signed today adds the Soviet Union to the growing list of countries which have joined in a determination to take practical measures to create a better world hereafter.

Molotov Note to Roosevelt, June 12, 1942

Before returning to my country I allow myself once more to express to you, Mr. President, the great satisfaction I feel in having reached a full understanding concerning the urgent tasks connected with the creation of a second front in Europe in 1942 for speeding up the rout of Hitlerite Germany and concerning co-operation of our countries in the post-war period in the interests of all freedom-loving peoples.

Soviet Ambassador Speaks in New York, June 22, 1942

The 22nd of June 1941 was a notable date in the history of the Second World War and will one day be seen to have been its turning point. On this

day Hitler carried out his fateful decision to attack the Soviet Union, a decision which was to determine the fate of all his undertakings, of Nazism, of
Fascism and of the other ideologies akin to them. On this day Hitler flung
down a challenge to the mightiest of the continental powers, a closely-knit
union of peoples with a joint population of a hundred and eighty million . . .

If Hitler had set any limit to his aggressive aspirations he would, of
course, have contented himself with the unexpectedly rapid, and quite considerable victories he had achieved up to the 22nd of June, 1941. But his
appetite is insatiable. The careful study of Hitler's political credo, as
expounded in Mein Kampf[15] and other Nazi literature, makes this quite clear.

. . . Nazism, as a foreign policy (that is to say the super-imperialism of
Hitler), set no limits to its aggressive aims, and was directed against the
whole world, toward the domination of the whole of Europe and its colonies,
and subsequently toward world domination. They did not understand that
while Hitler might change the order of his intended assaults, he would never
curtail their scope, and that the conquests of Austria, Czechoslovakia,
Poland, Belgium, Holland and other countries were mere stages on the road
to world domination.

In concluding a pact of non-aggression with the Soviet Union in 1939,
Hitler was moved by the sole aim of avoiding war on two fronts, which he
always feared. When he could sum up the position in the west as practically
a state of truce, from which he could anticipate no disturbances, he attacked
the Soviet Union . . .

While retreating, however, the Soviet armies inflicted upon the enemy
greater losses than they suffered themselves. The Hitler war machine lost its
best units and was sorely buffeted by continual fighting for a whole year. For
the first time the German theory of the blitzkrieg was exploded, and Hitler
was disappointed in his hopes of facile lightning victories by the Red Army's
prolonged and stubborn defense of its positions. The Red Army destroyed
the legend of the invincibility of the German Army, of the infallibility of Hitler's strategy, undermined the overweening self-confidence of Hitler's troops
and Hitler's people, instilling in them doubts of the sagacity of their Führer
and mistrust of his promises and of their final victory . . .

In the recently concluded agreements the Soviet, British and American
Governments have again, and in no uncertain tones, given mutual pledges not
to lay down their arms or cease from the struggle till the international terro-
rist Hitler, together with his henchmen, have been swept from the face of
the earth, till the ideological and material foundations for their criminal
aggressive intentions have been destroyed . . .

The Soviet Union today enters upon the second year of war. I think you
will agree with me that the activities in the country during this first year of
war, in the military, economic and cultural spheres, have shown the world
examples of the great achievements and boundless sacrifices of which a belligerent nation under proper leadership is capable, when firmly united, free

of internal saboteurs, conscious of the righteousness of its cause, inspired by patriotism and by other high ideals.

U.S. Note to U.S.S.R. on Anniversary of German Invasion, June 22, 1942

For one year the peoples of the Soviet Union have been engaging the armies not only of Nazi Germany but also of those other European countries the governments of which have accepted Nazi dictation. In this struggle the armed forces of the Soviet Union, with the heroic support of the entire population, have so acquitted themselves as to win the admiration of the liberty-loving peoples of the world and to earn a place in history beside those Russian Armies which over a century and a quarter ago did so much to ruin the plans of another aspirant to world conquest . . .

We are confident that before the end of another year the instigators of this war will have been given to understand how seriously they have underestimated the determination and the ability for effective action of the peace-loving nations and will have learned that in an aroused world aggressors can no longer escape the consequences of acts resulting in human suffering and destruction.

Churchill's Meeting with Stalin, August 12, 1942[16]

The Prime Minister then described the bombing activity over Germany and his hopes for substantial increase with American participation. Here came the first agreement between the two men. Stalin took over the argument himself and said that homes as well as factories should be destroyed. The Prime Minister agreed that civil morale was a military objective but the bombing of workmen's houses came as the by-product of near misses on factories. The tension began to ease and a certain understanding of common purpose began to grow. Between the two of them they soon destroyed most of the important industrial cities of Germany.

The Prime Minister with great adroitness took the occasion of the more friendly interchange to bring the discussion back to the second front. He explained the decision regarding Torch and its tactics emphasizing the need for secrecy . . .

About this time the Prime Minister drew a picture of a crocodile and pointed out that it was as well to strike the belly as the snout. The plans for the offensive in Egypt were described as well as the battle for Malta with details of the present naval engagement all of which interested Stalin greatly . . .

The conversation then came back to Torch and Stalin summed up its strategic advantages with masterful grasp of its implications. He showed real enthusiasm for the operation but he specifically asks that the political angle

be handled with the greatest delicacy and that it be started at the very earliest moment even earlier than you have in mind.

. . . Stalin has been much disappointed in our inability to be of greater
military assistance to him and although he was critical of us . . . he considered he was dealing with two nations with whom he had binding ties.

Stalin's Note to Churchill and Roosevelt, August 13, 1942

As the result of an exchange of views in Moscow which took place on the
12th August of this year, I ascertained that the Prime Minister of Great
Britain, Mr. Churchill, considered that the organization of a second front in
Europe in 1942 to be impossible.

As is well known, the organization of a second front in Europe in 1942
was pre-decided during the sojourn of Molotov in London, and it found
expression in the agreed Anglo-Soviet communiqué published on the 12th
June last.

It is also known that the organization of a second front in Europe had as
its object the withdrawal of German forces from the Eastern front to the
West, and the creation in the West of a serious base of resistance to the
German-Fascist forces and the affording of relief by this means to the situation of the Soviet forces on the Soviet-German front in 1942.

It will be easily understood that the Soviet Command built their plan of
summer and autumn operations calculating on the creation of a second front
in Europe in 1942.

It is easy to grasp that the refusal of the Government of Great Britain to
create a second front in 1942 in Europe inflicts a morale blow to the whole
of the Soviet public opinion, which calculates on the creation of a second
front, and that it complicates the situation of the Red Army at the front and
prejudices the plan of the Soviet Command . . .

It appears to me and my colleagues that the most favorable conditions
exist in 1942 for the creation of a second front in Europe, inasmuch as almost
all the forces of the German army, and the best forces to boot, have been
withdrawn to the Eastern front, leaving in Europe an inconsiderable amount
of forces and these of inferior quality. It is unknown whether the year of 1943
will offer conditions for the creation of a second front as favorable as 1942.
We are of the opinion, therefore, that it is particularly in 1942 that the creation of a second front in Europe is possible and should be effected.

In the Headlines

Le Figaro, Paris, August 21, 1942
IMPORTANT BRITISH MISSION IN DIEPPE REGION ENDS IN FAILURE
BERLIN ANNOUNCES THAT ATTACKERS ARE DEFEATED

Cassandre, Brussels, August 23, 1942 [collaborationist]
ANGLO-AMERICAN DECEPTIONS FROM DIEPPE TO MOSCOW

Stalin's Speech, November 6, 1942

Hence the chief reason for the tactical successes of the Germans on our front this year is that the absence of a second front in Europe enabled them to hurl on to our front all their available reserves and to create a large superiority of forces in the south-western direction.

Let us assume that a second front existed in Europe, as it existed in the first World War, and that a second front diverted, let us say, sixty German divisions and twenty divisions of Germany's allies. What would have been the position of the German troops on our front then? It is not difficult to guess that their position would have been deplorable. More than that, it would have been the beginning of the end of the German-fascist troops. . . . That means that in the summer of this year the German-fascist army would already have been on the verge of disaster. If that has not occurred, it is because the Germans were saved by the absence of a second front in Europe.

In the first World War Germany had to fight on two fronts: in the west, chiefly against Great Britain and France, and in the east against the Russian troops. Thus in the first World War there existed a second front against Germany.

I think that no other country and no other army could have withstood such an onslaught of the bestial bands of the German-fascist brigands and their allies. Only our Soviet country and only our Red Army are capable of withstanding such an onslaught. (Loud applause.) And not only withstanding it but also overpowering it.

It is often asked: But will there be a second front in Europe after all? Yes, there will be; sooner or later, there will be one. And it will be not only because we need it, but above all because our Allies need it no less than we do. Our Allies cannot fail to realize that since France has been put out of action, the absence of a second front against fascist Germany may end badly for all freedom-loving countries, including the Allies themselves . . .

The program of action of the Anglo-Soviet-American coalition is: the abolition of racial exclusiveness; the equality of nations and the inviolability of their territories; the liberation of the enslaved nations and the restoration of their sovereign rights; the right of every nation to arrange its affairs as it wishes; economic aid to the nations that have suffered and assistance to them in achieving their material welfare; the restoration of democratic liberties; the destruction of the Hitlerite regime.

There can be only one conclusion, namely that the Anglo-Soviet-American coalition has every chance of vanquishing the Italo-German coalition and undoubtedly will vanquish it.

Comrades, we are waging a great war of liberation. We are not waging it
alone, but in conjunction with our allies. It will bring us victory over the vile
enemies of mankind, over the German-fascist imperialists.

Stalin Interview with Associated Press, November 13, 1942

Q: What is the Soviet view of the Allied campaign in Africa?

A: The Soviet view of this campaign is that it represents an outstanding fact
of major importance, demonstrating the growing might of the armed
forces of the Allies and opening the prospect of the disintegration of the
Italo-German coalition in the nearest future . . .

Q: How effective has this campaign been in relieving pressure on the Soviet
Union, and what further aid does the Soviet Union await?

A: . . . What matters, first of all, is that, since the campaign in Africa
means that the initiative has passed into the hands of our Allies, this
campaign radically changes the military and political situation in Europe
in favor of the Anglo-Soviet-American coalition. It undermines the
prestige of Hitlerite Germany as the leading force in the system of
Axis powers and demoralizes Hitler's allies in Europe. It releases France
from her state of lethargy, mobilizes the anti-Hitler forces of France and
provides a basis for the organization of an anti-Hitler French army. It
creates conditions for putting Italy out of commission and for isolating
Hitlerite Germany. Finally, it creates the prerequisites for the organization
of a second front in Europe nearer to Germany's vital centers, which
will be of decisive importance for organizing victory over the Hitlerite
tyranny.

War in Eastern Europe

Fighting on the eastern front remained fierce, brutal, and bloody. The
German army failed to capture Moscow but continued to advance
through the Ukraine and in the direction of Stalingrad. Soviet forces
resisted everywhere, losing ground but taking a toll on an enemy that
was logistically stretched too thin.

In the Headlines

Cassandre, Brussels, May 31, 1942 [collaborationist]
NEW GERMAN VICTORY—BATTLE FOR KHARKOV IS OVER
THREE ARMIES DESTROYED, 240,000 PRISONERS, 1249 TANKS
    DESTROYED, 2026 CANONS, 538 PLANES: THESE ARE SOVIET LOSSES

Cassandre, Brussels, July 5, 1942
LARGE BOLSHEVIK FORCES ENCIRCLED IN KHARKOV AND KURSK
    SECTORS

Le Journal de Genève, Geneva, July 6, 1942
BATTLE RAGES BETWEEN KURSK AND KHARKOV

Le Figaro, Paris, August 29–30, 1942
BATTLE OF STALINGRAD REDOUBLES IN VIOLENCE

Le Journal de Genève, Geneva, September 6, 1942
FEROCIOUS RUSSIAN RESISTANCE AT THE DOORS OF STALINGRAD

Le Figaro, Paris, September 7, 1942
BATTLE OF STALINGRAD ENTERS DECISIVE PHASE
VIOLENT COMBAT IN SUBURBS OF THE CITY

Le Figaro, Paris, November 2, 1942
FIGHTING IN THE STREETS CONTINUES IN STALINGRAD

Testimony of Theodor Alexandrovich Klein—Soviet Driver

In August 1941, there followed the notorious "Fifth column decree," and in accordance to it all Russian-Germans were sent to the "labor army."[17] Simultaneously, all Russian-Germans were recalled from active army service, fearing that "Russian Germans" could desert to serve in the German army. My grandfather was sent to work in a mine. He rarely shared any memories about this horrible period of his life, trying to forget about all that. Yet he told us it was a real concentration camp. He stayed a year in the camp, and was caved in twice in the mine. People died like flies. My grandfather told us that he had mentally said good-bye to his wife, children and his life. By 1942, due to heavy casualties in the active army, there was a shortage of specialists. The military arrived at the camp. All inmates were lined up and they started finding out who had skills of any kind. My grandfather's friend was a driver before the war. He pointed at my grandfather and said he could drive cars too. That's how my grandfather got to the front as a driver in an artillery regiment.

Testimony of Mikhail Ilich Borodin[18]—Soviet Tank Driver

When the Stalingrad offensive started, I happened to take part in it. There was a dominant hill and the infantry couldn't take it without tank support. We got loaded with ammo and drove on. I always drove my tank with an open hatch. We blasted this little house, and from behind the hill, their mortars were firing. There was a flash; I was dazzled. My face was burnt. I felt neither pain nor anything at all. I drove over the trench, rode over the mortars, squishing them; the Germans were fleeing. I didn't fear death, didn't even think about it. Everything was broken in my mouth; I couldn't chew anything. That's how this battle episode finished for me.

Occupation and Holocaust

It took tremendous courage to challenge the Nazi regime, and as a result, the resistance movement in Germany was weak. Some members of the Reichmuth family engaged in acts of rebellion, but a short term in prison and threats of greater punishments ended those activities. Most ominously, the Nazi official Heydrich organized a meeting in the suburbs of Berlin (Wannsee) and established the procedures for the "final solution of the Jewish problem"—the Holocaust. The testimonies that follow only suggest the horror that awaited the population of Europe. As word spread about Nazi activities, Allied governments issued periodic warnings that such actions would be punished when the war ended. The Nazis did not take these admonitions seriously, as they continued to implement their war against civilians.

Testimony on Reichmuth Family—Gestapo Report, January 18, 1942[19]

Investigation of two students Klaus Rendtorff and Klaus Reichmuth, and also Katharina Reichmuth, the wife of the pastor Martin Reichmuth and mother of Klaus Reichmuth. The students were put under watch starting on the 13th and 14th of January 1942.

The students were children of fanatical pastors from the confessing church.

They both plan to become pastors in the confessing church. Rendtorff and Reichmuth have tried to convince the other seminary students of their religious views. Reichmuth has been the more forceful in the class. He has had some success using his propaganda to organize the other students. To achieve his goal he has taken the lead in discussions and copied pamphlets on the politics of the church that are hostile to the State. In the discussions that followed they stressed the idea that the contents of these propaganda tracts were truthful and mandated actions against the State. They continued to try to convince the other students of their views.

In their fanatical opinions and their rejection of the State, they have even gone on to insult and publicly slander Himmler, the head of the SS, in front of the entire class.

At the end of 1941 they distributed images of Himmler to the class. Rendtorff got hold of postcards of Himmler and stuck pins through his head and tore the cards. He attached another image to some bread and then pierced it. Reichmuth glued an image to the table and said "down with the bloody dog" and "he deserves the gallows." Then they destroyed the images and threw the pieces of paper in the trash to show their disdain.

They stated that they reject the person of Himmler himself because he is responsible for actions and measures against the clergy.

So that other students not in the class could know their views, Rendtorff distributed to several students who supported their ideas the insignia of an ancient organization of the church, so that each student could wear this illegal sign inside his jacket. This proved that Rendtorff and Reichmuth planned to create an illegal association.

For this reason we put them under surveillance starting in January 1942. During their interrogation, Reichmuth and Rendtorff openly admitted their opposition to the State. They are entirely responsible for their intrigues in view of their intellectual maturity, and I consider that it is absolutely necessary to make an example of them.

I demand a judgment against Rendtorff and Reichmuth and that they be held in protective custody for 6 months and be placed in a concentration camp. I will keep them in custody until further orders.

Katharina Reichmuth is the wife of Martin Reichmuth, the pastor of the confessing church. She gave the tracts to her son for copying. She created some of these tracts herself on her typewriter to spread her fanatical religious ideas within her parish; she has committed slanderous propaganda that is forbidden by the State police. She has been questioned here several times already as a fanatical adherent of this religious order and she has been put under surveillance several times.

For her, I have confiscated the typewriter that was used to create these tracts.

Signed: Müller[20]

Testimony of Danuta "Rad" Socha[21]—Polish Resistance Fighter

In 1942 she undertook conspiratorial activity in the Home Army under the pseudonym "Rad." Armed with binoculars and prior knowledge of the different types of German airplanes, she recorded their flights for the use of the Underground. She underwent communication, medical, and military training, which came in especially handy during the Operation Tempest, which was the liberation of Eastern Poland from under the Nazi occupation even before the Soviet invasion. Then, courier "Rad" and her friend, Olga Kruczek had an adventure that could have easily cost them their lives.

One day, before daybreak they decided to go, by bike, to Blazowa,[22] which was supposed to have been taken over by Soviets. They were to take part in the funeral of members of the local outpost, who had died in a skirmish with Germans. On the way, they were stopped by a small military detachment, which was moving towards Blazowa. Both couriers, Danuta and Olga took off their white-red armbands as a precautionary measure, but after identifying the vehicles as Soviet, Danuta put hers back on. However, the detachment proved to be a German penal unit on its way to pacify the local villages. After a short interrogation, during which Danuta was able to get rid of a small pistol hidden in her handbag, both women were put on a tank. Hanging on to the tank's barrel, they were transported to Blazowa.

The white-red armband on Danuta's sleeve was enough condemning evidence for the Germans. They placed her under a church wall and handed her a black scarf with an order to tie it around her eyes. She refused to execute this order, which did not hinder further preparations for her execution. It was stopped at the last moment by a higher-ranking officer who just happened to walk by. Both couriers were taken for further interrogation. Neither of them admitted to anything, saying that the Soviets had ordered them to put on the armbands after confiscating their identity documents. The oncoming Soviet offensive forced the Germans to stop their attempts to pacify Blazowa and to retreat. They also took both women with them with the intention to interrogate them. They spent part of the way on a truck full of ammunition and gasoline under Soviet fire. Taking advantage of a momentary commotion, caused by the enemy fire, both women were able to escape and returned to Blazowa on foot.

Wannsee Protocol, January 20, 1942

At the beginning of the discussion Chief of the Security Police and of the SD, SS-Obergruppenführer Heydrich, reported that the Reich Marshal[23] had appointed him delegate for the preparations for the final solution of the Jewish question in Europe and pointed out that this discussion had been called for the purpose of clarifying fundamental questions . . .

The Chief of the Security Police and the SD then gave a short report of the struggle which has been carried on thus far against this enemy, the essential points being the following:

(a)   the expulsion of the Jews from every sphere of life of the German people,

(b)   the expulsion of the Jews from the living space of the German people.

In carrying out these efforts, an increased and planned acceleration of the emigration of the Jews from Reich territory was started, as the only possible present solution . . .

The aim of all this was to cleanse German living space of Jews in a legal manner . . .

Approximately 11 million Jews will be involved in the final solution of the European Jewish question . . .

Under proper guidance, in the course of the final solution the Jews are to be allocated for appropriate labor in the East. Able-bodied Jews, separated according to sex, will be taken in large work columns to these areas for work on roads, in the course of which action doubtless a large portion will be eliminated by natural causes.

The possible final remnant will, since it will undoubtedly consist of the most resistant portion, have to be treated accordingly, because it is the product of natural selection and would, if released, act as a the seed of a new Jewish revival.

In the course of the practical execution of the final solution, Europe will be combed through from west to east . . .

The evacuated Jews will first be sent, group by group, to so-called transit ghettos, from which they will be transported to the East . . .

The beginning of the individual larger evacuation actions will largely depend on military developments.

The meeting was closed with the request of the Chief of the Security Police and the SD to the participants that they afford him appropriate support during the carrying out of the tasks involved in the solution.

Poem by Dutch Prisoner Jan Campert—"The Song of the Eighteen Dead"[24]

A cell is but six feet long
and hardly six feet wide,
yet smaller is the patch of ground,
that I now do not yet know,
but where I nameless come to lie,
my comrades all and one,
we eighteen were in number then,
none shall the evening see come.

O loveliness of light and land,
of Holland's so free coast,
once by the enemy overrun
could I no moment more rest.
What can a man of honor and trust
do in a time like this?
He kisses his child, he kisses his wife
and fights the noble fight.

I knew the task that I began,
a task with hardships laden,
the heart that couldn't let it be
but shied not away from danger;
it knows how once in this land
freedom was everywhere cherished,

before the cursed transgressor's hand
had willed it otherwise.

Before the oath can brag and break
existed this wretched place
that the lands of Holland did invade
and for ransom her ground has held;
Before the appeal to honor is made
and such Germanic comfort
our people forced under their control
and looted as a thief.

The Catcher of Rats who lives in Berlin
sounds now his melody—
as true as I shortly dead shall be
my dearest no longer see
and no longer shall the bread be broke
and share a bed with her—
reject all he offers now and ever
that sly trapper of birds.

For all who these words thinks to read
my comrades in great need
and those who stand by them through all
in their adversity tall,
just as we have thought and thought
on our own land and people—
a day does shine after every night,
as every cloud must pass.

I see how the first morning light
through the high window falls.
My God, make my dying light—
and so I have failed
just as each of us can fail,
pour me then Your grace,
that I may like a man then go
if I a squadron must face.

Testimony of Solomon Radasky[25]—Polish Holocaust Survivor

My father was killed in April 1942. He went to buy bread from the children who
were smuggling food into the ghetto. The children brought bread, potatoes and

cabbages across the wall into the Warsaw ghetto. A Jewish policeman pointed out my father to a German and told him that he saw my father take a bread from a boy at the wall. The German shot my father in the back.

The deportations started on July 22, 1942. My other 2 sisters and 2 brothers went to Treblinka. After that I never saw anybody from my family again.

Testimony of Father Leo Miechalowski[26]—Dachau Survivor

I was confined in Dachau . . .

I wore a red insignia which all those who had been arrested for political reasons had to wear this insignia.

. . . One man arrived and selected about thirty people for some easy labor. I also wanted to be selected for this assignment and those who had been selected for this work were led away. We went in the direction where the work was located and at the very last moment instead of going to the place of work we were led to the camp hospital. We did not know what was going to be done with us there. I thought to myself that perhaps this was going to be some detail for easier work in the hospital . . . there I was given malaria in such a manner that there were little cages with infected mosquitoes and I had to put my hand on one of the little cages and a mosquito stung me and afterwards I was still in the hospital for five weeks. Somewhat later, I don't exactly recall, two or three weeks, I had my first malaria attack. Such attacks recurred frequently and several medicines were given to us for against malaria. . . . It was approximately in the middle of 1942 when I was infected with malaria. . . . Towards the end I heard that approximately one thousand two hundred prisoners were subjected to these experiments.

Several days later, that was on the seventh of October 1942, a prisoner came and told me that I was to report to the hospital immediately. . . . I was led there, and there was a basin with water and ice which floated on the water. . . . Now wires had been taped to my back, also in the lower rectum. Afterwards I had to wear my shirt, my drawers, but then afterwards I had to wear one of the uniforms which were lying there. Then I had also to wear a long pair of boots with cat's fur and one aviator's combination. And afterwards a tube was put around my neck and was filled with air. And afterwards the wires which had been connected with me—they were connected to the apparatus, and then I was thrown into the water. All of a sudden I became very cold, and I began to tremble. I immediately turned to those two men and asked them to pull me out of the water because I would be unable to stand it much longer. However, they told me laughingly, "Well, this will only last a very short time." I sat in this water, and I had—and I was conscious for one hour and a half. I do not know exactly because I did not have a watch, but that is the approximate time I spent there.

When I was thrown into the water my temperature was lowered very slowly in the beginning and afterwards more rapidly. When I was thrown into the water my temperature was 37.6, then the temperature became lower.

Then I only had 33 and then as low as 30, but then I already became somewhat unconscious and every fifteen minutes some blood was taken from my ear. I was freezing very much in this water. Now my feet were becoming as rigid as iron, and the same thing applied to my hands, and later on my breathing became very short. I once again began to tremble, and afterwards cold sweat appeared on my forehead. I felt as if I was just about to die, and then I was still asking them to pull me out because I could not stand this much longer. Then I lost my consciousness.

Testimony of Eva Galler[27]—Polish Holocaust Survivor

This continued until September 1942. One day the drummer came. He announced that all the Jews had to take what they could carry and walk the seven kilometers to the next town of Lubaczow. There was a ghetto there.

All the Jews of Oleszyce and the neighboring villages were moved to the ghetto in Lubaczow.[28] The ghetto was the size of one city block for 7,000 people. We slept 28 people in a room that was about 12 by 15 feet. It was like a sardine box. People lived in attics, in basements, in the streets—all over. We were lucky to have a roof over our heads; not everyone did.

Testimony of Simon Igel—Polish-French Holocaust Survivor

I was born in Poland in August 1927 not far from Cracow, and my family moved first to Vienna in 1928 and then, as anti-Semitism spread throughout Austria, to Paris in 1937. Two years later the French police questioned our entry visas and sent us to Auxerre in the Bourgogne region. Following the defeat of France in 1940, our family situation deteriorated. In October 1940 the first "racial" laws were passed, prohibiting Jews from certain jobs in the government. The law was even harder on foreign Jews.

When my family was arrested in July 1942 (all of them died at Auschwitz), I was not taken because I was under 16 years old. Instead I was placed in an orphanage. Escaping from the orphanage, I at first hid with some neighbors. In the meantime the authorities decided to round up all of the Jewish children under 16 years old in the name of reuniting families. Of course my family was already on the train to Auschwitz. I went back into hiding.

I decided to flee to an area that was considered part of "free" France. Unfortunately I had to pay the guides who helped me cross the border into the Vichy zone all the savings that my parents had given to me—that is about 10,000 francs or the equivalent of two month's salary for a worker. In the non-occupied zone of France, the Vichy government issued a series of anti-Semitic decrees, further restricting freedoms, occupations, and ordering the wearing of yellow stars. I moved to Saint-Etienne and stayed there from September 1942 until August 1943. Without ration tickets for food, life was hard, but I managed to scrounge up whatever I could at the open markets.

Note to U.S.S.R. on Punishment of War Criminals, July 22, 1942

As the Government of the Union of Soviet Socialist Republics is aware, the Belgian Government, the Czechoslovak Government, the French National Committee, the Greek Government, the Luxembourg Government, the Netherlands Government, the Norwegian Government, the Polish Government and the Yugoslav Government signed, on January 13th, 1942, at St. James's Palace, London, a Declaration on the repression of war crimes. These Governments have now jointly examined the situation arising from the recrudescence of violations of international law, in particular of acts of oppression and terrorism in the European territories under enemy occupation.

These acts have, indeed, recently developed to such an extent and assumed such forms as to arouse the fear that as the defeat of the enemy countries approaches, the régime of occupation will assume an ever more barbarous and merciless character, not excluding the extermination of whole groups of people.

The above-mentioned Governments are, therefore, convinced that only very definite steps by the more powerful Allies can exert a deterrent influence . . .

In several notes, M. Molotov, People's Commissar for Foreign Affairs, has denounced to the civilized world the terrible wrongs which the Soviet people are enduring so heroically in their invaded lands. Out of such ordeals solidarity is being forged among the United Nations. This solidarity should strengthen itself through the repression of war crimes. Therefore, the above-mentioned Governments cherish the hope that the warning they seek to obtain will be of such a nature as to make the enemy understand that the will and power of the Soviet Union will guarantee that it will be implemented in full.

Roosevelt on War Crimes, August 21, 1942

The communication which I have just received from the chiefs of mission of the Netherlands, Yugoslavia and Luxembourg states that these acts of oppression and terror have taken proportions and forms giving rise to the fear that as the defeat of the enemy countries approached, the barbaric and unrelenting character of the occupational régime will become more marked and may even lead to the extermination of certain populations.

As I stated on October 25th, 1941:

The practice of executing scores of innocent hostages in reprisal for isolated attacks on Germans in countries temporarily under the Nazi heel revolts a world already inured to suffering and brutality. Civilized peoples long ago adopted the basic principle that no man should be punished for the deed of another. Unable to apprehend the persons involved in these attacks the Nazis characteristically slaughter fifty or a hundred innocent persons. Those who would "collaborate" with Hitler or try to appease him cannot ignore this ghastly warning . . .

The Government of the United States has been aware for some time of these crimes. Our Government is constantly receiving additional information from dependable sources and it welcomes reports from any trustworthy source which would assist in keeping our growing fund of information and evidence up-to-date and reliable.

The United Nations are going to win this war. When victory has been achieved, it is the purpose of the Governments of the United States, as I know it is the purpose of each of the United Nations, to make appropriate use of the information and evidence in respect to these barbaric crimes of the invaders, in Europe and in Asia. It seems only fair that they should have this warning that the time will come when they shall have to stand in courts of law in the very countries which they are now oppressing and answer for their acts.

Testimony of Paul Blobel[29]—Nazi Officer

[I]n June 1942 I was entrusted by Gruppenführer Müller with the task of obliterating traces of executions carried out by the Einsatzgruppen in the East.[30] My orders were that I should report in person to the commanders of the Security Police and SD, pass on Müller's orders verbally and supervise their implementation. This order was top secret . . .

During my visits in August I myself observed the burning of bodies in a mass grave near Kiev. This grave was about 55 m. long, 3 m. wide and 2-1/2 m. deep. After the top had been removed the bodies were covered with inflammable material and ignited. It took about two days until the grave burned down to the bottom. I myself observed that the fire had glowed down to the bottom. After that the grave was filled in and the traces practically obliterated.

Owing to the moving up of the front line it was not possible to destroy the mass graves farther south and east which had resulted from executions by the Einsatzgruppen.

According to my orders I should have extended my duties over the entire area occupied by the Einsatzgruppen, but owing to the retreat from Russia I could not carry out my orders completely.

Testimony of Pierre Lecostey[31]—Forced Labor

The construction of the blockhouses was very impressive: each morning hundreds of workers arrived for the labor. The French Jewish prisoners dug a trench in front of the house to hold water for washing. The Jews wore white clothes, which did not look it because of the dirt, with a yellow star. The Polish prisoners guarded them. Their numbers changed all the time.

Testimony of Dieter Wisliceny—Nazi Officer

I entered the SS in 1934. In 1934 I entered the SD [Gestapo]. I have known Eichmann since 1934. He ran Section IVA4. This department comprised two subsections: one for churches and another for Jewish matters. This Section IVA4b was concerned with the Jewish question. . . . Eichmann had special powers. . . . He was responsible for the so-called solution of the Jewish question in Germany and in all countries occupied by Germany. . . . The second phase was the concentration of all Jews in Poland and in other territories occupied by Germany in the East, in ghettos. This period lasted approximately until the beginning of 1942. The third period was the so called "final solution" of the Jewish question, that is, the planned extermination and destruction of the Jewish race. . . . Then at the end of July or the beginning of August [1942], I went to see him [Eichmann] in Berlin. . . . After a lengthy discussion Eichmann told me that my request to visit the Polish ghettos could not be granted under any circumstances whatsoever. In reply to my question "Why?" he said that most of these Jews were no longer alive. I asked him who had given such instructions and he referred me to an order of Himmler's. . . . The Führer had ordered the final solution of the Jewish question; the Chief of the Security Police and the SD and the Inspector of Concentration Camps were entrusted with carrying out this so-called final solution. This letter was signed by Himmler himself. I could not possibly be mistaken since Himmler's signature was well known to me. . . . Eichmann went on to explain to me what was meant by this. He said that the planned biological annihilation of the Jewish race in the Eastern Territories was disguised by the concept and wording "final solution."

Testimony of Ukrainian Representative, Events of September 23, 1942[32]

Our interest is narrowly focused at this point. We are focusing on the question of genocide. Approximately 14.5 million Ukrainians, including 600,000 Ukrainian Jews, were lost in the Second World War. The details include the fact that 459 villages were completely destroyed, in 27 villages . . . all the men, women and children in them were killed. For example, in the village of Kortelisy, 2,892 men, women and children were massacred and the village was destroyed.

Some other of the details of these losses include the following: 3,898,500 Ukrainians were killed by the German army on the territory of Ukraine; 1,366,699 Ukrainians were killed as war prisoners in concentration camps; in the period 1941–43, 2,244,000 Ukrainians were deported to work as slave laborers in German munitions factories and in Austria.

Roosevelt on War Crimes, October 7, 1942

I now declare it to be the intention of this Government that the successful close of the war shall include provision for the surrender to the United Nations of war criminals.

With a view to establishing responsibility of the guilty individuals through the collection and assessment of all available evidence, this Government is prepared to co-operate with the British and other Governments in establishing a United Nations Commission for the Investigation of War Crimes.

The number of persons eventually found guilty will undoubtedly be extremely small compared to the total enemy populations. It is not the intention of this Government or of the Governments associated with us to resort to mass reprisals. It is our intention that just and sure punishment shall be meted out to the ringleaders responsible for the organized murder of thousands of innocent persons and the commission of atrocities which have violated every tenet of the Christian faith.

Molotov on War Crimes, October 14, 1942

The Soviet Government and the entire Soviet people are imbued with feelings of fraternal solidarity and profound sympathy for the sufferings and courageous struggle of the peoples of the countries of Europe occupied by the Hitlerites.

The misery, degradation and privation inflicted on these peoples by Hitlerite tyranny is all the more understood by the peoples of the Soviet Union since the Hitlerite invaders, in the Soviet areas temporarily occupied by them, are perpetrating crimes and atrocities on a monstrous scale: mass murders of civilians, destruction of towns and villages, plunder and ruin of the population, brutal violation of women, children and the aged, enslavement of hundreds of thousands of people.

The Soviet Government once more confirms the universal and deliberate character of the bloody crimes of the Hitlerite invaders, which prove that the German Fascist Government and its accomplices, in striving to enslave the peoples of the occupied countries, to destroy their culture and debase their national dignity, have also made it their aim to carry out the direct, physical annihilation of a considerable section of the population of the territories captured by them . . .

It declared that the Hitlerite Government and its accomplices would not escape responsibility and deserved punishment for all the unprecedented atrocities perpetrated against the peoples of the U.S.S.R. and against all the freedom-loving countries.

The Soviet Government declared in addition, that its organs would make a detailed record of these crimes and atrocities of the Hitlerite Army, for which the outrages Soviet people justly demand and will obtain retribution.

Having received information about the monstrous atrocities perpetrated and being perpetrated by the Hitlerites, by order of the Government and military and civil authorities of Germany, on the territories of France, Czechoslovakia, Poland, Yugoslavia, Norway, Greece, Belgium, Holland and

Luxembourg, and giving the widest publicity to the information received from these countries, the Soviet Government once more declares to the world its inflexible determination that the criminal Hitlerite Government and all its accomplices must and shall suffer deserved, stern punishment for the crimes perpetrated against the peoples of the Soviet Union and against all freedom-loving peoples in territories temporarily occupied by the German army and its accomplices . . .

The Soviet Government considers it essential to hand over without delay to the courts of the special international tribunal, and to punish according to all the severity of the criminal code, any of the leaders of Fascist Germany who in the course of the war have fallen into the hands of States fighting against Hitlerite Germany.

Renewing at the present time its warning of the full weight of responsibility which the criminal Hitlerite leaders and all their accomplices bear for the monstrous atrocities perpetrated by them, the Soviet Government considers it opportune to confirm the conviction, expressed in its official declarations, that the Hitlerite Government, which recognizes only brute force, must be smashed by the all-powerful forces of the freedom-loving peoples, since the interests of the whole of mankind demand that as soon as possible the band of barefaced murderers called the government of Hitlerite Germany, shall be finished with once and for all.

CHAPTER 6

Victory at Stalingrad; Italy Invaded, 1943

Introduction to 1943

Many of the tensions that divided the western alliance in 1942 carried over into 1943: Would the U.S.S.R. drop out of the war? When would the invasion of France take place? And who would determine the status of Poland? This latter question on Poland's future was exacerbated by the German discovery of murdered Polish army officers in the Katyn Forest near Smolensk. German soldiers uncovered the burial ground of approximately 20,000 Poles and immediately claimed that Soviet agents had carried out the massacre. The Polish government in exile in London seconded the German accusation. The Soviet government protested this so-called German-Polish slander, and Roosevelt and Churchill were faced with a difficult political situation—they did not want to alienate Stalin in the middle of the war even though they suspected that Stalin was responsible. Stalin protested the accusations of the Polish government in London and used this pretext to break relations with it. He subsequently helped establish and then recognized his own puppet government in Poland. Roosevelt tried to convince Stalin to maintain relations with the Polish-London government. The conflict between the pro-western Polish government in exile in London and the pro-Soviet Polish government sponsored by Stalin poisoned relations among the Allies from this time on. Stalin knew of his own duplicity—Soviet culpability in the Katyn massacre was established after the war.

Diplomatically, two summit meetings dominated the year—the first in North Africa between Churchill and Roosevelt and the second in Iran that included Stalin as well. Roosevelt and Churchill met in Morocco in January to emphasize their control of North Africa after Operation Torch and the imminent defeat of both Italian and German forces there. The most important news that emerged from the protocol was the demand for "unconditional surrender." The Allies would not negotiate with the Axis powers and would accept nothing less than total capitulation. Sometimes criticized for prolonging the war, "unconditional surrender" was necessary to prevent a repetition of the aftermath of World War I, when an armistice left Germany intact and allowed unscrupulous politicians to claim that Germany had not been defeated.

Despite Stalin's statements on the destruction of Germany, the western Allies worried about his loyalty. Similarly, despite Franco's protestations of friendship, Hitler was concerned about American-British pressure on Spain to switch sides. The successful Allied landing in North Africa exacerbated the anxiety of the Axis powers. From the beginning of the war, Hitler had pressured Franco to enter the conflict, and Franco had repeatedly affirmed his support for the Fascist cause.

By 1943, Franco admitted to the German ambassador that his muted criticism of the Allies was due to economic aid that he had been receiving. Nevertheless, he assured Hitler that he remained firmly committed to a Fascist victory for a good reason:

Further, he knew for certain and was clearly conscious of the fact that only the victory of Germany would make possible the continued existence of the regime of Franco; a victory of the Anglo-Saxons, in spite of all the pacifying declarations which would be made to him from time to time in this respect by the English and American side, would mean his own annihilation. He therefore was hoping with all his heart for the victory of Germany and he had only one wish that this victory would come as soon as possible.[1]

In the end, Franco reasserted Spain's devotion to the Axis powers and promised to resist any Allied incursion on Spanish territory. Again insisting that his country had not yet recovered from its own civil war, Franco refused to bring Spain into the war despite his pro-Axis views.

Militarily, the most important events in 1943 took place in the U.S.S.R. All participants as well as observers recognized the crucial nature of the battle for Stalingrad. Soviet victory came in February, shortly after the meeting between Roosevelt and Churchill in North Africa. Roosevelt congratulated Stalin on a battle that would be considered the turning point of the war in Europe. Soviet newspapers celebrated the event with nearly identical headlines in *Pravda* and *Izvestiia*: "Our forces have concluded the liquidation of the German fascist troops surrounded in the Stalingrad region."[2] Following the Soviet triumph at Stalingrad, the Red Army went on the offensive, while Germany remained on the defensive for the rest of the war. Several months later (July and August) the Red Army defeated the German forces in a massive tank battle at Kursk.[3] In military importance, the battles of Stalingrad and Kursk have to be considered among the greatest events of the war, ranking alongside Germany's total domination of the west in 1940 and the Normandy landings that would come in 1944.

For good reasons, Stalin's Order of the Day on May 1, 1943, sounded more optimistic than his pronouncements of previous years. The German army had suffered a devastating defeat at Stalingrad and the Soviet army was on the offensive. Stalin revealed that Germany responded to Stalingrad and western victories in North Africa with suggestions for peace talks (the worst fear of the United States and Britain), but the Soviet ruler dismissed these offers. To the relief of the American and British governments, Stalin's speech included significant praise for his western allies and affirmed his desire to annihilate the Nazi regime.

On the second anniversary of the German invasion of the U.S.S.R., Roosevelt and Secretary of State Cordell Hull[4] sent messages to Stalin extolling the strength and success of the Soviet Union in its struggle against the Nazi invaders. Although these messages were part of a continuing campaign to encourage goodwill, Stalin responded by again pressing for the promised second front. The timing of the invasion of France remained a source of contention among the Allies and led to a change in diplomatic representation in Washington. Analogous to his action in 1939 when he viewed Litvinov as a liability preventing a Soviet-German deal, Stalin removed Litvinov as ambassador to the United States in 1943 for not convincing the Allies to open the second front. The appointment of A. Gromyko[5] was a signal that the U.S.S.R. would push harder for aggressive military action in the west.

Although the Allies were not prepared to open a second front in France in 1943, they successfully completed their military actions in North Africa and moved from there into Sicily (Operation Husky) in July. The Allied landings were successful, and in response to Italian military defeats, the Fascist Grand Council voted to remove Mussolini from office. The king appointed Pietro Badoglio[6] as the new premier. One month later, the Allies announced that Italy had switched sides and joined the fight against Germany. Mussolini was put under house arrest, only to be rescued by the Nazis and moved to northern Italy where he proclaimed a new state, the so-called Italian Social Republic. The German army refused to surrender Italy, and the fight for control of the country was intense and brutal. Under Field Marshal Kesselring,[7] German forces fought tenaciously and slowed Allied forces. Unable to drive the Germans out of Italy before the end of 1943, Allied troops suffered a hard winter in the mountainous center of the country.

While fighting continued on all fronts, Allied foreign ministers met in Moscow in October for the Tripartite Conference. Although a few problems and differences surfaced, the meeting was in general a diplomatic success. The foreign ministers (Hull, Eden, and Molotov, joined by Chinese ambassador to Moscow Foo Ping-sheung[8]) agreed that they would pursue the war to its conclusion and that there would not be any separate peace or armistice with the Fascist states (a sign that they were still worried about such a possibility). They acknowledged that the only way to hasten the end of the war was through continued cooperation in both military and economic arenas, and in this regard, they decided to talk further on a variety of postwar issues, including the treatment of Italy and of Austria, and the establishment of an international organization to maintain peace. Finally, the foreign ministers cleared the way for a major summit in Iran's capital.

The summit in Tehran marked the first time that Roosevelt, Churchill, and Stalin met together. This conference focused on the conduct of the war and the postwar period. The Allied leaders reiterated their determination to continue the war until all Fascist states had been defeated, and they pledged to work together to create a peaceful world order after victory had been achieved. While the timing for a second front could not be announced, they reached agreement on an invasion of France in the spring of 1944. Finally, the Allied leaders signed a communiqué promising the punishment of war criminals.

Before the Tehran Conference, Stalin celebrated the Russian Revolution with a speech that focused on the continuing struggle against Germany. He correctly identified 1943 as the turning point in the war, with Soviet victories at Stalingrad and Kursk forcing the Germans to begin a slow but steady retreat from the Soviet Union. At the same time, Stalin praised his allies for their actions and victories in North Africa and in Italy. He looked forward to the next step in the confrontation: "Now the united countries are filled with determination to strike joint blows against the enemy which will result in final victory over him."[9] With the war going well, Stalin turned to the postwar situation, when liberated countries would be free to choose their own forms of government (so he claimed) and when war criminals would be held accountable for their actions.

The United States also warned Germany about its treatment of prisoners and civilians. As Secretary of State Hull stated after returning from Iran:

The Conference also served as an occasion for a solemn public declaration by the heads of the three Governments with regard to the perpetrators of the bestial and abominable crimes committed by the Nazi leaders against the harassed and persecuted inhabitants of occupied territories—against people of all races and religions, among whom Hitler has reserved for the Jews his most brutal wrath. Due punishment will be administered for all these crimes.

None of these warnings mattered to the Nazi leaders. Despite the deteriorating military situation, the Germans gave priority to their policies of racial extermination. The Nazis planned to liquidate the remaining population in the Warsaw Ghetto, home to nearly half a million Jews in 1941 but less than 100,000 by 1943. The trapped residents inside the ghetto had been collecting and making weapons, and when the Nazis moved to close the ghetto in April by shipping the population to concentration camps, an uprising broke out led by Jewish resistance organizations. Despite their miserable living conditions, starvation, and rampant disease, the self-defense force held off the German army for nearly three weeks. In charge of German military operations, General Stroop[10] filed a lengthy and repetitive report delineating the operations of his forces day by day. Unable to track down all the Jewish resistors, some of whom used the sewers for shelter, the Germans resorted to burning the ghetto block by block, and this brutality culminated in the destruction of the Great Synagogue of Warsaw. Later that summer, the Nazis proceeded with the destruction of the remaining ghettos in Poland.

The Jews of Eastern Europe were not the only civilians targeted for the final solution. Testimony at the Nuremberg Trials indicated that Himmler was determined to exterminate the Jewish population of Western Europe, including France, Holland, and Denmark as well. His representatives in Denmark told him that the local population would not respond well to this plan, but Himmler insisted on it anyway. In the end, most of Denmark's Jews escaped to Sweden.

Rudolf Hoess served as the commandant of Auschwitz concentration camp from May 1940 until December 1943.[11] In this capacity, Hoess was intimately involved in all aspects of the camp process. His Nuremberg testimony was revealing in this regard, although he tried to obscure the truth on the more sinister aspects of the final solution. He knowingly lied, first by claiming that the primary focus in the camps was armaments production and that excess deaths were due to normal war shortages. He continued along these lines by stating that the large number of deaths was the result of Allied destruction of railways that supplied the camps with food and medical supplies, and he further lied when he asserted that he never witnessed the ill treatment of prisoners. Overall, he blamed Himmler and Eichmann as the driving forces behind the camp system. Convicted of war crimes, Hoess was hanged in 1947.

THE SOURCES

Stalingrad: The Turning Point

The battle for Stalingrad raged from the fall of 1942 through the winter of 1943. The fighting was watched closely throughout Europe, and it was widely recognized as crucial to German success or Soviet survival. With the exception of the battle for Moscow in December 1941, the German military had enjoyed extraordinary success in Russia. Stalingrad, for symbolic and strategic reasons, was the city that Hitler wanted to capture and that the Soviets were determined to hold. Finally in February 1943, the remnants of the German and Romanian armies assaulting the city were forced to surrender. While a French collaborationist newspaper (*Le Petit Parisien*) still predicted German victory, the Soviet press celebrated the destruction of the Axis forces. President Roosevelt congratulated Stalin on the victory, and Soviet combat veterans testified to the fierceness of the fighting.

In the Headlines

Le Petit Parisien, Paris, January 19, 1943 [collaborationist]
AFTER 2 MONTHS OF BRUTAL COMBAT THE GERMAN ARMY
  EVERYWHERE STOPS VIOLENT SOVIET ATTACKS

Le Petit Parisien, Paris, February 3, 1943
SOVIET ATTEMPTS TO PIERCE GERMAN LINES ARE REPULSED

Izvestiia, Moscow, February 3, 1943
OUR FORCES HAVE FULLY CONCLUDED THE LIQUIDATION OF THE
  GERMAN FASCIST FORCES SURROUNDED IN THE STALINGRAD
  REGION

Izvestiia, Moscow, February 4, 1943
THE GREAT STALINGRAD EPIC HAS BEEN VICTORIOUSLY COMPLETED!

Roosevelt Congratulates Stalin, February 22, 1943

For many months, in spite of tremendous losses in men, supplies, transportation and territory, the Red Army denied victory to a most powerful enemy. It checked him at Leningrad, at Moscow, at Voronezh, in the Caucasus, and finally, at the immortal battle of Stalingrad, the Red Army not only defeated the enemy but launched the great offensive which is still moving forward along the whole front from the Baltic to the Black Sea. The enforced retreat of the enemy is costing him heavily in men, supplies, territory, and especially in morale.

Such achievements can only be accomplished by an army that has skillful leadership, sound organization, adequate training, and above all, the determination to defeat the enemy, no matter what the cost in self-sacrifice.

At the same time, I also wish to pay tribute to the Russian people from whom the Red Army springs, and upon whom it is dependent for its men, women and supplies. They, too, are giving their full efforts to the war and are making the supreme sacrifice.

The Red Army and the Russian people have surely started the Hitler Forces on the road to ultimate defeat and have earned the lasting admiration of the people of the United States.

Testimony of Fedor Pavlovich Ivanov—Soviet Cavalry

Sent to an officer-training course that lasted only for a few months in 1942 due to the military crisis, Fedor was certified as an artillery officer and quickly sent to Stalingrad.

On his way to the front, German planes bombed Fedor's train, and he lost all of his documents. When all of the survivors were assembled, Russian officers asked each man to declare his area of specialization. Fedor, more comfortable with horses than with artillery pieces, announced that he was with the cavalry. In addition to his preference for riding, he had also decided that the cavalry was potentially safer than artillery.

Rather than serving as an artillery officer, Fedor became a private in the cavalry and was assigned to reconnaissance, a position he held for the rest of the war.

Fedor participated in the battle of Stalingrad and continued his service in the 8th Guards Army commanded by General Vasily Chuikov.[12]

Fedor prided himself on his horsemanship. When one of his commanders needed new horseshoes for his mount, Fedor repaired the shoes and received extra privileges from his commander. He would use such expertise several times during the war to win leaves and other special treatment.

Fedor loved his horses, and although he had several killed beneath him, he always considered himself fortunate to ride such fine animals. All of his horses were named Dunai for the Danube River, the goal of the Russian advance. He laughed when his trusted horses intimidated and even bit German prisoners.

As the war moved west from Stalingrad, the 8th Guards Army fought a hard battle in November 1943 at the Dniepr River. Despite the high death rate on both sides, Fedor himself was unhurt; nevertheless he lost another horse in the struggle.

For his heroics in the crossing of the Dniepr, Fedor received the Order of the Patriotic War 2nd Degree. This would not be Fedor's last medal, for as the war continued westward he won a certificate of bravery.

Fedor often demonstrated initiative and resourcefulness. He remembered an order to find and catch a German soldier in order to extract information. During a relative period of calm between battles, Fedor thought about this situation. Scouts from his platoon had not been able to entrap a German, but Fedor knew that his commander wanted the information.

Fedor and his friend Nephed, who was from Siberia and was big and strong, decided to fulfill the order themselves because they were promised rewards for catching any German prisoner. Their friend, a good painter, drew on a white sheet a picture of a Russian soldier without pants and showing his bare ass, with Hitler kissing the Russian soldier's butt.

Fedor and Nephed placed the sheet in the neutral zone between the forces, attaching it to some barbed wire.

Next day they saw Germans looking at the sheet and some Germans were insulted and emerged to retrieve the sheet. Fedor and Nephed waited in ambush, and Nephed was able to grab one soldier but struck him too hard and killed him.

Fedor and Nephed remained in hiding and when another German soldier attempted to remove the sheet, Nephed captured him and took him to the Russian commander. The satisfied commander called the head of division to report that the mission had been accomplished, and then awarded Fedor and his friend a leave as a reward . . .

Finally Fedor returned to his platoon and participated in major battles in 1944 and 1945.

In March 1944, Fedor received his second decoration—the prestigious Decoration of Fame—in recognition of his personal bravery and courage. Fedor always remained proud of this medal because of its association with personal courage.

As the battle moved into Belorussia, Fedor again set a trap in order to capture a potential informer. Waiting near a creek that separated German and Russian lines, Fedor watched and studied the Germans as they moved toward the creek to collect water. Riding quickly through the German lines he was able to knock one enemy soldier unconscious and lift the German onto his horse. Despite German small arms and mortar fire, Fedor escaped and delivered the prisoner to his platoon.

Fedor received another brief leave as a reward but he soon returned to battle.

Fedor received decorations for his participation in the battles for Poland and Warsaw, and he then moved forward with the Russian army into Germany and toward Berlin. After Berlin he received a Red Star Decoration.

Debate about Bolshevism

With the Soviet victory at Stalingrad, Germany and its allies, including the Vichy government in France, attempted to win popular support by warning Europeans of the threat of Communism. This attempt failed because of the brutality of Nazi occupation. President Roosevelt directly praised the Soviet military for its sacrifices and its victories, and a Belgian resistance newsletter pointed out that the oppressors of Belgium were the Nazis and that the Russians were too far away to be considered a threat.

In the Headlines

Le Petit Parisien, Paris, February 1, 1943 [collaborationist]
ADOLF HITLER HAS POSED THE FOLLOWING ALTERNATIVES: EITHER GERMANY AND ITS ALLIES WILL ENJOY VICTORY OR A WAVE OF BOLSHEVISM WILL DESTROY EUROPE [article accompanied by idealized photo of Hitler]

Le Petit Parisien, Paris, February 2, 1943
ALL FRENCH PEOPLE MUST KNOW THAT COMMUNISM IS TODAY'S TRUE RISK TO EUROPE AND TO FRANCE—DECLARES PRESIDENT LAVAL[13]

Le Petit Parisien, Paris, February 4, 1943
THE VANGUARD OF THE EUROPEAN ARMIES AGAINST BOLSHEVIK BARBARISM: DEFENDERS OF STALINGRAD FIGHT TO THE END BEFORE SUCCUMBING TO OVERWHELMING NUMBERS

Le Petit Parisien, Paris, February 19, 1943
IN A MAJOR SPEECH DR. GOEBBELS SAYS: THE REICH ALONE CAN EFFECTIVELY OPPOSE THE BOLSHEVIK THREAT TO OUR CONTINENT[14]

Bolsheviks or Nazis—article in *La Voix des Belges*, Brussels, April 1943 [resistance]

The Soviet peril: this has been the theme of German propaganda for several weeks. They say that only Germany is capable of defending us . . . "The Russians—I don't know the Russians," says a brave merchant, "but I know the Germans and that is sufficient." Let's review the German record: arbitrary arrests, massacre of hostages, the deportation of men, women, and the young, general misery—these are the results of their presence. After that they try to pretend that they are the heroes of civilization—permit us to smile at this. . . . The Soviets may be difficult but they are far away.

    If the Germans are worried about the Soviet peril, it is above all a military issue. For the first time in this war the German army has found an adversary that resists and gives them difficulty. . . . We follow the progress of the war on the radio. . . . We applaud Stalin and Timoshenko[15] because their success hastens the hour of our deliverance.

All enemies of Hitler are our friends. Each blow against him is a step toward our own liberation . . .

Supporting Germany in the struggle is simply forging the chains of our own enslavement. The traitor who fights in German armies struggles against the interests of his own nation. The worker who volunteers to work for German industry permits the Reich to free a soldier who is an oppressor of others. . . . We have an enemy, a single enemy: he who since 10 May 1940, violated Belgium, and since then has kept Belgium in servitude that grows more cruel each day.

Roosevelt Praises Soviet Army, June 21, 1943

Two years ago tomorrow by an act of treachery in keeping with the long record of Nazi duplicity the Nazi leaders launched their brutal attack upon the Soviet Union. They thus added to their growing list of enemies the mighty forces of the Soviet Union. These Nazi leaders had underestimated the extent to which the Soviet Government and people had developed and strengthened their military power to defend their country and had utterly failed to realize the determination and valor of the Soviet people during the past two years. The freedom-loving peoples of the world have watched with increasing admiration the history-making exploits of the armed forces of the Soviet Union and the almost incredible sacrifices which the Russian people are so heroically making. The growing might of the combined forces of all the United Nations which is being brought increasingly to bear upon our common enemy testifies to the spirit of unity and sacrifice necessary for our ultimate victory. This same spirit will, I am sure, animate us in approaching the challenging tasks of peace, which victory will present to the world.

Battle for North Africa and Italy

The Axis powers fought as long as possible to hold North Africa, but in 1943, they were forced to abandon this struggle as British and American forces surrounded and overwhelmed them. To celebrate Allied victory, Roosevelt and Churchill met in Casablanca and famously proclaimed the doctrine of "Unconditional Surrender."[16] Using North Africa as a launching pad, the Allies then attacked Sicily and the mainland of Italy. Italian defeats led to the removal of Mussolini as premier. Testimony of those who fought in Italy acknowledged the brutality of combat in the mountainous terrain.

Casablanca Conference Protocol, February 12, 1943

In an attempt to ward off the inevitable disaster, the Axis propagandist are trying all of their old tricks in order to divide the United Nations. They seek to create the idea that if we win this war, Russia, England, China, and the United States are going to get into a cat-and-dog fight.

This is their final effort to turn one nation against another, in the vain hope that they may settle with one or two at a time—that any of us may be so gullible and so forgetful as to be duped into making "deals" at the expense of our Allies.

To these panicky attempts to escape the consequences of their crimes we say—all the United Nations say—that the only terms on which we shall deal with an Axis government or any Axis factions are the terms proclaimed at Casablanca: "Unconditional Surrender." In our uncompromising policy we mean no harm to the common people of the Axis nations. But we do mean to impose punishment and retribution in full upon their guilty, barbaric leaders.

In the Headlines

Corriere Della Sera, Milan, May 8, 1943
BATTLE RAGES IN TUNISIA
HEROIC RESISTANCE OF AXIS TROOPS AGAINST MASS ENEMY
 ATTACK

The Times, London, May 13, 1943
FINAL AXIS COLLAPSE IN TUNISIA
ALL ORGANIZED RESISTANCE AT AN END

Corriere Della Sera, Milan, July 11, 1943
ATTACK ON SICILY

Corriere Della Sera, Milan, July 12, 1943
FIERCE FIGHTING ALONG THE SOUTHEAST COAST OF SICILY

Testimony of Warren G. Hirt[17]—American Seabees

In North Africa as I explained earlier, our outfit was kept busy making the pontoon causeways and training people in how they were used. And then the invasions started taking place. First it was Sicily and our boys had to ride these open pontoons ashore before H-Hour. They were really completely unprotected riding these pontoon causeways in the invasion, exposed to the open fire of the German artillery and so they really did themselves proud. We had a lot of casualties there. We had about 70% of injuries or death in one form or another. But the first invasion was in Sicily. And then they came back to North Africa and rearmed again for the invasions in Italy. Salerno was a bloody invasion, which is notable for the fact that it was so difficult. Our guys were involved in that. And they were involved in the Anzio Beach invasion, which is also another bloody one.[18] So the guys really had tough

times and they really did many heroic things. But they did the job. And after
the two invasions instead of thinking that maybe we'd be going home, they
packed us all up and sailed us to England to be prepared for the invasion of
France.

In the Headlines

Corriere Della Sera, Milan, July 22, 1943
HORROR IN THE WORLD FOR THE VANDAL-LIKE DESTRUCTION IN
   ROME [reference to Allied bombing]
BATTLE RAGES IN THE CENTRAL SECTOR IN SICILY

Corriere Della Sera, Milan, July 26, 1943
RESIGNATION OF MUSSOLINI
BADOGLIO IS HEAD OF GOVERNMENT

Journal de Genève, Geneva, July 26, 1943
IL DUCE DISMISSED
VICTOR EMMANUEL APPEALS TO MARSHAL BADOGLIO

Izvestiia, Moscow, July 27, 1943
THE BANKRUPTCY OF ITALIAN FASCISM

Le Petit Parisien, Paris, July 28, 1943
EVENTS IN ITALY—NOTHING HAS CHANGED IN THE DESIRE OF THE
   REICH TO LEAD THE STRUGGLE TO VICTORY

Corriere Della Sera, Milan, July 29,1943
FASCIST PARTY DISSOLVED

Corriere Della Sera, Milan, September 8, 1943
ARMISTICE: HOSTILITIES END BETWEEN ITALY AND ENGLAND AND
   UNITED STATES

The Times, London, September 9, 1943
ITALY SURRENDERS—COMPLETE SUBMISSION TO THE ALLIES
IMMEDIATE END OF HOSTILITIES
BADOGLIO ORDERS RESISTANCE TO THE GERMANS

Testimony of Michael John Donoghue[19]—British Army

"A SLEEP ON A MOUNTAIN"

A personal remembrance.
We trudged, slipped and strained up, ever up.
A mule track, sometimes only a few feet wide.
Night, freezing, misty, yet the sweat poured from us.
An enemy m/g [machine gun] opens up,
the Italian muleteers run to safety.

Some of the mules fall off the track.
Stumbling and cursing with our loads, m/g's, rifles,
all the paraphernalia for killing men who had
the emblem 'Gott mit uns' [God is with us] on their belt buckles.
So, he was with them too!
Yet still we murdered each other.
I have never found the answer, and gave up God—
that was the easiest solution to my problem!
After some hours we were allowed to halt.
And as we crouched there, slowly freezing,
I felt around and found a blanket rolled round a body,
who I presumed was one of our men.
I gradually pulled the blanket around me for a little warmth.
Then, not long after, we were ordered
to move up the mountain.
The man who I had shared the blanket with was
a young German, with most of his head missing!
Yet I felt nothing, only grateful for the warmth of the blanket!
As we staggered up, ever higher, ever colder,
a tall l/c [lieutenant-colonel] was shot in the shoulder.
It was only a flesh wound, yet he died a few hours later.
Another soldier gradually went mad with fear.
Cursing obscenely, crying and muttering,
shouting and then screaming.
He had to be clubbed with an m/g butt.
The Germans opened up with star shells
and then came the mortars and m/g's.
We crouched beneath the rocks, sweating and freezing,
feeling certain that every bullet was directed at us,
and that rock and shell splinters were searching for us.
So we spent the night, climbing and lurching,
every limb crying with pain and exhaustion.
Our faces crusted with frost
and dirt mingled with our sweat.

Testimony of Raymond Chow[20]—American Army in Italy

So we went up the road and we walk a little bit and we saw some guy lighting a cigarette. They were Germans. They were with a motorcar with a sidecar. There were two or three of them. And we went up there and the Lieutenant pointed to one guy and told him to go up and check it out and if anything happened he was to just drop down. He fired and killed a guy then we all fired. I think we killed them all. We had good officers, that guy—the officer was looking for souvenirs anyway. We went up there. We wanted to destroy the motorcycle. We cut the tires, we set it on fire and he took the pistol from the guy the other guy shot. He said, "Sir, I killed that guy, it should be mine." The officer said, "Ok." He gave it back to him. So, he was good; he did not pull rank or anything. He was just a platoon leader.

It was just part of the job. Either kill him or he was going to kill me. I was behind a big rock, I had my M-1, this trail just comes down. Too bad I didn't have the BAR machine gun so I could have got the other guys too. The M-1 just fires single.

Well Anzio—they did not tell us anything about Anzio. They did not give us any picture, no briefing on that. All they say is that it will be flat land. The next morning we come in; it's just Naples. You know Naples is not very far from Anzio and we went by boat. We didn't jump or anything. We went by LST. It was nothing—no resistance. All day just walked and took a couple of houses. We occupied a couple and stayed there all that night. The next morning it was hell. The Germans somehow sneaked into the next house. They were shelling us, that's when I got hit in the back. I went to see a doctor. "I can't help you; you got shrapnel in your back—I can't dig it out so I'll have to send you back to the hospital."

Testimony of John Torreano[21]—82nd Airborne in Italy

I enlisted in 1942 and was first sent overseas in 1943. We landed in Casablanca in North Africa but did not see any combat at that time. Our first combat mission was in Sicily, which was a badly coordinated campaign. For example, as we were flying over Sicily in our C-47s preparing for our drop, German planes appeared above us to drop bombs on our navy ships off the coast. The navy fired at the German planes; we were between the Germans and our own navy and we lost 22 planes, many due to friendly fire.

The fighting on Sicily was intense. General Patton was in charge, but he was not popular with the troops. He was very gung ho but was mostly interested in his own image and promotion and wanted attention for himself at any cost. As they used to say—his guts and our blood. The incident when he slapped some soldiers was well-known and hurt his reputation even more with the guys.[22]

Anyway after Sicily we went back to Africa for a short time before the invasion of Italy. We dropped into Salerno and then worked our way to Naples. That fighting in Italy was real tough because of the hills. By the way since I was from north Italy, General [James] Gavin[23] asked me to translate for him but I really couldn't understand that south Italian accent too well.

Testimony of Keith Campbell, December 1943[24]—American Army

It took us thirty-one days to cross the Atlantic Ocean. And we landed at Taranto, Italy which is on the toe. Now the captain of our ship refused to go the last 90 miles or so up the Adriatic Coast to the town of Bari where we were supposed to go because on the 2nd of December of '43 the Germans came in on a low level raid and bombed all of the ships in the harbor of Bari. And they sunk 17 ships and heavily damaged 8 of them and 1 of the ships was carrying a full load of mustard poison gas and that poison gas was completely hushed up 99 and 9/10s percent and people didn't know about it at all. Now there were over 1,000 men killed in that bombing of those ships and about half of them were killed because they jumped off the ships into the water to swim to shore and that mustard gas was in the water. They got burned from that mustard gas, but when they got to the hospitals, the hospitals didn't know about the mustard gas and they treated them for shell shock. It took about 7 days before General Eisenhower sent the number one medical doctor in the whole United States military to Bari and he found out real quick that these people were suffering from this mustard gas and then they got good treatment, but in the meantime as I said almost 1,000 people died.

Well, when we landed at Taranto—there were no trains there. And they just dumped us off the ships. So somebody got some boxcars and an engine and they put us—they jammed us in these boxcars and we had to go over about 100 miles from Taranto up to Bari. And there was no heat and no water, no toilets or anything else in those boxcars.

Italy Joins the Allies, October 13, 1943

The Governments of Great Britain, the United States and the Soviet Union acknowledge the position of the Royal Italian Government as stated by Marshal Badoglio and accept the active cooperation of the Italian nation and armed forces as a co-belligerent in the war against Germany. The military events since September eighth and the brutal maltreatment by the Germans of the Italian population, culminating in the Italian declaration of war against Germany have in fact made Italy a co-belligerent and the American, British and Soviet Governments will continue to work with the Italian Government on that basis. The three Governments acknowledge the Italian Government's pledge to submit to the will of the Italian people after the Germans have been driven from Italy, and it is understood that nothing can detract from the absolute and untrammeled right of the people of Italy by constitutional means to decide on the democratic form of government they will eventually have.

Soviet-American Friendship

The United States and Britain decided not to jeopardize relations with Stalin over the disclosure of a mass burial ground where Soviet agents had executed Polish officers and intellectuals.[25] When German soldiers announced the discovery near Smolensk, the Soviet government denied the accusation and the western Allies chose to ignore the situation for the sake of the alliance. Despite continuing differences on several issues, the western Allies and the U.S.S.R. publicly praised each other through much of 1943. There were good reasons for this apparent improvement in relations: the Soviet victory at Stalingrad suggested that Germany would lose the war on the eastern front, the bombing of Germany was bringing destruction to those responsible for the war, the Allied victory in North Africa and Italy put additional pressure on Axis nations, and finally the British and Americans were ready to commit to an invasion of France in 1944. The Germans were retreating in Russia, in Africa, and in Italy. By the end of the year, Stalin was congratulating his allies for their actions, and the "big three" met for the first time in Iran to put the final touches on the plan for a second front the following spring.

In the Headlines

Cassandre, Brussels, April 25, 1943 [collaborationist]
12,000 CORPSES AT KATYN
MASSACRE BY THE BOLSHEVIKS

Ambassador Gromyko Addresses Roosevelt, October 4, 1943

During the entire two years of this stubborn struggle, in which the heaviest burden of effort and sacrifices has fallen upon the Soviet Union, the peoples of the Soviet Union received and are receiving from the friendly American people not only moral, but substantial material support as well, in the form of airplanes, tanks, guns, and other military material, and also foodstuffs. The Soviet people highly values this support, for which I express to you, Mr. President, and through you to the whole American people, the warm gratitude of my Government and the peoples of my country.

The armed forces of the Allies, including those of the United States of America, are taking an increasingly greater part in our common struggle against Hitlerite Germany, and have already inflicted a number of heavy defeats upon the cunning foe. The successes of the Red Army in its struggle against the Hitlerite hordes during more than two years, its present victorious advance on the Soviet-German front, the remarkable successes of

Anglo-American arms in North Africa and Sicily, as well as the developing military operations of the Anglo-American forces on the territory of Italy, have created a favorable military-political situation for inflicting decisive blows upon the hated enemy.

It is now clear that the war is turning in favor of the United Nations. However, for delivery of the final blow upon the enemy, exertion of the total strength of our countries and also of all the United Nations, will be required.

Communiqué of Tripartite Conference in Moscow, November 1, 1943[26]

This declaration, published today, provides for even closer collaboration in the prosecution of the war and in all matters pertaining to the surrender and disarmament of the enemies with which the four countries are respectively at war. It sets forth the principles upon which the four governments agree that a broad system of international cooperation and security should be based. Provision is made for the inclusion of all other peace-loving nations, great and small, in this system.

Declaration on Austria, November 1, 1943

Austria is reminded, however, that she has a responsibility which she cannot evade for participation in the war on the side of Hitlerite Germany, and that in the final settlement account will inevitably be taken of her own contribution to her liberation . . .

Declaration Regarding Italy, November 1, 1943

. . . Allied policy towards Italy must be based upon the fundamental principle that Fascism and all its evil influences and emanations shall be utterly destroyed and that the Italian people shall be given every opportunity to establish governmental and other institutions based upon democratic principles . . .

Declaration of German Atrocities, November 1, 1943

At the time of the granting of any armistice to any government which may be set up in Germany, those German officers and men and members of the Nazi party who have been responsible for, or have taken a consenting part in the above atrocities, massacres and executions, will be sent back to the countries in which their abominable deeds were done in order that they may be judged and punished according to the laws of these liberated countries and of the free governments which will be created therein. Lists will be compiled in all possible detail from all these countries having regard especially to the invaded parts of the Soviet Union, to Poland and

Czechoslovakia, to Yugoslavia and Greece, including Crete and other islands, to Norway, Denmark, the Netherlands, Belgium, Luxemburg, France, and Italy.

Thus, the Germans who take part in wholesale shootings of Italian officers or in the execution of French, Dutch, Belgian, or Norwegian hostages or of Cretan peasants, or who have shared in the slaughters inflicted on the people of Poland or in territories of the Soviet Union which are now being swept clear of the enemy, will know that they will be brought back to the scene of their crimes and judged on the spot by the peoples whom they have outraged. Let those who have hitherto not imbrued their hands with innocent blood beware lest they join the ranks of the guilty, for most assuredly the three allied Powers will pursue them to the uttermost ends of the earth and will deliver them to their accusers in order that justice may be done.

Stalin's Speech, November 6, 1943

The victories of the Red Army have had results and consequences far beyond the limits of the Soviet-German front. They have changed the whole further course of the world war and acquired great international significance. The victory of the Allied countries over the common enemy has come nearer, while relations among the Allies and the fighting partnership of their armies, far from weakening, have, contrary to the expectations of the enemy, become stronger and more consolidated.

This year the Red Army's blows at the German-fascist troops were supported by the military operations of our Allies in North Africa, in the Mediterranean Basin and in Southern Italy. At the same time the Allies subjected and are still subjecting important industrial centers of Germany to heavy air bombing and thus considerably weakening the enemy's military power. If we add to all this the fact that the Allies are regularly supplying us with various armaments and raw materials, it can be said without exaggeration that, by doing all this, they have considerably facilitated the successes of our summer campaign. Of course, the present operations of the Allied armies in south Europe cannot yet be regarded as a second front. But still it is something in the nature of a second front. Obviously, the opening of a real second front in Europe, which is not far off, would considerably hasten victory over Hitlerite Germany and still further consolidate the comradeship-in-arms of the Allied countries . . .

The cause of German fascism is lost, and the sanguinary "New Order" it has established is approaching collapse. In the occupied countries of Europe an outburst of the people's wrath against the fascist enslavers is developing. Germany's former prestige in the countries of her allies and in the neutral countries is lost beyond recovery; and her economic and political ties with neutral states have been undermined . . .

Hitlerite Germany and her vassals stand on the verge of catastrophe . . .

The Red Army and the Soviet people during the past year have achieved great successes in the struggle against the German invaders. We have achieved a radical turning-point in the war in favor of our country, and the war is now proceeding to its final climax. But it is not the habit of Soviet people to rest satisfied with their achievements, to exult over their successes. Victory may elude us if complacency appears in our ranks. Victory cannot be won without struggle and effort. It is achieved in fighting. Victory is now near, but to win it there must be a fresh strenuous effort, self-sacrificing work throughout the rear and skillful and resolute actions of the Red Army at the front. It would be a crime against the Motherland, against the Soviet people who have fallen temporarily under the fascist yoke, against the people of Europe, languishing under German oppression, if we failed to use every opportunity of hastening the enemy's defeat. The enemy must not be allowed any respite. That is why we must exert all our strength to finish off the enemy.

In the Headlines

Izvestiia, Moscow, November 16, 1943
THE STRENGTHENING OF SOVIET-AMERICAN FRIENDSHIP

Declaration of Tehran Conference, December 1, 1943

As to war—our military staffs have joined in our round table discussions, and we have concerted our plans for the destruction of the German forces. We have reached complete agreement as to the scope and timing of the operations to be undertaken from the east, west and south.

The common understanding which we have here reached guarantees that victory will be ours.

And as to peace—we are sure that our concord will win an enduring peace. We recognize fully the supreme responsibility resting upon us and all the United Nations to make a peace which will command the goodwill of the overwhelming mass of the peoples of the world and banish the scourge and terror of war for many generations . . .

No power on earth can prevent our destroying the German armies by land, their U Boats by sea, and their war plants from the air.

Our attack will be relentless and increasing.

Emerging from these cordial conferences we look with confidence to the day when all peoples of the world may live free lives untouched by tyranny, and according to their varying desires and their own consciences.

We came here with hope and determination. We leave here, friends in fact, in spirit and purpose.

Spanish Problem

At the beginning and at the end of 1943, Germany pressured Franco
to enter the war. The Spanish leader remained hesitant, pledging
friendship but refusing direct military involvement.

Spanish-German Protocol Against Allies, February 10, 1943

At the time in which the intention of the German Government to deliver to the
Spanish Army in the shortest time possible arms, war equipment, and war material of modern quality and in sufficient quantity is to be realized, the Spanish
Government, at the request of the Reich Government, declares that it is determined to resist every entry by Anglo-American forces upon the Iberian Peninsula or upon Spanish territory outside of the Peninsula, that means, therefore, in
the Mediterranean Sea, in the Atlantic and in Africa as well as in the Spanish Protectorate of Morocco, and to ward off such an entry with all the means at its
disposal.

German Ambassador on Talks with Franco, December 15, 1943

He [Franco] would like to emphasize at once that there was no question of
the Spanish foreign policy changing. He knew quite certainly that the German
policy was pursuing the objective of strengthening Spain, while the English
and American policies traditionally aimed at weakening Spain. Further, he
knew for certain and was clearly conscious of the fact that only the victory
of Germany would make possible the continued existence of the regime of
Franco; a victory of the Anglo-Saxons, in spite of all the pacifying declarations
which would be made to him from time to time in this respect by the English
and American side, would mean his own annihilation. He therefore was hoping with all his heart for the victory of Germany and he had only one wish
that this victory would come as soon as possible. . . . He emphasized, however, that the attitude of the Spanish Government against Bolshevism and
Communism would thereby be altered in no way; and that at home as well
as abroad this struggle was continuing, just as against Jewry and Freemasonry.
. . . The Chief of State concluded the conversation in a very cordial fashion,
by emphasizing again his hope for the German victory and his friendship for
Germany and very warmly requested me to greet the Führer most cordially
on his behalf.

Bombing

As 1943 progressed, the Allies achieved air superiority over the
Luftwaffe. The result was the large-scale bombing of German cities,
armaments factories, oil repositories and other strategic targets. In

preparation for the planned invasion of France in 1944, the Allies hit strategic targets there as well, a military action that was condemned by Marshal Pétain. Several Allied air force personnel testified to the danger inherent in these missions.

In the Headlines

Le Petit Parisien, Paris, April 5, 1943 [collaborationist]
MARSHAL PÉTAIN OFFERS WITHERING CONDEMNATION OF ANGLO-AMERICAN BOMBING OF FRANCE

CHIEF OF STATE DENOUNCES THOSE IN THE EMIGRATION AS WELL AS THOSE IN FRANCE WHO ARE TRYING TO REESTABLISH THE GOVERNMENT THAT LOST THE COUNTRY [criticism of General de Gaulle and French *Resistance*]

Testimony of Jozef Nowak, March 1943[27]—Polish Air Force

Target—Essen, the hub of German war industry. The briefing-officer made it clear and the crews knew it already, that this was the area fiercely defended from air attacks and thus, the most saturated with anti-aircraft artillery. The crew of Nowak's Wellington, marked BH-S, received an additional task—after dropping their own bomb load, they were to circle the air raid zone for twenty minutes and direct the on coming waves of bombers to their target. That mission and those twenty minutes Nowak remembered as the hardest moments of his life—a barrage of anti-aircraft artillery fire blowing up all around; the waves of on coming bombers—many of them almost instantly annihilated by the explosion of their own lethal charge hit by enemy fire before being discharged. Nowak's plane seemed to be immune from enemy fire—one long second followed by another for twenty eternal minutes—and miraculously survived. Out of five crews sent by the 300 Bomber Squadron on that mission, only one came back.

Testimony of Benjamin Witten, July 1943[28]—American Air Force

Well, we flew one mission, I think it was to Hamburg, maybe further south. And we were going over a city in France, called Amiens. Amiens, France. Well, I'd been there before and there was a lot of flak coming up. So a colonel was flying our co-pilot, and I called up the colonel and I said, "permission to deviate from the course." He says, "why?" I said, "I've been over Amiens before and there's a lot of flak." And he says, "S.O.P, S.O.P," meaning standard operating procedure. Well, I've got all these planes behind me, and I did not go over Amiens. I went ten miles south of Amiens, France, and we did miss the flak.

Now the stepped up formations we flew was actually devised by Colonel Curtis LeMay.[29] He was my CO when I first got there. And he devised that. And here's how he introduced himself. He said, "I am the best pilot, the best navigator and the best bombardier in the ETO." And he was. LeMay was good, chewing his cigar and smoking.

Testimony of Roland J. Eggebeen, 1943[30]—American Air Force

Oh we were up one night and you're flying up at 20,000 feet, and you're flying under oxygen. And they have what they call oxygen checks. It's every two minutes, the pilot would call out "oxygen check." And so each one of us had a number. Well, they went through oxygen checks; I didn't answer. So they told the waist gunners to cut the power off my turret and use cranks to help me, open up and find out what was the matter. And this happened to be that the valve on my oxygen mask froze, and I wasn't getting any oxygen and I passed out. So they had spare oxygen there, masks there that they put on me, and then they brought me to again.

Testimony of Oliver Stork[31]—B-17 Flying Fortress

I was in the service for two and a half years but I only spent eight months over there and did the 30 missions in about five to six months and then you just sit around and wait. When we were going to have a mission our orders would come down at our base. Anyways our orders would come down and the operations people would have to give orders to different people like the pilots and the radio operators and navigation and bombardiers. Then there were other people getting their guns ready and all that took hours. They'd come around and wake us up at midnight. Then we'd go and eat breakfast because it was a long mission before we came back. Sometimes it would take about nine to ten hours. They gave us a good, hardy breakfast if you weren't nervous enough to eat it. After breakfast you had what was called a briefing and you'd go into the briefing room and I'd be real nervous cause you'd never know where you would go. They had a very big wall map to stake out the course on the map. It'd be a devious route so you'd never know where you were going so we'd take diversions. Everyone would be excited when they'd tell you the target. They tried to maintain secrecy. And after the briefing was completed, the navigator would have to go into a separate place to pick up his maps, which were prepared. The rest of the crew would get their guns and vests and heavy suits. It got as cold as 50 degrees below zero up high in 30,000 ft but the highest I've went was 29,600 ft. I flew my first five missions in a row so after that they sensed people cracking up so they'd give you a little recreation and give you a little pass.

We used the highly explosive bombs—the 500 pounders. Then we had fragmentation bombs which were any anti-personnel type bombs used along the front lines in France when the invasion was going on and along the German line. We tried to hit as many Germans as we could. Then we had incendiary bombs, which started fires.

Nearing the target I was looking out the window and planes right on the side of me, and two of them collide. And both of those guys were in our barracks, so the next morning their beds were empty. I mean that could really, really get to you, you know. They were very good. Otherwise the mission wasn't that dangerous. We figured out that possibly one was hit by flak causing him to lose control and hit the plane causing them both to go down. We could only see two chutes open. The tail gunner kept watching because I was at the front and couldn't see. So I couldn't see what happened after they went down. That was very, very tragic; I'll never forget that sight. Those guys were good, good fellows, slept in the bed right next to us; they weren't on my crew but we knew them pretty well.

Testimony of Charles Joseph Cilfone[32]—American Air Force

Well, most of the targets were in France, Belgium, and Holland. Most of our bombing at that time, which was the middle of 1943 and through the first part of 1944, were actually mostly marshalling yards where the railroads gather all their trains to break them up and distribute to various destinations. And bridges that were crossing rivers that were highways, and intersections of highways where we would bomb intersections of those various highways to cause a disruption of military movement.

They were shooting at us all the time. One thing them Germans, they might have been dirty rotten sons of guns but they sure knew how to shoot.

Accuracy is a word that does not apply. It's persistence and tremendous amounts of ammunition is what applies. Accuracy they may not have had but they still scared the hell out of us. They had lots of ammunition, they had gunners that knew what they were doing, they knew how to fire those guns so that the shells would burst right close to your airplane, not necessarily hit you but the shells would burst. When a shell burst it threw out tiny pieces of metal, thousands and thousands of tiny pieces of metal that might pierce the aircraft and possibly do damage to the men and kill some of the men in the airplanes. . . .

[M]any men were killed and in these types of operations I saw people lose their leg. I was in the same airplane, over the 72 missions we brought back 4 dead men in the same airplane where I was. Four separate bodies.

Most of the time they were shooting at us with heavy guns. Any time they were shooting at you, you had at least some wounded or killed in action. Yes, most of the time we had people wounded and many times we had people killed in action. That's correct.

Once in awhile you might see a guy jump out but most of the time you didn't see anybody jump out.

We all had parachutes, but that does not mean you were able to use it because if the airplane got pretty well torn up, it was very possible that the men themselves were very badly damaged and incapable of using their parachutes.

Well, I was wounded a couple of times but the main time was the flak which is the burst of the shell. The German shells that were shot at us, these were generally shells that were about 4 feet long and 6 inches wide but they had little meters on them that allowed them to set the time of explosion which was generally a few feet from the airplane or from the formation. And that thing would explode and when it exploded, pieces went all over. Pieces as big as your fingernail, pieces as big as a finger. Various sizes and it was very sharp metal. And when it tore into an airplane and tore into a body it would do damage. I was wounded in the backs of both hands as I was setting my manipulation for the bombing mission. It was the last few seconds of the bombing mission when that thing hit my hand. And the guy sitting behind me, he was the co-pilot, he lost his leg. He lost his right leg right there; he didn't have a leg left. But these things happen and we were able to come back anyway.

They went after the big bombers because the big bombers were going into Germany itself, not necessarily France, Belgium, and Holland where the Germans were the occupants. The big bombers were going into Germany to hit the factories and other things and those fighter planes, their main job was to hit those guys.

Testimony of Willard Reese[33]—8th Air Force

On one mission we were hit by flak right up in the front of the ship. You know, they have a Plexiglas nose up there where the bombardier sits and looks out. He is sitting up right in the front and we had just passed the target. The anti-aircraft were tracking us; it was a clear day. When they track you (they were pretty good, the gunners were) you could tell they were tracking you because they would follow right in front of you or right along side you at the same altitude. This one was following us and we took evasive action and peeled off and dove down somehow and the tracking followed us. All of a sudden, ba-boom and it hit right in the nose of the ship! The Plexiglas nose was shattered; of course air and fumes and everything came (fumes and smoke from the explosion) came right up through the ship. I thought, "Oh boy, we have had it!" But the bombardier wasn't hurt at all. It was a strange thing; some pieces of flack came through and hit a canister of ammunition (for the gun) on the floor and the ammunition exploded. The bullets were shooting out through the sides of the ship, fortunately. I couldn't see them and I didn't know what happened and I thought, "Man they are both gone!" The bombardier's head popped up pretty soon and he said, "We are OK!" he was off oxygen then and he was looking for an oxygen bottle. They [crew] all went to the rear of the ship then because it was too cold. Temperatures were like minus forty degrees at that altitude. If you had your face or hands exposed to the weather just for a few minutes you could get frostbite or worse. We flew back that way; that was the worst condition we experienced, I guess; the closest call we had.

Occupation and Atrocities

Throughout 1943, the Germans continued their war against the civilian population of Europe. They targeted Jews primarily, but also sectors of almost every nationality group in Europe. The extensive testimonies included here describe Nazi practices.

Testimony of Karol Wierzbicki[34]—Polish Prisoner of War

On July 15, 1943, he was sent to Carcassonne, near the French-Spanish border, to command the route to the Pyrenees transfer outpost—a part of the Polish Evacuation Service (code "Eva" from "eva-cuation"). The aim of this undertaking was to transfer the Allied military personnel (those, who were not evacuated in time following France's collapse in 1940 and remained in hiding; escapees from German POW camps; airmen, who managed to avoid capture after being shot down over German-occupied territories) from France to England. Also, to maintain a transfer route, available for couriers and special assignment agents.

Second Lieutenant Wierzbicki and his outpost's activities did not go unnoticed by the Germans. On September 16, 1943, due to the action of a German agent, who infiltrated the organization, Wierzbicki and two of his collaborators were arrested by the Gestapo. Wierzbicki was accused of smuggling people and after two weeks of investigation and a stay in solitary confinement in Carcassonne prison, as well as four weeks in the Compiègne concentration camp, he was sent to Buchenwald concentration camp. He was then transferred to the Dora-Mittelbau camp, known for its use of inmates as slave labor on the production lines of V1 and V2 missiles.[35]

Testimony of Eva Galler[36]—Polish Holocaust Survivor

Then, beginning on January 4, 1943, the Gestapo and the Polish and Ukrainian police started to chase all the Jews out from their houses. The deportation took several days. People ran and hid. The Jewish police helped to find the people in hiding. They had been promised that they would stay alive if they cooperated.

We knew where we were going. A boy from our town had been deported to Belzec camp. He escaped and came back to our town. He told us that Belzec had a crematorium. Deportation trains from other cities had passed by our city and people had thrown out notes. These notes were picked up by the men forced to work there. The notes said, "Don't take anything with you, just water."

They took us to a cattle train. People started to run away from the train, but they were shot. Once on the train we had to stand because there was no room to sit down. A boy tore the barbed wires from the train window. The young people started to jump out of the window. Many jumped. The SS on the rooftop of the train shot at them with rifles. My father told us, the oldest three, "Run, run—maybe you will stay alive. We will stay here with the small children because even if they get out, they will not be able to survive."

My brother Berele jumped out, then my sister Hannah, and then I jumped out. The SS men shot at us. I landed in a snowbank. The bullets did not hit me. When I did not hear anything anymore, I went back to find my brother and my sister. I found them dead. My brother Berele was 15. My sister Hannah was 16. I was 17.

I took off my star and I promised myself that never again would I ever wear a star. I ran back to the city where we lived. We had a Gentile friend there, a lady to whom we gave a lot of our belongings. She was scared to keep me. Gentile families who were found to be hiding Jews would be killed. She hid me behind a cedar-robe in the corner. I was standing there listening to people come in. They were discussing how they were killing the Jews, how the Jews were running away, who had been shot. It was a small city. They felt sorry for the Jews. It was a sensation, a thing to talk about. They felt sorry but they forgot right away.

In the evening when it became dark she gave me half a loaf of bread and 25 Polish zlotys. She told me to go.

I wanted to go to the train station, but I was afraid to go in our city because everybody knew me. So I went to the woods and walked to the next station 32 kilometers away. At that time it was thought that there were partisans in the woods. People were afraid to go in the woods, but I was not afraid.

Testimony of Marie Vaillant-Couturier[37]—French Holocaust Survivor

I was arrested on 9 February 1942 by Pétain's French police, who handed me over to the German authorities after six weeks. . . . At the end of my interrogation they wanted me to sign a statement, which was not consistent with what I had said. I refused to sign it. The officer who had questioned me threatened me, and when I told him that I was not afraid of death or of being shot, he said, "But we have at our disposal means for killing that are far worse than merely shooting." And the interpreter said to me, "You do not know what you have just done. You are going to leave for a concentration camp in Germany. One never comes back from there." . . .

I left for Auschwitz on the 23 of January 1943, and I arrived there on the 27. I was with a convoy of 230 French women.

In the convoy there were some elderly women. I remember one who was 67, and had been arrested because she had in her kitchen her husband's shotgun, which she kept as a souvenir and had not declared, because she did not want it to be taken from her. She died after a fortnight at Auschwitz.

There were also cripples, among them a singer who had only one leg. She was taken out and gassed at Auschwitz.

It was a terrible journey. We were 60 in a wagon and we were given no food or drink during the journey. At the various stopping places we asked the Lorraine soldiers of the Wehrmacht who were guarding us, whether we would arrive soon, and they replied: "If you knew where you are going you would not be in a hurry to get there."

We arrived at Auschwitz at dawn. The seals on our wagons were broken, and we were driven out by blows with the butt end of a rifle, and taken to the Birkenau camp, a section of the Auschwitz camp.

We were led to a large shed, then to the disinfecting station. There our heads were shaven and our registration numbers were tattooed on the left forearm . . .

After that we were taken to the block where we were to live. There were no beds but only bunks, and there nine of us had to sleep without any mattress, and the first night without any blanket. We remained in blocks of this kind for several months.

At 3 in the morning the shouting of the guards woke us up and with cudgel blows we were driven from our bunks to go to roll call. Nothing in the world could release us from going to the roll call; even those who were dying had to be dragged there . . .

During the work the SS men and women who stood guard over us would beat us with cudgels, and set their dogs on us. Many of our friends had their legs torn by the dogs. I even saw a woman torn to pieces and die under my very eyes when a member of the SS, encouraged his dog to attack her and grinned at the sight . . .

One saw stacks of corpses piled up in the courtyard, and from time to time a hand or a head would stir amongst the bodies, trying to free itself; it was a dying woman attempting to get free and live . . . in the courtyard, there were rats as big as cats running about and gnawing the corpses and even attacking the dying, who had not enough strength left to chase them away . . .

The Jewish women, when they arrived in the first months of pregnancy, were subjected to abortion. When their pregnancy was near the end, after confinement, the babies were drowned in a bucket of water. Then the mothers and their babies were called to the infirmary, they were put in a lorry and taken away to the gas chamber.

There was one block where the Polish and Russian mothers were. One day the Russian mothers, having been accused of making too much noise, had to stand for roll call all day in front of the block, naked, with their babies in their arms.

The system employed by the SS of degrading human beings to the utmost by terrorizing them and causing them through fear to commit acts which made them ashamed of themselves, resulted in their being no longer human. This was what they wanted—it took a great deal of courage to resist this atmosphere of terror and corruption . . .

There was also, in the spring of 1944, a special block for twins. It was during the time when large convoys of Hungarian Jews—about 700,000—arrived. Dr. Mengele,[38] who was carrying out the experiments, kept back from each convoy twin children and twins in general, regardless of their age, so long as both were present . . .

One night we were awakened by terrifying cries, and we discovered, on the following day from the men working in the "Sonderkommando" (the "Gas Kommando") that on the preceding day, the gas supply having run out, they had thrown the children into the furnaces alive.

Testimony of Venezia Kamhi—Bulgarian Survivor

My first home was in the Jewish neighborhood in Sofia.

On May 24, 1943, there was great unrest. Members of the Brannik organization[39] appeared on horses in the town. They did not have any restrictions—they could beat and destroy, and we were very oppressed by them once Hitler started the war . . .

We got the message to leave Sofia on May 24, 1943, and on the 25th and 26th, we were already on our way to Kiustendil. There was not enough time to pack properly. We put only clothes and blankets into those 20 kilos of luggage. The officials sent us a message with the date and time we had to go to the railway station. People said we had to be assembled in different towns so that they could easily transport us to the Aegean region. The 11,000 Yugoslavian Jews who were deported there had died. Meanwhile, there were many protests by the Bulgarian public against the deportation of Bulgarian Jews to Poland. A great part of the population protested. . . . More than 50 members of the Parliament signed a petition against the deportation of Bulgarian Jews to concentration camps in Poland and that's how we were saved.

Testimony of Lily Arouch—Greek Survivor

In July 1942 an order came out that all Jewish males aged eighteen to forty-five had to gather up at Eleftheria Square. . . The view was horrifying. It was a square full of men without tops or hats and the sun was burning hot. They had been lined up on the central side. The Germans were positioned in front of a big bank and they were making rounds and pointing at people. They would shout, "you, you" and make them do cartwheels and hit them. They forced them to stay there for many hours until the sun went down; they were standing since dawn and being tortured one after the other. I have to admit I was terrified . . .

In April 1943 we were forced to wear the Star of David, even the children, and we were moved to the ghetto. . . . In the ghetto each family, regardless of how many members, had one room. We spent about two months there. The bad news just kept on coming: they started arresting and sending people to the train station and then put them on trains and shipped them off somewhere . . .

On 12th April 1943 I left the ghetto with my two sisters; we stayed alone that night. Before we left my father told me, "Listen child, you have two younger sisters and you need to take care of them." We didn't know what was going to happen next. Thankfully my parents came the following night and then the morning after that everyone in the ghetto, where we had also been before, was gathered and taken to the ghetto next to the train station. From there they were forced into trains and left. My grandmothers and aunties were taken too. We found that out when we were hiding, because we had a Christian friend who would come and tell us some news. We remained hidden in that house for nineteen months, even though the original plan was to move further away from the center . . .

These people saved us; they were very special . . .

Testimony of General Stroop on Warsaw Ghetto Destruction, May 1943

The Ghetto thus established in Warsaw was inhabited by about 400,000 Jews. It was separated from the rest of the city by partition and other walls and by walling-up of thoroughfares, windows, doors, open spaces, etc.

It soon became clear, however, that not all dangers had been removed by this confining the Jews to one place. Security considerations required removing the Jews from the city of Warsaw altogether. . . . Before the large-scale action began, the limits of the former Ghetto had been blocked by an external barricade in order to prevent the Jews from breaking out. This barricade was maintained from the start to the end of the action and was especially reinforced at night.

When we invaded the Ghetto for the first time, the Jews and the Polish bandits succeeded in repelling the participating units, including tanks and armored cars, by a well-prepared concentration of fire. . . . Although firing commenced again, we now succeeded in combing out the blocks according to plan. The enemy was forced to retire from the roofs and elevated bases to the basements, dug-outs, and sewers. In order to prevent their escaping into the sewers, the sewerage system was dammed up below the Ghetto and filled with water, but the Jews frustrated this plan to a great extent by blowing up the turning off valves. Late the first day we encountered rather heavy resistance, but it was quickly broken by a special raiding party. In the course of further operations we succeeded in expelling the Jews from their prepared resistance bases, sniper holes, and the like, and in occupying during the 20 and 21 April the greater part of the so-called remainder of the Ghetto to such a degree that the resistance continued within these blocks could no longer be called considerable . . .

In every case these passages and dug-outs were connected with the sewer system. Thus, the Jews were able to maintain undisturbed subterranean traffic. They also used this sewer network for escaping subterraneously into the Aryan part of the city of Warsaw. Continuously, we received reports of attempts of Jews to escape through the sewer holes. . . . Time and again Polish bandits found refuge in the Ghetto and remained there undisturbed, since we had no forces at our disposal to comb out this maze. Whereas it had been possible during the first days to catch considerable numbers of Jews, who are cowards by nature, it became more and more difficult during the second half of the action to capture the bandits and Jews. Over and over again new battle groups consisting of 20 to 30 or more Jewish fellows, 18 to 25 years of age, accompanied by a corresponding number of women kindled new resistance. These battle groups were under orders to put up armed resistance to the last and if necessary to escape arrest by committing suicide . . .

The resistance put up by the Jews and bandits could be broken only by relentlessly using all our force and energy by day and night. I therefore decided to destroy the entire Jewish residential area by setting every block on fire, including the blocks of residential buildings near the armament works. The Jews then emerged from their hiding places and dug-outs in almost every case. Not infrequently, the Jews stayed in the burning buildings until, because of the heat and the fear of being burned alive they preferred to jump down from the upper stories after having thrown mattresses and other upholstered articles into the street from the burning buildings. With their bones broken, they still tried to crawl across the street into blocks of buildings which had not yet been set on fire or were only partly in flames. Often Jews changed their hiding places during the night, by moving into the ruins of burnt-out buildings, taking refuge there until they were found by our patrols. Their stay in the sewers also ceased to be pleasant after the first week . . .

Only through the continuous and untiring work of all involved did we succeed in catching a total of 56,065 Jews whose extermination can be proved. To this should be added the number of Jews who lost their lives in explosions or fires but whose numbers could not be ascertained.

During the large-scale operation the Aryan population was informed by posters that it was strictly forbidden to enter the former Jewish Ghetto and that anybody caught within the former Ghetto without valid pass would be shot. At the same time these posters informed the Aryan population again that the death penalty would be imposed on anybody who intentionally gave refuge to a Jew, especially lodged, supported, or concealed a Jew outside the Jewish residential area.

Permission was granted to the Polish police to pay to any Polish police-man who arrested a Jew within the Aryan part of Warsaw one third of the cash in the Jew's possession. This measure has already produced results.

The Polish population for the most part approved the measures taken against the Jews . . .

The large-scale action was terminated on 16 May 1943 with the blowing up of the Warsaw synagogue at 2015 hours.

Testimony of Dieter Wisliceny—Nazi Officer[40]

In January 1943 Eichmann ordered me to come to Berlin and told me that I was to proceed to Salonika to solve the Jewish problem there in co-opera-tion with the German Military Administration in Macedonia . . .

In Salonika the Jews were first of all concentrated in certain quarters of the city. There were in Salonika about 50,000 Jews of Spanish descent. At the beginning of March, after this concentration had taken place, a teletype mes-sage from Eichmann to Brunner ordered the immediate evacuation of all Jews from Salonika and Macedonia to Auschwitz . . .[41]

They were without exception destined for the so-called final solution. The cash which the Jews possessed was taken away and put into a common account at the Bank of Greece. Eichmann had explained to me under the term "final solution," that is, they were annihilated biologically. As far as I could gather from my conversations with him, this annihilation took place in the gas chambers and the bodies were subsequently destroyed in the crematories.

Testimony of Solomon Radasky[42]—Polish Holocaust Survivor

At Majdanek they took our clothes and gave us striped shirts, pants and wooden shoes.

We had to walk 3 kilometers to work. I had to hold myself up straight without limping and walk out of the gate of the camp. I was scared. If I limped, they would take me out of line. At Majdanek they hung you for any little thing. I did not know how I would make it. We had to walk to work barefoot. There were little stones on the road that cut into your skin and blood was running from the feet of many people. The work was dirty field work. After a few days some people could not take it anymore, and they fell down in the road. If they could not get up, they were shot where they lay. After work we had to carry the bodies back. If 1,000 went out to work, 1,000 had to come back.

One day as we were standing at roll call, a man in the back of the line smoked a cigarette. The camp commandant looked down at us and demanded to know who had smoked a cigarette. No one answered. "I am going to hang 10 dogs," he said. "I will give you 3 minutes." They called us dogs because we had tags with our numbers on them; my number was 993. We looked from one to the other, but no one answered.

The camp commandant did not wait 3 minutes; he did not wait 2 minutes. He took his whip and he cut off 2 rows of 5 prisoners. I was in the group of 10.

He asked, "Who wants to go up first on the bench?" You had to go stand on the bench and put the rope around your neck. I was in the first three to go up on the bench. I climbed up and put the rope around my neck . . .

The soldier took off the rope that had been around my neck. All it would have taken was a few seconds more and I would have been dead. He just had to kick out the bench. The soldier beat us until we jumped down from the bench and got back into the line.

Testimony of Louis Villette[43]—French Forced Labor

I left for Germany for required work there on 8 June 1943. Our camp in Germany included Russians, French POWs, and civilian French workers. I was a civilian French worker, and our group went about its work without guards. Otherwise our treatment was identical to the other prisoners. We slept in a room with 40 men per barracks, on bunk beds filled with straw in a camp under surveillance. I worked for one year in a train car factory, and then we were turned over to factories or farms in the area for various tasks that lasted about two weeks. The climate was much colder than in France, although there was less wind.

We had to move the train cars that were finished. One time when we were moving several cars I discreetly shoved a piece of wood into the rail so that the cars were derailed and blocked the movement on the road. A German guard took me to the office. I claimed that I had not seen the piece of wood on the rail but I was told in French to report back in two hours when I would be sent to a place where I would learn to work correctly.

I was saved by the bombardment of the camp. There was an alert with sirens announcing the arrival of a bombing attack. The whole office burned as a result of the attack of the incendiary bombs. We were in a bomb shelter and were not injured. Several buildings burned down and the officer in charge forgot about me.

Testimony of Vladislava Karolewska[44]—Polish Holocaust Survivor

In the hospital we were put to bed and the hospital room in which we stayed was locked. We were not told what we were to do in the hospital and when one of my comrades put the question she got no answer but she was answered by an ironical smile. Then a German nurse arrived and gave me an injection in my leg. After this injection I vomited and I was put on a hospital cot and they brought me to the operating room. Then I lost my consciousness and when I revived I noticed that I was in a regular hospital room. I recovered my consciousness for a while and I felt severe pain in my leg. Then I lost my consciousness again. I regained my consciousness in the morning and then I noticed that my leg was in a cast from the ankle up to the knee and I felt a very strong pain in this leg and the high temperature. I noticed also that my leg was swollen from the toes up to the groin. The pain was increasing and the temperature, too, and the next day I noticed that some liquid was flowing from my leg. The third day I was put on a hospital cart and taken to the dressing room. A blanket was put over my eyes and I did not know what was done with my leg but I felt great pain and I had the impression that something must have been cut out of my leg. Two weeks later we were all taken again to the operating room and put on the operating tables. The bandage was removed, and that was the first time I saw my leg. The incision went so deep that I could see the bone. . . . I could not walk. The puss was draining from my leg; the leg was swollen up and I could not walk.

Testimony of Rudolf Mildner—Nazi Officer

I was made the commander of the Sipo and SD[45] in Denmark on 15 September 1943. A few days after I arrived in Copenhagen an order from Himmler . . . arrived demanding the arrest of all Danish citizens of Jewish faith and their shipment to Theresienstadt . . . I sent a telegram to the RSHA Gruppenführer Müller, asking to have the Jewish persecutions stopped. As reasons for this I mentioned that the Jews in Denmark had not yet shown themselves unfriendly toward the Reich, that the whole Danish nation would reject measures taken against the Jews, that action would have an unfavorable effect in Scandinavia, England, and the U.S., that the trade relationship between Germany and Sweden would be disturbed, as well as that with Denmark. In Denmark one could then expect political strikes and the amount of sabotage would increase, etc. The answer to my telegram was an order by Himmler that the anti-Jewish actions were to be carried out. . . .

This command had chartered two ships for the deportation of the Jews. This action failed, however, and there was great bitterness in Berlin.

Hitler and Himmler had raged when they received the report.

Testimony of Simon Igel—Polish-French Holocaust Survivor

The situation changed again in November 1942 when the Nazis occupied Saint-Etienne. Eventually my luck ran out, and I was arrested on August 18, 1943, my sixteenth birthday. To this day I'm not sure if I was turned in by a friend under torture or by neighbors who collaborated. I was taken to the Fort Montluc prison in Lyon, where Klaus Barbie,[46] known as the "butcher of Lyon," was in charge. Three weeks later, I was sent to Drancy outside of Paris, the holding and transfer point for Jews before deportation.

In early October 1943 I was shipped to Auschwitz with about 1,000 other Jews. When we arrived almost half of our group was gassed immediately, while the other half was selected for slave labor. I believe that I was designated for slave labor because at sixteen I was in decent physical shape and I spoke German well. The number 157085 was then tattooed onto my left arm. I worked at various jobs—hard labor all—until my hands were bloody and my body broken.

Testimony of Rudolf Hoess—Nazi Commandant of Auschwitz

Dr. Kauffmann [Dr. Kurt Kauffmann was counsel for the defendant Ernst Kaltenbrunner]:[47] From 1940 to 1943, you were the Commander of the camp at Auschwitz. Is that true?

Hoess: Yes . . .

Dr. Kauffmann: Is it furthermore true that Eichmann stated to you that in Auschwitz a total sum of more than 2 million Jews had been destroyed?

Hoess: Yes.

Dr. Kauffmann: Men, women, and children?

Hoess: Yes.

Dr. Kauffmann: When were you commander at Auschwitz?

Hoess: I was commander at Auschwitz from May 1940 until December 1943.

Dr. Kauffmann: Is it true that in 1941 you were ordered to Berlin to see Himmler? Please state briefly what was discussed.

Hoess: Yes. In the summer of 1941 I was summoned to Berlin to Reichsführer SS Himmler to receive personal orders. He told me something to the effect—I do not remember the exact words—that the Führer had given the order for a final solution of the Jewish question. We, the SS, must carry out that order. If it is not carried out now then the Jews will later on destroy the German people. He had chosen Auschwitz on account of its easy access by rail and also because the extensive site offered space for measures ensuring isolation.

Dr. Kauffmann: And after the arrival of the transports were the victims stripped of everything they had? Did they have to undress completely; did they have to surrender their valuables? Is that true?

Hoess: Yes.

Dr. Kauffmann: And then they immediately went to their death?

Hoess: Yes.

Dr. Kauffmann: I ask you, according to your knowledge, did these people know what was in store for them?

Hoess: The majority of them did not, for steps were taken to keep them in doubt about it and suspicion would not arise that they were to go to their death. For instance, all doors and all walls bore inscriptions to the effect that they were going to undergo a delousing operation or take a shower. This was made known in several languages to the internees by other internees who had come in with earlier transports and who were being used as auxiliary crews during the whole action.

Dr. Kauffmann: And then, you told me the other day, that death by gassing set in within a period of 3 to 15 minutes. Is that correct?

Hoess: Yes.

Dr. Kauffmann: You also told me that even before death finally set in, the victims fell into a state of unconsciousness?

Hoess: Yes. From what I was able to find out myself or from what was told me by medical officers, the time necessary for reaching unconsciousness or death varied according to the temperature and the number of people present in the chambers. Loss of consciousness took place within a few seconds or a few minutes.

Dr. Kauffmann: Did you yourself ever feel pity with the victims, thinking of your own family and children?

Hoess: Yes.

Dr. Kauffmann: How was it possible for you to carry out these actions in spite of this?

Hoess: In view of all these doubts which I had, the only one and decisive argument was the strict order and the reason given for it by the Reichs-führer Himmler.

Dr. Kauffmann: I ask you whether Himmler inspected the camp and convinced himself, too, of the process of annihilation?

Hoess: Yes. Himmler visited the camp in 1942 and he watched in detail one processing from beginning to end. Eichmann came repeatedly to Auschwitz and was intimately acquainted with the proceedings . . . At the end of the war there were still 13 concentration camps. . . . Medical experiments were carried out in several camps.

Col. Amen [Colonel John Harlan Amen was Associate Trial Counsel for the United States]: Witness, you made an affidavit, did you not, at the request of the Prosecution?

Hoess: Yes.

Col. Amen: "I was appointed Commandant of Auschwitz. I commanded Auschwitz until 1 December 1943, and estimate that at least 2,500,000 victims were executed and exterminated there by gassing and burning, and at least another half million succumbed to starvation and disease making a total dead of about 3,000,000. This figure represents about 70 or 80 percent of all persons sent to Auschwitz as prisoners, the remainder having been selected and used for slave labor in the concentration camp industries; included among the executed and burned were approximately

20,000 Russian prisoners of war (previously screened out of prisoner-of-war cages by the Gestapo) who were delivered at Auschwitz in Wehrmacht transports operated by regular Wehrmacht officers and men. The remainder of the total number of victims included about 100,000 German Jews, and great numbers of citizens, mostly Jewish, from Holland, France, Belgium, Poland, Hungary, Czechoslovakia, Greece, or other countries. We executed about 400,000 Hungarian Jews alone at Auschwitz in the summer of 1944." That is all true, Witness?

Hoess: Yes, it is.

Col. Amen: "Mass executions by gassing commenced during the summer of 1941 and continued until fall 1944. I personally supervised executions at Auschwitz until first of December 1943 and know by reason of my continued duties in the Inspectorate of Concentration Camps, WVHA, that these mass executions continued as stated above." Are those statements true and correct, Witness?

Hoess: Yes, they are.

Col. Amen: "The 'final solution' of the Jewish question meant the complete extermination of all Jews in Europe. I was ordered to establish extermination facilities at Auschwitz in June 1941. At that time, there were already in the General Government three other extermination camps: Belzek, Treblinka, and Wolzek. These camps were under the Einsatzkommando of the Security Police and SD. I visited Treblinka to find out how they carried out their exterminations. The camp commandant at Treblinka told me that he had liquidated 80,000 in the course of one-half year. He was principally concerned with liquidating all the Jews from the Warsaw Ghetto. He used monoxide gas, and I did not think that his methods were very efficient. So when I set up the extermination building at Auschwitz, I used Cyklon B [Zyklon B], which was a crystallized prussic acid which we dropped into the death chamber from a small opening. It took from 3 to 15 minutes to kill the people in the death chamber, depending upon climatic conditions. We knew when the people were dead because their screaming stopped. We usually waited about one-half hour before we opened the doors and removed the bodies. After the bodies were removed our special Kommandos took off the rings and extracted the gold from the teeth of the corpses." Is that all true and correct, Witness?

Hoess: Yes.

Col. Amen: Incidentally, what was done with the gold which was taken from the teeth of the corpses, do you know?

Hoess: This gold was melted down and brought to the Chief Medical Office of the SS at Berlin.

Col. Amen: "Another improvement we made over Treblinka was that we built our gas chamber to accommodate 2,000 people at one time whereas at Treblinka their 10 gas chambers only accommodated 200 people each. The way we selected our victims was as follows: We had two SS doctors on duty at Auschwitz to examine the incoming transports of prisoners. The prisoners would be marched by one of the doctors who would make spot decisions as they walked by. Those who were fit for work were sent into the camp. Others were sent immediately to the extermination plants. Children of tender years were invariably exterminated since by reason of their youth they were unable to work. Still another improvement we made over Treblinka was that at Treblinka the victims almost always knew that they were to be exterminated and at Auschwitz we endeavored to fool the victims into thinking that they were to go through a delousing process. Of course, frequently they realized our true intentions and we sometimes had riots and difficulties due to that fact. Very frequently women would hide their children under the clothes, but of course when we found them we would send the children in to be exterminated. We were required to carry out these exterminations in secrecy but of course the foul and nauseating stench from the continuous burning of bodies permeated the entire area and all of the people living in the surrounding communities knew that exterminations were going on at Auschwitz." Is that all true and correct, Witness?

Hoess: Yes.

Charles de Gaulle, leader of the Free French during the war. Known as a prickly, stubborn man, de Gaulle was protective of France's—and his own—interests, and his relations with other allies were marked by mutual mistrust. NATIONAL ARCHIVES

With the Arc de Triomphe in the background, French civilians line the Champs Élysées to cheer Free French troops after the liberation of Paris in August 1944.
LIBRARY OF CONGRESS

German officers taken prisoner after the liberation of Paris. NATIONAL ARCHIVES

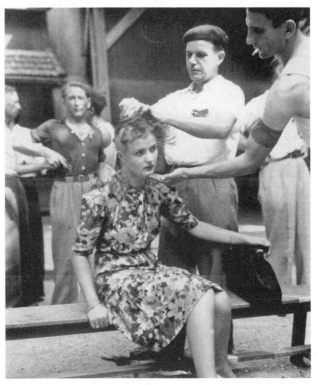

A French woman has her hair shorn off—the penalty for
having personal relations with the Germans. NATIONAL ARCHIVES

Members of the French resistance, followed by newly liberated local civilians, escort a pair of French women accused of collaborating with the ousted German occupiers. They are touching their hair, which will likely be shaved off as punishment. NATIONAL ARCHIVES

Female war correspondents, 1944. From left to right: Ruth Cowan, Associated Press; Sonia Tomara, *New York Herald Tribune*; Rosette Hargrove, Newspaper Enterprise Association; Betty Knox, *London Evening Standard*; Iris Carpenter, *Boston Globe*; and Erika Mann, *Liberty* magazine. NATIONAL ARCHIVES

Members of the Maquis near Boulogne, France, September 1944. The Maquis were guerrilla bands associated with the French Resistance.
NATIONAL ARCHIVES CANADA / PA 166396 / GRANT

Paratroopers, part of the Allied 1st Airborne Army, land in Holland during Operation Market Garden. Conceived by Field Marshal Bernard Montgomery, the operation failed to achieve its goals.
NATIONAL ARCHIVES

Scouts of the Queen's Own Cameron Highlanders of Canada in Belgium, October 1944. NATIONAL ARCHIVES CANADA / PA 138416 / BELL

The Dutch city of Nijmegen, target of the U.S. 82nd Airborne Division in Operation Market Garden in September 1944. Nijmegen was hit by Allied and German bombardment and shelling. The bridge over the Waal River was a key objective of the airborne drop. NATIONAL ARCHIVES

An American B-17 damaged during a bombing raid on Cologne. The German city was the target of more than 250 Allied raids throughout the war.
U.S. ARMY AIR FORCES

Cologne as seen in April 1945. The cathedral in the background still stands despite receiving several direct hits and sustaining severe damage.
NATIONAL ARCHIVES

Men of the U.S. 8th Infantry Regiment are pinned down by German small-arms fire in the Belgian town of Libin. NATIONAL ARCHIVES

Pipers perform at the burial of fifty-five members of The Black Watch of Canada in the Netherlands, October 1944. After achieving success in Normandy, the push to Germany took longer and cost more men than many Allied commanders suspected. NATIONAL ARCHIVES CANADA / PA 136820 / BELL

During the Battle of the Bulge, which the Germans launched in December 1944, men of *Kampfgruppe Peiper* walk on the road to Malmedy, Belgium. Peiper's battle group served as the spearhead of the German offensive and murdered eighty-four American prisoners at Malmedy. U.S. ARMY CENTER FOR MILITARY HISTORY

American GIs taken prisoner by the Germans. NATIONAL ARCHIVES

Paratroopers of the U.S. 82nd Airborne Division march through a snowstorm in Belgium during the Battle of the Bulge, January 1945. Initially surprised by the German offensive, the Americans regrouped and mounted stiff resistance, inflicting a decisive defeat on the Third Reich. U.S. ARMY

American soldiers push through the snow during the Battle of the Bulge. U.S. ARMY

Iconic photograph of the Big Three—Churchill, Roosevelt, and Stalin—at the Yalta Conference, February 1945. The meeting dealt with postwar Europe, including the division of Germany and Polish elections. It would be the last meeting of the threesome as Roosevelt died two months later and Churchill was ousted as prime minister in July. NATIONAL ARCHIVES

C-47 transports and CG-4 gliders lined up for Operation Varsity, the Allied attempt in March 1945 to establish bridgeheads across the Rhine River.
U.S. AIR FORCE

Canadian infantrmyen march through Holland, April 1945. NATIONAL ARCHIVES

American infantrymen take shelter next to a tank in the German town of Geich, which shows damage by heavy shelling. Even as the war approached its conclusion, Allied forces still faced difficult fighting. NATIONAL ARCHIVES

After liberation, members of the Dutch National Socialist Party and young female collaborators (whose heads have been shaved as punishment) are marched down a street by the Dutch Resistance, April 1945. NATIONAAL ARCHIEF / ANEFO / WILLEM VAN DE POLL

Members of The Black Watch of Canada in a Dutch village, April 1945. NATIONAL ARCHIVES CANADA / PA 133160 / GURAVICH

With his mother pushing from behind, a German boy pulls a cartload of their possessions out of a German town. NATIONAL ARCHIVES

A Russian slave laborer, liberated by the U.S. 3rd Armored Division, points out a Nazi guard who beat prisoners. NATIONAL ARCHIVES

A box of wedding rings Germans removed from concentration camp victims at Buchenwald. NATIONAL ARCHIVES

A starving inmate of Camp Gusen, Austria, liberated by Americans in the spring of 1945. NATIONAL ARCHIVES

An American and a Soviet soldier embrace, April 1945. U.S. and Soviet forces met at Torgau, Germany, but many intra-Allied disputes over postwar Europe—and eventually the Cold War—lay in the future. NATIONAL ARCHIVES

Field Marshal Wilhelm Keitel signs the surrender terms for Germany, May 7, 1945. NATIONAL ARCHIVES

Senior American military commanders at the end of the war. Seated, left to right: William H. Simpson (Ninth Army); George S. Patton (Third Army); Carl A. Spaatz (U.S. Strategic Air Forces); Dwight D. Eisenhower (Supreme Allied Commander); Omar Bradley (12th Army Group); Courtney Hodges (First Army); and Leonard T. Gerow (Fifteenth Army). Standing, left to right: Ralph Stearley (IX Tactical Air Command), Hoyt Vandenberg (Ninth Air Force), Walter Bedell Smith (Eisenhower's chief of staff), Otto P. Weyland (XIX Tactical Air Command), and Richard E. Nugent (XXIX Tactical Air Command).

Soviet soldiers hoist their flag at the conclusion of the battle for Berlin. Even though Germany's fate had been sealed, the dying Reich fought bitterly for its capital city.

An American sailor and airman celebrate Germany's surrender with British civilians in London, May 1945. NATIONAL ARCHIVES

VE Day celebration in Toronto, 1945. CITY OF TORONTO ARCHIVES / BOYD

CHAPTER 7

Allies Invade France, 1944

Introduction to 1944

In his New Year message published in Soviet newspapers on January 1, 1944, President M. Kalinin[1] praised his own country's military efforts as well as those of the western Allies. Always worried about Soviet commitment to the alliance, the American and British governments viewed these comments as a positive sign of unity as they entered the new year.

Continuing to accentuate the theme of Allied cooperation, Roosevelt reported to Congress on the Tehran Conference. He made extensive references to the mistakes of World War I and emphasized that such errors would not be repeated after the current conflict ended. He asserted that the Allies were committed to real peace after the war, a goal that was strengthened by meetings such as those at Tehran where long-range planning and cooperation had taken place. To maintain peace in the future, Roosevelt pledged that the United States would never return to a policy of isolationism.

In reality, relations between the Allies were strained, particularly on the subject of the future of Poland. Realizing that a break between the Soviet government and the Polish government in exile (pro-western) was approaching, Roosevelt tried to convince Stalin to be more patient and to allow the Polish government to make changes in its membership that would be acceptable to Soviet needs. Roosevelt suggested territorial adjustments that Stalin wanted as an incentive.

Despite Roosevelt's plea for patience, Stalin reiterated his objections to the pro-western Polish government and indicated that his relations with that entity could not continue. Specifically, Stalin rejected the Polish demand for the restoration of the 1921 border and the inclusion, from Stalin's point of view, of "pro-fascist, imperialist elements hostile to the Soviet Union" in the exile government in London.[2]

After the head of the Polish government in exile visited Roosevelt in Washington, Roosevelt wrote to Stalin to assure the Soviet leader of Poland's friendly intentions toward the U.S.S.R. Stalin restated the problems: the Polish government had not accepted the border desired by the U.S.S.R., and the Polish government had not been reconstituted to include pro-Soviet cabinet members. With Soviet troops approaching eastern Poland just as Stalin was preparing to break with the Polish government in exile, the entire issue of the status of Poland was nearing a breaking point. Over the next two years, the Polish issue remained the most difficult for the Allies to resolve diplomatically.

The Polish crisis continued into the summer and reached a new level of urgency in August. The Polish Home Army, the underground resistance force Allied with the pro-western Polish government in exile, rose against German control of Warsaw. The timing was crucial—an attempt to take power in Warsaw before the Soviet army arrived. The uprising lasted for two months, and Roosevelt and Churchill asked Stalin to provide military assistance to the Poles. Stalin promised to do what he could to defeat Germany, but offered no specific assistance to the Polish Home Army. He saw the Polish force as an instrument of the Polish government in exile that he distrusted. In the end, the Soviet army paused east of the Vistula River and did not provide any aid for the uprising. Nazi forces eventually crushed the rebellion of the Polish Home Army, using many of the same methods they had employed against the Warsaw Ghetto uprising the year before. The Soviet army insisted that it could not provide direct help because of logistical problems and extended supply lines; it finally entered Warsaw in January 1945.

After the Polish Home Army was defeated, Churchill visited Stalin in Moscow. Their talks were cordial, especially since Churchill acquiesced to most Soviet demands in Eastern Europe. Stalin wrote to Roosevelt sharing his assessment of the successful talks. He alluded to the prospects for a positive resolution of the situation in Poland and other related issues. Stalin did not mention Churchill's suggestion that most of Eastern Europe would naturally fall under Soviet influence in the postwar period (in exchange for British supremacy in Greece). With this understanding and the war going well on the eastern front, Stalin was finally prepared for a summit with his allies; he invited Roosevelt to meet, perhaps in November, at a Black Sea location. This invitation eventually led to the Yalta Conference in February 1945.

A new area of contention emerged as Allied armies moved through Axis countries and encountered increasing numbers of Soviet prisoners of war being held by Germany and other nations. Stalin feared that some of these prisoners would seek asylum in the west, and the Soviet leader became obsessed with recovering all Soviet military personnel. His ambassador in Washington claimed that the liberated prisoners were being mistreated, deprived of food, enlisted in western armies, and subjected to anti-Soviet propaganda. He demanded that the United States agree to the immediate repatriation of all Soviet prisoners. The United States denied any interference, but the dispute added to the growing tensions in the alliance.

Militarily, four stories dominated the year. The Soviet advance on the eastern front continued, as the Red Army finally broke the siege of Leningrad and pushed into Poland and other areas in Eastern Europe; the Allies confronted the stubborn German resistance in Italy that led to the controversial destruction of the monastery at Monte Cassino but also the liberation of Rome on the eve of the D-Day landing; American, British, Canadian, and French troops landed in

northern France and opened the long awaited second front; and at the
end of the year, German forces tried to break through the Allied lines
in the west, initiating one of the bloodiest battles of the war—the
Bulge.

As the invasion of the U.S.S.R. approached its third anniversary,
Soviet newspaper headlines celebrated the end of the siege of
Leningrad and Red Army victories against German forces throughout
the country. This reversal of military fortune, from massive German
dominance in 1941 to the Soviet advances of 1944, was one of the
remarkable achievements of the war. Fortunately for the United States
and Britain, unrelenting Soviet progress in Eastern Europe kept
German forces pinned down and limited the number of Axis soldiers
available to contest the fighting in Italy or the landing in France. As
the Russians moved forward, the Allies collectively encouraged
Bulgaria, Finland, Hungary, and Romania to withdraw from the war,
stop their assistance to Germany, and begin the process of resisting
Nazi control. All of the friends of the Axis were warned that they
would face due consequences for their loyalty to Germany. These
warnings were well timed, as the Soviet army methodically moved into
the Baltic States, Belorussia, the Crimea, Finland, Hungary, Poland,
and Romania.

The second important military event in 1944 involved the fighting in
Italy. Early in the year, Allied forces landed at Anzio, lost their
advantage due to hesitant leadership and German resistance, and
destroyed the monastery at Monte Cassino in a controversial bombing
raid. Finally, German Field Marshal Kesselring's so-called Gustav Line
was broken and Allied troops liberated Rome in June 1944.[3]

D-Day in northern France was one of the most significant events of
the war. The Normandy coast was divided into five landing beaches—
Utah and Omaha for the Americans, Sword and Gold for the British,
and Juno for the Canadians. Free French and units from other nations
joined in the attack. Civilians who lived in this part of France
experienced the Allied invasion in many different ways—some of them,
living in strategic villages, were eyewitnesses to the battles and killing
that took place. While the vast majority of French civilians were happy
to be liberated, the Allied advance often inflicted a cost on the local
population as well as on the opposing armies. These personal
memories of the impact of the invasion on family or friends provide an
important perspective on understanding the realities of war.

American and German soldiers all testified to the brutality of the
battle. Cities such as Cherbourg, Caen, and St.-Lô were practically
destroyed in brutal fighting; eventually the Allies made progress across
northern France through difficult hedgerow country. Paris was
liberated in August with the assistance of the Free French Forces and

the Resistance; General de Gaulle was able to make a triumphant entry into the city that had been occupied for four years. Despite the celebration of freedom in the French capital, the Allied objective still remained Germany; progress in that direction met with a major setback in an airborne assault in Holland in September (Operation Market Garden).[4]

The last important military event of 1944 occurred in December, when Hitler gambled on a final offensive action, attacked through the Ardennes Forest, and caught Allied forces off guard. At first German forces made progress, but their advance eventually was halted and reversed. The Battle of the Bulge was Germany's last chance to stop the Allies in the west. While Allied forces ultimately advanced toward their goals on both eastern and western fronts, the fighting was hard and vicious, with the Germans putting up a tenacious defense in Belgium, France, Holland, Italy, and Russia and Eastern Europe.

Despite Germany's military setbacks and warnings issued by the Allies about the treatment of civilians, the brutal occupation continued to claim its victims. In the east, Hungarian Jews were rounded up and sent to Auschwitz. In the west, few people survived the German massacre of the civilian population of Oradour-sur-Glane, a small town in central France. On June 10, 1944, men, women, and children were herded into barns, garages, and even the church, where some were killed by machine gun fire and others were burned alive. More than 640 people were slaughtered.[5] After the war, the French government used this event as one item of indictment against the German occupation. Eventually some of the perpetrators of this crime were put on trial. In another notorious case, the Nazis discovered the hiding place used by Anne Frank's family in Amsterdam; she died at the age of fifteen in the Bergen-Belsen concentration camp.[6]

As the year ended, Stalin used his annual speech on the anniversary of the Russian Revolution to praise the western allies and the Soviet army. He indicated that the rapid advance of Soviet troops against Germany was directly connected to the opening of a second front in France. Stalin looked forward to Allied victory, the continuation of cooperation, and the creation of a new international organization to replace the League of Nations. The Soviet leader praised the Red Army for its "devastating blows at the enemy" and again acknowledged the "consummate skill by the armies of our Allies." He anticipated the imminent defeat of the "fascist beast."[7]

THE SOURCES

Soviet-American Relations

The Soviet government was pleased with military events in 1943, including the victory at Stalingrad, the Allied battle for North Africa, and the invasion of Italy. At the beginning of 1944, Soviet President Kalinin sent a warm greeting to the American and British people. As the year progressed and victory seemed more likely, differences over the postwar political settlement took precedence over purely military considerations. The most significant issue was the makeup of the future Polish government, a dispute that continued throughout 1944 and intensified in the last months of the war. The Soviet government also expressed its concerns about the treatment and return of liberated Soviet prisoners, some of whom wanted asylum in the west. Stalin wanted the return of all Soviet prisoners. By the end of the year, Soviet satisfaction with Allied progress in France led to Stalin's praise of his allies and plans for a summit conference early in 1945.

President Kalinin on Allied Success, January 1, 1944

Parallel with the blows of the Red Army our Allies also conducted an uninterrupted struggle with the German Fascist troops this year. Anglo-American troops drove the Germans from North Africa, Sicily, Sardinia and Corsica. Now the battle has been transferred to southern Italy where the Allied troops are steadily advancing toward the capital of Italy, Rome. The Anglo-American Air Forces have been working effectively destroying strategic industrial targets in Germany.

The strongest ally of Germany in Europe, Italy, has capitulated and the Italian people are increasingly being drawn into the struggle with the Germans.

The joint struggle against German fascism has led to the close political rapprochement of the Allies.

The Tehran Conference is in reality the greatest event of our times, a historical landmark in the struggle with the German aggressor. All the efforts of the Germans to separate the freedom loving nations failed. The leaders of the three great powers reached full agreement on questions of war and peace. Namely they achieved that for which the popular masses in the occupied countries suffering under the heel of the German boot are thirsting.

Roosevelt to Congress on Tehran Conference, January 11, 1944

All our Allies want freedom to develop their lands and resources to build up industry, to increase education and individual opportunity, and to raise standards of living.

All our Allies have learned by bitter experience that real development will not be possible if they are to be diverted from their purpose by repeated wars—or even threats of war . . .

The best interests of each nation, large and small, demand that all freedom-loving nations shall join together in a just and durable system of peace. In the present world situation, evidenced by the actions of Germany, Italy, and Japan, unquestioned military control over disturbers of the peace is as necessary among nations as it is among citizens in a community. And an equally basic essential to peace is a decent standard of living for all individual men and women and children in all nations. Freedom from fear is eternally linked with freedom from want.

In the Headlines

Le Journal de Genève, Geneva, January 31, 1944
SYSTEMATIC BOMBING OF LARGE CITIES OF THE REICH
RAPID ADVANCE OF RUSSIAN ARMIES TOWARD NARVA [Estonia]

Roosevelt and Stalin Letters on Poland, June 1944

Roosevelt to Stalin: . . . The vital necessity for the establishment of the fullest kind of collaboration between the Red Army and the forces of the Polish underground in the common struggle against our enemy is his [reference to Polish prime minister] primary immediate concern. He believes that coordination between your armies and the organized Polish underground is a military factor of the highest importance not only to your armies in the East but also to the main task of finishing off the Nazi beast in his lair by our combined efforts.

It is my impression that the Prime Minister is thinking only of Poland and the Polish people and will not allow any petty considerations to stand in the way of his efforts to reach a solution with you. In fact it is my belief that he would not hesitate to go to Moscow, if he felt that you would welcome such a step on his part, in order to discuss with you personally and frankly the problems affecting your two countries, particularly the urgency of immediate military collaboration.

Stalin to Roosevelt: If we have in view military cooperation between the Red Army and the Polish underground forces fighting the Hitler invaders, that, undoubtedly, is vital to the final defeat of our common enemy. Certainly, the proper solution of the problem of Soviet-Polish relations is of great importance in this respect. You are aware of the Soviet Government's point of view and of its desire to see Poland strong, independent and democratic, and Soviet-Polish relations good-neighborly and based on lasting friendship. A vital condition for this, in the view of the Soviet Government, is a reconstruction of the Polish émigré Government that would ensure participation of Polish leaders in Britain, the U.S.A. and the U.S.S.R., and more particularly of Polish democratic leaders inside Poland, plus recognition by the Polish Government of the Curzon Line as the new frontier between the U.S.S.R. and Poland.

Allied Leaders Exchange Notes on Poland, August 1944[8]

Roosevelt and Churchill to Stalin: We are thinking of world opinion if anti-Nazis in Warsaw are in effect abandoned. We believe that all three of us should do the utmost to save as many of the patriots there as possible. We hope that you will drop immediate supplies and munitions to the patriot Poles of Warsaw, or will you agree to help our planes in doing it very quickly? We hope you will approve. The time element is of extreme importance.

Stalin to Roosevelt and Churchill: Sooner or later the truth about the handful of power-seeking criminals who launched the Warsaw adventure will out. Those elements, playing on the credulity of the inhabitants of Warsaw, exposed practically unarmed people to German guns, armor and aircraft. The result is a situation in which every day is used, not by the Poles for freeing Warsaw, but by the Hitlerites, who are cruelly exterminating the civilian population.

From the military point of view the situation, which keeps German attention riveted to Warsaw, is highly unfavorable both to the Red Army and to the Poles. Nevertheless, the Soviet troops, who of late have had to face renewed German counterattacks, are doing all they can to repulse the Hitlerite sallies and go over to a new large-scale offensive near Warsaw. I can assure you that the Red Army will stint no effort to crush the Germans at Warsaw and liberate it for the Poles. That will be the best, really effective, help to the anti-Nazi Poles.

U.S.S.R. on Soviet Prisoners, September 1944[9]

Practice has shown that the attitude of certain Allied authorities to freed Soviet citizens is characterized by a whole series of irregularities. Thus at times freed Soviet citizens are considered as prisoners of war and there is established for them a regime at times even more severe than for German prisoners of war. The legal and material conditions in which freed Soviet citizens find themselves are in a number of cases unsatisfactory. There are cases of propaganda hostile to the Soviet Union in the camps in which freed Soviet citizens are placed. Attempts are made to recruit freed Soviet citizens for foreign military units. A certain number of freed Soviet citizens by the unilateral decision of the Allied authorities were sent from Europe to Canada and Africa. Certain other irregularities have also occurred.

. . . In this connection, [the Soviet Government] expresses the firm conviction that the Government of the United States of America will take immediate and effective measures to prevent similar facts in the future. The

Soviet Government expects that the authorities of the United States will immediately issue the following instructions:

1. That freed Soviet citizens will be regarded by all authorities not as prisoners of war but as free citizens of an Allied power. . . .

2. That the recruitment of freed Soviet citizens for foreign armed forces will not take place.

3. That all necessary measures will be taken for the facilitation of the most speedy return of freed Soviet citizens to their country.

Stalin to Roosevelt on Future Meeting, October 19, 1944

During the conversations it has been clarified that we can, without great difficulties, adjust our policy on all questions standing before us, and if we are not in a position so far to provide an immediate necessary decision of this or that task, as for example, on the Polish question, but nevertheless, more favorable perspectives are opened. I hope that these Moscow conversations will be of some benefit from the point of view that at the future meeting of three of us, we shall be able to adopt definite decisions on all urgent questions of our mutual interest.

. . . you could arrive in the Black Sea at the end of November to meet with me on the Soviet Black Sea coast. I would extremely welcome the realization of this intention. From the conversation with the Prime Minister, I was convinced, that he also shares this idea. Thus the meeting of three of us could take place at the end of November in order to consider the questions which have been accumulated since Teheran. I would be glad to receive a message from you on this matter.

Stalin Speech, November 6, 1944

What must be regarded as a new factor in the war against Hitler Germany this past year is that this year the Red Army has not been operating against the German forces single-handed, as was the case in previous years, but together with the forces of our Allies. The Teheran Conference was not held for nothing. The decision of the Teheran Conference on a joint blow at Germany from west, east and south began to be carried out with astounding precision. Simultaneously with the summer operations of the Red Army on the Soviet-German Front, the Allied forces launched the invasion of France and organized powerful offensive operations which compelled Hitler Germany to wage war on two fronts. The troops and Navy of our Allies accomplished a mass landing operation on the coast of France that was unparalleled in history for scope and organization, and overcame the German fortifications with consummate skill.

Thus, Germany found herself gripped in a vice between two fronts.

As was to be expected, the enemy failed to withstand the joint blows of the Red Army and the Allied forces . . .

The task is to keep Germany gripped in this vice between the two fronts.

. . . Differences of opinion occur even among people in one and the same Party. They are all the more bound to occur between representatives of different States and different Parties. The surprising thing is not that differences exist, but that they are so few, and that as a rule in practically every case they are resolved in a spirit of unity and coordination among the three Great Powers. What matters is not that there are differences, but that these differences do not transgress the bounds of what the interests of the unity of the three Great Powers allow, and that, in the long run, they are resolved in accordance with the interests of that unity. It is known that more serious differences existed between us over the opening of the Second Front. But it is also known that in the end these differences were resolved in a spirit of complete accord . . .

To win the war against Germany is to accomplish a great historic task. But to win the war does not in itself mean to ensure for the peoples a lasting peace and guaranteed security in the future. The task is not only to win the war but also to make new aggression and new war impossible—if not for ever, then at least for a long time to come.

Battle for Italy

Bitter fighting in Italy continued into 1944. Trapped on the coast because of the higher ground occupied by German defenders, the Allies decided to bomb a monastery where they believed enemy troops had taken refuge. The monastery of Monte Cassino was destroyed, but the Allies were mistaken—the Germans had not used the landmark for protection. The event led to charges that the Allies had not shown proper respect for Italian monuments, an accusation repeated later in the year when the Allies bombed Rome. The liberation of Rome came on the eve of the Allied landing in Normandy in June.

In the Headlines

Le Journal de Genève, Geneva, January 31, 1944
GERMAN TROOPS ABANDON ROME

Le Journal de Genève, Geneva, February 17, 1944
DESTRUCTION OF THE MONTE CASSINO MONASTERY

Corriere Della Sera, Milan, February 17, 1944
CYNICAL AMERICAN CLAIMS ABOUT THE RUIN OF THE FAMOUS
   MONASTERY

Corriere Della Sera, Milan, June 6, 1944
AMERICANS BRING THE WAR TO THE STREETS OF THE CITY [ROME]

Testimony of Franciszek Kurak, January 1944—Monte Cassino

One day, during the fight over Monte Cassino Corporal Kurak and his twenty-man strong patrol were caught in the crossfire of enemy artillery, which prevented their retreat and threatened to kill off the patrol. On top of that, they lost their radio communication equipment, destroyed by enemy fire, and with that the ability to effectively direct their own artillery fire on to the enemy's positions. In this hopeless situation, Corporal Franciszek Kurak, in civilian life a born athlete, took upon himself a mission, which today he thinks of as the most difficult and the longest run of his life. He ran under constant enemy fire a distance of about half a kilometer on a mountainside overgrown with thorny bushes. He did it twice, in order to deliver new radio communication equipment to the patrol held at bay. They were saved. Only after the operation was over did the corporal realize that his body was punctured with hundreds of thorns from the bushes he forced his way through, and what was stranger still, he did not feel any pain from them during the runs.

Testimony of Jesse E. Foster, June 1944[10]—Air Force

We were shot down on June 5, 1944.

Bologna—that's the bridge we—the target we had to bomb, and I think it was right after I said, "Bombs away," that we got hit, and the plane started spinning. . . . I said, "to heck with it. I'm getting out of here." So I went to the escape hatch, which was underneath the pilot's and right near our compartment, and I noticed the navigator was sitting on his map table. And I opened the escape hatch, and I must have been the first one out. Now you can imagine that all of this happened in seconds. I don't know how many seconds, but really fast.

So I got out, and then I realized that I was all alone. . . . But anyway, I made it to the ground and the co-pilot in his chute landed a few yards from me, almost about the same time. So the two of us were together, and he told me that the pilot was killed instantly . . . we landed in a very mountainous area near Bologna, and the other crew landed in another part of the mountain area, and the partisans got a hold of them and hid them.

We landed next to a farmhouse. It was pretty rustic, and the farmer came out. He didn't speak—his language was not very good, but understandable. And he said, "You have to get out of here." He says, "I can't help you." And he pointed across the valley to the hillside on the other side, and there were a few burned down—burned up ruins of some farmhouses. He said, "If I help you, the Germans are going to burn my house down." So he says—he pointed to a little path. He says, "You better go that way as soon as possible." So we walked a few yards down the path, and then we decided we better hide the chutes. And we bundled up the chutes and just hid them in the bushes . . . we heard "click-click-click." And we looked up, and there was—there were three German soldiers pointing rifles and machine guns at us. Now these were very young; they must have been 17–18 year old boys. And, well, we were captured. That was it. So we had to follow them down the path—down the hill . . .

You'd see these officers—well dressed with knee-length leather boots clicking their heels and hailing Hitler. So we were strip-searched.

Invasion of France

The long-awaited invasion of France—the opening of the second front—started early in June. The fighting in Normandy was divided along five beaches, with two each assigned to the British and Americans and another given to the Canadians. At the same time, additional Allied forces joined the assault—Free French Forces, members of the resistance, Polish soldiers, and others. Allied newspapers celebrated the successful landing, whereas Axis voices focused on heavy Allied losses and German defensive measures. As the Allies moved inland and drove toward Paris in August, several collaborationist newspapers ceased publication. Nevertheless, the extensive testimonies included here honor the intensity of the battle. Voices from Allied soldiers, German soldiers, and French civilians are all included to provide a total picture of this crucial event.

British Views of the Invasion of France

In the Headlines

The Times, London, June 7, 1944
THE GREAT ASSAULT GOING WELL
ALLIES SEVERAL MILES INLAND
MASS ATTACK BY AIRBORNE TROOPS

The Times, London, June 9, 1944
FIERCE FIGHTING IN NORMANDY
ENEMY RESERVES ENGAGED ON WHOLE FRONT

The Times, London, June 15, 1944
VIOLENT BATTLES NEAR CAEN
ALLIES WITHSTANDING STRONG COUNTER-ATTACKS

The Times, London, June 23, 1944
ALL-OUT ATTACK ON CHERBOURG

The Times, London, June 26, 1944
AMERICAN TROOPS ENTER CHERBOURG
STREET BY STREET ADVANCE TOWARD DOCKS

Testimony of Maurice Clancy, June 6, 1944—Royal Navy

My ship was called H.M.S. *Bleasdale*. It was a hunt-class destroyer of small size—about 1200 tonnes and although it was not very fast it was highly maneuverable.

. . . Twenty-four hours before D Day all shore leave was stopped and the crews of all ships were told that the big event was "on."

In the early hours of 6th of June our flotilla was moved out together with many other destroyers. The weather was not good but we had seen worse. The minesweeping vessels had, a few hours earlier, swept a channel across to France and we passed them as they returned down the route which had been marked with small buoys.

We were the first naval fighting ships to arrive at the scene and for all of us it was our first sight of France . . .

Our attack was to move in within a few kilometres of the shore which was at Bernières Sur Mer (Juno Beach).[11] Since we were never allowed any maps we had only a vague notion where we were. Our task was to bombard the German gun emplacements in that area and, if possible, to put them out of action. For hour after hour we pounded the German massive concrete structures and also plastered the landing beaches to explode any mines. In all we fired about 150 tonnes of 10 cms shells until the ships magazines were totally empty. We then were recalled to Portsmouth. . . . On our way back to Britain we saw the vast armada creeping forward—filled with troops for whom we felt very sorry. I was glad then, as we all were, that I had joined the navy and not the army . . .

. . . we returned escorting the battleships HMS *Rodney* and HMS *Nelson* with the other heavy gun vessels where we were sent to Sword Beach in the area of Ouistreham.[12] The invading British and Canadian armies had come up against very fierce German opposition in the areas of Caen—mainly I believe from Panzer (German tanks) troops.

The battleships started a tremendous bombardment with broadsides from their huge guns in various combinations between their 3 turrets of 3 guns each. We had never seen these awesome weapons fired before and, since we were guarding them with a continuous sonar vigilance against possible u-boat attack and within a hundred or so metres of their guns, we were shattered by the noise and flames which are inherent in such weaponry. The guns were pointing at a steep angle to the sky and we knew that the range of their target was well inland. It was in fact some 25 kilometres away out to the town which we eventually knew to be Caen. Although hardened by war it is difficult to describe the feelings that ran through our emotions as we witnessed this giant demonstration of sea power that was raining huge shells weighing 1 tonne each upon a people we regarded as our friends and allies. I can still picture that dreadful scene.

The British and Canadian landings and construction of the Mulberry harbours had gone well at our Sword and Juno Beach-heads but the weather conditions to the west had deteriorated and the Americans we heard had had a bad time at their Omaha landing point.[13] Occasionally we saw bodies floating past on the tide but we were told to leave them. We were glad of that.

American Views of the Invasion of France

Testimony of Jean Gragg—Nurse

On that day I was a 23-year-old U.S. Army Nurse . . .

By dawn on the 6th of June we were told that our troops were landing in France. Within the next three weeks our hospital had received three thousand wounded men. They were not all Americans—we also had British and French. Casualties were expected to be high and they were. As each trainload of wounded arrived from France we worked around the clock till every man was cared for.

Testimony of Dalton Eastus[14]—Hedgerow Country

So on the 6th is when they actually made the invasion. It was still stormy, but they couldn't hold off any longer, they said. They went ahead as scheduled, but I'll tell you, the seas were awful rough. We had to go down off the side of the ship on cargo nets, and these boats were coming up 8 and 10 feet high. The swell was real high, and you had to catch it coming up. And, of course, the Eighth Infantry Regiment was the first regiment to make the initial assault on Utah Beach. Some reason or another our general figured the Eighth was the best regiment, so he usually picked it out for the assault regiment. Went along pretty good until the second or third day and then things began to get rough. Matter of fact, the Germans had an area flooded with water—to keep us from crossing. But the engineers had made a pontoon bridge. We got across on that. And hedgerows were pretty rough, because you couldn't see and Germans would be on one side and you would be on the other side.

You're just scared to death. You don't know what to do, you know. You just wonder how long you're going to be there. It's more or less automatic with you, because you've been trained for that for months on end. I got along pretty good up until we got up around—well, Sainte-Mère-Église is where we joined up with the 101st Airborne Aviation. And we joined up with them. To go from there to Cherbourg. But after Sainte-Mère-Église, why, we went on into Montebourg. That's where I got wounded, in Montebourg, just on the outskirts of Montebourg. And we're still in the hedgerow country. We never got out of the hedgerow . . .

[T]hey were just like fences all over the fields, and they have a gate now and then in between them, but you don't dare to look over that gate, you know, because the snipers would be zeroed in on it. But what they did, somebody come up with the idea that you put some—we call them cow catchers on trains. You put them on tanks. You hit these hedgerows, and they just cut right through. And that's the way they got through some of them. They just plow right through. And of course, we had to go through these hedgerows and that's where I got hurt, in the hedgerow. Because I don't know whether the Germans were shelling 88s or mortars or what, but they would make it so they would hit in the top of the hedgerow and then the shrapnel would come down on you. I got an injury in my right leg and left heel and I got some in my back. I was there all night until the medics picked me up the next day.

Testimony of Harold Shebeck—Supply Officer

The glider troops of the British Army landed in Normandy on June 6 and American glider troops were supposed to go the same day but for some reason orders were changed and we did not go until early on June 7. On June 6 we spent all day writing letters, checking and re-checking weapons and equipment, and visiting a large tent where models of the area in Normandy we were supposed to land in had been built by our Engineers. Every road, town, river, tree, hedgerow in that part of Normandy was built according to scale for us to study and I remember every street in Valognes, Montebourg, Ste-Mère-Église, and Chef-du-Pont very well.

When we left England and crossed the English Channel there were so many ships below us that it looked as though one could have walked across the Channel without getting wet feet. Our glider was towed by a C-47 plane by means of a 300 foot nylon rope and the sky was full of planes and gliders. Our glider carried my jeep, driver, a supply sergeant, and myself. We had been given pills for air sickness but my driver was lying on the floor under the jeep and was vomiting all the way across the channel from being air sick. The Germans had placed large poles throughout many of the fields of Normandy connected with wires on which were fixed explosives to blow up a glider on landing. Our pilot found a field which did not seem to have any poles and prepared to cut us loose from the plane towing us. He misjudged the height of the hedgerows and knocked the wheels off the glider. So here we were traveling about 70 miles an hour, about 16 to 20 feet off the ground and no wheels and, of course, we had to crash but nobody was hurt. In all the while I was in Normandy I only saw one glider that looked as though it could fly again otherwise they were all smashed up. In nearly every case it was because of wheels being knocked off. Before we left England we had studied aerial photographs of Normandy but I think many of the pilots misjudged the height of the hedge-rows. There were snipers all around at this time but we assembled at our Command Post between Ste-Mère-Église and Chef-du-Pont but it was a couple of days before our regiment got together. We were about six miles inland from Utah Beach as I remember. The mission of our regiment—as well as all of the Airborne—was to seize and hold the roads leading into Normandy from northern France so the enemy could not arrive in such force to be able to throw the people landing on the beaches back into the sea.

Testimony of James Faust—Omaha Beach

I was at Omaha Beach June 6, 1944. We went ashore at 6 A.M. French time, before the infantry and other army equipment came in. I was the first man in my company to set foot on French soil as I drove one the three trucks. We were supposed to have our trucks engines "water proofed" so we could drive them off the landing craft through five feet depth of water on to the beach.

The soldiers had to wade out in the water on to land. My truck was the only one of the trucks that made it out on its own power. The other two had to be pulled onto the beach by a bulldozer as their motors drowned out. So myself and one military policeman were the only two on the beach for several moments. I asked him what I was supposed to do, and he said "seek cover" as German shells were falling all around on the beach. But our men were lucky since none of our company was injured during the landing. The other troops were not so fortunate as many, many casualties occurred. Our main purpose was to scour the land with mine detectors and detonate them so the rest of the army could get in. There were numerous mines and we got all we could find but there were so many we missed some. A few of our men were even killed by mines that were unseen.

Testimony of Warren G. Hirt[15]—American Seabees

June 6th the landing took place in the early hours of the morning. Sometime during the next morning we arrived at the landing area and then we landed. But we were stationed along the beach because all of our activity had to do with helping all of the troop ships unload and then supply ships unload over our pontoon causeways. We were living on top of one of the cliffs that they had such a hard time climbing up and capturing on Omaha Beach. But I remember thinking on the next day when I looked out and saw how much material—thousands and thousands of pieces of equipment were being unloaded constantly, day and night, 24 hours a day. That was the first time that I realized that there was no way we were going to lose this war. The Germans and no one else could stand up to that kind of equipment and man-power. It was really thrilling to see all that being unloaded.

Testimony of John Torreano—82nd Airborne

After Italy we had to prepare for the invasion of France. We were sent to Ireland for some rest before shipping to England. About midnight on June 5, 1944, the 82nd parachuted out of our C-47s into France at Ste.-Mère-Église.[16] I landed in a tree right next to the famous church in the center of town. We quickly got gathered together and headed for some small bridge at the Merderet River that we had to hold and wait for the units that landed on Utah Beach. The fighting was hard and the bridge changed hands a couple of times but we finally held it. After that we were sent back to England again for some rest.

Testimony of Eric Strauss, June 1944[17]—Utah Beach

Now we boarded the ships on the 5th of June . . .

Now we were the second wave that landed on our segment of Utah Beach. The first wave came in about two hours before we landed, and their mission was to go somewhat inland along the beach and dig in and be ready for any German counter attack.

In contrast to what happened at Omaha Beach, the beach was not well defended by the Germans and the Navy gun barrage and bombings from aircraft before the invasion had softened them up and the Germans had, they retreated when their fortifications came under fire so we really met no opposition on the beach.

Well, earlier paratroopers had landed inland. And our mission was to move through the first wave and relieve or reinforce the paratroopers inland. . . . unfortunately the Navy landed us on the sandbank and so, off we ran from the ship onto the sandbank and into the water and it turned out the water was up to our neck.

We kept moving and I remember meeting up with the paratroopers and then we moved into a town called Ste-Mère-Église, and there's a famous story—this was in the vicinity where the paratroopers had landed. And one was caught on the church steeple. And he sort of couldn't move. He was hanging—his parachute caught up on the steeple of the church and he was sort of caught there for awhile until his fellow soldiers finally were able to cut him loose and free him. And, but this was all over by the time we got there. But there was a German sniper up in the church steeple, and he started firing at us and everybody, well that was really our first fire fight so to speak so everybody took out their rifle and started pelting the church steeple. . . . And everybody started firing at the church steeple. I don't know whether we hit the German sniper, but he sort of ducked out of the way.

We started running into trouble because we now moved into the French farm country. And French farmers marked off their land with hedgerows around the perimeter of their land. And, the whole of their land and their neighbor's land was very symmetrical. So here is all this land and there's a hedgerow around it and this was ideal for Germans to hide behind with their machine guns, and wait for the Americans to show up and that's where we really took our casualties.

And, eventually, now what American ingenuity came up with, they took tanks and they welded bulldozer blades to the front of the tank, and then the tanks were first and the infantry followed a good distance behind the tanks and the tanks plowed through the hedgerows, and destroyed the hedgerows so now we could see if anybody was hiding behind them.

Testimony of John Misa[18]—35th Division

I landed in Normandy on D+6. And, from Normandy we headed towards St.-Lô. And going there was lots of hedgerows. When we landed in Normandy, we were going to relieve the 29th division at St.-Lô. And as we were going there, we were in a ravine and this 188-millimeter howitzer blasted off. I just about dropped a load in my pants.

. . . when we came on the beach, everything was taped off. It was all mined. We had to go, just stay within the tape perimeter or else we would have been blown up.

My job assignment was to drive the radio truck.

Went through combat everyday, shot at, shelled, bombed, strafed. Wasn't a day that we didn't go through that. The unit was replaced 250%. We were always getting new guys. And they didn't know a darn thing about combat. Lot of them would get shot before they even hit the front lines.

Testimony of Arthur Gross[19]—Air Force

So we were the replacements for the people that were lost on that, which isn't a very pleasant thing to do, to move right in where somebody had just been cleared out . . .

And the complete tour of missions at that time was 25 and the estimated life of a crew was twelve and a half missions. After 21 missions, they upped the ante and the tour now became 30 missions. So, it was very disappointing when we were four missions away from completing a tour and now they added another five.

On June 14, 1944, which incidentally is Flag Day, we had a mission to Le Bourget Airfield, which was the airfield that Lindbergh landed when he flew across the ocean in his single engine plane. But, we were approaching the target area, so the leader of the squadron or the group decided to go around and try it again and see if the bombardier could get a clear shot at the target. Flak was very heavy and at the time I was flying in the ball turret, just to observe our bomb pattern.

I had a few choice words for the people that decided to make a go-around and wondered why they didn't bypass that and go to an alternate target, which was normally the plan. But, we made our turnaround and I think the German gunners were after the lead aircraft and we were flying on the right wing of the lead aircraft. They missed him and we got hit. And we were hit in the wing. Fortunately the projectiles just went through the aircraft wing and didn't explode. If it exploded, that would have been it for everybody. Nobody would have gotten out because it would have blown the wing off immediately. As it was, it pierced the fuel tanks and, as the fuel leaked out and hit the engine exhaust, it brought fire. And before too long, the entire left wing was covered in white flame; it was so hot. .

Actually I didn't open my parachute until I got into the clouds, anticipating an escape.

Testimony of William Masterson—Engineers

On June 16 we boarded a train for Southampton. At Southampton we boarded an LST (Landing Ship, Tank). We left for France at 11:30 P.M. About 7 A.M. on June 17 we were several hundred meters off the Omaha (Easy Red) Beach but the ship's commander would not let us debark because of the high and rough seas. While on deck I witnessed a truck full of soldiers leave the LST next to ours and drive about three hundred meters before it disappeared under the water, drowning a number of men. After riding the storm out for four or five days and watching the artificial harbors being demolished by the storm we were allowed to make our landing and waded through the water to the beach. I was an engineer attached to an infantry replacement company assigned to the U.S. 2nd Infantry Division. Several other engineers and myself kept our infantry company out of the mine fields and we didn't get hurt. A company behind us lost a squad of 13 men when they wandered into a mine field . . .

From then on we cleared mines in the lodgment area and were assigned to open the ports of Barfleur and St. Vaast la Hougue.[20] This involved mine removal, blowing road blocks, demolishing German fortifications, repairing dock areas and removing ship wrecks. Other companies in our regiment were used to open the ports of Cherbourg, Isigny and Grand Camp. While traveling up the peninsula to Barfleur I remember seeing either Valognes or Montebourg in flames and burning after they had been shelled. One of our jobs was to remove a German concrete road block at Barfleur without blowing up an adjacent house. We managed to do this without damage to the house.

Testimony of [Alfred] Scott Bates[21]—Americans Occupy France

Finally in February 1944 they sent us overseas in a huge convoy—about 200 ships that took 21 days to cross the North Atlantic. We arrived in England and everything was getting ready for D-Day. My group was a civil affairs unit—that is not combat but preparing to run the occupation of France and Germany. England was an armed camp at that time, and I watched the sky full of gliders heading for Normandy on June 6.

About a week or so after D-Day, I was sent to France. We marched toward St.-Lô, and I was serving as an interpreter trying to help our lieutenant, who was totally incompetent, to find our unit. We stayed out of combat but basically followed the infantry wherever it went so we could translate and set up local governments. In St.-Lô and Avranches it was clear that de Gaulle had told the French officers to make sure that only pro-Gaullist officials were given power and to keep the communists out.

Although I saw lot of bombing and strafing and dead horses all over the fields, I really had a great job in a hotel as a liaison to the French officers and officials. The Gaullists were looking for collaborators and already started shaving the heads of women who had been with Germans. I got to stay in this hotel. Lots of GIs were bringing prostitutes into the hotel rooms, and my sergeant was shacked up with a prostitute/collaborator and he got gonorrhea from her. Lots of French women were trying to get by, so some did our laundry for a fee but others just "serviced" the GIs. I think I remember two bordellos in Cherbourg and there were always lines of GIs outside. Near St.-Lô two French girls just laid in a field while soldiers had sex with them. Everyone was getting laid.

German Views of the Invasion of France

In the Headlines

Der Angriff, Berlin, June 7, 1944
FIERCE FIGHTING ON THE COAST BETWEEN LE HAVRE AND
    CHERBOURG

Der Angriff, Berlin, June 8, 1944
THE SECOND NIGHT ON THE CHANNEL COAST: SEVERAL
    BRIDGEHEADS DESTROYED—SUCCESS AGAINST THE BATTLESHIP
    FLEETS

Tübinger Chronik, Tübingen, June 8, 1944
BIG BATTLE ON NORMAN PENINSULA
OUR TROOPS ANSWER THE ENEMY WITH STRONG
    COUNTERATTACKS
HUGE LOSSES FOR BRITISH AND NORTH AMERICANS

Tübinger Chronik, Tübingen, June 9, 1944
GERMAN TANKS COUNTERATTACK AT BAYEUX

Der Angriff, Berlin, June 9, 1944
HEAVY LOSSES FOR THE ENEMY NEAR CARENTAN
ANGLO-AMERICAN TROOPS EAST OF ORNE, DRIVEN AWAY FROM
    THE COAST

Der Angriff, Berlin, June 11, 1944
INTENSITY OF INVASION BATTLES INCREASES
REINFORCEMENTS ADDED ON BOTH SIDES

Der Angriff, Berlin, June 13, 1944
SITUATION IN NORMANDY REMAINS UNCHANGED
HEAVY ATTACKS FROM OUR AIR FORCE (LUFTWAFFE) ON THE
   INVASION FLEETS

Tübinger Chronik, Tübingen, June 13, 1944
FRONTLINE IS CLOSING IN ON INVADERS

Völkischer Beobachter, Berlin, June 13, 1944
EISENHOWER'S PLAN RUINED

Testimony of Wolfgang Geritzlehner, June 5–6, 1944[22]

At dusk, trouble started. There were hundreds of flares at sea.

We were sitting there quietly, drinking our Calva [fermented apple cider] and watching. We thought: "That's some show!" Later, a liaison officer arrived shouting "Alarm, alarm! Enemy paratroopers in Wolfgang!"

He was right, as the sky filled with planes flying over us in close order. From the sea, the uproar was deafening. It sobered us up. We alerted all the officers and everything started. All of a sudden, there were soldiers coming out from everywhere. We prepared ourselves quickly. We blackened our faces as we had been ordered to in case we'd have to fight at night, and we took some tinned food with us.

To be frank, we were not afraid. We were so sure that the situation would be settled within a few hours, that we didn't even take our personal belongings.

Testimony of Heinz Perschke, June 6, 1944[23]

The landing of the Allies on 6 June 1944 was for me only one event in a series of German military defeats, starting with Stalingrad and followed by Allied landings in North Africa and in Italy. Nevertheless I thought at that time that the war would not be lost by Germany, in the sense that we would have to give up about half our conquests in Europe, but that we could defend our country, our homeland. I had the opinion with many other soldiers that the shorter the front lines and the more quickly the "miracle army" (that is what we called the V1 and V2 rockets at that time) were put into use, the better our chances would be. The invasion of Normandy in this perspective was a relatively insignificant event. To be fair, I have to say that the term "invasion" is not really appropriate, as France was an occupied country, and the military action of the Allies was intended to be an act of liberation. In any case from the Nazi point of view it was an invasion.

Testimony of Walter Schad, June 6, 1944[24]

At Gonfreville, early in the morning on June 6, I heard the call of the sentry who announced "enemy parachutes approaching." The infirmary immediately became a first-aid post: the first ones to be injured were the cows of the Fossey family; and then American parachutists arrived, and finally injured from both sides started showing up.

The first battalion of our regiment entered the heat of battle facing the bridgehead at Utah Beach, and it was almost completely annihilated in the area of Sainte-Marie-du-Mont.

The second battalion got the order to scout in the direction of Sainte-Mère-Église. The 3rd battalion remained in place as a reserve for a while. Our first-aid post was shifted on June 6 toward Carentan. . . . Our units had to withdraw from their positions toward the north and east of Carentan because of the heavy casualties and because we were threatened with encirclement.

From June 12 on, the regiment occupied the area northwest of the road from Carentan to Périers, in the region of Méautis. After the severe fighting and the heavy casualties we had suffered (within 24 hours, 800 injured had come to see us), the area of Méautis was much calmer.

After the capture of Cherbourg, a new offensive started in our area. The casualties were heavier and heavier. The doctors were stationed at the front lines not far from the active battalions. My hands were burned there on July 7, and I was evacuated. When the regiment withdrew from the front, only about 60 men were still standing. All the others—more than 3,000—had been killed, injured, taken prisoners, or were missing.

Testimony of Rudolf Schuebl, June 1944[25]

I was 17 when the allies landed. I was an Austrian enlisted in the German army. A little before June 6, we were stationed at Brest, and the order arrived to go to Normandy. But there were no trucks and no gas to take us there, so we had to go on foot or by bike, and of course when we got to Normandy we were not in good shape for the fight that was coming. On the evening of June 5, we were near Barneville. I clearly remember seeing hundreds of planes flying over, heading inland at top speed. I was taken prisoner at Saint-Sauveur-le-Vicomte, and I spent two years in England before I could go home. Of course we were frightened during combat—we are human beings.

Testimony of G. Moeller, June 6, 1944[26]

On 6 June 1944 we were in combat but retreating about 30 kilometers from the Bug River, not far from the small town of Vladimir in Ukraine. I was an artillery gunner in support of the 342nd tank division.

The news of the invasion of France came to us at noon with the supply vehicles that brought us lunch and other cold meals during the day. While we had been expecting an invasion, the news still took us by surprise. Among the many thoughts that ran through my head and those of my comrades was the hope that, in light of the ongoing retreat and the heavy losses we were suffering, the invasion would move quickly to end the war and we could leave the hell we were in while still alive.

Testimony of Joachim Hübener, June 1944[27]

When we heard about the invasion by the English in Normandy, I was a soldier on the eastern front. I swear that it is true that I had already for a long time thought about the defeat of Germany as a possibility. During the years 1941–45, I was able to visit my home two times and I had a couple of occasions when I engaged in conversations that took my mind off of the daily life of being a soldier. Some examples:

At the railway station at Güstrow I met my cousin who was an officer cadet. In this short exchange he told me about a secret movement of resistance against Hitler.

A friend at the front, who later became a protestant minister, like me, and who was also a member of the confessional church (like Niemöller),[28] told me in a private conversation: We cannot be victorious!

By military courier, I received a letter from my uncle in Danzig in which he scolded me: you are participating in a criminal war. This letter came in 1944. Blind to the real situation, I answered: What will happen to the children, women, and old people in our country if we do not hold on at the front?

I don't remember any more about my feelings when I received the news of the invasion.

It was only little by little that I woke up from my ignorance. The defeat at Stalingrad, the failed assassination attempt against Hitler, the German retreat back to the Oder River, and finally the surrender of Germany all contributed to my awakening.

Even at the age of 22 at the time of the landing, I only understood a small amount and this was even in spite of the arrest and imprisonment of my own father in 1937–38 because of his membership in the confessional church. In 1940 I volunteered to join the army.

Our retreat and the assassination attempt against Hitler on 20 July 1944 came as shocks to me. The idea of nationalism was too deeply driven into all Germans. But if the assassination attempt had succeeded, Hitler would have been venerated as a martyr by all Nazis. And it is difficult to imagine the results, as one can see even today the crazy imbeciles who listen to the words of the neo-Nazis.

Testimony of Sabine Leibholz-Bonhoeffer[29]—Exile in England

Finally the end of the war seems a bit closer. On 6 June 1944, like every day, we left our house and our neighbor's son was sitting in the garden in the sun and he told us: this is D-Day. We did not totally understand what he was saying but we did not want him to know that we did not understand so we just said: "yes of course" and we continued on our way. Several minutes later Marian arrived on a bike with the news: the English and the Americans have landed in France. Everyone in town was nervous. No one spoke of anything else, and everyone waited with impatience for the newspaper. The schoolboys were singing "It's a long way to Tipperary" and "Roll out the barrel." Overall everyone felt enormous anxiety.

French Newspapers Debate the Invasion of France

Views within France were sharply divided. The government of Marshal Pétain tried to rally the French people against the Allied invasion. Collaborationist newspapers echoed the position of Vichy and Germany. Opposition and resistance groups welcomed the invasion as the beginning of liberation. French civilians, most of whom welcomed liberation, were caught in the middle of the fighting, and they experienced the Normandy landing with anticipation mixed with fear.

In the Headlines

La Croix, Paris, June 8, 1944 [conservative]
SOLEMN WARNING BY CHIEF OF STATE AND GOVERNMENT—
   "FRANCE CAN ONLY SAVE HERSELF BY PRACTICING MORE
   RIGOROUS DISCIPLINE" PROCLAIMS THE MARSHAL [reference to Pétain]

Le Petit Parisien, Paris, June 8, 1944 [collaborationist]
VIGOROUS GERMAN DEFENSE
MARSHAL PÉTAIN APPEALS TO THE NATION TO OBEY THE ORDERS
   OF THE GOVERNMENT AND FOR EACH PERSON TO REMAIN
   LOYAL TO HIS DUTY

La Croix, Paris, June 15, 1944
IN NORMANDY, DESPITE THEIR EFFORTS, ANGLO-AMERICANS HAVE
   NOT BROKEN GERMAN RESISTANCE NORTH OF ST.-LÔ

La Croix, Paris, June 16, 1944
ANGLO-AMERICAN NAVY HAS SUFFERED SUBSTANTIAL LOSSES

Le Petit Parisien, Paris, June 16, 1944
SINCE THE BEGINNING OF THE OPERATIONS IN NORMANDY THE
   ANGLO-AMERICANS HAVE LOST MORE THAN 400 TANKS AND
   1,000 PLANES AND 400,000 TONS OF SHIPS

La Renaissance du Bessin, Bayeux, July 4, 1944 [pro-Allies]
CHERBOURG'S LIBERATION ACCLAIMED

France Amérique, New York, July 16, 1944 [pro-Allies]
1789—JULY 14—1944: LIBERATION!

La Presse Cherbourgeoisie, Cherbourg, August 24, 1944 [pro-Allies]
PARIS AND MARSEILLE LIBERATED
GENERAL LECLERC'S TANK DIVISION HAS ENTERED THE CAPITAL

Le Figaro, Paris, August 26, 1944 [pro-Allies]
PARIS IS CARRIED AWAY WITH ENTHUSIASTIC ACCLAIM FOR
    GENERAL DE GAULLE

Le Figaro, Paris, August 27, 1944
FROM THE ARC DE TRIOMPHE TO NOTRE DAME—ACCLAIM BY HUGE
    AND EXCITED CROWDS ALONG THE PROCESSION OF GENERAL
    DE GAULLE

Belgique, Paris, August 29, 1944 [resistance]
DISCOVERY OF CORPSES OF HEROES TORTURED BY BOCHES
    [KRAUTS]
34 MUTILATED CORPSES IN MASS GRAVE IN THE FORT OF
    VINCENNES
LONG LIVE DE GAULLE! LONG LIVE EISENHOWER! LONG LIVE
    LECLERC! LONG LIVE OUR LIBERATION!

French Civilians on June 6, 1944

Testimony of Henri-Jean Reynaud[30]

Through the window, we caught a glimpse of the planes and some men jumping out of them, but we didn't realize right away what it was.

Around 6 o'clock, through the bedroom window, we could see some
shadows striking matches to light cigarettes. Some of those shadows were
lying on the ground.

With my father and my eldest brother, we went out to see the house
that had been burning. It was then, while crossing the square, that I saw my
first dead body—a German. And then I saw other corpses, spread all over,
and this time some of them were Americans.

Then I saw my first American parachutist, and I was surprised to see
their faces smeared with soot and their hairstyles like Iroquois Indians.

Later in the morning, when the Americans were able to make contact
with the people of our town, they helped us understand that the Germans
would probably counter-attack.

A few bullets hissed by. Quickly, the streets were empty. We took shelter
in a ditch. Three or four houses were completely destroyed, their roofs blasted.

We couldn't see the church from the place we were in, but we could hear its bells. The sound reassured us since this was not the noise of war, and we thought that in spite of everything the church was still standing.

Testimony of Raymond Paris[31]

Mr. Maury, the notary at Sainte-Mère-Église, who was my boss but also the head of the local resistance network, had told me that when I heard the message "les dés sont sur le tapis" (the dice are on the carpet), that would mean the landings would soon take place. When I heard that message on my radio, it was June 5 and I couldn't help shouting out, "The landings are happening!" I began talking with my parents; then we all went to bed. I was incredibly excited: I went to bed fully clothed and of course I could not get to sleep. At 10 P.M. I heard someone calling me outside. Two friends of mine were in the street, telling me there was a fire at Julia Pommier's house. My father and I went down to join them, and then we ran off to the fire station. We woke up a fireman so he could ring the alarm bell. We got out the hand pump with the pipes, nozzles, and buckets and began to pull it along. While we were getting our breath back after we got to the square, a wave of planes flew over very low. We set off again, and arrived at the burning house. About sixty locals had come out on hearing the bell, and they'd already formed a chain to pass buckets of water. Then there were about thirty Germans there, keeping an eye on the operation.

A second wave of planes arrived. The chain stopped operating as everyone looked up, afraid that bombs would be falling. The Germans shot at the planes. Two minutes went by, and then another wave of planes flew over very low. We could see their doors were open, but there was no time to think about anything else before the boys jumped. The Germans immediately opened fire. I threw my arms to the sky and shouted, "The landings are happening!" Twenty or so paras [paratroopers] fell into the square and all hell broke loose: the Germans fired in all directions and the bullets were whistling past our ears. The soldiers who landed in the trees were killed by the Germans, but the others managed to get rid of their parachutes and hide in the surrounding streets and gardens. The whole thing only lasted a few minutes, in a deafening, racket: the church bell, the planes, the crack of bullets, the shouts and screams. We civilians stood petrified a few moments before coming to our senses and running for shelter.

The whole village was outside before long, and for a few hours we really celebrated victory. But at 8:15, the Germans began bombing the village. We found ourselves in the trench I'd dug two days before, with the neighbors. There was a series of explosions very close by.

Testimony of Renée Couppey[32]

On June 6 in the morning, we saw our first parachutists arriving through the woods next to my parents' house. They were frightening because they were all blackened, with leaves on their helmets, and knives along their legs, and always chewing gum! The next day was even noisier. The Germans and the Americans were fighting all around the house, and some came in through a window, went from room to room, and then went out the other side. We stayed there, 11 members of the same family. Outside, there were awful cries. A bit later, 5 Americans set up a machine-gun in the road. I could see the Germans watching them from a house not too far away. Once the machine-gun was installed, the Germans started shooting. I saw the 5 men jump in the air as their flesh was practically embedded in the wall of the house. One body landed in a tree, while another was buried under a slab of debris with only the arm still moving.

The entire family left for Sainte-Mère-Église. On the road, I saw a German and an American who had stabbed each other with their bayonets. They remained in that position, connected to each other and both dead.

Testimony of Renée Caillemer[33]

Still, four Germans came into my house to hide in a small cellar under the stone staircase. Around 2 A.M., two American parachutists [paras] came in and asked: "Germany?" My daughter and my maid pointed at the cellar. The door resisted, so the two parachutists shot through it. Then the door opened—one German was dead and another was wounded. The paras took the others out to the road to kill them. It was very quick.

Testimony of René Lecalier[34]

I was a member of a resistance group.

As soon as the Americans arrived, they enrolled me. I was sent on a mission to St.-Lô to contact the local resistance leaders and get information about German defenses. I crossed the lines several times, crawling along the ground out of sight. Sometimes I would pose as a farmer with a rope and a bucket so the Germans would think I was looking for a cow. Once they questioned me and shut me up in a barn, but I managed to escape during a bomb attack.

Testimony of Jeanine Gazengel[35]

During the night, we heard the planes and the bombardments. As the time went on, the bombardments were getting louder and louder until it became a deafening uproar. Everything had collapsed in the house. We went out to look for shelter in a trench with two other families. We could hardly breathe because of the smell of gunpowder in the air. . . . About 8 o'clock, my father said: "be quiet! I can hear someone talking!" And a few minutes later, he cried out "but he is talking English!" He went out of the trench right away and a soldier pointed his gun at him. The soldier advanced to the trench and saw the children, so he put down his gun. I was quite impressed.

Testimony of Geneviève Onfroy[36]

All night long, we heard rattling noises and shots. There were also flares. It was beautiful. We saw the first tanks arrive around 10:30 A.M., with the soldiers too. We were afraid they would be Germans, because we didn't recognize their helmets that had leaves on them. They were black all over, and they almost frightened us. They asked, "Germans?" then they searched all through the house.

In the field on the other side of the road, they installed a signal center. There was also an infirmary, just next to it. At the beginning, the Americans were distrustful; we had to taste the water before they would drink because they were afraid of being poisoned. But I also remember a soldier who was walking on the road, and my father said, "the war is over for us," and the soldier answered, "it's just starting for us."

Testimony of Charles Gosselin[37]

There was a 9 P.M. curfew. At 9:30, the bombing started, and we went out to the German shelter just next to the house. The sky was lit up as if by multicolored fireworks. The bombs stopped at about 11:30, and just after that, the planes came to drop their paratroopers. We crawled back into the house then, and I went up into the tower. From up there, I could see the men jumping and falling in the neighboring field. I don't know what they did once they landed. In another nearby field, a glider had hit some trees and flipped over before it reached the ground: all the paras were killed and the plane was full of blood.

In the morning, we saw soldiers going along the road, coming from the beach. They were searching the buildings for Germans. We knew they were Americans because they gave us Camel cigarettes.

From the tower, I also saw Americans attacking the battery behind the house. They were marching with their weapons slung over their shoulders or ready for action, when a shot rang out: one soldier fell to the ground and the others all threw themselves down. Then an officer came up into the tower to shoot at the Germans with his rifle: he killed half of them, and the other half surrendered.

Testimony of Claude Dreno[38]

On June 7th at 8:30 P.M. we heard a muffled sound that was getting louder and closer. Then we saw 45 bombers in three rows of fifteen, then black dots falling away from the planes towards us. My mother and I instantly went to take shelter outside. We knew that when you couldn't hear the bombs whistling, it was a bad sign, because it meant they were heading for you. And we couldn't hear anything until they exploded. It made a terrible racket, like an earthquake. I don't know how long the bombing went on—no doubt only a few minutes, but you lose all sense of time. Obviously, you're frightened and you don't know what's going on. When it's over, you come out pretty well stunned. There's a strange atmosphere over everything: after all that noise, it's silent, you can't hear anything, or it's like hearing through cotton wool. Then there's the dust: everything is yellow. I was so terrified during that air raid, nothing has really frightened me since.

Testimony of Roger Lelaisant[39]

I was an apprentice mechanic at Villedieu. I was 19. And I had belonged to the Villedieu's resistance network since 1942. After taking part in the derailment of the Paris-Granville train, I was arrested by the Gestapo on March 31, 1944. I was interrogated, beaten up, and finally sent to St.-Lô prison on April 4. I shared a cell with ten other prisoners.

On the evening of June 6, the first air raid made us very hopeful. The bombs were falling sort of around the prison, and we were thinking: this is it—we are going to be freed.

We thought a bomb would blow the doors open and we would be able to escape. We could hear it all, but we couldn't see anything: we felt full of hope, without fear, even though the fact of being in prison doesn't make you feel safe from bombs.

I ran away and got involved in resistance work again, mainly helping the Americans.

Testimony of Louis Bihel[40]

In the evening, an officer came by to tell us we shouldn't stay where we were because they were preparing to attack. We went to a stable 500 meters away; there were about 150 people there. We stayed eight nights. In the daytime, we went out to take care of the animals. And while we were doing that, the Germans and Americans were fighting. The Americans would take some ground and the Germans would recapture—it was a constant to and fro. The fighting went on during the night, from midnight until 3 or 4 in the morning. In the morning, they took away their dead. In the afternoon, they rested.

When they came back, it was obvious there were gaps in their ranks. I saw a truck go by full of bodies, Germans and Americans all mixed up, held on by ropes and piled as high as a cart at hay making time. There was a truce when it was time to bring in the dead. The Germans surrendered when they had no more ammunition and food. The battle lasted eight days.

Testimony of Suzanne Duchemin[41]

On June 5, we found out the landings would take place soon because we heard the radio messages for the resistance groups. A few moments later, two paratroopers came into the yard, asking for directions to Sainte-Mère-Église. My husband showed them the way, and then came home to bed.

Of course, we heard the planes, as they skimmed just over the house. We quickly went out onto the first floor balcony to see what was going on. Hundreds of paras [paratroopers] were coming down. It was fantastic; we were totally euphoric: me, my brother, my father and a friend who had not heard any of the racket made by the planes. I woke him up by opening the shutters and, shouting, "François, the Allies are landing!"

Some paras fell into the château grounds. One of them got stuck in a tree and fell quite a way when he cut his parachute straps. We helped him regain consciousness, took all his heavy gear off and carried him into the house, where we made a fire to keep him warm. Other soldiers came by during the morning, stopping just long enough to have a drink before setting off again. In a field 300 meters away there was an injured para, so we went to get him with a stretcher. As we got back to the château, we suddenly heard a group of Germans coming down the road, singing. That's when the battle began. The Germans were on the grounds, fighting with the Americans. We could hear the machine guns, and in the distance the noise of naval cannon fire and the German artilleries. We kept out of sight, moving to a different room whenever bullets started coming through the windows.

Testimony of Georges Dumoncel[42]

Before D-Day, the Germans had requisitioned us to construct their defense line. There were trenches and blockhouses made out of big tree trunks covered in earth.

After two days, I came back to the house to look for some meat: in a field, I saw about fifty German soldiers ready for battle, lined up along a hedge. Near the road there was a machine gun. There wasn't a sound, and you could feel the tension. It was clear the slightest thing could spark it all off. I didn't feel too comfortable. An officer told me the Americans were three kilometers away, and he was right because in the afternoon, around three o'clock, we saw the Americans arriving from Vasteville and Héauville.

They approached the crossroads over the grassy areas, without taking cover. The first five were gunned down. The fighting lasted four days. We could hear the bombs and machine guns, and we could see the dust and smoke. After two days, the Americans called their air force in: first the fighter planes, then the dive-bombers. The German positions were annihilated; the trenches were filled in with the earth thrown up by the explosions, and we were still coming across bodies a week after the fighting was over.

Testimony of Julien Le Bas[43]

Soon we saw two formations of Flying Fortresses approaching from the east, at very high altitude. Two white rockets were fired by the lead plane, and immediately the bombs were dropped. They were just small black dots at first, but got bigger as we watched, falling diagonally with a frightful noise towards the town center. I was petrified, yet I couldn't take my eyes off this loud bombing run.

There was a horrible crash, followed by a cloud of dust so thick that you couldn't make out the town from our vantage point. People were running all over the place trying to find their loved ones, shouting. We heard that a neighboring family was trapped in a concrete trench, and another had been wiped out by a bomb that fell right into their dining room.

We returned to St.-Lô on August 20, not knowing what we should expect. The town had been annihilated, and we were relatively pleased to find our house was only half destroyed. We cleared the rubble and sealed the windows with tar-paper. My father repaired his blacksmith's forge and soon got down to work for the farmers who needed horseshoes.

Testimony of Maurice Nordez[44]

You can say we had a good time at the Liberation. When the Americans arrived, we formed a group of about 20 people to announce it to the people of the village. We woke Alfred Mouchel up, who opened the door with his nightgown on and then uncorked a bottle of cider for the occasion.

Everybody came to the square to see the Americans. Everybody was applauding. . . . As a mechanic, I was very impressed by the Americans and their equipment. Usually, my father did not smoke, but he succumbed to the taste of American cigarettes for a while.

Testimony of Célestin Pellé[45]

[T]he Germans camped in our fields ready for battle. The village was bombed on the night of June 9–10, and then the fighting really began. For three weeks, our farm was between the two lines. The Germans were 50 meters away at the mill, and the Americans were at the bottom of the field on the other side. They often fired at each other, and we were stuck in the middle, along with a lot of people who had fled the village. As soon as the shooting began, we went indoors. A friend of mine had managed to get through to the American lines. When he came back, he had some cigarettes and he offered me one. I'd only just lit it when some Germans arrived, and of course recognized the smell of American tobacco. They questioned us for quite a long time before finally letting us go . . . the guns were always firing, and we regularly saw dead soldiers being brought back from battle.

Testimony of Jean Taboué[46]

On June 10, the whole family—about 15 people—went up to my grandmother's, in La Glacerie. Above all, we wanted to escape the bombardments. As a whole, there were between 150 and 200 people in this quarry. Even if we didn't know each other, there was a great solidarity among us all from the beginning.

We were caught in the middle, the shells passed just above our heads and we had long conversations to try to figure out where the Americans were, according to the trajectory of the shells and the explosions. Beyond these very random speculations, we had no information about how the battle was developing and many of us were anxious. One day, two jeeps turned up in the quarry. The soldiers aimed their guns at us but put them down immediately when the girls climbed up the jeeps and kissed them. It was over.

Testimony of Claude Haize[47]

On June 12, an engineering battalion set up camp, and four days later the work began. My parents had no option: of the 38 hectares covered by our farm, the Americans took 37 for their airfield. In three days, the ground was ready: they pulled out trees and hedges like you or I would pull out a post. In one week I had changed centuries. The first sorties began on June 25th, and the day after that the base was completely finished.

It was the 50th Fighter Group that was stationed there: four squadrons of twenty planes each. At first there were Thunderbolts and then twin fuselage P38s. There were about 2,000 soldiers over the whole base: pilots, mechanics, flak units, and more. The runway was 1,800 meters long and every plane had its own parking area. Then there were mechanical workshops, security services, and sanitary facilities. It was like a small town in the middle of the countryside. We made friends with a lot of the Americans. . . . In the first few days, when the planes returned from their missions, we hurried to count them, to make sure they were all back. When Operation Cobra was on, the activity was continuous: we counted 280 take-offs and landings in a single day.

Testimony of André Gidon[48]

When the first bulldozer arrived in the garden and began its maneuvers, we were amazed. We did not even have a tractor on our farm, so you can imagine the impression a bulldozer made! They used dynamite to get rid of the hedges. We lived right next to the airfield. The landing strip went just behind the house through the garden. Right beside it was the space reserved for a plane called Pee Wee. Every plane had a name, and a pin-up girl painted on its cockpit. They used the runway both ways, depending on the wind.

My mother washed clothes for the mechanics and did everything she could to help them. I spent all my time hanging around them. They were a bit like big brothers for me. I remember one who was called Larry, and then there was Blackie, Tommy, and others. They let us drive their Jeeps. When the planes went on sorties, the mechanics would hook two bombs under the wings, and then the plane would take off and come back half an hour later. It stayed just long enough to hook up two more bombs, and then it would take off again. And that's how it went on all the time, without a break.

Testimony of Paul Bedel[49]

On Wednesday, June 28, an artillery duel went on without a break until Thursday afternoon. The Americans stopped their fire completely at 3 or 4 o'clock. Just then, the heavy bombers turned up—several waves of them. It had been bearable up till then, but now the noise was terrifying, a totally deafening buzz.

As soon as the planes had gone, the firing started up again even more fiercely, and we couldn't believe our ears. Just after that came a massive racket, a tank attack with small shells falling everywhere. There were crashes and bangs all around us. Then at around 7 or 8 o'clock in the evening, things calmed down.

We thought it was the end: the 105 mm guns started shooting again, and so did the tanks. Near the German positions, it was like fireworks with big explosions, fires, crackling sounds. Everything was blown up into the air and smashed to pieces. It was a long and extremely noisy night, a storm of metal and gunfire. I cannot describe the noise, the whistling, the constant sounds. On and on—on and on . . .

A minute later, we saw Allied soldiers coming down the main road, seemingly from all over the place. What surprised us was that unlike the German soldiers, they marched in silence. Their shoes had rubber soles. Then the Jeeps, GMCs and half-tracks arrived. It was all over.

Two hours later, columns of German soldiers began arriving from all directions, without weapons or helmets or cartridge belts, all untidy, their hands on their heads.

Testimony of Raymond Bertot[50]

We left the farm on the night of June 5–6 for a house a bit further away. There were three or four families together there. Around 4 o'clock in the morning, there was a loud banging. The navy and air force really gave it all they had! Looking out of the windows, we could see cows that had been blown into the trees by the explosions. Then suddenly it stopped and there was silence.

We saw the first soldiers walking by on the roads. Two of us were hurt, so we waved to them and a few crawled over to treat the wounded. They were very surprised to find us there, because before the landings the allies had asked all the population of the coastal areas to evacuate. So they thought we were spies. And my father, who had spent all night helping paras, giving them directions and telling them where the Germans were, was carted off immediately. He left France with the first few German prisoners and spent ten days being questioned in England.

Testimony of Raymond Gardie[51]

On June 7 at about 7 o'clock in the evening, we were in the garden outside our house at La Haye-du-Puits. A squadron of planes flew towards us from the southeast. My father and I counted them: there were 17. My father said they hadn't come for us, but just after that we heard the whistle of falling bombs. My father took me and my mother to shelter under the stairs, but before we could get there, I was thrown to the ground by the blast of an explosion. You couldn't see anything; it was dark as night despite the daylight. The bombs had fallen thirty meters from our house. Immediately afterwards, everyone or nearly everyone left the town. There was no panic, but it all happened very quickly. We made up bundles of sheets and clothes, chucked them through the window, and set off on foot. The men kept a low profile so they couldn't be requisitioned by the Germans to dig foxholes for them. This time it was Allied planes that bombed us—twin fuselage P38s—and a whole family from Periers was killed. The Germans made us move on again, to Anneville-sur-Mer, and that's where the Americans liberated us. When we got back to La Haye-du-Puits, it was in ruins. My father said, "we're lucky, our house is still standing!" The whole place had been flattened, but we had regained our freedom. During the occupation, we had been nothing more than pawns, but now we could do what we wanted, even if it was something as simple as just chatting in the street.

Testimony of Emile Bisson[52]

On the night of June 5–6, bombs surrounded Les Martins farm 500 meters from our house. The walls trembled, and the sky outside was lit up with multicolored rockets. In the morning, I went to see my uncle at Saint-Vaast. With his telescope, we could see the ships in the distance.

We could figure out more or less where the Americans were from the noises we heard. It was clear that the battle was getting nearer. The next day, the Americans arrived. It was about 8 P.M., and I was coming home from hay work. We saw a truck parked in front of the house and soldiers. From where we were, we couldn't see whether they were German or not, and we were a bit worried. But as we got nearer, we saw they were American. The whole family was outside—my father gave them cider, and the farmhand took every packet of cigarettes the soldiers gave him. And I smoked my first cigarette.

Testimony of Raymond Lereculey[53]

They arrived in the night. The dogs were barking and we heard someone knocking at the door. There were four of them. Because of their soot-covered faces, we thought they were black. The water dripping off their uniforms was turning our earthen floor into mud. My father lit a fire and offered them some calva. One of them tried it, but managed to make us understand that if they drank too much, they would not feel well. So they had some milk. They left after half an hour.

On Sunday at mass, Madame Bazire came into the church shouting "The boches [krauts] are coming, everyone!" The paras asked us to stay in the church while they went out to fight. People were praying and talking.

We stayed there until mid-afternoon, when a Canadian who could speak French said we could leave if we stayed close to the hedges, and we weren't to say anything about Americans if by chance we passed any Germans. We ran off, seven or eight at a time. I came upon a dead German in the next field, covered in blood. That really upset me.

Testimony of Marie Couespel[54]

The first American vehicle that came to Saint-Pierre-Église just passed through very fast—by the time we realized what had happened, they were already out of sight. Then the jeep turned back and stopped at the road junction near the church right in front of our shop. During the Occupation, I had taken English lessons with a lady who used the Assimil method [short for assimilation—a methodology for learning a foreign language developed in France], and I'd asked her to tell me how you would say "Je suis si contente de vous voir" in English. I wanted to learn this phrase because I was sure that one day the Allies would arrive, and I wanted to greet the first Allied soldier I saw. When I saw the jeep had stopped, I elbowed my way through the twenty or so people that had gathered. They were all talking at once and the soldier was sitting in the jeep with his back to me, so to make myself heard over the noise I practically shouted: "So happy to see you!" The soldier turned round and kissed me on my right cheek. He was unshaven, and I felt the imprint of his kiss on my cheek for a long time. It was a moment of pure happiness.

Testimony of Yves De La Rüe[55]

Two days after the landings, an officer arrived at the farm and asked us to find some men to bury the dead. He also told us we had to bury them in the field opposite the farm. The Americans had known ever since March 1944 that they would set up a cemetery here, because they knew there was not a single pebble or stone in that field. Trucks went through the countryside picking up the bodies, and brought them to us. My job was to collect the personal belongings and put them in a little bag tied up with parachute string. We took the weapons too, and the cigarettes, and at the end of the day, we divided the packets up between all the men who had been digging the graves. To begin with, we buried them in their parachutes, then afterwards in special bags. Later the coffins arrived, so then we had to dig up the ones we'd wrapped in parachutes and bags and put them into their coffins. I did that for two whole weeks.

It was very upsetting work. For the first few days, it made me sick to look at them. I found two soldiers who had come to the farm on June 6 and had given me sweets while I poured them some cider. Both of them were burnt almost beyond recognition—it was horrible, monstrous. But after a bit I got used to handling all these dead men.

We buried six thousand American soldiers, and they stayed here until the Colleville cemetery was opened in 1947.

Testimony of Anne-Marie Lecostey, June 1944[56]

The Americans stayed several days. . . . There were a lot of them. They gave us cigarettes, candy, chocolates, all sorts of things that we did not have for a long time and which gave us real pleasure. It was amazing how much they gave out: they had an abundance that contrasted with the shortages we were used to. They left a lot of food for us when they moved out.

Testimony of French Government—Oradour-Sur-Glane

And the crowning event in these German atrocities—we now come to it will be the destruction of Oradour-sur-Glane, in the month of June 1944. On Saturday, 10 June, beginning in the afternoon, a detachment of SS, belonging very likely to the "Das Reich" Division which was present in the area,[57] burst into the village after having surrounded it entirely, and ordered the population to gather in the central square. It was then announced that a denunciation had indicated that explosives had been hidden in the village and that searches and verifications of identity were about to take place. The men were invited to group together in four or five units, each of which was locked into a barn. The women and children were led into and locked in the church. It was about 1400 hours. A little later machine-gunning began and the whole village was set on fire, as well as the surrounding farms. The houses were set on fire one by one. The operation lasted undoubtedly several hours, in view of the extent of the locality and the town.

In the meantime the women and the children were in anguish as they heard the echoes of the fire and of the shootings. At 1700 hours, German soldiers penetrated into the church and placed upon the communion table an asphyxiating apparatus which comprised a sort of box from which lighted fuses emerged. A little time shortly thereafter the atmosphere became unbreathable. Someone was able to break the door which brought the women and children back to consciousness. The German soldiers then started to shoot through the windows of the church, and they came in to finish off the survivors with machine guns. Then they spread upon the soil inflammable material. One woman was able to escape; she reached the window when the cries of a mother who tried to give her child to her, drew the attention of one of the guards, who fired on the would-be fugitive and wounded her seriously. She saved her life by simulating death and she was later cared for in a hospital of Limoges.

At about 1800 hours the German soldiers stopped the Departmental train which was passing in the vicinity. They told the passengers going to Oradour to get off, and, having machine-gunned them, threw their bodies in the furnace.

Testimony of Marguerite Rouffanche, June 10, 1944[58]—Massacre Survivor

Shoved together in the holy place, we became more and more worried as we awaited the end of the preparations being made for us. At about 4 P.M. some soldiers, about 20 years old placed a sort of bulky box in the nave, near the choir, from which strings were lit and the flames passed to the apparatus which suddenly produced a strong explosion with dense, black, suffocating smoke billowing out. The women and children, half choked and screaming with fright rushed towards the parts of the church where the air was still breathable. The door of the sacristy was then broken in by the violent thrust of one horrified group. I followed in after but gave up and sat on a stair. My daughter came and sat down with me. When the Germans noticed that this room had been broken into they savagely shot down those who had tried to find shelter there. My daughter was killed near me by a bullet fired from outside. I owe my life to the idea that I had to shut my eyes and pretend to be dead.

Firing burst out in the church then straw, sticks and chairs were thrown onto bodies lying on the stone slabs. I had escaped from the killing and was without injury so I made use of a smoke cloud to slip behind the altar. In this part of the church there are three windows. I made for the widest one in the middle and with the help of a stool used to light the candles, I tried to reach it. I don't know how but my strength was multiplied. I heaved myself up to it as best I could and threw myself out of the opening that was offered to me through the already shattered window. I jumped about nine feet down.

When I looked up I saw I had been followed in my climb by a woman holding out her baby to me. She fell down next to me but the Germans, alerted by the cries of the baby, machine-gunned us. The woman and the baby were killed and I too was injured as I made it to a neighboring garden and hid among some rows of peas and waited anxiously for someone to come to help me. That wasn't until the following day at 5 P.M.

Testimony of Survivor, June 10, 1944

At around 4 o'clock, an explosion in the village signaled the start of the massacre. It began simultaneously in each site. The SS fired low, at the men's legs. The executioners continued until nothing moved. They then climbed over the bloody bodies and finished off those unfortunates who were still moving. Then, quite calmly, chatting to each other, they covered the bodies with straw, hay, wood and anything that would burn.

The SS lit the fire they had prepared, and as the flames started to take hold, they moved away.

The fire roared. It was dreadful. The dying and the mortally wounded were burned alive.

Testimony of Germain Voisset, June 6, 1944[59]—Resistance

I was arrested on 14 October 1943 for acts of resistance and imprisoned in the Garonne area. On 6 June 1944 all political prisoners were being transferred to Compiègne. We were guarded by the famous SS division "Das Reich" which was later infamous for burning down the town of Oradour-sur-Glane in France.

On 6 June we could hear bombing taking place and by use of an illegal radio we learned that some train stations had been bombed and that the landing had begun. As a result we hoped that our transfer to a concentration camp would no longer be possible but our hopes were crushed and we were sent to Dachau.

Allied Attempt to Cross the Rhine

In September, Allied forces were moving through Belgium, and under the leadership of newly promoted Field Marshal Montgomery planned a daring paratroop landing in Holland to try to cross the Rhine River, outflank German defenses, and potentially end the war quickly. Operation Market Garden ran into stiff German resistance, and the bridge at Arnhem later became notorious as "a bridge too far." The Allied assault had to be called off after about ten days.[60]

In the Headlines

Belgique, Paris, September 4, 1944
BRUSSELS IS LIBERATED

Belgique, Paris, September 18, 1944
ALLIED PARATROOPERS LANDING IN HOLLAND

The Times, London, September 18, 1944
AIRBORNE ARMY LANDS IN HOLLAND

Extract from a *Diary for Two Dutch Children Written by Their Parents*[61]

On the 18th of September 1944 the town of Eindhoven was liberated by the Second British Army after more than four years and four months of German oppression . . .

The days before the 18th of September: The British Army is fighting in Belgium . . . German resistance is stiff. . . . During the night you would hear gunfire in the distance . . . the very small number of pro-German people flee with many Germans panic-stricken from the city and it is rumored that the English troops will be here now very soon . . .

The activity of Allied aircraft in the air reached a new climax. The gigantic air-armadas form a magnificent sight and the steady drone of their engines sets the windows rattling. . . . But then all of a sudden we don't see anymore Germans, we hear the shouts of joy from the town and in no time flags and orange pennants fly from the houses . . .

The entry of the second British army into Eindhoven! It is a fantastic show. It is unforgettable . . .

They are greeting us with the V-sign or with their thumbs up. . . . Have we ever been so thankful towards complete strangers. . . . They asked us how the Germans treated us and they couldn't believe what we tell them. They shake their heads and say: "Well, that's all over now, you're free again."

. . . In the morning I went up and had with a few friends a glass of champagne in a restaurant packed with people discussing the enormous events of the day before and all of them smiling happily now that the strain of the German oppression had been lifted from their hearts. . . . The public in the restaurant consisted of all sorts of people: civilians, members of the Dutch resistance army who were justly proud of showing themselves for the first time in public with the insignia on their arms and last but not least American paratroopers and British soldiers mixed up with the Dutch people and often wearing orange and red, white and blue in honor of our liberation.

In the Headlines

Le Figaro, Paris, September 19, 1944
LARGE NUMBERS OF ALLIED PARATROOPERS LAND IN HOLLAND
GENERAL MONTGOMERY ATTACKS ON THE BELGIAN-DUTCH
   BORDER

The Times, London, September 21, 1944
BRITISH REACH THE RHINE
FIERCE STRUGGLE FOR BRIDGE AT NIJMEGEN

Belgique, Paris, September 24, 1944
FIERCE BATTLE IN HOLLAND

The Times, London, September 28, 1944
2,000 MEN RETURN FROM ARNHEM
LAST OF AIRBORNE DIVISION WITHDRAWN

Le Figaro, Paris, September 29, 1944
GERMAN RESISTANCE REMAINS STRONG

Testimony of John Torreano, September 1944—82nd Airborne

The next battle I remember was the one they call "a bridge too far" when
General Montgomery wanted to cross into Germany. General Gavin led us
to a bridge near Nijmegen on a beautiful Sunday afternoon but the battle
turned real ugly and then the British unit didn't show up. They couldn't get
to us like they were supposed to and we had to pull back. That was real bad.

Battles Of Hürtgen and Bulge

Two of the most difficult battles on the western front took place in the
late fall and winter of 1944: the Battles of Hürtgen and Bulge.[62] Allied
forces were convinced that the Germans were facing defeat, but the
closer the Allies moved toward German territory the harder the
Germans seemed to fight. Both of these battles—Hürtgen and the
Bulge—fought in foggy, freezing, and snowy conditions, were
remembered by all participants as among the most brutal of the war.

Testimony of Chester Mikus, Fall–Winter 1944[63]—Hürtgen Forest

We went there [Normandy], we broke out of St.-Lô with some of the three
divisions landed. After we broke out it was pretty easy going until we hit the
Hürtgen Forest. Then we had to wait for our supplies to catch up with us.
And then in the Hürtgen Forest those Germans really mauled us. And then
they pulled us off the line. And the next morning we got orders to go to the
Bulge, and that's when the Germans broke there.

Oh yeah, I brought back a rifle, a helmet, and a pistol that we took from
a prisoner. And that's about it.

Testimony of Leroy D. "Whitey" Schaller, Fall–Winter 1944[64]—Hürtgen Forest

I did join the 28th Division as a rifleman and I was pretty happy with that.
I saw a lot of combat. I was in Hürtgen Forest and that is a terrible place.
That's where—in the Ardennes? It's in an area where the Germans had
come through in World War I and again in World War II. It was before the

Battle of the Bulge. It was in—actually it was mostly from September to November—September to November of '44 I believe.

Actually the whole division suffered 107 percent casualties. We lost five thousand killed in action. And there were several other divisions that lost the same number there. We lost that in two weeks. So, we would get 200 men and I know one time we had 200 men come in in the afternoon and in the morning there were only 90 fit for duty. I don't remember a whole lot about the Hürtgen Forest Campaign. Actually I thought I came in on the morning of the 16th, the 15th and left on the morning of the 16th. Forty years later they proved to me that I actually spent six days there. If you were alive two hours after you were there, you were a veteran. And because I didn't realize I was in Hürtgen there. I froze my feet there. Well we left there on the 16th and I froze my feet sometime in that time and I didn't know it until Thanksgiving.

In the Headlines

Atlanta Journal, Atlanta, December 17, 1944
NAZIS COUNTERATTACK ALONG WIDE FRONT
HEAVY FIGHTING RAGES IN ARDENNES FOREST

Le Journal de Genève, Geneva, December 18, 1944
GERMAN COUNTER-OFFENSIVE IN THE ARDENNES AND ALSACE

Le Journal de Genève, Geneva, December 19, 1944
MARSHAL RUNDSTEDT'S OFFENSIVE GAINS TERRITORY IN BELGIUM
    AND LUXEMBURG[65]

Le Figaro, Paris, December 19, 1944
GERMAN ARMY LAUNCHES FIRST GREAT OFFENSIVE ON THE
    WESTERN FRONT
FIRST AMERICAN ARMY ON GERMAN-BELGIAN BORDER ABSORBS
    THE SHOCK

Le Monde, Paris, December 19, 1944
THE GERMAN ARMY COUNTER-ATTACKS ALONG BORDERS OF
    BELGIUM-LUXEMBURG

La Presse Cherbourgeoisie, Cherbourg, December 21, 1944
THE GERMAN COUNTER-OFFENSIVE CONTINUES BUT THE
    AMERICAN ARMY OPPOSES IT WITH A LARGE FORCE OF MEN AND
    EQUIPMENT

Bruxelles-Paris [formerly *Belgique*], Paris, December 21, 1944
STRONG COUNTER-ATTACK BY 1ST AMERICAN ARMY

Le Figaro, Paris, December 22, 1944
GERMAN OFFENSIVE CONTINUES IN SECTORS OF MONTJOIE AND
    MALMÉDY

Le Monde, Paris, December 25, 1944
THE ALLIES COUNTER-ATTACK ON THE FLANKS OF THE GERMAN
   OFFENSIVE

Bruxelles-Paris, Paris, December 28, 1944
GERMAN OFFENSIVE PROGRESSES TOWARD THE MEUSE

Le Figaro, Paris, December 29, 1944
ALLIES FOLLOW THEIR ADVANTAGE TO THE SOUTH OF THE ENEMY
   SALIENT—CONTROL BASTOGNE AND ECHTERNACH

Testimony of Glen Brutus, December 1944[66]—Battle of the Bulge

And then we walked and rode up into the Ardennes. And we were there
when the Battle of the Bulge started on the 16th of December. We were the
first outfit hit by the Germans in the Battle of the Bulge. We covered a
27-mile front. My division, that's 15,000 men. You're only supposed to be
covering a five-mile front when you're under attack, so they went through us
like . . . The morning of the 19th about daylight, the colonel come by and
said, "You better get dug in. All hell is going to break loose." And it did. And
he got killed the 19th of December. 1500 men in a battalion. When we were
walking down the road as 1500 men, he was number 1, and I was number 2.
I was the second guy behind him. After the lieutenant colonel got killed, the
major took over. He had never been in combat so we didn't listen to him
much. We listened to a lieutenant who had been in combat in the South Pacific. So somebody, one sergeant hollered out, "We might as well surrender.
We're surrounded with Germans, machine guns." We didn't surrender right
away. I was crawling through the evergreens to get away from the rest of my
buddies, because they were drawing fire in on top of us. So I got underneath
a little evergreen there with my carbine. While I was laying underneath there
to wait to see what happened, I thumbed through my English-German translation book to figure out what I was going to say if the Germans came up to
me. Came to word—*nicht schiessen*—that's don't shoot.
   So when he [German soldier] got about even with me, I hollered at him,
"nicht schiessen!" He come over and stuck his head under there and his
mouth dropped open. "Raus!" I come up with my hands up. A kraut took a
pot shot at me. Somebody shot. It had to be a German, because all Americans quit firing.
   . . . I dumped my duffel—my gas mask container out on the ground. I
had D-bars and some personal stuff in it. And he picked up what he wanted
out of it off the ground and put it in his pocket, this German did. Cigarettes,
yeah, he took them too. And then we got down to the bottom of the hill
and walked over towards an old barn there. And they had a bunch of
Germans and Americans there, been wounded there in the barn. That's
where our first—that's when I run onto my first sergeant there. He'd been

captured too. And it wasn't long before some officer come up and motioned us to start down the road. So, it got dark, of course. This happened a little bit before dark. Next morning they shoved us out on the road, and there was GIs as far as you could see in both directions about six abreast. "Jesus Christ, they caught the whole American army." That's hard to handle.

Testimony of John Torreano, December 1944—82nd Airborne

They pulled us back into France for some rest but then the Battle of the Bulge started. This time we didn't jump into battle—they trucked us to Belgium but we didn't have the right coats or gloves or boots for that weather. Basically we just scavenged for equipment—if you saw a dead soldier, didn't matter if he was American or German, you would take his coat or boots or whatever. The whole battle was not organized. We had one incident where 5 of us entered an abandoned Belgian farmhouse and surprised 4 Germans who were hiding in the barn. So we made a deal with them. We told them to sleep downstairs and we slept upstairs and in the morning they went on their way and we went on ours. That was because it was pretty impossible to take prisoners—what were we going to do with them and we didn't want to just shoot them. But plenty of prisoners just were shot by both sides at that time.

Testimony of John J. Bertram, Jr., December 1944[67]—Battle of the Bulge

We were then transported by truck to Eastern Belgium to a small town called Krinkelt where we set up the headquarters for the 924th Field Artillery. In, say about December 19, 1944, the 1st Sergeant came into the headquarters and said, "There's been a small breakthrough, and we need to pack up and get out." About the time we were ready to leave, the German tanks pulled into the town, and this turned out to be the Battle of the Bulge. I spent several hours in a foxhole in the backyard of our headquarters until our commanding officer surrendered after a German tank pointed its gun into the basement where the personnel from our group were hiding, period. We were marched eastward. I don't recall the town where we stopped, but we were subsequently loaded onto German boxcars to the—to be transferred to a POW camp. This being December, it was very cold.

Testimony of David Saltman, December 1944[68]—Battle of the Bulge

In December 1944, I radioed my unit and got a sharp message from the battalion commander: "Silence your radio and return immediately. Out." About twenty minutes later I came across the 638th Tank Destroyer

Battalion passing me in the opposite direction. I made a u-turn and joined the column, which I later learned was en route to Belgium.

They were wailing and moaning about the fall of Malmédy. We wound around narrow country roads en route to the town of Marche. We were attached to the 84th Infantry Division. It was foggy and very cold.

The Germans lost no time greeting us with artillery fire. The next day was a beehive of activity. Troops pulled out of town and the civilians left in droves. The 84th Division headquarters pulled back, felling trees as road blocks.

The fighting was fierce. Task forces were sent out in every direction and the American soldier performed far beyond expectation.

The front line was a semi-circle around Marche with the Germans holding the high ground. They had complete control and knocked out two of our tank destroyers, burning in an open field. I went up a dirt road heading for high ground in a jeep. A German tank shell fired at me, lost its target and exploded down the far side of the hill. There were many close calls like that in the Battle of the Ardennes.

In the next seven days we changed from the defensive to the offensive and captured that important ridgeline. The siege of Marche had ended.

The weather became very cold, as low as −20 degrees. Water in my canteen froze into solid ice.

Buzz bombs flew 100 feet overhead, probably headed for England where they did considerable damage on impact.

Slowly but surely we drove the Germans back with heavy casualties on both sides.

Of particular interest in this battle was the Belgian city of Bastogne. While the Germans were overrunning Belgium, the 101st Airborne Division was surrounded, completely cut off in Bastogne. When the Germans demanded the surrender of the town, Major General Anthony McAuliffe[69] gave his famous reply, "Nuts!" Bastogne was one of the few Belgian cities that was never occupied by the Germans.

Eastern Front, Occupation, Concentration Camps

Throughout the year, the eastern front remained a center for fierce combat and brutality. For Allied bombers, the Ploesti oil fields in Romania were an important target. The Soviet military advanced and liberated German occupied areas. As the Red Army moved west, the Allies took the opportunity to warn Axis powers that their punishment would be lessened if they dropped out of the war. Nevertheless, the Nazis continued their racial policy of eliminating populations in the concentration camp system. The testimonies of survivors from different countries provide an indication of the barbarity of German actions.

Testimony of Fred Litty[70]—B-17 Over Romania

I flew a B-17. The first thing to do was to wipe out their [German] Air Force. And the big thing was, when the 15th [Air Force] was formed, that was one of the assignments, was to destroy their petroleum facilities. But that wasn't very easy to do because of the distance we had to fly and the fact that we didn't have—our fighter escort wasn't capable, because of fuel limitations, of following us for the—for that distance.

You asked did you fly every day? This is the February flight log. And 10, 14, 15, 17, 20th, 22nd, 24th . . . if you counted these all up, it wouldn't come to 50. Yet I'm credited with 50 missions. When they exceeded a certain distance or whatever or timewise—I think it was all based on distance—we were credited with two missions. And the Ploesti oil fields—they usually counted as two missions because of the distance involved.

The antiaircraft, I think, would get to almost 30,000, I think, to maybe— or I'm going to say 25,000. And some of them, I know, were higher than that. But I think that's what they considered the maximum height for antiaircraft fire . . . we never flew straight courses. And—but the target—they were always very, very thick with antiaircraft.

We've got in our squadron nine airplanes. And the fighters [German] come in on you—usually they like to come head-on, sometimes six abreast. And so every gun in the front of the airplane and on top of the airplane is firing at them.

You can only have so much gross weight in an airplane. If you're using all but 4,000 pounds for fuel, what can you do? You're limited on bomb load.

Allies Warn German Partners on Staying in War, May 1944

1. The Axis satellites, Hungary, Romania, Bulgaria, and Finland, despite their realization of the inevitability of a crushing Nazi defeat and their desire to get out of the war are by their present policies and attitudes contributing materially to the strength of the German war-machine.

2. These nations still have it within their power, by withdrawing from the war and ceasing their collaboration with Germany and by resisting the forces of Nazism by every possible means, to shorten the European struggle, diminish their own ultimate sacrifices, and contribute to the Allied victory.

3. While these nations cannot escape their responsibility for having participated in the war at the side of Nazi Germany, the longer they continue at war in collaboration with Germany the more disastrous will be the consequences to them and the more rigorous will be the terms which will be imposed upon them.

4. These nations must therefore decide now whether they intend to persist in their present hopeless and calamitous policy of opposing the inevitable Allied victory, while there is yet time for them to contribute to that victory.

Testimony of Samuel Pisar, June 6, 1944[71]—Polish Survivor

The famous and heroic day, the landing in Normandy on 6 June 1944, was in Auschwitz a day like all others in the camp. The number of inmates who were gassed to death exceeded the losses of the Allies on the beaches of northern France on "the longest day."

In terms of Poland, which aided the SS in its deliveries to the camps, the news arrived a bit later that a landing had taken place someplace in the west.

Some prisoners whispered that the Russians were also engaged in a counterattack on the eastern front—it seemed unimaginable.

The British resistance, the advance of the Red Army, the American mobilization had stopped the inevitable conquest of the world by the Reich. Unbelievable.

Testimony of Stanislav Mikhailovich Severinovsky[72]—Soviet Army

I was drafted in March of 1943. I was sent to a machine-gun school which I completed in April of 1943. I was awarded the rank of second lieutenant and sent to the 1st Belorussian Front to take a position as a platoon commander.

When I arrived, I was assigned to Regiment 321 of Division 15 in the 65th Army. In May of 1944, there were preparations going on for the offensive to liberate Belorussia. In mid-May, the offensive of the 1st and the 2nd Belorussian Fronts began. Our regiment participated in the liberation of such cities as Baranovichi and Osipovichi. By August, we reached the border with Poland. In Polish territory, I was especially struck by the concentration camp Treblinka: huge piles of shoes, personal belongings, and human hair. The fields around the camp were covered with ashes, and human figures could be seen in the fields—people wondering in the fields and trying to find gold dentures in the ashes.

We were proud of the fact that we were in the military and in action. What were we fighting for? For the Motherland, for Stalin. Were we scared? It varied. At first, every explosion would startle us. Later we got used to explosions, shooting, seeing disfigured dead human bodies.

What did we think about the Germans? We thought: kill him or he will kill you. Eye for eye, tooth for tooth. About Americans we were talking in the context of the Second Front.

In October 1944, we crossed the Narev and the Vistula rivers, to the north of Warsaw, and after severe fighting took control of the front line.

For us Hitler was the epitome of evil on earth due to persecution of communists, Jews, book burning, and invasion of neighboring countries.

For us Stalin was the leader of the world proletariat, the friend of all children.

Testimony of Leslie Werwicki—Buchenwald

I happened to be on June 6, 1944 a Polish political prisoner of the Nazis, number 10941 in the extermination camp of Buchenwald in Thuringia, thousands of kilometers away from the Normandy beaches.

As usual in the camp every prisoner had to work, and at that time I was doing compulsory work in an irrigation commando involving hundreds of prisoners like me.

We learned about the Normandy Allied landing because the SS camp command decided to relay the news at noontime from the main gate via a speaker system that carried the sound throughout the camp for everybody to hear.

Naturally the official German broadcast stipulated that the Allied invasion would be defeated. To me and all my fellow prisoners this German announcement raised our spirit and assured us that Germany will be defeated for sure and we will be certainly liberated before too long by the victorious Allies. The liberation came 10 months later on April 11, 1945.

In the Headlines

Belgique, Paris, September 5, 1944
FINLAND SURRENDERS

Le Journal de Genève, Geneva, September 26, 1944
THREE RUSSIAN ARMIES MARCH ON RIGA

Le Journal de Genève, Geneva, September 30, 1944
NEW RUSSIAN ADVANCES IN SLOVAKIA AND TRANSYLVANIA

Le Monde, Paris, December 19, 1944
FRANCE AND U.S.S.R. SIGN TREATY OF ALLIANCE AND MUTUAL
   ASSISTANCE

Le Journal de Genève, Geneva, December 27, 1944
RUSSIAN TROOPS OCCUPY SUBURBS OF BUDAPEST

Testimony of Alexandra Petrovna Medvedeva-Nazarkina[73]— Soviet Sniper

When the war started, I had just finished the second year of high school. I was directed to the female school of sniper training. I successfully finished this school and arrived at the front at the end of 1943. Sometimes we could only wash ourselves with snow. I remember how I killed my first fascist. While observing enemy positions, I spotted a machine gunner. I aimed and shot. Everyone was joyous; they hurried to congratulate me. And I wept, for I had killed a man. For the killing of my 10 first Hitlerites I was awarded with the medal "For Courage." The battles were hard and bloody. In 1944 there was heavy fighting in Poland. An enemy sniper appeared in one location, and we suffered appreciable losses: our commander, a scout, and many signalmen were killed. There came an order: "Destroy fascist sniper!" Three of us went to carry out the order. We soon discovered the lair of the enemy sniper and eliminated him, as well as other positions of the Germans. Our task was fully accomplished! I had 43 eliminated fascists on my personal account.

Stalin Order of the Day, November 7, 1944

The Red Army and the Soviet people are ready to strike new devastating blows at the enemy. The days of the blood-stained Hitlerite regime are numbered. Under the blows of the Red Army the fascist bloc has finally crumbled to pieces. Hitlerite Germany has lost most of its Allies. The large-scale operation in Western Europe, carried out with consummate skill by the armies of our Allies, brought about the defeat of the German forces in France and Belgium, and the liberation of these countries from fascist occupation. The allied troops have crossed Germany's western frontiers. The joint blows of the Red Army and the Anglo-American troops against Hitlerite Germany have brought nearer the hour of the victorious conclusion of the war. The encirclement of Hitlerite Germany is being completed. The den of the fascist beast has been invested on all sides, and no tricks of the enemy will save him from imminent complete defeat.

The Red Army and the armies of our Allies have taken up the initial positions for the decisive offensive against the vital centers of Germany. Now the task is to crush Hitlerite Germany within the shortest possible time, through a vigorous onslaught of the armies of the United Nations.

Testimony of Karol Wierzbicki[74]—Polish Camp Survivor

For some reason, unknown to him even today, the Gestapo was convinced, that 2nd Lieutenant Wierzbicki was familiar with plans for the Allied invasion of Western Europe. One day, in the early stage of the invasion, Wierzbicki was transported from Dora-Mittelbau to nearby Gestapo headquarters, where they attempted to obtain information of this operation from him. Of course, this interrogation did not contribute anything new to the Gestapo's intelligence about the invasion. However, during the interrogation, Wierzbicki had enough time to acquaint himself with a wall map, where current developments of the invasion were shown in detail. He was filled with a renewed sense of hope.

As a prisoner in concentration camps, Karol Wierzbicki witnessed the unimaginable moral degeneration of the oppressors and the utter physical deterioration of their victims. Although he survived, the threat of death was ever-present, as he witnessed the deaths of inmates every day. A particularly deep impression was left on him when the Hitlerites hung twenty prisoners accused of sabotage. Fellow-inmates were forced to watch the execution, which was done to prevent any future acts of sabotage.

Freedom, which came on April 15, 1945, was preceded by a transfer to another concentration camp—Bergen-Belsen, known for its horrible living conditions.

Testimony of Maurice Lampe[75]—French Prisoner Of War

The journey lasted three days and three nights under particularly vile conditions—104 deportees in a cattle truck without air . . . we arrived at Mauthausen on the morning of 25 March 1944, in temperature 12 degrees below zero.[76]

I mention, however, that from the French border we traveled in trucks, naked.

When we arrived at Mauthausen, the SS officer who received this convoy of about 1,200 Frenchmen informed us in the following words, which I shall quote from memory almost word for word: "Germany needs your arms. You are, therefore, going to work, but I want to tell you that never again will you see your families. Who enters this camp, will leave it only by the chimney of the crematorium."

. . . I was then selected to work in a work gang in a stone quarry. The quarry at Mauthausen was in a hollow about 800 meters from the camp proper. There were 186 steps leading down to it.

It was a particularly hard Calvary, because the steps were so rough-hewn that even to go up without a load was extremely tiring . . .

We started work at seven o'clock in the morning. By eight o'clock, one hour later, two of my comrades had already been murdered. They were murdered because they had not understood the order, given in German, detailing them for a task. We were frequently beaten because of our inability to understand the German language.

On the evening of that first day—15 April 1944, we were told to carry the two corpses to the top, and we had to go up 186 steps with a corpse, and we all were beaten before we reached the top.

Life in Mauthausen was one long cycle of torture and of suffering . . .

During September—I think it was on 6 September 1944 there came to Mauthausen a small convoy of 47 British, American and Dutch officers. They were airmen who had come down by parachute. They had been arrested after they had tried to make their way back to their country. Because of this they were condemned to death by a German Court. They had been in prison about a year and were brought to Mauthausen for execution.

On their arrival they were transferred to the "bunker," the camp prison. They were made to undress and had only their pants and a shirt. They were barefooted.

The following morning they answered the roll-call at seven o'clock. The working gangs went to their tasks. The 47 officers were assembled in front of the office and were told by the commanding officer of the camp that they were all under sentence of death.

I must mention that one of the American officers asked the commander that he should be allowed to meet his death as a soldier. In reply, he was lashed with a whip and beaten. The 47 were led barefoot to the quarry.

For all the prisoners at Mauthausen the murder of these men has remained in their minds like a scene from Dante's Inferno. The procedure was: At the bottom of the steps they loaded stones on the backs of these poor wretches and they had to carry them to the top. The first ascent was made with stones weighing 25 to 30 kilos and was accompanied by blows. Then they were made to run down. For the second ascent the stones were still heavier, and whenever the poor wretches sank under their burden, they received kicks and blows with a bludgeon—even stones were hurled at them.

In the evening when I rejoined the gang with which I was then working, the road which led to the camp was a path of blood. I almost stepped on a lower jaw of a man. Twenty-one bodies were strewn along the road. Twenty-one had died on the first day. The twenty-six others died the following morning . . .

I would like to cite another example of an atrocity which remains clearly in my memory. This also took place during September 1944. That evening the roll call took longer than usual. Someone was missing. After a long wait and searches carried out in the various blocks, they found a Russian, a Soviet prisoner, who perhaps had fallen asleep, and had forgotten to answer roll call; what the reason was we never knew, but at any rate he was not present at the roll call. Immediately the dogs and the SS went, seized the poor wretch, and before the whole camp—I was in the front row, not because I wanted to be, but because we were arranged like that—we witnessed the fury of the dogs let loose upon this unfortunate Soviet man. He was torn to bits in the presence of the whole camp.

I should add that this man, in spite of his sufferings, faced his death in a particularly brave manner.

Testimony of Solomon Radasky[77]—Polish Holocaust Survivor

Twice a day we carried sand to Birkenau to cover the ashes of the dead. The sand was to cover the ashes that came from the crematoria. I did this for more than a year.

The ovens were on one side of the crematoria, and the ashes came out this side. The other side was where the gas chamber was. The Sonderkommando took the ashes out of the ovens. There were big holes for the ashes and we covered the ashes with sand.

I saw when the transports came. I saw the people who were going in, who to the right and who to the left. I saw who was going to the gas chambers. I saw the people going to the real showers, and I saw the people going to the gas. In August and September of 1944 I saw them throw living children into the crematorium. They would grab them by an arm and a leg and throw them in.

The Russians were pushing back the Germans at Stalingrad. Transports were coming from the Lodz ghetto.[78] That is when we saw them grab the little children by the head and the leg and throw them into the crematoria alive. Then the Hungarian people were coming.

Testimony of Victor Dupont[79]—French Buchenwald Survivor

When I arrived at Buchenwald I soon became aware of the difficult living conditions. The regime imposed upon the prisoners was not based on any principle of justice . . .

Every imaginable kind of beating, immersion in bath-tubs, squeezing of testicles, hanging, crushing of the head in iron bands, and the torturing of entire families in each other's sight. I have, in particular, seen a wife tortured before her husband, and children were tortured before their mothers.

. . . At Buchenwald various elements described as "political," "national"—mainly Jews and gypsies—and "social"—especially criminals— were herded together under the same regime. There were criminals of every nation: Germans, Czechs, Frenchmen, etc., all living together under the same regime. I shall give one example: In 1944 a convoy of several hundred gypsy children arrived at Buchenwald—by what administrative mystery we never knew. They were assembled during the winter of 1944 and were to be sent on to Auschwitz to be gassed.

One of the most tragic memories of my detention is the way in which these children, knowing perfectly well what was in store for them, were driven into the vans, screaming and crying. They went on to Auschwitz the same day . . .

Later on, the executions in Buchenwald took place in the camp itself. To my own knowledge they began in September 1944. . . . The men were done away with by means of inter-cardiac injections. The execution was performed by injecting phenol into the heart in the most brutal manner. The bodies were then carted to the crematorium mostly during roll-calls or at night.

The prisoners were forced to be present at hangings under threats of the most cruel beatings. When they hanged the poor wretches, the prisoners had to give the Hitler salute.

Worse still, one prisoner was chosen to pull away the stool on which the victim stood. He could not evade the order, as the consequences to himself would have been too grave. When the execution had been carried out, the prisoners had to file in front of the victims between 2 SS men. They were made to touch the body and look the dead man in the eyes . . .

Testimony of Rudolf Mildner[80]—Nazi Officer

Probably in July or August of 1944 the commanders received an order by Himmler with the contents that the members of all English-American commando groups should be turned over to the Sipo [security police] by the armed forces. The Sipo was to interrogate these men and then shoot them after the questioning. The shooting was to be made known to the armed forces in the communiqué saying that the commando force had been annihilated in battle.

The decree indicated that it had been drawn up by Himmler and the supreme commander of the ground forces Keitel.[81] The decree was classified "top secret." It was to be destroyed immediately after reading.

It made no difference whether the member of the commando unit was in civilian clothes or in uniform.

I believe I can remember a decree by R.F. SS Himmler ordering all agents dropped by parachute in uniform or civilian clothes, to be treated like members of commando units.

Testimony of Dieter Wisliceny —Nazi Officer

After the entry of the German troops into Hungary, Eichmann went there personally with a large command. I was assigned to Eichmann's command. Eichmann began his activities in Hungary at the end of March 1944. The first measure adopted by Eichmann in co-operation with these Hungarian Government officials was the concentration of the Hungarian Jews in special places and special localities. The action was initiated in mid-April 1944.

. . . Eichmann suggested to the Hungarians that these Jews be transported to Auschwitz and other camps. The evacuation was carried out by the Hungarian Police.

This operation affected some 450,000 Jews.

They were, without exception, taken to Auschwitz and brought to the final solution.

In October-November 1944 about 30,000 of these Jews, perhaps a few thousand more, were removed from Budapest and sent to Germany. They were to be used to work on the construction of the so-called Southeast Wall, a fortification near Vienna. They were mostly women.

They had to walk from Budapest to the German border—almost 200 kilometers. They were assembled in marching formations and followed a route specially designated for them. Their shelter and nutrition on this march was extremely bad. Most of them fell ill and lost strength . . .

Q: Approximately how many Jews were affected by measures of the Secret
     Police and SD in those countries about which you have personal
     knowledge?
     Wisliceny: In Slovakia there were about 66,000, in Greece about 64,000,
                and in Hungary more than half a million. . . . In Bulgaria, to my
                understanding about 8,000; in Croatia I know of only 3,000
                Jews who were brought to Auschwitz in the summer of 1942
                . . .
Q: . . . did you gain any knowledge or information as to the total number of
     Jews killed under this program?
     Wisliceny: Eichmann personally always talked about at least 4 million
                Jews. Sometimes he even mentioned 5 million. According to
                my own estimate I should say that at least 4 million must have
                been destined for the so-called final solution. He [Eichmann]
                said he would leap laughing into the grave because the feeling
                that he had 5 million people on his conscience would be for
                him a source of extraordinary satisfaction.

CHAPTER 8

Allied Victory, 1945

Introduction to 1945

The summit at Yalta in February 1945 was one of the most important meetings of the twentieth century. Roosevelt, Churchill, and Stalin tried to resolve a long list of issues while they awaited Germany's defeat. As Allied armies advanced through France and Eastern Europe, the Yalta Communiqué reaffirmed general principles on unconditional surrender and continued military consultation. The "big three" agreed to the postwar division of Germany into zones of occupation, reparation payments by Germany, creation of a United Nations, a pledge to help rebuild a free and economically viable Europe, a similar pledge to create a democratic Poland, and a plan to establish a coalition government in Yugoslavia.

Following the Yalta Communiqué, the general principles that had been announced were elaborated in the Protocol, signed by the foreign ministers (Stettinius, Molotov, and Eden)[1] of the three Allied nations. The Protocol was the specific implementation of the principles of the Communiqué. To underscore the importance of particular details, Roosevelt, Stalin, and Churchill signed the special addenda on reparations from Germany and an agreement on Japan.

Roosevelt's health, already deteriorating at the beginning of 1945, was adversely affected by the strains of the long trip to Yalta. The ailing president considered the Yalta agreements extremely important, and he spent his last six weeks trying to convince Congress and the American public of the importance of the accords. He did so despite his own valid concerns that Stalin would not live up to his promises, especially on Poland and the democratization of Eastern Europe. Despite positive rhetoric on the Polish issue coming out of Yalta, this item had not been resolved and continued to be one of the most important and bitter disputes of 1945 (and after). In the period between the Yalta summit and his death in April, Roosevelt registered his disappointment with the lack of Soviet-American consultation on the Polish issue. Roosevelt sent message after message to Stalin asking the Soviet Union to honor its commitment on the creation of a democratic Poland. Stalin continually shifted the issue and even claimed that he was powerless to prevent his own government (Presidium of the Supreme Soviet) from recognizing the Provisional Government of Poland (the pro-Soviet or Lublin government).

Roosevelt felt that reasonable procedures had been established at Yalta for transforming the Lublin (Warsaw) Government into a coalition regime (Polish Provisional Government of National Unity) that would include all Polish parties. Because of the military reality of Soviet occupation of Polish territory, the United States accepted the prominent role that members of the Lublin Government would play in any new government; nevertheless Roosevelt protested Soviet attempts to block the inclusion of other Polish representatives. Roosevelt correctly predicted the negative consequences for postwar cooperation if the Allies split over Poland. Responding forcefully to Roosevelt's objections, Stalin insisted that problems in this area had been caused by American and British attempts to violate the Yalta agreements. The Soviet government claimed that it would accept the reconstitution of the Polish government, but only if a majority of the members were from the Lublin Government and if all new members accepted other Soviet conditions.

Despite the split on the Polish issue, Roosevelt focused publicly on the positive aspects of the Protocol, including plans for the disarmament and de-Nazification of Germany. While punitive measures were planned for Germany's leaders, Roosevelt assured the German people that the Allies favored the rehabilitation of that country as soon as possible. Mindful of Germany's isolation after World War I, Roosevelt did not want a repetition of that situation and its negative consequences.

The conversation among Allied leaders halted temporarily on April 12 with the death of President Roosevelt. Later the same month, Axis rulers perished—Mussolini at the hands of Italian partisans and Hitler by suicide as the Reich crumbled around him. At the same time Allied armies met in Germany; new president Harry Truman[2] issued a statement praising President Roosevelt for his wartime leadership while looking forward to the final victory ahead. Stalin also celebrated the meeting of Soviet and American forces in Germany and promised that the Allies would continue to work together to destroy the enemy.

Despite this seeming cordiality, the fate of Poland continued to dominate Allied discourse and haunted the possibility for true postwar cooperation. After Roosevelt's death, Truman and Churchill objected to Soviet obstruction on the creation of a democratic Polish government. They recommended that Poles representing all political positions be invited to Moscow for consultation, but like Roosevelt, their options were constrained by the military situation in Eastern Europe.

Stalin's response on Poland foreshadowed the hardening of positions on both sides.[3] Complaining that the United States and Britain were ignoring the Soviet Union's security needs, Stalin pointed out that he had not been consulted and had not attempted to intervene in the formation of the governments of Belgium and Greece because of their importance to the British. He accepted British influence in those countries. Similarly, he argued that the U.S.S.R. "is entitled to seek in Poland a Government that would be friendly to it."[4] The disagreement continued into (and exacerbated) the Cold War era.

While this debate raged, the Allies made military progress toward
the final defeat of Germany. At the beginning of the year, American
and British forces brought the Battle of the Bulge to an end at the
same time that the Red Army entered Warsaw. In March, the western
Allies crossed the Rhine River at Remagen (the Ludendorff Bridge)
and other locations while the Russians continued their advance in
Poland. In liberating all of this territory, the Allies uncovered the full
extent and horror of German occupation policies. By mid-April Soviet
forces were closing in on Berlin, and with the war in Europe nearing
conclusion, the Allies again warned the Germans that they would be
held responsible for the mistreatment of prisoners, internees, and
deportees.

With Germany defeated and occupied, and aware that the mistakes
of 1918 and 1919 had allowed future German leaders to claim that
they had not lost the Great War, the Allies made sure that the German
military signed the articles of surrender. The American, British,
French, and Soviet occupying forces ordered all Germans to cooperate
in the transfer of property, transportation, and communications to
Allied control. All Nazi military organizations were abolished, and
Germans were not allowed to leave the country without Allied
permission.

After Japan's defeat, Truman appealed for Stalin's help in settling
outstanding issues related to the peace treaties to "stop the
undermining of confidence in the ability of the Great Powers to work
together and [to] give renewed hope to a world longing for peace."
The president further recommended the creation of a commission
under United Nations auspices to examine "the control of atomic
energy in the interest of world peace."[5]

As the year ended, Stalin asserted that the conference of ministers in
Moscow was moving in a positive direction and contributing to
"proper mutual understanding between our countries in this period of
transition from war to peace." The Soviet leader claimed that he was
looking forward to "further opportunities for coordinating the policies
of our countries on other issues."[6] In reality, there was little to hold
this alliance together. Once the common enemy had been defeated, the
conflicting interests and ideologies of the United States and the
U.S.S.R. emerged and drove the one-time allies toward the Cold War.

THE SOURCES

Allied Agreements and Differences

At the Yalta summit of the "big three" in February, the Allies agreed on a list of crucial items: occupation zones in Germany, the trial of war criminals, the creation of a United Nations, and the timing of the war against Japan. They also accepted language on the establishment of a postwar Polish government, but Stalin had a different understanding of the meaning of that agreement from that of Roosevelt and Churchill. President Roosevelt spent the last two months of his life arguing with Stalin on that subject; Stalin refused to accept western interference on his border. After Roosevelt's death, Truman took up the Polish cause, but the United States and U.S.S.R. never resolved the issue.

Stalin Defends Views on Poland, January 1, 1945

I am very sorry that I have not succeeded in convincing you of the correctness of the Soviet Government's stand on the Polish question. Nevertheless, I hope events will convince you that the National Committee has always given important help to the Allies, and continues to do so, particularly to the Red Army, in the struggle against Hitler Germany, while the émigré Government in London is disorganizing that struggle, thereby helping the Germans.

Of course I quite understand your proposal for postponing recognition of the Provisional Government of Poland by the Soviet Union for a month. But one circumstance makes me powerless to comply with your wish. The point is that on December 27 the Presidium of the Supreme Soviet of the U.S.S.R., replying to a corresponding question by the Poles, declared that it would recognize the Provisional Government of Poland the moment it was set up. This circumstance makes me powerless to comply with your wish.

Roosevelt Warns of Split over Poland, February 6, 1945

In so far as the Polish Government is concerned, I am greatly disturbed that the three Great Powers do not have a meeting of minds about the political set up in Poland. It seems to me that it puts all of us in a bad light throughout the world to have you recognizing one government while we and the British are recognizing another in London. I am sure this state of affairs should not continue and that if it does it can only lead our people to think there is a breach between us, which is not the case. I am determined that there shall be no breach between ourselves and the Soviet Union. Surely there is a way to reconcile our differences . . .

I have had to make it clear to you that we cannot recognize the Lublin Government as now composed, and the world would regard it as a lamentable outcome of our work here if we parted with an open and obvious divergence between us on this issue.

I hope I do not have to assure you that the United States will never lend its support in any way to any provisional government in Poland that would be inimical to your interests.

It goes without saying that any interim government which could be formed as a result of our conference with the Poles here would be pledged to the holding of free elections in Poland at the earliest possible date. I know this is completely consistent with your desire to see a new free and democratic Poland emerge from the welter of this war.

Communiqué of the Yalta Conference, February 11, 1945

The Defeat of Germany

Nazi Germany is doomed. The German people will only make the cost of their defeat heavier to themselves by attempting to continue a hopeless resistance.

The Occupation and Control of Germany

. . . Under the agreed plan, the forces of the Three Powers will each occupy a separate zone of Germany . . .

It is our inflexible purpose to destroy German militarism and Nazism and to ensure that Germany will never again be able to disturb the peace of the world. We are determined to disarm and disband all German armed forces; break up for all time the German General Staff that has repeatedly contrived the resurgence of German militarism; remove or destroy all German military equipment; eliminate or control all German industry that could be used for military production; bring all war criminals to just and swift punishment and exact reparation in kind for the destruction wrought by the Germans; wipe out the Nazi Party, Nazi laws, organizations and institutions, remove all Nazi and militarist influences from public office and from the cultural and economic life of the German people; and take in harmony such other measures in Germany as may be necessary to the future peace and safety of the world. It is not our purpose to destroy the people of Germany, but only when Nazism and militarism have been extirpated will there be hope for a decent life for Germans, and a place for them in the comity of nations.

Reparation by Germany

We have considered the question of the damage caused by Germany to the Allied Nations in this war and recognized it as just that Germany be obliged to make compensation for this damage in kind to the greatest extent possible . . .

United Nations Conference

We are resolved upon the earliest possible establishment with our allies of a general international organization to maintain peace and security. We believe that this is essential, both to prevent aggression and to remove the political, economic and social causes of war through the close and continuing collaboration of all peace-loving peoples.

Declaration on Liberated Europe

. . . The establishment of order in Europe and the rebuilding of national economic life must be achieved by processes which will enable the liberated peoples to destroy the last vestiges of Nazism and Fascism and to create democratic institutions of their own choice. This is a principle of the Atlantic Charter—the right of all peoples to choose the form of government under which they will live—the restoration of sovereign rights and self-government to those peoples who have been forcibly deprived of them by the aggressor nations . . .

By this declaration we reaffirm our faith in the principles of the Atlantic Charter, our pledge in the Declaration by the United Nations, and our determination to build in cooperation with other peace-loving nations a world order under law, dedicated to peace, security, freedom and the general well-being of all mankind.

Poland

. . . We reaffirm our common desire to see established a strong, free, independent and democratic Poland. As a result of our discussions we have agreed on the conditions in which a new Polish Provisional Government of National Unity may be formed in such a manner as to command recognition by the three major powers.

The agreement reached is as follows:

A new situation has been created in Poland as a result of her complete liberation by the Red Army. This calls for the establishment of a Polish Provisional Government which can be more broadly based than was possible before the recent liberation of western Poland. The Provisional Government which is now functioning in Poland should therefore be reorganized on a broader democratic basis with the inclusion of democratic leaders from Poland itself and from Poles abroad. This new Government should then be called the Polish Provisional Government of National Unity.

This Polish Provisional Government of National Unity shall be pledged to the holding of free and unfettered elections as soon as possible on the basis of universal suffrage and secret ballot. In these elections all democratic and anti-Nazi parties shall have the right to take part and to put forward candidates.

The three Heads of Government consider that the eastern frontier of Poland should follow the Curzon Line.[7]

In the Headlines

Izvestiia, Moscow, February 13, 1945
CONFERENCE OF THE THREE ALLIED POWERS—SOVIET UNION, UNITED STATES OF AMERICA AND GREAT BRITAIN

La Presse Cherbourgeoise, Cherbourg, February 14, 1945
THE CRIMEAN CONFERENCE CONDEMNS NAZI GERMANY TO DEFEAT

Roosevelt Reports on Yalta, March 1, 1945

The German people, as well as the German soldiers, must realize that the sooner they give up and surrender, by groups or as individuals, the sooner their present agony will be over. They must realize that only with complete surrender can they begin to reestablish themselves as people whom the world might accept as decent neighbors.

We made it clear again at Yalta, and I now repeat—that unconditional surrender does not mean the destruction or enslavement of the German people . . .

We did, however, make it clear at this conference just what unconditional surrender does mean for Germany.

It means the temporary control of Germany by Great Britain, Russia, France, and the United States. Each of these nations will occupy and control a separate zone of Germany. . . . Unconditional surrender also means the end of Nazism, and of the Nazi Party—and all of its barbaric laws and institutions.

It means the termination of all militaristic influence in the public, private, and cultural life of Germany.

It means for the Nazi war criminals a punishment that is speedy and just—and severe.

It means the complete disarmament of Germany; the destruction of its militarism and its military equipment; the end of its production of armament; the dispersal of all of its armed forces; the permanent dismemberment of the German General Staff, which has so often shattered the peace of the world.

It means that Germany will have to make reparations in kind for the damage which it has done to the innocent victims of its aggression.

By compelling reparations in kind—in plants, and machinery, and rolling stock, and raw materials—we shall avoid the mistake made after the last war of demanding reparations in the form of money which Germany could never pay.

Roosevelt to Stalin on Poland, April 1, 1945

So far there has been a discouraging lack of progress made in the carrying out, which the world expects, of the political decisions which we reached at the Conference particularly those relating to the Polish question. I am frankly puzzled as to why this should be and must tell you that I do not fully understand in many respects the apparent indifferent attitude of your Government. . . . I intend, therefore, in this message to lay before you with complete frankness the problem as I see it . . .

In the discussions that have taken place so far your Government appears to take the position that the new Polish Provisional Government of National Unity which we agreed should be formed should be little more than a continuation of the present Warsaw Government. I cannot reconcile this either with our agreement or our discussions. While it is true that the Lublin Government is to be reorganized and its members play a prominent role it is to be done in such a fashion as to bring into being a new Government. This point is clearly brought out in several places in the text of the agreement. I must make it quite plain to you that any such solution which would result in a thinly disguised continuance of the present Warsaw regime would be unacceptable and would cause the people of the United States to regard the Yalta agreement as having failed . . .

Stalin to Roosevelt on Poland, April 7, 1945

In order to break the deadlock and reach an agreed decision, the following steps should, I think, be taken:

(1) Affirm that reconstruction of the Polish Provisional Government implies, not its abolition, but its reconstruction by enlarging it, it being understood that the Provisional Government shall form the core of the future Polish Government of National Unity.

(2) Return to the provisions of the Crimea Conference and restrict the number of Polish leaders to be invited to eight persons, of whom five should be from Poland and three from London.

(3) Affirm that the representatives of the Polish Provisional Government shall be consulted in all circumstances, that they be consulted in the first place, since the Provisional Government is much stronger in Poland compared with the individuals to be invited from London and Poland whose influence among the population in no way compares with the tremendous prestige of the Provisional Government . . .

(4) Only those leaders should be summoned for consultation from Poland and from London who recognize the decisions of the Crimea Conference on Poland and who in practice want friendly relations between Poland and the Soviet Union.

(5) Reconstruction of the Provisional Government to be effected by replacing a number of Ministers of the Provisional Government by nominees among the Polish leaders who are not members of the Provisional Government.

In the Headlines

Izvestiia, Moscow, April 13, 1945
DEATH OF PRESIDENT OF THE UNITED STATES OF AMERICA
  FRANKLIN ROOSEVELT [article accompanied by flattering picture and
  obituary]

Allies Warn Germany on Prisoners, April 23, 1945

The Governments of the United Kingdom, United States of America, and U.S.S.R., on behalf of all the United Nations at war with Germany, hereby issue a solemn warning to all commandants and guards in charge of Allied prisoners of war, internees or deported citizens of the United Nations in Germany and German occupied territory and to members of the Gestapo and all other persons of whatsoever service or rank in whose charge Allied prisoners of war, internees or deported citizens have been placed, whether in battle zones, on lines of communication or in rear areas. They declare that they will hold all such persons, no less than the German High Command and competent German military, naval and air authorities, individually responsible for the safety and welfare of all Allied prisoners of war, internees or deported citizens in their charge.

Any person guilty of maltreating or allowing any Allied prisoners of war, internees or deported citizens to be maltreated, whether in battle zone on lines of communication, in a camp, hospital prison or elsewhere, will be ruthlessly pursued and brought to punishment. They give notice that they will regard this responsibility as binding in all circumstances and one which cannot be transferred to any other authorities or individuals whatsoever.

Stalin to Truman on Poland, April 24, 1945

Another circumstance that should be borne in mind is that Poland borders on the Soviet Union, which cannot be said about Great Britain or the U.S.A.

Poland is to the security of the Soviet Union what Belgium and Greece are to the security of Great Britain.

You evidently do not agree that the Soviet Union is entitled to seek in Poland a Government that would be friendly to it, that the Soviet Government cannot agree to the existence in Poland of a Government hostile to it. This is rendered imperative, among other things, by the Soviet people's blood freely shed on the fields of Poland for the liberation of that country. I do not know whether a genuinely representative Government has been established in Greece, or whether the Belgian Government is a genuinely democratic one. The Soviet Union was not consulted when those Governments were being formed, nor did it claim the right to interfere in those matters, because it realizes how important Belgium and Greece are to the security of Great Britain. . . .

To put it plainly, you want me to renounce the interests of the security of the Soviet Union; but I cannot proceed against the interests of my country.

War on the Western Front

While diplomatic discussions went on in an attempt to resolve Allied differences, fighting continued on both fronts. Those living under German occupation suffered through the winter of 1944–1945. After breaking the German offensive that started in December 1944 but concluded only in January 1945, Allied forces finally crossed the Rhine in February and moved into German territory. With the Germans retreating, resistance forces joined and supported the Allied invasion of Germany. More and more Germans were captured, such as Heinz Perschke, one of the few who admitted the attraction of Nazi ideology. As Allied troops made progress, a large number of American prisoners were freed and many testified about life in German camps.

Testimony on Winter Privations in Holland[8]

Household difficulties were many in this last winter of the war.

No gas, electricity, telephone or telegraph, slow and restricted postal traffic, little fuel. . . .

The communal kitchen provides us with one-half litre of watery soup a day. . . . a few potatoes and some vegetables . . .

No electrical current. In the darkest months of the year after 4 P.M. struggling in darkness with an old-fashioned floating-wick with liquid brilliantine instead of oil. A column of black smoke arises from it . . .

As misery grows more grinding wood robbery goes up. The woodwork is even stolen from the houses that are left by the inhabitants on account of obliged evacuation or damage from bombs or V's. Anything fit for burning disappears . . .

Death rate is abnormally high on account of underfeeding, and the staff of the undertakers are transported to Germany . . . no wood for coffins. . . . Among the poorest the corpse is taken from the coffin after the mourners have left the churchyard and is buried in a paper bag. The coffin is used again for the next one . . .

The schools are closed during the winter months owing to fuel shortage.

The black market is flourishing . . .

Everybody knows what we suffered under *razzias* [roundups] and bombs, V's and evacuation, requisition of houses and goods. . . . I meant only to give you a glimpse of the daily troubles in this dark war winter.

In the Headlines

Le Figaro, Paris, January 2, 1945
AMERICANS ATTACK AND MAKE PROGRESS WEST OF BASTOGNE

La Presse Cherbourgeoise, Cherbourg, January 4, 1945
AMERICANS ADVANCE IN THE ARDENNES

Le Monde, Paris, January 9, 1945
AMERICANS AND BRITISH CONTINUE TO PROGRESS NORTH OF
    ARDENNES SALIENT

La Presse Cherbourgeoise, Cherbourg, January 9, 1945
THE THREE ALLIED ARMIES DESTROY GERMAN FORCES IN THE
    ARDENNES

Bruxelles-Paris [formerly Belgique], Paris, January 11, 1945
BERLIN ANNOUNCES: GREAT BATTLE IN PROGRESS IN ARDENNES

Bruxelles-Paris, Paris, January 12, 1945
GERMANS EVACUATE ARDENNES SALIENT

The Times, London, January 17, 1945
NEW BRITISH ATTACK ON WESTERN FRONT

The Times, London, January 18, 1945
AMERICAN ARMIES LINKING IN ARDENNES

Testimony of Franklin E. Kameny, 1945[9]—Americans Invade Germany

It was bitter cold. There had been some nasty fighting around before we ever got there. The Americans had taken all of our dead with them. The Germans hadn't . . . we used to wander around, there were trenches and so on, and things were covered with snow when we got there. Some of that began to melt, and every so often you would see two boots, boot tips sticking up out of the snow, and underneath it was the body of a dead German soldier.

. . . near the end of January, they moved us up north into Holland. We went through the area of the Battle of the Bulge late at night. It was a moonlit night, we went through the Ardennes . . .

But anyway, around the beginning of March, we headed east into the Rhineland in Germany . . .

We crossed the Rhine and headed out into the Ruhr Pocket. The Ruhr, of course, was an industrial area. It was considered important, our troops were rounding the Ruhr—that's where we really got into full-fledged, nonstop combat, for quite a while. And all the usual things, we lost quite a number of men. You learn after a while, as we did quickly enough—their artillery was coming in—that as long as you hear an artillery shell, you're all right. But the shells travel faster than sound, so if it's going to come very close to you, before it gets there, you stop hearing it. Then you know you may be hit! And you have a few extra seconds, maybe five, ten at the most, and you hear it land somewhere near you and you're thankful it didn't land on you.

Europe was being sorted out one way or another. And we were shipped south to Czechoslovakia and became, instead of army of occupation, we became army of liberation, and headed on south into Bohemia, western Czechoslovakia, and we were stationed for about a month, probably two.

Testimony of Raymond Chow, April 1945—Americans Invade Germany

We went into Germany and we crossed a river, Elbe I think. They say it was supposed to be a secret mission and everything like that. They had a river raft. Every time we land we usually land in the morning time—right before dawn. We crossed the river. We were supposed to take a bunch of houses, which we did. It was getting light so we started advancing towards those houses we were supposed to take. I already heard we lost two guys; there was this sniper—two sergeants. Then we go across the fields. There was a guy standing in plain view leaning up against a fence post. So I took a shot at him. I didn't aim or anything—just brought my rifle up and hit him. He wasn't dead. When I went up to him, my sergeant say, "Hey, you did a bum job—hit him; you are supposed to kill him." "Why don't you do it for me?" So he just threw him into the ditch.

Testimony of Margriet—Dutch Resistance Regiment

When one night a German patrol under covering fire crosses the Waal, a house-to-house fight starts by which two men of the 1st platoon are taken as prisoners of war by the Germans. At the end of February the company is pulled back to Oss for a period of rest . . . after three days the company leaves as the first one of the Brabant Regiments for Germany. "To Berlin" is written on the trucks. Nevertheless, Nijmegen is the first stop. Everything must now be loaded in DUKW's (amphibious vehicles),[10] because the area further on is flooded. . . . Montgomery was preparing in this area to cross the Rhine—"Operation Plunder."[11] Patrol was part of the daily work. One night the company received heavy artillery fire, but due to the order at the time of arrival to dig in deep, the shelling fortunately has no consequences. At the beginning of April the "Margriet" crosses the Rhine.

In the Headlines

La Presse Cherbourgeoise, Cherbourg, February 5, 1945
A THOUSAND BOMBS POUND BERLIN DURING THE DAY
FIRES RAGE IN THE GERMAN CAPITAL

Le Monde, Paris, February 28, 1944
AMERICANS ADVANCE AT THE SAME TIME ON COLOGNE AND
   DUSSELDORF

The Times, London, March 6, 1945
AMERICANS BREAK INTO COLOGNE

La Presse Cherbourgeoise, Cherbourg, March 9, 1945
THE AMERICANS REACH THE NORTHERN RHINE
NEAR COBLENCE AFTER AN ADVANCE OF 100 KM.

Le Monde, Paris, March 27, 1945
DARMSTADT TAKEN, FRANKFORT MENACED BY TANKS OF GENERAL
   PATTON

La Presse Cherbourgeoise, Cherbourg, March 29, 1945
FIVE ALLIED ARMIES ADVANCE INTO THE HEART OF GERMANY

La Journal de Genève, Geneva, April 5, 1945
ALLIES MARCH QUICKLY TOWARD NORTH AND CENTRAL GERMANY

Testimony of Jesse E. Foster[12]—American Prisoner of War

We went to the—what they call Stalag III, which, in the German way of the military customs—the Air Force was in charge of holding Air Force prisoners. And then the camps were run by the German Army. So this camp was in Sagan, which was—I keep forgetting where that was—Poland?[13]

   And this was the main Luftwaffe camp where they had—I think it was about 40–50 thousand Air Force prisoners, enemy Air Force, and of course, that included the British and other nationalities. And they kept us in separate barbwire compounds by nationalities.

Due to the problems in supplying and getting these huge quantities of food through the country to the prison camps, when I was captured, it was one carton for two men per week. And when things got very bad, 15 men per carton per week. And then finally, nothing per week. But anyway, the German ration was a piece of bread, which was 50%—actually 50% wood. And a lot of it was moldy by the time we got it. And then we got some—one cup of soup a day. And we got some hot water to make coffee, because in these food parcels, there was instant coffee. And we got some German log sausage, which is a sausage made partially—with a partial amount of blood. But ours was a hundred percent blood. Nobody ate it except me. And we get the one small piece of margarine every few days and a few other things, but, as I said, there was only 700 calories a day. So we were always hungry. And if anybody left a slight speck of food in his bowl, someone else would scrape it out with his finger. And so anyway, when you were starving, the only thing you think of is food.

Anyway, late at night on that evening, I think it was in January right after Christmas, over the loud speakers, we got the notice camp will be evacuated and everything within 30 minutes. And so we got our things together and got outside and prepared to march out, which we did.

The guards and all the German military were in command. And we had to line up, like in a parade. I don't know, three or four deep in long lines and started marching. And it was taking us West.

. . . we were put into box cars that you see in movies that carry the concentration camp victims; exactly the same. And we were loaded the same. In other words, stand up, pack us in, impossible to sit down, no toilet facilities. So people were—it was a mess, to say the least.

. . . But it was really a very tough experience. Of course, men got very sick; men died. Also, men died on the forced march. Many didn't have real good shoes, and they had to wrap their feet in rags, and they froze. I think—I can't remember exactly, but I think some were actually shot that couldn't keep up.

. . . we were now occupants of this prison camp. In this prison camp, the conditions there were really terrible. There were no toilets. At night, we were locked up; we couldn't go out. And they had an empty metal—like a paint can. I guess it must have been about, say, ten gallons or so. And this was placed at the—inside the door, and this is what became the toilet at night when we were locked up. And by morning, it was over-flowing, and it was a mess. And we had to take turns emptying it, and I had the wonderful experience of emptying it one day. The other regular toilet was unbelievable. It was a sort of a septic tank made out of con-crete. It was square. It was about, oh, maybe a meter and a half on each side, and it was about one meter off the ground. And in order to defecate, you had to hop up on it and put your backside over the edge. And this was very high, and it happened where someone had lost their balance and fell in. So this was the toilet facilities for the whole camp. Only one of these, and that was it. There was very little food. It was very, very bad conditions.

Testimony of Leroy Schaller—American Prisoner of War

I became a prisoner of war after the Battle of the Bulge which was in December. I lasted two days. Our last message was hold at all cost and we did.

... we were marched eventually to—well, marched about seven or eight days. That first night they put us in a cave and a lot of the men were convinced that they were going to blow the entrance to the cave after they got us, got everybody in there, but it didn't happen. And they kept us there two nights and then they put us on the road the next day and told us for every one that escaped they'd shoot 10. We took them at their word. We marched through Prum where the townspeople threw rocks and spit at us. One little brat came out, I guess he was maybe 8 or 9 years old and kicked a man ahead of me in the shins just as hard as he could. And then we were—we marched over to a church town and then we were put in boxcars and sent to Bad Orb in Germany. And that was Stalag IXB. I was there 115 days. We all lost around 45 percent of our weight in that time. The Jewish—well actually there were about 50 that were really Jewish, but they took 350 men out of there and they ended up in a Holocaust Camp which was known as Berga. Most of those men did not come out.

Testimony of Glen Brutus—American Prisoner of War

Took us to Hildesheim, Germany, a railroad intersection. Loaded us on boxcars. Put so many in that boxcar, you couldn't even all sit down at once. You had to take turns about standing up. Finally they stopped us Christmas Eve 1944 in Hildesheim, Germany.

Used the helmet for a commode. We had them helmets lined up by the door. And when they slid the door open, the helmets dumped out on the ground. Shit and piss splattered out.

They shoved us in a building after we got to this prison camp. And that was about the first of January '45. Got registered as a prisoner of war. We had to wait in line to get registered as a prisoner of war and there were several hundred of us. Well, they were slow getting it done, of course. It was dirt floor, colder than hell than even in the building, down around zero. Piled up in a pile there like a bunch of hogs and went to sleep. I think that's when I got my feet frostbitten. Wake up the next morning and left foot here was swollen up. I had to walk around on it a while before—until the swelling go down before you could lace up your shoes. And then they vaccinated us for typhus, the Germans did. Your body lice spread that typhus disease. We was crawling with body lice. You wore them same clothes for six months.

It was liberated by the Russians. It was the Russians. 40 miles south of Berlin in a place called Hildesheim, Germany.

The Russians were in control. Couldn't get anybody to get anything out of the Russian general. Figured he was drunk. Now, they did drive in some cattle they confiscated off the Germans, shot them down. We butchered them. That's what we was going to eat was them damn cattle. I was down to about 120 pounds. Brother, about got shot [by Germans] for stealing two potatoes. That's how tough it was. That's pretty tough going. The Germans left the day before the Russian army showed up.

There wasn't actually any fighting around the prison camp, because the Germans had left the night before. But the Germans stayed out in the perimeter in the woods. And I remember the Germans sent word in if the Russians didn't show up, they come back into the camp, for every gun they found they were going to shoot 100 of us.

Testimony of Alex Haddon, May 3, 1945[14]—American Prisoner of War

I was captured and taken to Stalag 17. Now in Stalag 17 there were 4,200 of us and the unique thing was that we were all fliers, ex-fliers really, and all non-commissioned officers. Under the Geneva Convention we were not compelled to work, but we found ourselves within the confines of the barbed wire with not much to do but wait. So it was clear to me that we needed programs of diversion, diverting minds away from the wire. The Germans had made it very clear to us if we even so much as touched a wire that was still inside the compound, that we would be shot without notice.

Some prisoners were shot; we lost about a dozen men for that reason. We were liberated by the 13th Armored Division of the 3rd Army (Patton's group).[15] It happened on May 3, 1945 and it happened quite suddenly one morning. Seven jeeps pulled into that area with three [American] soldiers in each. They were just beautiful people. They were solid and we were all scrawny, with tattered, torn clothes and so on. It was quite a contrast, but almost to a man we crawled up to those jeeps. We could touch the tires or touch their boots. It was a very emotional moment!

. . . by nightfall, we met the Russians and they were coming toward us. That was an extremely interesting thing because they said, "Nyet (no)! No further! This is Russian territory now." We realized that there wasn't anything that we could do about it. Before we turned our vehicles around they broke out the vodka and there in the street we were toasting. We were turned around and we didn't want to make an international incident out of it, so back we went.

Testimony of John J. Bertram, Jr., 1945[16]—American Prisoner of War

It was the town of Hammelburg where our train stopped. There we were given some hot tea and a piece of black bread, and we were then moved to a POW camp, No. 13C. The camp contained officers, which I never saw, and Russian prisoners, and we were barracked in a former cavalry horse stable. This was in the middle of January 1945. We stayed in this horse stable until late April. We were loaded on boxcars again for transport to a camp farther south in Germany. One day as we were chugging along, our train was strafed by one of the American planes. The train stopped immediately and we all jumped out and waived at the plane and he recognized us as POWs, wiggled his wings, and went on his business. The commandant of the train said we could paint POW on top of the boxcars, and we could either continue on the train or walk to the next camp where we were to be held. I chose to walk. We were formed into a column and were guarded by several of the older Germans who had been drafted in the last days of the war. We eventually arrived at a huge POW camp near Regensburg, which had Italian, Russian, English, Australian prisoners. After several days in the sick bay, our camp was liberated by my old friends from the 99th division. We were evacuated by air to Paris.

Testimony of [Alfred] Scott Bates—Americans Occupy Germany

Our next job was to study the city of Munich. We were given maps of the city because Eisenhower was already planning for the occupation. In 1945 we moved behind the 8th Army into Germany. I saw the American soldiers looting everything. I couldn't believe it and it made me sick. Officers and regular soldiers were stealing everything. Everyone wanted a lugar or some other German souvenir. I was stationed in the Rathaus and the message center so I saw all the boxes of loot ready to be shipped back to the United States. A lot of German women were looking to become mistresses of the Americans as the best way to survive.

So we moved into Munich. There was still lots of shooting and chaos and settling of scores. Our job was first to repatriate the Russian POWs. We were under orders to send them all back to Russia. Even in Munich we could smell the awful stench from Dachau.

A lot of us hated our officers. We especially didn't like Patton because he would even arrest our own GIs who were not in uniform. A lot of us cheered when we heard he died.

So after Munich I went to Marseilles and that was also chaotic. But at the end of 1945 I was sent back to the U.S.—first to Norfolk and then Chicago—and then back to college to study French.

In the Headlines

La Presse Cherbourgeoise, Cherbourg, April 19, 1945
GENERAL PATTON'S TROOPS ENTER CZECHOSLOVAKIA

The Times, London, April 19, 1945
BRITISH TANKS 17 MILES FROM HAMBURG
THE CAPTIVES OF BELSEN: INTERNMENT CAMP HORRORS

Testimony of Heinz Perschke, January 1945[17]—German Soldier

My opportunity to defend my homeland took place in January 1945—but in a different way than I had imagined. I was transferred to the western front, and I found myself for the first time confronting Allied forces. Near the first day of the mission I was badly wounded and I became a prisoner of war of the Americans. I received very good medical treatment, and after about two months in the hospital, I was sent to a camp for prisoners in Cherbourg.

About 8 days after I had been wounded a young American soldier, full of hate, called me a Nazi and an assassin. This had a profound impact on me. Was I a Nazi? Until this moment I had only thought of myself as a German soldier.

Since that moment, I have never stopped thinking about that question. Today I know that I really started thinking about that question even before the American said that to me. But I was without doubt under the influence of the State, without the least bit of contact with other ways of thinking and without being informed on a deeper level, and after all, I was only 18 years old. Where could I hear any different information? What was the predominant view in Germany?

I was passionate about National Socialism because it promised to give to Germany its proper place in the world after the defeat of the First World War, which was lost by treason (the legend of the stab in the back). In addition, National Socialism promoted a "community of people" in which social justice would prevail—for those who came from a modest social class and consequently those who did not have a lot of money—this was a definite promise.

As a result we accepted—with more or less enthusiasm—the second-ary effects of this promise—that were considered a necessity. These included the concentration camps and the putting to death of those people "unworthy of life." When I was 10 years old my grandmother took me one time to a church meeting where there was a protest against this kind of killing, and they cited especially the examples of the Bethel hospital and the persecution of the Jews.

Already in 1934 I saw on a post in a window the anti-Jewish propa-ganda newspaper "Der Stürmer" with a photo showing my grandmother in the process of making a purchase in a store owned by a Jew.[18] One of our Jewish doctors was forced to stop treating us. One time I saw a crowd in our street. No one was speaking. After a while I learned that they had come for a Jewish family. The typical rich Jews did not live in our part of the town, that is it was not the "plutocrats" that propaganda talked about, but rather simple folks like us.

So did we have knowledge of the persecution of the Jews? Of course, we knew about it, and we did not do anything about it. It was a very seri-ous situation. I remember two exceptions to this inaction. After the night that is called *Kristallnacht*, our professor who was a nationalist told us the next day in language very precise and formal: "What happened yesterday, the destruction by fire of synagogues and the destruction of Jewish stores, is not worthy of Germans." I don't know if he was punished for this. Sev-eral days later, our pastor told us in his sermon: "Whether we like it or not the Jews are the elect people of God and they are under His protec-tion." This may have been a simple religious statement but in the atmos-phere of the time it was a very dangerous statement. This pastor was arrested several times for taking this position.

We were all aware of the persecution of the Jews. What the majority of Germans did not know was the atrocities committed in the concentra-tion camps. We could not imagine that they were killing the people. That does not exonerate us, we are guilty also, but it is necessary to tell the historical truth.

Was I therefore a Nazi and an assassin? In spite of my youth I cannot totally exonerate myself. Perhaps the loss of East Prussia and all that my family owned is a sort of punishment. But I believe also that God gives new starts in life to those who understand their errors and mistakes.

My captivity was the first step toward my new life.

War on the Eastern Front

While the western Allies advanced across the Rhine into Germany, the Soviet army moved along a broad front toward Berlin. Fighting throughout Eastern Europe remained difficult and brutal. As they pushed the German army back, Soviet forces freed many of the concentration camps and their starving prisoners. While greeted as liberators throughout much of Eastern Europe, the Red Army soon replaced the Germans as a new occupying force. Many Polish resistance fighters now turned their animosity toward the Russians; Tadeusz Wichrowski escaped Poland ahead of the Soviet army.

Testimony of Markov Vladimir Protasovich—Soviet Pilot

In January 1945 we were part of the air cover provision for the troops fighting for Krakow. On the 20th we completed 5–6 sorties in a day, and as evening approached we arrived at Krakow airfield. The aerodrome had been mined and we had to land to the right of the landing strip. *Lavochkins* [Soviet fighters] were coming in to land head on. Everyone just got down as best they could. The town was ablaze.

In the Headlines

La Presse Cherbourgeoise, Cherbourg, January 5, 1945
THE RUSSIANS OCCUPY MOST OF BUDAPEST

La Presse Cherbourgeoise, Cherbourg, January 13, 1945
THE RUSSIANS CONQUER THE HUNGARIAN CAPITAL

The Times, London, January 17, 1945
DOUBLE OFFENSIVE SOUTH OF WARSAW

Pravda, Moscow, January 18, 1945
WARSAW LIBERATED

The Times, London, January 18, 1945
RUSSIANS SWEEP ACROSS POLAND
WARSAW FALLS TO MARSHAL ZHUKOV[19]

La Presse Cherbourgeoise, Cherbourg, January 19, 1945
THE SOVIET ARMY ADVANCES RAPIDLY THROUGH POLAND

Le Monde, Paris, January 19, 1945
WARSAW, CRACOW, CZESTOCHOWA FREED BY SOVIET ARMY

Testimony of Tadeusz "Wicher" Wichrowski[20]—Polish Soldier

In January 1945 the Holy Cross Brigade began its dramatic war march to the West. Pressed hard by the Soviets and Germans, in cold and hunger, through Silesia and Czechoslovakia, the Brigade finally reached the western front. As the only military unit of Underground Poland, it combatively collaborated with the Allies (the American Army) in combat with the enemy, helping to destroy a Nazi division. The Brigade also freed female prisoners from a concentration camp in Holysov.

In that final period, the Brigade's Command did not forget about Wicher and assigned him to a four-person patrol with the mission to cross the frontline and make contact with General Patton's Americans. Stealing through difficult, unknown terrain amidst amassed German army units and outposts took almost two days, but ended with a success—the American soldiers greeted the Underground Poland's patrol emerging from the woods not only with great surprise, but also with quite understandable disbelief.

In the Headlines

La Presse Cherbourgeoise, Cherbourg, January 30, 1945
SOVIET TROOPS ADVANCE INTO GERMAN TERRITORY

Le Figaro, Paris, January 30, 1945
ARMY OF ZHUKOV IS 130 KM. FROM BERLIN

Le Figaro, Paris, January 31, 1945
ZHUKOV AND KONEV CONVERGE ON BERLIN[21]
HITLER EXHORTS GERMANY TO RESIST

Volontés de Ceux de la Resistance, Paris, February 14, 1945
THE MOST TERRIBLE PLACE IN THE WORLD: THE KILLING FACTORIES OF MAJDANEK[22]

Testimony of Simon Igel—Polish-French Holocaust Survivor

Finally in January 1945, with the Russians approaching the camp, we were taken on a forced march in snow and sub-zero temperatures to the train station at Gleiwitz.[23] Our numbers were decimated by cold and snow, fatigue and the blows of the SS, and finally the killing of those who faltered. I survived because of the help of another prisoner, Sigi Hartmeyer, who was from Berlin originally. From Gleiwitz, we were put on trains without food or drink and taken to the Dora-Mittelbau concentration camp in eastern Germany. By the time we arrived there, three-quarters of our original group had already died. This time my slave labor involved working in an underground factory on bomb elements for the V1 rockets. I remained in this camp from January until April 1945. About April 1, we were moved again, this time by train in the direction of Bergen-Belsen. Whenever the trains could not proceed further due to Allied bombing raids, we were forced to march on foot by the SS guards. On 13 April, more than 1,000 prisoners were pushed into a barn and burned to death. Two days later the British liberated the camp at Bergen-Belsen.

In the Headlines

Le Figaro, Paris, February 16, 1945
IN 48 HOURS 20,000 ALLIED PLANES BOMBARD GERMANY IN UNISON
  WITH RUSSIAN ARMY TACTICS [reference to bombing of Dresden]

The Times, London, March 6, 1945
MARSHAL ZHUKOV DRIVING FOR LOWER ODER

Le Monde, Paris, March 27, 1945
IN THE EAST, RUSSIANS HAVE BROKEN ENEMY RESISTANCE AND
  ADVANCE RAPIDLY TOWARD VIENNA

La Journal de Genève, Geneva, April 5, 1945
ENCIRCLEMENT OF VIENNA BEGINS

Le Monde, Paris, April 27, 1945
BERLIN TOTALLY ENCIRCLED

Testimony of Maria Stepanovna Nidilko—Soviet Medic

In the battle for a German city, our soldiers had to fight against large
forces of desperately resisting Germans. A lot of wounded were delivered
to my front line medical facility. Wounded fighters were dying. I carried
them over to a German church to save them. Being preoccupied with the
wounded, I hadn't noticed our men were forced to retreat. There were
Germans all around. There was only one escape—to defend ourselves. I
bolted the door. Several wounded soldiers and I prepared for combat. The
Germans tried to break into the church. We opened fire in response. I
tried to make aimed shots. The handful of soldiers and wounded wouldn't
have survived, had our men not come to aid us in time—there really are
some lucky minutes in war.

Testimony of Ivan Ivanovich Konovalov—Soviet Pilot

We almost never saw Germans. In reality they had all been moved out. If
there were incidences of looting, then we were severely punished. On one
occasion—I'm not going to talk about it—well, not to put too fine a point
on it, one lad whose family had all been wiped out during the occupation
shot dead an elderly German woman. The court-martial gave him ten
years, commuted to a penal battalion. Obviously, we would go into houses,
looking for hard liquor basically. Their houses all followed a typical pattern
and we soon learned where to look. Rank-and-file and sergeants were
allowed to send home 5kg parcels, officers 10kg. I used to give my

allowance to ranks and sergeants who basically were older than myself and had families. Just before my return to the U.S.S.R. I got together a lot of crockery and crystal and loaded it into my two bomb bays. We flew back from East Prussia and were immediately sent on leave, but when I got back the bomb bays were empty. So I didn't bring back any trophies! I personally had no contact with prisoners of war.

Kultur! [photo of concentration camp victims]—article in *La Voix des Belges*, Brussels, May 1945

The conquest of Germany has liberated one after the other the camps of political prisoners. Slowly, piece by piece, the veil has lifted, that the Nazis had carefully used to hide their barbaric practices. The atrocities committed are revealed, the instruments of torture are discovered. And throughout the Reich there is an odor of pestilence and of savagery, and the world wonders about this sadism and is overcome by disgust. . . . Each new advance of the Allies opens a new piece of this terrible dossier of charges against the Nazis, of new proof of their insane rage of destruction. . . . Each day the sinister litany grows longer: Maidanek, Auschwitz, Bergen-Belsen, Ahlem, Wolfenbutel, Nordhausen, Klein-Gladbach, Sieburg, Buchenwald, Dachau, Lebenstern, etc.

Victory

The American and Soviet armies met in April 1945, and Allied leaders exchanged congratulatory notes on the occasion. With Soviet forces moving into Berlin, Hitler committed suicide; Mussolini was captured and executed by Italian partisans. At the end of the first week of May, German forces surrendered. The Allies did not repeat the mistakes of World War I—this time, they marched across Germany so that no future leader could claim that Germany had not been defeated in war—and this time, they made sure that the German military surrendered so that future civilian governments could not be blamed.

Truman Statement on Meeting of Allied Armies, April 27, 1945

The Anglo-American Armies under the command of General Eisenhower have met the Soviet forces where they intended to meet—in the heart of Nazi Germany. The enemy has been cut in two . . .

It means, first, that the last faint, desperate hope of Hitler and his gangster government has been extinguished. . . . Nothing can divide or weaken the common purpose of our veteran armies to pursue their victorious purpose to its final Allied triumph in Germany.

Nations which can plan and fight together shoulder to shoulder in the face of such obstacles of distance and of language and of communications as we have overcome can live together and can work together in the common labor of the organization of the world for peace.

Finally, this great triumph of Allied arms and Allied strategy is such a tribute to the courage and determination of Franklin Roosevelt as no words could ever speak, and that could be accomplished only by the persistence and the courage of the fighting soldiers and sailors of the Allied nations.

Stalin Statement on Meeting of Allied Armies, April 27, 1945

In the name of the Soviet Government, I address you, commanders and men of the Red Army, and of the armies of the Allies.

The victorious armies of the Allied Powers, waging a war of liberation in Europe, have routed the German troops and linked up on the territory of Germany.

Our task and our duty are to complete the destruction of the enemy, to force him to lay down his arms and surrender unconditionally. The Red Army will fulfill to the end this task and this duty to our people and to all freedom-loving peoples.

I greet the valorous troops of our Allies, which are now standing on the territory of Germany shoulder to shoulder with the Soviet troops, and which are full of determination to carry out their duty to the end.

Testimony of Jack Bowen, May 1945[24]—Americans Meet Russians

The plane was shot down near Vienna, Austria. On the bomb run, they were hit by flak and one of the engines caught fire. And two of the other engines were also hit and out of commission. They were flying with one full engine and a part of another engine when they came off the bomb run. They knew that they couldn't get back to the base. The pilot asked for a heading to the nearest friendly point they could get to, which was across the Russian lines in Hungary, to a little fighter strip on the other side of the front, to a place called Pecs, Hungary. As they were landing, the Russian soldiers shot at them with rifles. The strip was too short for their plan and they ended up on the side of a hill. Before they got out of the plane, they smashed the bomb site and radio equipment and loaded all the 50 machine guns.

They did not care much for the Russians and the Russians did not care much for the Americans. They boasted that once they defeat Germany, they would take over England and all of Europe.

The Russian major gave their pilot a receipt for the plane. They stayed there for a short period in a farm house owned by an elderly Hungarian couple whose granddaughter was living with them. Their daughter (or daughter in law) had been taken by the Germans when they evacuated and their son was killed during the war. Jack gave them his parachute before he left and told them to use the material to make clothes for their grand-daughter. They treated them very well. Three of them stayed there and the others stayed at various other farm houses in the area.

They first gave the Russians their names, ranks, and serial numbers and asked them to notify their base that they were safe. They did that at every location they went to, but when they got back to the base, nobody knew where they had been. Evidently, the Russians never did anything with the information given them.

Eventually, the Russians put them on a freight train in a box car with a pile of straw and rolls of bread, salami and a big bag of tobacco and European newspapers.

Testimony of Joseph A. Gautsch, May 1945[25]—Americans Meet Russians

Well, from there we just went east. It was a big rush. We'd just move during the daytime, and the Germans were retreating so we were just following them. There would be a little fire fight now and then or something like that. Every night we'd stop in a town, go into a house and kick everybody out and everybody'd move. It was nice. We tried to find the best house, because you knew the best wine would be there. That went on until the end of the war in Europe. And then in Linz, Austria—nice town on the Danube River—beautiful town—city, really. We were just chasing the Germans. That's where we stopped because the Russians were there.

We met the Russians. And Linz was—had a big railroad and yards and had a lot of camps there, and there were workers from Russia every-where, and they were in reasonably good shape because they needed them to work there. And then after the fighting was over with, why, then one of my jobs was to—we had to inspect all these people before the Russians would accept them back, their own people. So we had to delouse them and that. But there were some big factories there, and they had big show-ers, and we'd line everybody up and push them through there, give them a bar of soap. We'd give them a bar of soap to start with, but that quit soon because they ate the soap, they were so hungry. And then they'd take a shower, and we'd spray DDT all over their clothes and delouse them. And then the Russians would take them.

In the Headlines

The Times, London, April 30, 1945
MUSSOLINI PUT TO DEATH BY PARTISANS
BODY BROUGHT TO MILAN DAY BEFORE ALLIES ENTER

La Presse Cherbourgeoise, Cherbourg, May 1, 1945
THE END OF NAZI GERMANY
HIMMLER OFFERS TO SURRENDER TO GREAT BRITAIN AND THE
   UNITED STATES

Journal de Genève, Geneva, May 2, 1945
CHANCELLOR HITLER IS DEAD

Pravda, Moscow, May 3, 1945
FLAG OF VICTORY RAISED OVER BERLIN

La Presse Cherbourgeoise, Cherbourg, May 4, 1945
BERLIN HAS FALLEN

Atlanta Journal, Atlanta, May 7, 1945
NAZIS SURRENDER

La Presse Cherbourgeoise, Cherbourg, May 8, 1945
THE ALLIES HAVE DESTROYED THE MONSTER
ITS ARMIES VANQUISHED, ITS TERRITORY OCCUPIED
GERMANY SURRENDERS WITHOUT CONDITIONS

Testimony of Naum Kravets

Suddenly one of the pilots rushed into the room and cried, 'Victory! Victory!' and shot a string of bursts in the ceiling. We always slept in underpants, so I hurriedly put my pants and jacket on and rushed outside. The pilots of our regiment were aligned. They were shooting in the air and crying, 'Victory, Victory, the war is over!' I took out my pistol and started shooting as well. I wasted all cartridges. That was the way I celebrated victory day. Then our squad commander came and took a picture of us. On the occasion of the victory I was awarded an Order of the Great Patriotic War of the 2nd class and a Medal 'For Victory in the Great Patriotic War' . . .

   Patriotic spirit was very high at the front. We were raised as patriots of our country. What we had to deal with at war nurtured this spirit even more. It was written on board of our plane: 'For the Motherland, For

Stalin!' Those words were written only on those planes, whose crews distinguished themselves in battle and I took pride that there was such an inscription on ours. On our torpedoes it said 'For Stalingrad!', 'For Leningrad!' We fought for the whole country, for our kin and certainly for our favorite leader, Stalin.

Act of Surrender, May 8, 1945

1. We the undersigned, acting by authority of the German High Command, hereby surrender unconditionally to the Supreme Commander, Allied Expeditionary Force and simultaneously to the Supreme High Command of the Red Army all forces on land, at sea, and in the air who are at this date under German control.

2. The German High Command will at once issue orders to all German military, naval and air authorities and to all forces under German control to cease active operations at 2301 hours Central European time on 8th May 1945, to remain in the positions occupied at that time and to disarm completely, handing over their weapons and equipment to the local allied commanders or officers designated by Representatives of the Allied Supreme Commands . . .

3. In the event of the German High Command or any of the forces under their control failing to act in accordance with this Act of Surrender, the Supreme Commander, Allied Expeditionary Force and the Supreme High Command of the Red Army will take such punitive or other action as they deem appropriate.

Testimony of Tamara Aronovna Zeveke[26]

I cannot forget the night before May 9. Nobody was asleep. The radio was on all night. We were expecting the news about the capitulation of Germany. We rushed outside, ran to the post office to send telegrams to family and friends. People who did not know each other were embracing on the street. People were crying with happiness and grief.

Stalin Victory Speech, May 9, 1945

The great day of victory over Germany has come. Fascist Germany, forced to her knees by the Red Army and the troops of our Allies, has acknowledged herself defeated and declared unconditional surrender . . .

Being aware of the wolfish habits of the German ringleaders, who regard treaties and agreements as empty scraps of paper, we have no reason to trust their words. However, this morning, in pursuance of the act of surrender, the German troops began to lay down their arms and

surrender to our troops en masse. This is no longer an empty scrap of paper. This is actual surrender of Germany's armed forces . . .

Now we can state with full justification that the historic day of the
final defeat of Germany, the day of the great victory of our people over
German imperialism has come . . .

Hitler's crazy ideas were not fated to come true—the progress of the
war scattered them to the winds. In actual fact the direct opposite of the
Hitlerites' ravings has taken place. Germany is utterly defeated. The
German troops are surrendering. The Soviet Union is celebrating Victory,
although it does not intend either to dismember or to destroy Germany.

Comrades! The Great Patriotic War has ended in our complete
victory. The period of war in Europe is over. The period of peaceful
development has begun.

In the Headlines

Le Monde, Paris, May 9, 1945
THE TRIUMPH OF THE ALLIES
THE WAR IS WON! HERE IS VICTORY!

Pravda, Moscow, May 9, 1945
HITLER'S GERMANY CRUSHED
SOVIET PEOPLE CELEBRATE GREAT VICTORY

Izvestiia, Moscow, May 9, 1945
CONGRATULATIONS ON THE VICTORIOUS COMPLETION OF THE
   GREAT PATRIOTIC WAR, COMRADES!

Truman Reports on Potsdam Conference, August 9, 1945

They seek to rid Germany of the forces which have made her so long
feared and hated, and which have now brought her to complete disaster.
They are intended to eliminate Nazism, armaments, war industries, the
German General Staff, and all its military tradition. They seek to rebuild
democracy by control of German education, by reorganizing local government and the judiciary, by encouraging free speech, free press, freedom of
religion, and the right of labor to organize.

   . . . German economic power to make war is to be eliminated. The
Germans are not to have a higher standard of living than their former victims, the people of the defeated and occupied countries of Europe.

We are going to do what we can to make Germany over into a decent
nation, so that it may eventually work its way from the economic chaos it
has brought upon itself, back into a place in the civilized world . . .

We do not intend again to make this mistake of exacting reparations in money and then lending Germany the money with which to pay. Reparations this time are to be paid in physical assets from those resources of Germany which are not required for her peacetime subsistence.

The first purpose of reparations is to take out of Germany everything with which she can prepare for another war. Its second purpose is to help the devastated countries to bring about their own recovery by means of the equipment and material taken from Germany.

. . . That basis was a total amount of reparations of 20 billion dollars. Of this sum, one half was to go to Russia, which had suffered more heavily in the loss of life and property than any other country.

Truman Seeks Soviet Cooperation, December 19, 1945

I repeat my assurance to you that it is my earnest wish, and I am sure it is the wish of the people of the United States, that the people of the Soviet Union and the people of the United States should work together to restore and maintain peace. I am sure that the common interest of our two countries in keeping the peace far outweighs any possible differences between us . . .

This hope will also be greatly strengthened if your Government will join in the proposals to have a commission created under the United Nations Organization to inquire into and make recommendations for the control of atomic energy in the interest of world peace.

Stalin's Response to Truman on Cooperation, December 23, 1945

I agree with you that the peoples of the Soviet Union and the United States should strive to work together in restoring and maintaining peace, and that we should proceed from the fact that the common interests of our two countries far outweigh certain differences between us.

The conference of the Ministers now in session in Moscow has already yielded good results. . . . We may take it that agreement on these important points has been reached and that the conference has done work that will play a prominent part in establishing proper mutual understanding between our countries in this period of transition from war to peace.

The subject of atomic energy is still under discussion. I hope that on this matter, too, we shall establish unity of views and that by joint effort a decision will be reached that will be satisfactory to both countries and to the other nations.

End Matter

World War II in Europe Timeline

1935

March: German Rearmament

Anglo-German Naval Agreement

French-Soviet-Czech Mutual Assistance Pact

1936

March: Germany reoccupies Rhineland

1937

Stalin purges Red Army

1938

March: Germany annexes Austria (Anschluss)

September: Hitler demands Sudetenland—claims Czechs are killing Sudeten Germans

Hitler sets deadline for transfer of Sudetenland for October 1

Czech government rejects Hitler's demands

Hitler, Chamberlain, Daladier, and Mussolini sign Munich Pact

Hitler-Chamberlain promise not to go to war against each other

Chamberlain proclaims "peace for our time"

October: German army moves into Sudetenland

President Beneš resigns

November: *Kristallnacht* in Germany

1939

March: German army occupies rest of Czechoslovakia

Britain and France give guarantee to Poland

April: Spanish Civil War ends; Franco is new leader of Spain

Hitler demands Danzig and Polish Corridor

May: Stalin removes Litvinov as foreign minister

Molotov becomes foreign minister

Polish foreign minister rejects German demands

Germany and Italy sign alliance—Pact of Steel

August: Nazi-Soviet Nonaggression Pact and Secret Protocol

Belgian, American, and Vatican leaders call for peace

Hitler rejects Daladier's pleas; blames English guarantee to Poland

Germany claims Polish atrocities

September: Germany invades Poland

England and France mobilize

England and France issue ultimatum to Germany on Poland

State of war between England/France and Germany

Chamberlain and Daladier address parliaments to explain actions and causes of war

Mussolini calls for peace talks

Nazi occupation and atrocities in Poland begin

Soviet army occupies eastern Poland

Germans occupy Warsaw

U.S.S.R. pressures Estonia

October: U.S.S.R. pressures Lithuania

U.S.S.R. pressures Latvia

November: Warsaw ghetto established

Polish government in exile established in London

U.S.S.R. demands border changes with Finland

U.S.S.R. breaks diplomatic relations with Finland

U.S.S.R. invades Finland; Winter War begins

December: Winter War continues in Finland

League of Nations expels U.S.S.R.

1940

January: Germany plans spring offensive

February: Winter War continues

March: Finland signs treaty with U.S.S.R.

Daladier resigns in France; Paul Reynaud is new premier

April: Spring offensive begins

Germany invades Denmark and Norway

British land in Norway

May: British begin to leave Norway

Germany invades Belgium, Luxemburg, Holland, and France

Winston Churchill replaces Chamberlain as prime minister

German paratroopers take major Belgian fort

Rotterdam bombed

Dutch government moves to London

Holland surrenders

German army occupies Brussels and Antwerp

Belgium surrenders to the Germans

France suffers defeats along Maginot Line

Premier Reynaud adds Marshal Pétain to cabinet

Allied forces retreat to Dunkirk; evacuation begins

June: Dunkirk evacuation ends; more than 200,000 British and 100,000 French rescued

Germans bomb Paris

Norway surrenders

Italy declares war on France and England

Paris occupied

Pétain replaces Reynaud as French premier

General de Gaulle calls for resistance

France signs armistice; surrenders to Germany

Hitler visits Paris

U.S.S.R. occupies Baltic States—Estonia, Latvia, and Lithuania

U.S.S.R. occupies parts of Romania

July: Vichy government under Pétain set up

German air force (*Luftwaffe*) begins bombing of England

Germany plans invasion of Britain (Operation Sealion)

August: Vichy government sentences General de Gaulle to death in absentia

U.S.S.R. annexes Baltic States

Germany increases bombing of England; Battle of Britain under way

Churchill praises Royal Air Force pilots

September: Italian forces move from Libya into Egypt

Tripartite Pact (Axis) signed by Germany, Italy, and Japan

October: German army moves into Romania

Hitler postpones invasion of Britain

Hitler meets Franco

Italy invades Greece

Jews in Warsaw ordered into ghetto

November: President Roosevelt reelected for a third term

Greeks counterattack; drive Italian army out of Greece

British torpedo attack on Italian fleet at Taranto

Germans bomb Coventry and famous cathedral

Hungary joins Tripartite Pact

Romania joins Tripartite Pact

Slovakia joins Tripartite Pact

December: Franco refuses to enter the war

Hitler plans invasion of U.S.S.R.

Germans bomb London

1941

January: British and Australian troops take Tobruk from Italian forces

February: German General Rommel sent to head Afrika Korps in North Africa

Franco exchanges views with Hitler and Mussolini

March: Rudolf Hoess takes command of Auschwitz concentration camp

Yugoslavia joins Axis (Tripartite Pact)

Lend Lease Act passed in United States

Germans bomb London

Rommel attacks in North Africa; drives British back

Yugoslavia overthrows pro-Axis government

April: Rommel advances in North Africa; moves toward Egypt

Germany invades Yugoslavia and Greece

Yugoslavia surrenders to Germany

Greece surrenders to Germany

May: Rudolf Hess flies to Scotland and is captured

German battleship *Bismarck* sinks British ship HMS *Hood*

British planes cripple battleship *Bismarck*

June: Germany invades U.S.S.R. (Operation Barbarossa)

Molotov (not Stalin) announces invasion

Germans advance rapidly and capture Minsk

July: Stalin addresses nation and calls for scorched earth policy

British-Soviet Mutual Assistance Pact

Germans reach Smolensk

Einsatzgruppen (killing squads) begin killing of Jews in U.S.S.R.

August: Germans capture Smolensk

Roosevelt and Churchill sign Atlantic Charter

September: Leningrad under siege

Germans capture Kiev

Germans murder 33,000 Jews near Kiev at Babi Yar

October: Germans move toward Moscow

Germans take Odessa and Kharkov

November: Battle for Moscow continues

December: Red Army holds Moscow

Japan attacks Pearl Harbor

United States and Britain at war with Japan

Germany and Italy declare war on United States

Hitler issues Night and Fog Decree on treatment (disappearance) of prisoners

1942

January: Twenty-six countries (United Nations) sign declaration against Axis

Heydrich heads Wannsee Conference on the final solution

May: Rommel launches offensive in North Africa

Heydrich wounded in attack in Prague

June: Heydrich dies from wounds

German retaliation destroys Lidice, Czechoslovakia

Auschwitz begins using gas for mass extermination

British retreat to El Alamein in Egypt

United States promises aid to U.S.S.R.

Molotov asks for second front in 1942

July: First Battle of El Alamein

Germans take Crimea and Sevastopol

Anne Frank family in hiding in Amsterdam

Treblinka concentration camp opened

Jews from Warsaw ghetto sent to concentration camps

August: General Montgomery takes charge of British Eighth Army in North Africa

Canadian forces attack Dieppe, France; raid fails

Churchill visits Stalin; Stalin again asks for second front

Roosevelt warns Germany about war crimes

September: Germans move toward Stalingrad

October: Second Battle of El Alamein; British advance

United States and U.S.S.R. warn Germany about war crimes

November: British advance in North Africa continues; Rommel retreats

United States forces land in Morocco and move into Algeria (Operation Torch)

British retake Tobruk

Battle of Stalingrad continues with Soviet attack (Operation Uranus)

December: British-American offensive in North Africa continues

1943

January: Battle of Stalingrad continues

Roosevelt and Churchill meet at Casablanca Conference; "unconditional surrender"

Allies take Tripoli in Libya

February: Battle of Stalingrad ends with German surrender

United States forces retreat at Kasserine Pass in Tunisia

March: Germans pushed out of Tunisia

Greek Jews sent to Auschwitz

April: Allied victory in North Africa

Warsaw ghetto uprising by Jewish resistance forces

Discovery of murdered Polish officers at Katyn Forest near Smolensk

May: Allies complete takeover in Tunisia

German and Italian forces in North Africa surrender

Warsaw ghetto destroyed

July: Allies invade Sicily; Palermo falls

Allies bomb Rome

Mussolini deposed; replaced by Marshal Pietro Badoglio

Massive tank confrontation in Battle of Kursk ends in Soviet victory

Allies bomb Hamburg; firestorm results

Warsaw ghetto Jews sent to Treblinka

August: Allies occupy Sicily

General Patton slaps soldier who suffers from shell shock

Soviets complete victory at Kursk and liberate Kharkov

September: Allies invade Italy

Italy surrenders

Germans occupy Rome

Germans paratroopers rescue Mussolini

Mussolini proclaims Italian Social Republic

Soviets retake Smolensk; move toward Kiev

Danes save Jewish population with boatlift to Sweden

October: Allies liberate Naples

            Italy declares war on Germany

November: Soviets liberate Kiev

            Allied foreign ministers meet in Moscow

            Roosevelt, Churchill, and Stalin meet at Tehran Conference

            Invasion of France set for spring 1944 (Operation Overlord)

December: Franco refuses to enter war

            General Eisenhower chosen to command Allied forces for Operation Overlord

1944

January: Allies attack Monte Cassino in Italy

            Allies land at Anzio in Italy

            Soviet troops enter Poland

            Siege of Leningrad lifted after 900 days

February: Battle of Anzio continues

            Allies bomb monastery of Monte Cassino

            Soviet forces move into Baltic States

March: Soviet troops advance in Belorussia and Ukraine

            Battle in Italy continues

May: Soviet forces liberate Sevastopol and Crimea

            Allies take Monte Cassino and break out at Anzio

            Allies prepare for invasion of France

June: Allies liberate Rome

            Allied bombing of Normandy increased

            Allied paratroopers dropped in Normandy night before invasion

            Allied invasion (Operation Overlord) begins—D-Day

            D-Day puts 150,000 Allied troops on beaches on first day

            Germans destroy French town of Oradour-sur-Glane

            Allies take port of Cherbourg

            Red Army launches offensive in Belorussia (Operation Bagration)

July: Soviets liberate Minsk

            Allies fight in hedgerows of Normandy

            British liberate Caen

            United States troops liberate St.-Lô

            Allied break out from Normandy (Operation Cobra)

            Assassination attempt of Hitler fails

            Red Army liberates Majdanek concentration camp

August: Polish Home Army uprising in Warsaw; Soviet advance halted

            Roosevelt and Stalin disagree about Poland

            Allied forces land in Southern France

            Nazis arrest Anne Frank and family in Amsterdam

            Hitler would-be assassins tortured and killed

            French Resistance uprising against German occupation

           Allies liberate Paris; General de Gaulle enters city

           Red Army takes Romania

September: Allies liberate northern France, Brussels, and Antwerp

           Allies attempt airborne attack in Holland (Operation Market Garden); Germans hold

           U.S.S.R. and Finland sign armistice

           Red Army invades Bulgaria

           Red Army advances in Baltic States, Poland

October: Germans defeat Warsaw uprising by Polish Home Army

           Red Army enters Yugoslavia, Hungary, and Slovakia; continues into Baltic States

           Churchill meets Stalin in Moscow; agrees to Soviet influence in Eastern Europe

           Allies liberate Athens

           Rommel commits suicide

           Battle in Hürtgen Forest

November: Roosevelt reelected for fourth term

December: Battle of the Bulge

           Germans drive for Antwerp

           Germans kill Americans in Malmédy massacre

           Bastogne surrounded; General McAuliffe says, "nuts"

           General Patton moves Third Army to relieve Bastogne

           Weather clears and Allied planes bomb German forces

           Red Army assaults Budapest; Hungary joins Allies

1945

January: Battle of the Bulge ends

           Red Army liberates Warsaw, Auschwitz concentration camp

           Red Army retakes Lithuania; moves into East Prussia

February: Yalta Conference of Roosevelt, Churchill, and Stalin

           Allied bombing of Dresden

March: Red Army still fighting in Hungary

           Allies cross Rhine River at Remagen

           Red Army assaults Berlin, Austria

           Allies liberate Frankfurt

April: Red Army moves toward Vienna; takes Slovakia

           Allies surround German forces in Ruhr pocket

           Allies liberate Buchenwald and Bergen-Belsen concentration camps

           Roosevelt dies; Harry Truman becomes president

           Battle of Berlin rages

           Mussolini captured and executed by Italian partisans

           Allies liberate Dachau concentration camp

           Hitler commits suicide

May: Goebbels and family commit suicide

Red Army occupies Berlin

German forces in Italy surrender

German forces in Holland surrender

Red Army moves toward Prague

German military surrenders at Reims, France

Red Army liberates Prague

Göring captured, Himmler commits suicide, and Eichmann escapes

June: United Nations charter signed

July: United States atomic test successful

Potsdam Conference meets

Attlee replaces Churchill as prime minister

August: Atomic bombs dropped on Japan

September: Japan signs unconditional surrender

November: Nuremberg war crime trials begin

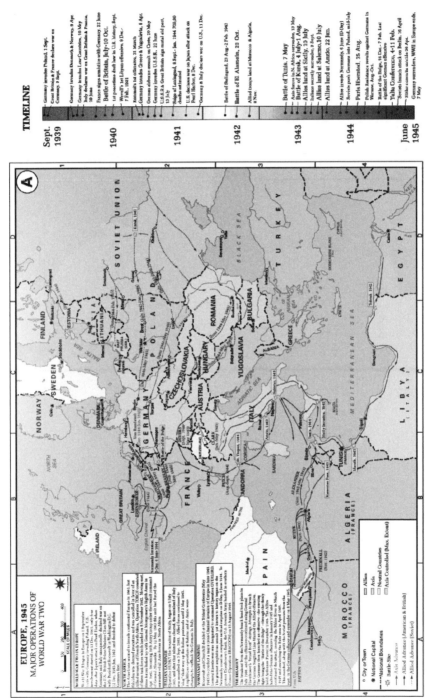

MILITARY CAMPAIGNS OVERVIEW

EUROPE, 1945
MAJOR OPERATIONS OF
WORLD WAR TWO

TIMELINE

CAMPAIGN IN POLAND

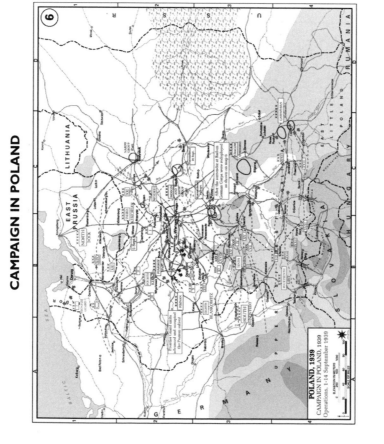

POLAND, 1939
CAMPAIGN IN POLAND, 1939
Operations, 1–14 September 1939

WINTER WAR FINLAND

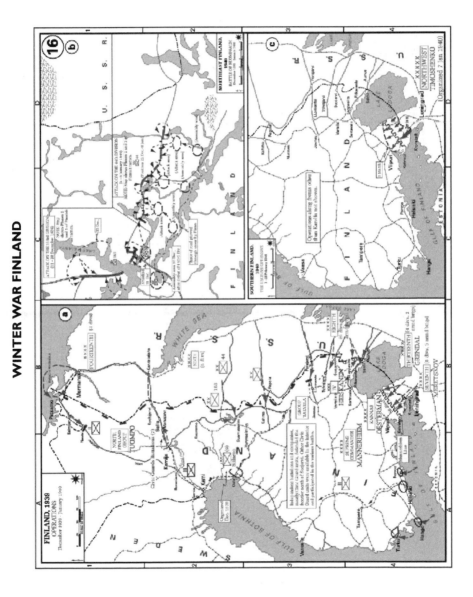

CAMPAIGN IN NORWAY

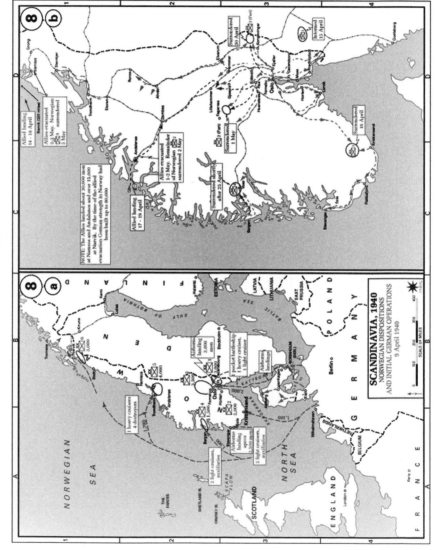

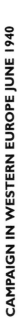
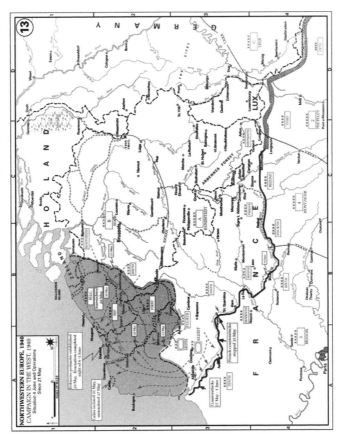

CAMPAIGN IN WESTERN EUROPE JUNE 1940

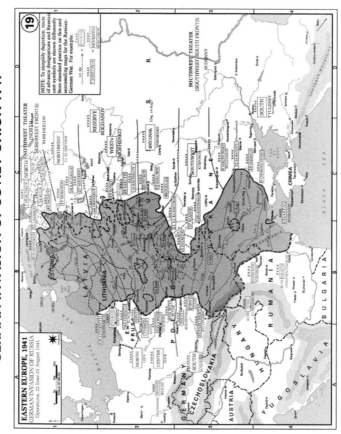

GERMAN INVASION OF SOVIET UNION 1941

BATTLE OF STALINGRAD

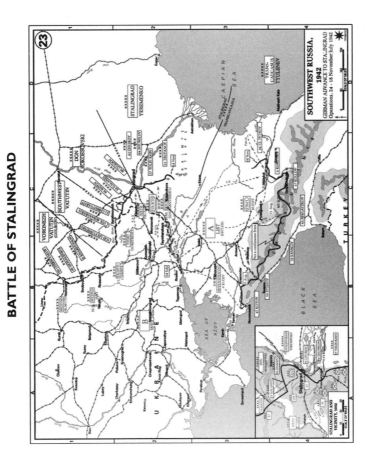

SOUTHWEST RUSSIA, 1942
GERMAN ADVANCE TO STALINGRAD
Operations, 24 - 18 November July 1942

STALINGRAD AND
VICINITY, 1942

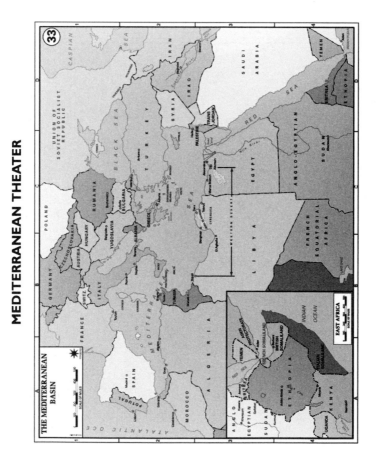

MEDITERRANEAN THEATER

CAMPAIGN IN SICILY, 1943

ALLIED LANDING IN ITALY, 1943

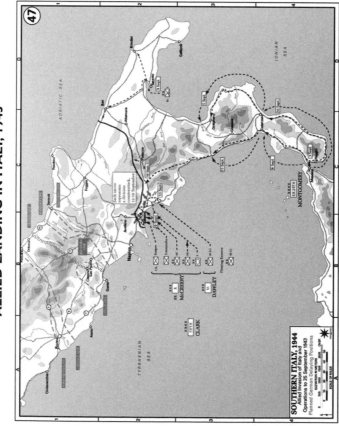

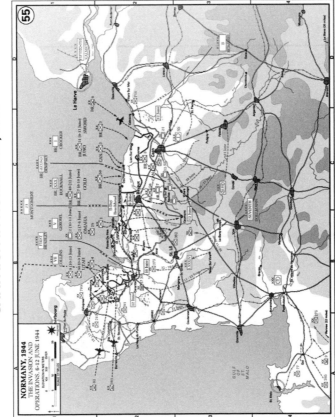

CAMPAIGN IN NORMANDY, 1944

EUROPE MID-DECEMBER, 1944

EUROPE, 1944
ALLIED GAINS IN EUROPE
6 June - 24 July 1944
25 July - 14 September 1944
15 September - 15 December 1944

60

BATTLE OF THE BULGE, DECEMBER 1944

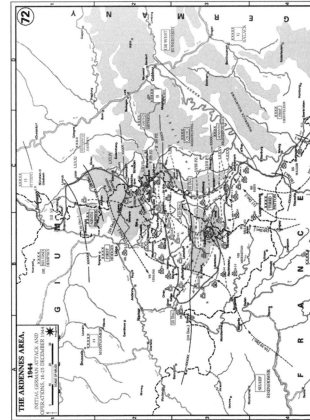

THE ARDENNES AREA,
1944
INITIAL GERMAN ATTACK AND
OPERATIONS, 16-25 DECEMBER 1944

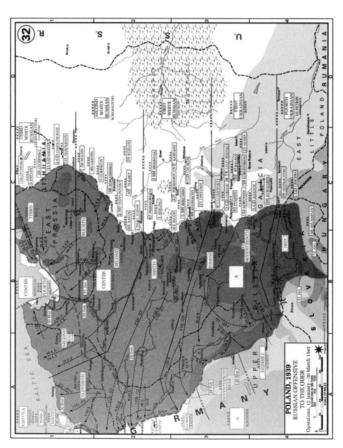

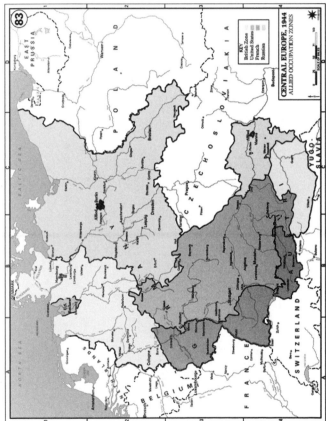

ALLIED OCCUPATION ZONES, 1945

Sources and Copyright Holders

Most of the official documents included in this book, such as treaties, speeches, and newspaper headlines, are in the public domain or follow the concept of fair use. The editor expresses his gratitude to all copyright holders who granted permission to reproduce personal accounts, interviews, Web site information, and other sources. Every effort has been made to contact all copyright holders, and any omissions will be rectified in subsequent printings if notice is given to the publishers.

Chapter One: Appeasement in Munich, 1938

1. The Munich Agreement. Avalon Project, Yale University Law School.
2. Hitler-Chamberlain Declaration. Avalon Project, Yale University Law School.
3. Testimony of Ladislav Homola Permission of Ladislav Homola. Interview and translation by Zachary Goldberg and Alena Švejdová.
4. Testimony of Bohuslav Krajíček. Permission of Bohuslav Krajíček. Interview and translation by Zachary Goldberg and Alena Švejdová.

Chapter Two: War Is Declared, 1939

1. Chamberlain Guarantee to Poland. *The British War Bluebook*. Avalon Project, Yale University Law School.
2. Hitler's Speech to Reichstag on Poland. *The British War Bluebook*. Avalon Project, Yale University Law School.
3. Beck's Speech to Polish Parliament. *The British War Bluebook*. Avalon Project, Yale University Law School.
4. Chamberlain to Hitler. *The British War Bluebook*. Avalon Project, Yale University Law School.
5. Hitler to Chamberlain. *The British War Bluebook*. Avalon Project, Yale University Law School.
6. Nazi-Soviet Nonaggression Pact. *Nazi-Soviet Relations 1939–1941*. Avalon Project, Yale University Law School.
7. Secret Protocol. Nazi-Soviet Nonaggression Pact. *Nazi-Soviet Relations 1939–1941*. Avalon Project, Yale University Law School.
8. Appeal of King of Belgium. *The British War Bluebook*. Avalon Project, Yale University Law School.
9. Roosevelt to King of Italy. *The British War Bluebook*. Avalon Project, Yale University Law School.
10. Pope's Appeal for Peace. *The British War Bluebook*. Avalon Project, Yale University Law School.
11. Polish President's Note. *The British War Bluebook*. Avalon Project, Yale University Law School.
12. Hitler Remarks to French Ambassador in Berlin. *The French Yellow Book*, No. 242. Avalon Project, Yale University Law School.

13. Daladier Appeal to Hitler. *The French Yellow Book*, No. 253. Avalon Project, Yale University Law School.
14. Hitler's Response to Daladier. *The French Yellow Book*, No. 261. Avalon Project, Yale University Law School.
15. Hitler to British Government. *The British War Bluebook*. Avalon Project, Yale University Law School.
16. Chamberlain's Speech to House of Commons. *The British War Bluebook*. Avalon Project, Yale University Law School.
17. Hitler to German Army. *The British War Bluebook*. Avalon Project, Yale University Law School.
18. Hitler Addresses Reichstag. *The British War Bluebook*. Avalon Project, Yale University Law School.
19. Daladier to Chamber of Deputies. *The French Yellow Book*, No. 356. Avalon Project, Yale University Law School.
20. Daladier to People of France. *The French Yellow Book*, No. 370. Avalon Project, Yale University Law School.
21. Chamberlain to House of Commons. *The British War Bluebook*. Avalon Project, Yale University Law School.
22. Hitler to German People. *The British War Bluebook*. Avalon Project, Yale University Law School.
23. Hitler to German Army on the Western Front. *The British War Bluebook*. Avalon Project, Yale University Law School.
24. Chamberlain's Broadcast to German People. *The British War Bluebook*. Avalon Project, Yale University Law School.
25. Mussolini's Call for Peace. *The British War Bluebook*. Avalon Project, Yale University Law School.
26. Testimony of Shep Zitler. Interview and permission by John Menszer. www.holocaustsurvivors.org.
27. Testimony of Eva Galler. Interview and permission by John Menszer. www.holocaustsurvivors.org.
28. Testimony of Nikolai Konstantinovich Shishkin. Interview and permission by Artem Drabkin. www.iremember.ru.

Chapter Three: Germany Conquers Western Europe, 1940

1. Testimony of Group Captain C. Brian Kingcome. Permission of Imperial War Museum, Code 10152, 10–11.
2. Testimony of Air Vice Marshal Harold A. C. Bird-Wilson. Permission of Imperial War Museum, Code 10093, 12–14.
3. Testimony of Group Captain Denys Edgar Gillam. Permission of Imperial War Museum, Code, 10049, 6–7.
4. Mussolini Declares War on Allies. www.historicalresources.org.
5. Armistice Agreement between Germany and France. Avalon Project, Yale University Law School.
6. Testimony of Marcel Tison. Permission of La Presse de la Manche, *In the Name of Freedom*, 113.
7. Testimony of Henri Hervieu. Permission of La Presse de la Manche, *In the Name of Freedom*, 113.
8. Testimony of Karol Wierzbicki. Permission of Electronic Museum; translation by Agnieszka K. Marszalek. www.electronicmuseum.ca/Poland-WW2_ww2.html.
9. Testimony of Jozef Franciszek Nowak. Permission of Electronic Museum; translation by Agnieszka K. Marszalek. www.electronicmuseum.ca/Poland-WW2_ww2.html.

10. Testimony of Tadeuz "Wicher" Wichrowski. Permission of Electronic Museum; translation by Agnieszka K. Marszalek. www.electronicmuseum.ca/Poland-WW2_ww2.html.
11. Testimony of Emil Reuter at Nuremberg Trials, February 1, 1946.
12. Testimony of Charles Couppey. Permission of Agnès Lelion, *Sillons de vie Gréville-Hague 1939–1944 et demain*, 15.
13. Testimony of Marie Dubost. Permission of Agnès Lelion, *Sillons de vie Gréville-Hague*, 15.
14. Testimony of Paul Roser at Nuremberg Trials, January 29, 1946.
15. Franco to Mussolini. Avalon Project, Yale University Law School.
16. Mussolini to Franco. Avalon Project, Yale University Law School.
17. Franco to Hitler. Avalon Project, Yale University Law School.
18. Conversation between Franco and Hitler. Avalon Project, Yale University Law School.
19. Testimony of Group Captain C. Brian Kingcome. Permission of Imperial War Museum, Code 10152, 23–24.
20. Testimony of Group Captain Denys Edgar Gillam. Permission of Imperial War Museum, Code 10049, 13, 19.
21. Testimony of Wing Commander Eustace Holden. Permission of Imperial War Museum, Code 11198, 23.

Chapter Four: Invasion of the Soviet Union, 1941

1. Hitler Seeks Spanish Participation. Avalon Project, Yale University Law School.
2. Mussolini Speech in Rome. Jewish Virtual Library, www.jewishvirtuallibrary.org.
3. Franco Answers Hitler on War. Avalon Project, Yale University Law School.
4. Testimony of Ivan Ivanovich Konovalov. Interview and permission by Artem Drabkin. www.iremember.ru.
5. Testimony of Naum Kravets. Permission of Central Europe Center for Research and Documentation. www.centropa.org.
6. Treaty between Britain and U.S.S.R. Avalon Project, Yale University Law School.
7. Treaty between U.S.S.R. and Polish Government in Exile. Avalon Project, Yale University Law School.
8. The Atlantic Charter. *The Axis in Defeat: A Collection of Documents on American Policy Toward Germany and Japan*, 1–2.
9. Testimony of Naum Kravets. Permission of Central Europe Center for Research and Documentation. www.centropa.org.
10. Testimony of Samouil Borisovich Lelchitski. Interview and permission by Michael Lelchitski.
11. Testimony of Polina Gregoryevna Lelchitski. Interview and permission by Michael Lelchitski.
12. Testimony of Naum Kravets. Permission of Central Europe Center for Research and Documentation. www.centropa.org.
13. Germany Declares War on the United States. Avalon Project, Yale University Law School; Historical Resources about the Second World War, www.historicalresources.org.
14. Hitler Speech to Reichstag. Historical Resources about the Second World War, www.historicalresources.org.
15. Italy Declares War on the United States. Historical Resources about the Second World War, www.historicalresources.org.
16. Axis Pact on War. Avalon Project, Yale University Law School.
17. Poland's Commitment to Allies. Avalon Project, Yale University Law School.

18. Testimony of Marie Dubost. Permission of Agnès Lelion, *Sillons de vie Gréville-Hague*, 23.
19. Testimony of Pierre Lecostey. Permission of Agnès Lelion, *Sillons de vie Gréville-Hague*, 26.
20. Testimony of Charles Couppey. Permission of Agnès Lelion, *Sillons de vie Gréville-Hague*, 27.
21. Testimony of Marie Madeleine Leneveu. Permission of Agnès Lelion, *Sillons de vie Gréville-Hague*, 31.
22. Testimony of Fania Brantovskaya. Permission of Central Europe Center for Research and Documentation. www.centropa.org.
23. Testimony of Otto Ohlendorf at Nuremberg Trials, January 3, 1946.
24. Testimony of Eva Galler. Interview and permission by John Menszer. www.holocaustsurvivors.org.
25. Testimony of Hans Cappelen at Nuremberg Trials, January 29, 1946.
26. Testimony of Nisim Navon. Permission of Central Europe Center for Research and Documentation. www.centropa.org.
27. Testimony of Alois Hollriegel at Nuremberg Trials, January 4, 1946.
28. Testimony of Abram Suzkever at Nuremberg Trials, February 27, 1946.
29. Night and Fog [*Nacht und Nebel*] Decree. Permission of Jewish Virtual Library www.jewishvirtuallibrary.org and Avalon Project, Yale University Law School.

Chapter Five: Occupation and Terror in Europe, 1942

1. Testimony of Warren G. Hirt. Permission of Veterans History Project, The Library of Congress.
2. Declaration by United Nations. *Peace and War 1931–1941*, 850–853.
3. Memorandum of Conference at White House. *Foreign Relations of the United States, 1942*, Vol. 3, 575–578.
4. Mutual Aid Agreement between U.S. and U.S.S.R. Department of State, *Bulletin*, June 13, 1942, Vol. 6, no. 155, 531, 535.
5. Molotov Note to Roosevelt. *Foreign Relations of the United States, 1942*, Vol. 3, 594.
6. Soviet Ambassador Speaks in New York. *One Year of Soviet Struggle against German Invasion*, 25–30.
7. U.S. Note to U.S.S.R. on Anniversary of German Invasion. Department of State, *Bulletin*, 27 June 1942, Vol. 6, no. 157, 562.
8. Churchill's Meeting with Stalin. *Foreign Relations of the United States, 1942*, Vol. 3, 618–620.
9. Stalin's Note to Churchill and Roosevelt. *Foreign Relations of the United States, 1942*, Vol. 3, 621–622.
10. Stalin's Speech. Stalin, *War Speeches*, 38–49.
11. Stalin Interview with Associated Press. Stalin, *War Speeches*, 51–53.
12. Testimony of Theodor Alexandrovich Klein. Interview and permission by Artem Drabkin. www.iremember.ru.
13. Testimony of Mikhail Ilich Borodin. Interview and permission by Artem Drabkin. www.iremember.ru.
14. Testimony of Reichmuth Family. Permission of Peter Reichmuth.
15. Testimony of Danuta "Rad" Socha. Permission of Electronic Museum; translation by Agnieszka K. Marszalek. www.electronicmuseum.ca/Poland-WW2_ww2.html.
16. Wannsee Protocol. Avalon Project, Yale University Law School.
17. Poem by Dutch Prisoner Jan Campert. Permission and copyright: © Jan Campert from Dat ik van binnen brandt, De Bezige Bij, Amsterdam, 2004.

18. Testimony of Solomon Radasky. Interview and permission by John Menszer. www.holocaustsurvivors.org.
19. Testimony of Father Leo Miechalowski at Nuremberg Trials, October 1946.
20. Testimony of Eva Galler. Interview and permission by John Menszer. www.holocaustsurvivors.org.
21. Testimony of Simon Igel. Permission of Simon Igel.
22. Note to U.S.S.R. on Punishment of War Criminals. *Punishment for War Crimes*, 22.
23. Roosevelt on War Crimes. *Punishment for War Crimes*, 26–27.
24. Testimony of Paul Blobel at Nuremberg Trials, June 18, 1947.
25. Testimony of Pierre Lecostey. Permission of Agnès Lelion, *Sillons de vie Gréville-Hague*, 37.
26. Testimony of Dieter Wisliceny at Nuremberg Trials, January 3, 1946.
27. Testimony of Ukrainian Representative. Ukrainian Canadian Civil Liberties Association.
28. Roosevelt on War Crimes. *Punishment for War Crimes*, 27–28.
29. Molotov on War Crimes. *Punishment for War Crimes*, 23–25.

Chapter Six: Victory at Stalingrad; Italy Invaded, 1943

1. Roosevelt Congratulates Stalin. *Foreign Relations of the United States, 1943*, Vol. 3, 505; *Correspondence between the Chairman of the Council of Ministers of the U.S.S.R. and the Presidents of the USA and the Prime Ministers of Great Britain during the Great Patriotic War of 1941–1945*, February 22, 1943, Vol. 2, 48.
2. Testimony of Fedor Pavlovich Ivanov. Permission of Elena Zvereva.
3. Bolsheviks or Nazis. *La Voix des Belges*, Brussels.
4. Roosevelt Praises Soviet Army. *Correspondence between the Chairman of the Council of Ministers of the U.S.S.R. and the Presidents of the USA and the Prime Ministers of Great Britain during the Great Patriotic War of 1941–1945*, Vol. 2, 67.
5. Casablanca Conference Protocol. Avalon Project, Yale University Law School.
6. Testimony of Warren G. Hirt. Permission of Veterans History Project, The Library of Congress.
7. Testimony of Michael John Donoghue. Permission of Patrick Donoghue.
8. Testimony of Raymond Chow. Permission of Veterans History Project, The Library of Congress.
9. Testimony of John Torreano. Permission of John Torreano.
10. Testimony of Keith Campbell. Permission of Veterans History Project, The Library of Congress.
11. Italy Joins the Allies. Department of State, *Bulletin*, October 16, 1943, Vol. 9, no. 225, 254.
12. Ambassador Gromyko Addresses Roosevelt. Department of State, *Bulletin*, October 9, 1943, Vol. 9, no. 224, 245–247.
13. Communiqué of Tripartite Conference in Moscow. *Foreign Relations of the United States, 1943*, Vol. 1, 558–561, 755–769.
14. Stalin's Speech. Stalin, *War Speeches*, 79–83.
15. Declaration of Tehran Conference. Department of State, *Bulletin*, December 11, 1943, Vol. 9, no. 233, 409.
16. Spanish-German Protocol against Allies. Avalon Project, Yale University Law School.
17. German Ambassador on Talks with Franco. Avalon Project, Yale University Law School.
18. Testimony of Jozef Nowak. Permission of Electronic Museum; translation by Agnieszka K. Marszalek. www.electronicmuseum.ca/Poland-WW2_ww2.html.

19. Testimony of Benjamin Witten. Permission of Veterans History Project, The Library of Congress.
20. Testimony of Roland J. Eggebeen. Permission of Veterans History Project, The Library of Congress.
21. Testimony of Oliver Stork. Permission of Veterans History Project, The Library of Congress.
22. Testimony of Charles Joseph Cilfone. Permission of Veterans History Project, The Library of Congress.
23. Testimony of Willard Reese. Permission of Veterans History Project, The Library of Congress.
24. Testimony of Karol Wierzbicki. Permission of Electronic Museum; translation by Agnieszka K. Marszalek. www.electronicmuseum.ca/Poland-WW2_ww2.html.
25. Testimony of Eva Galler. Interview and permission by John Menszer. www.holocaustsurvivors.org.
26. Testimony of Marie Vaillant-Couturier at Nuremberg Trials, January 28, 1946.
27. Testimony of Venezia Kamhi. Permission of Central Europe Center for Research and Documentation. www.centropa.org.
28. Testimony of Lily Arouch. Permission of Central Europe Center for Research and Documentation. www.centropa.org.
29. Testimony of General Stroop on Warsaw Ghetto Destruction. Avalon Project, Yale University Law School.
30. Testimony of Dieter Wisliceny at Nuremberg Trials, January 3, 1946.
31. Testimony of Solomon Radasky. Interview and permission by John Menszer. www.holocaustsurvivors.org.
32. Testimony of Louis Villette. Permission of Agnès Lelion, *Sillons de vie Gréville-Hague*, 54–56.
33. Testimony of Vladislava Karolewska at Nuremberg Trials, December 22, 1946.
34. Testimony of Rudolf Mildner at Nuremberg Trials, November 16, 1945.
35. Testimony of Simon Igel. Permission of Simon Igel.
36. Testimony of Rudolf Hoess at Nuremberg Trials, April 15, 1946.

Chapter Seven: Allies Invade France, 1944

1. President Kalinin on Allied Success. *Foreign Relations of the United States, 1944*, Vol. 4, 801–802.
2. Roosevelt to Congress on Tehran Conference. Department of State, *Bulletin*, January 15, 1944, Vol. 10, no. 238, 76–77.
3. Roosevelt and Stalin Letters on Poland. *Correspondence between the Chairman of the Council of Ministers of the U.S.S.R. and the Presidents of the USA and the Prime Ministers of Great Britain during the Great Patriotic War of 1941–1945*, June 19 and 24, 1944, Vol. 2, 137–139.
4. Allied Leaders Exchange Notes on Poland. *Correspondence between the Chairman of the Council of Ministers of the U.S.S.R. and the Presidents of the USA and the Prime Ministers of Great Britain during the Great Patriotic War of 1941–1945*, August 20 and 22, 1944, Vol. 2, 147–148.
5. U.S.S.R. on Soviet Prisoners. *Foreign Relations of the United States, 1944*, Vol. 4, 1251–1255.
6. Stalin to Roosevelt on Future Meeting. *Foreign Relations of the United States, 1944*, Vol. 4, 1019–1020.
7. Stalin Speech. Stalin, *War Speeches*, 104–114.

8. Testimony of Franciszek Kurak. Permission of Electronic Museum; translation by Agnieszka K. Marszalek. www.electronicmuseum.ca/Poland-WW2_ww2.html.
9. Testimony of Jesse E. Foster. Permission of Veterans History Project, The Library of Congress.
10. Testimony of Maurice Clancy. Permission of Peter Reichmuth.
11. Testimony of Jean Gragg. Permission of Peter Reichmuth.
12. Testimony of Dalton Eastus. Permission of Veterans History Project, The Library of Congress.
13. Testimony of Harold Shebeck. Permission of Peter Reichmuth.
14. Testimony of James Faust. Permission of Peter Reichmuth.
15. Testimony of Warren G. Hirt. Permission of Veterans History Project, The Library of Congress.
16. Testimony of John Torreano. Permission of John Torreano.
17. Testimony of Eric Strauss. Permission of Veterans History Project, The Library of Congress.
18. Testimony of John Misa. Permission of Veterans History Project, The Library of Congress.
19. Testimony of Arthur Gross. Permission of Veterans History Project, The Library of Congress.
20. Testimony of William Masterson. Permission of Peter Reichmuth.
21. Testimony of [Alfred] Scott Bates. Permission of Scott Bates.
22. Testimony of Wolfgang Geritzlehner. La Presse de la Manche, *Notre été 44*, 20.
23. Testimony of Heinz Perschke. Permission of Peter Reichmuth.
24. Testimony of Walter Schad. La Presse de la Manche, *Notre été 44*, 46.
25. Testimony of Rudolf Schuebl. La Presse de la Manche, *In the Name of Freedom*, 66.
26. Testimony of G. Moeller. Permission of Peter Reichmuth.
27. Testimony of Joachim Hübener. Permission of Peter Reichmuth.
28. Testimony of Sabine Leibholz-Bonhoeffer. Permission of Peter Reichmuth.
29. Testimony of Henri-Jean Reynaud. La Presse de la Manche, *Notre été 44*, 25.
30. Testimony of Raymond Paris. La Presse de la Manche, *In the Name of Freedom*, 26.
31. Testimony of Renée Couppey. La Presse de la Manche, *Notre été 44*, 28.
32. Testimony of Renée Caillemer. La Presse de la Manche, *Notre été 44*, 23.
33. Testimony of René Lecalier. La Presse de la Manche, *In the Name of Freedom*, 55.
34. Testimony of Jeanine Gazengel. La Presse de la Manche, *Notre été 44*, 31.
35. Testimony of Geneviève Onfroy. La Presse de la Manche, *Notre été 44*, 30.
36. Testimony of Charles Gosselin. La Presse de la Manche, *In the Name of Freedom*, 31.
37. Testimony of Claude Dreno. La Presse de la Manche, *In the Name of Freedom*, 39.
38. Testimony of Roger Lelaisant. La Presse de la Manche, *In the Name of Freedom*, 46.
39. Testimony of Louis Bihel. La Presse de la Manche, *In the Name of Freedom*, 70.
40. Testimony of Suzanne Duchemin. La Presse de la Manche, *In the Name of Freedom*, 25.
41. Testimony of Georges Dumoncel. La Presse de la Manche, *In the Name of Freedom*, 70.
42. Testimony of Julien Le Bas. La Presse de la Manche, *In the Name of Freedom*, 45.
43. Testimony of Maurice Nordez. La Presse de la Manche, *Notre été 44*, 53.
44. Testimony of Célestin Pellé. La Presse de la Manche, *In the Name of Freedom*, 84.
45. Testimony of Jean Taboué. La Presse de la Manche, *Notre été 44*, 59.
46. Testimony of Claude Haize. La Presse de la Manche, *In the Name of Freedom*, 53.
47. Testimony of André Gidon. La Presse de la Manche, *In the Name of Freedom*, 53.
48. Testimony of Paul Bedel. La Presse de la Manche, *In the Name of Freedom*, 78.
49. Testimony of Raymond Bertot. La Presse de la Manche, *In the Name of Freedom*, 34.
50. Testimony of Raymond Gardie. La Presse de la Manche, *In the Name of Freedom*, 82.

51. Testimony of Emile Bisson. La Presse de la Manche, *In the Name of Freedom*, 64.
52. Testimony of Raymond Lereculey. La Presse de la Manche, *In the Name of Freedom*, 38.
53. Testimony of Marie Couespel. La Presse de la Manche, *In the Name of Freedom*, 65.
54. Testimony of Yves de la Rüe. La Presse de la Manche, *In the Name of Freedom*, 30.
55. Testimony of Anne-Marie Lecostey. Permission of Agnès Lelion, *Sillons de vie Gréville-Hague*, 101.
56. Testimony of French Government at Nuremberg Trials, January 31, 1946.
57. Testimony of Marguerite Rouffanche at trial in Bordeaux, France in 1953.
58. Testimony of survivor. *Oradour-sur-Glane*, Édition de l'Association des Familles des Martyrs d'Oradour-sur-Glane.
59. Testimony of Germain Voisset. Permission of Peter Reichmuth.
60. Extract from a *Diary for Two Dutch Children Written by Their Parents*. Permission of Nederlands Instituut voor Oorlogsdocumentatie, Document II (99C-a, 1).
61. Testimony of John Torreano. Permission of John Torreano.
62. Testimony of Chester Mikus. Permission of Veterans History Project, The Library of Congress.
63. Testimony of Leroy D. "Whitey" Schaller. Permission of Veterans History Project, The Library of Congress.
64. Testimony of Glen Brutus. Permission of Veterans History Project, The Library of Congress.
65. Testimony of John Torreano. Permission of John Torreano.
66. Testimony of John J. Bertram, Jr. Permission of Veterans History Project, The Library of Congress.
67. Testimony of David Saltman. Permission of Peter Reichmuth.
68. Testimony of Fred Litty. Permission of Veterans History Project, The Library of Congress.
69. Allies Warn German Partners on Staying in the War. Department of State, *Bulletin*, May 13, 1944, Vol. 10, no. 255, 425.
70. Testimony of Samuel Pisar. Permission of Peter Reichmuth.
71. Testimony of Stanislav Mikhailovich Severinovsky. Permission of Irina Willis.
72. Testimony of Leslie Werwicki. Permission of Peter Reichmuth.
73. Testimony of Alexandra Petrovna Medvedeva-Nazarkina. Interview and permission by Artem Drabkin. www.iremember.ru.
74. Stalin Order of the Day. Stalin, *War Speeches*, pp. 115–17.
75. Testimony of Karol Wierzbicki. Permission of Electronic Museum; translation by Agnieszka K. Marszalek. www.electronicmuseum.ca/Poland-WW2_ww2.html.
76. Testimony of Maurice Lampe at Nuremberg Trials, January 25, 1946.
77. Testimony of Solomon Radasky. Interview and permission by John Menszer. www.holocaustsurvivors.org.
78. Testimony of Victor Dupont at Nuremberg Trials, January 26, 1946.
79. Testimony of Rudolf Mildner at Nuremberg Trials, June 27, 1945.
80. Testimony of Dieter Wisliceny at Nuremberg Trials, January 3, 1946.

Chapter Eight: Allied Victory, 1945

1. Stalin Defends Views on Poland. *Correspondence between the Chairman of the Council of Ministers of the U.S.S.R. and the Presidents of the USA and the Prime Ministers of Great Britain during the Great Patriotic War of 1941–1945*, Vol. 2, 173–174.
2. Roosevelt Warns of Split over Poland. *Correspondence between the Chairman of the Council of Ministers of the U.S.S.R. and the Presidents of the USA and the*

Prime Ministers of Great Britain during the Great Patriotic War of 1941–1945, Vol. 2, 177–179.

3. Communiqué of the Yalta Conference. *Foreign Relations of the United States, The Conferences at Malta and Yalta 1945,* 969–975; *The Axis in Defeat: A Collection of Documents on American Policy toward Germany and Japan,* 6–8; Department of State, *Bulletin,* February 18, 1945, Vol. 12, no. 295, 213–216.

4. Roosevelt Report on Yalta. *The Axis in Defeat: A Collection of Documents on American Policy toward Germany and Japan,* 8–10.

5. Roosevelt to Stalin on Poland. *Foreign Relations of the United States, 1945,* Vol. 5, 194–196; see also *Correspondence between the Chairman of the Council of Ministers of the U.S.S.R. and the Presidents of the USA and the Prime Ministers of Great Britain during the Great Patriotic War of 1941–1945,* Vol. 2, 191–193.

6. Stalin to Roosevelt on Poland. *Correspondence between the Chairman of the Council of Ministers of the U.S.S.R. and the Presidents of the USA and the Prime Ministers of Great Britain during the Great Patriotic War of 1941–1945,* Vol. 2, 200–202.

7. Allies Warn Germany on Prisoners. Department of State, *Bulletin,* April 29, 1945, Vol. 12, no. 305, 811.

8. Stalin to Truman on Poland. *Correspondence between the Chairman of the Council of Ministers of the U.S.S.R. and the Presidents of the USA and the Prime Ministers of Great Britain during the Great Patriotic War of 1941–1945,* Vol. 2, 208–209.

9. Testimony on Winter Privations in Holland. Permission of Nederlands Instituut voor Oorlogsdocumentatie, Document II (332-L, 13).

10. Testimony of Franklin E. Kameny. Permission of Veterans History Project, The Library of Congress.

11. Testimony of Raymond Chow. Permission of Veterans History Project, The Library of Congress.

12. Testimony of Margriet. Permission of The Dutch Underground. msbeliever.tripod.com/Underground.html.

13. Testimony of Jesse E. Foster. Permission of Veterans History Project, The Library of Congress.

14. Testimony of Leroy Schaller. Permission of Veterans History Project, The Library of Congress.

15. Testimony of Glen Brutus. Permission of Veterans History Project, The Library of Congress.

16. Testimony of Alex Haddon. Permission of Veterans History Project, The Library of Congress.

17. Testimony of John J. Bertram, Jr. Permission of Veterans History Project, The Library of Congress.

18. Testimony of [Alfred] Scott Bates. Permission of Scott Bates.

19. Testimony of Heinz Perschke. Permission of Peter Reichmuth.

20. Testimony of Markov Vladimir Protasovich. Interview and permission by Artem Drabkin. www.iremember.ru.

21. Testimony of Tadeusz "Wicher" Wichrowski. Permission of Electronic Museum; translation by Agnieszka K. Marszalek. www.electronicmuseum.ca/Poland-WW2_ww2.html.

22. Testimony of Simon Igel. Permission of Simon Igel.

23. Testimony of Maria Stepanovna Nidilko. Interview and permission by Artem Drabkin. www.iremember.ru.

24. Testimony of Ivan Ivanovich Konovalov. Interview and permission by Artem Drabkin. www.iremember.ru.

25. Kultur! *La Voix des Belges.*

26. Truman Statement on Meeting of Allied Armies. Department of State, *Bulletin*, April 29, 1945, Vol. 12, no. 305, 808.
27. Stalin Statement on Meeting of Allied Armies. Stalin, *War Speeches*, 127–128.
28. Testimony of Jack Bowen. Permission of Veterans History Project, The Library of Congress.
29. Testimony of Joseph A. Gautsch. Permission of Veterans History Project, The Library of Congress.
30. Testimony of Naum Kravets. Permission of Central Europe Center for Research and Documentation. www.centropa.org.
31. Act of Surrender. *The Axis in Defeat: A Collection of Documents on American Policy toward Germany and Japan*, 24–25; see also *A Decade of American Foreign Policy*, 1941–1949, 505–506; see also *United States Statutes at Large*, 79th Congress, 1st Session, 1945, Vol. 59, Part 2, 1858–1859.
32. Testimony of Tamara Aronovna Zeveke. Permission of Irina Willis.
33. Stalin Victory Speech. Stalin, *War Speeches*, 135–137.
34. Truman Reports on Potsdam Conference. *The Axis in Defeat: A Collection of Documents on American Policy toward Germany and Japan*, 18–21.
35. Truman Seeks Soviet Cooperation. *Correspondence between the Chairman of the Council of Ministers of the U.S.S.R. and the Presidents of the USA and the Prime Ministers of Great Britain during the Great Patriotic War of 1941–1945*, Vol. 2, 267–268.
36. Stalin's Response to Truman on Cooperation. *Correspondence between the Chairman of the Council of Ministers of the U.S.S.R. and the Presidents of the USA and the Prime Ministers of Great Britain during the Great Patriotic War of 1941–1945*, Vol. 2, 268–269.

Notes

Introduction

1. Churchill, Winston S. *Their Finest Hour*. Boston, Houghton Mifflin Co., p. 42.
2. Winston Churchill, Speech to House of Commons, June 4, 1940.
3. Winston Churchill, Speech to House of Commons, August 20, 1940.

Chapter One: Appeasement in Munich, 1938

1. Adolf Hitler (1889–1945) was appointed Chancellor of Germany in 1933; he ruled until his suicide in 1945; Weimar Republic refers to the constitutional democratic system that governed Germany from the end of World War I until 1933. The Treaty of Versailles was signed in 1919 to end World War I and was criticized as a humiliation for Germany by the Nazis as well as many other Germans.
2. Rhineland was demilitarized by the Treaty of Versailles to create a buffer zone between France and Belgium on one side and Germany on the other. Hitler sent the German army into this area in 1936; he was not challenged by the western powers. The Treaty of Versailles prohibited *Anschluss*, the union of Austria with the German state. Germany and Austria united in 1938.
3. Sudetenland was the German name for a part of western Czechoslovakia inhabited by a German-speaking population. Hitler falsely claimed that the Czechs mistreated the German population.
4. Edvard Beneš (1884–1948) served as president of Czechoslovakia from 1935–1938 and from 1945–1948.
5. Neville Chamberlain (1869–1940) was prime minister of Britain from 1937–1940; Edouard Daladier (1884–1970), who had been premier of France two previous times, was premier again from 1938–1940; Benito Mussolini (1883–1945) ruled Italy from 1922 until 1943.
6. Hitler-Chamberlain Declaration, September 30, 1938.
7. Joseph Stalin (1878–1953) was the ruler of the U.S.S.R.; he held the post of general secretary of the Communist Party.
8. *Kristallnacht* took place in November 1938. The Nazi attack on Jewish establishments led to the rounding up of thousands of people who were sent to concentration camps, the burning of about 200 synagogues, and the deaths of approximately ninety people. The broken glass in the streets gave this event its name.
9. The *People's Observer* was the official newspaper of the Nazi Party.
10. *The Czech Word*.
11. *Evening Czech Word*.
12. *The Evening Messenger*.
13. Ladislav Homola was born in 1920 in Choltice, Czechoslovakia. Only eighteen years old at the time of the Munich Pact, Homola was not particularly interested in politics at the time.
14. Terezín (Theresienstadt) was a concentration camp in northern Czechoslovakia not far from the German border.
15. Bohuslav Krajíček was eighteen years old when the war started. He saved his harshest criticism for the Russians.
16. Emil Hácha (1872–1945) succeeded Beneš as president of Czechoslovakia in 1938.
17. Reinhard Heydrich was a high-ranking SS officer involved in the plan to exterminate Europe's Jewish population.

Chapter Two: War Is Declared, 1939

1. Danzig was established as a free city administered by Poland after World War I. In 1939, Hitler pressured Poland to accept German control over Danzig and the Corridor.
2. Josef (Józef) Beck (1894–1944) was the Polish foreign minister.
3. Beck's Speech to Polish Parliament, May 5, 1939.
4. M. Litvinov (1876–1951) was Soviet foreign minister from 1930–1939 and later ambassador to the United States; V. Molotov (1890–1986) replaced Litvinov as Soviet foreign minister in 1939 and signed the nonaggression pact with Germany.
5. Joachim von Ribbentrop (1893–1946) was Hitler's foreign minister from 1938 until the end of the war. He was sentenced to death at the Nuremberg Trials.
6. Leopold III (1901–1983) was king of Belgium from 1934–1951; his statement was issued on behalf of Belgium, Denmark, Finland, Luxemburg, the Netherlands, Norway, and Sweden.
7. Robert Coulondre was French ambassador in Moscow before becoming ambassador in Germany.
8. Daladier Appeal to Hitler, August 26, 1939.
9. Hitler's Response to Daladier, August 27, 1939.
10. Hitler used the word "unbearable" at least twice. See Hitler Remarks to French Ambassador, August 25, 1939 and Hitler to British Government, August 29, 1939.
11. Pope Pius XII (1876–1958) became pope in 1939.
12. *Time.*
13. *Polish Daily.*
14. Ignacy Moscicki (1867–1946) was president of Poland from 1926–1939. Marshal Pilsudski (1867–1935) held actual power in the country from 1926–1935.
15. French ambassador Coulondre sent these comments to Georges Bonnet (1889–1973), French foreign minister under Premier Daladier. Bonnet served in the Vichy government during the war.
16. *The Capital Newspaper.*

Chapter Three: Germany Conquers Western Europe, 1940

1. Maginot Line refers to French defensive forts built between the wars. The forts did not protect the entire border; the Germans broke through at Sedan.
2. Whether Hitler actually danced a jig is disputed today, but in any case the population of the Allied countries accepted the idea of Hitler's pettiness.
3. In November 1940, more than 500 German planes bombed the city of Coventry, destroying most of the city as well as the cathedral. A postwar controversy charged that Churchill knew of the attack in advance but allowed it to proceed to protect Britain's code-breakers. In reality, the warnings of a German attack did not specify the city; the British government and Royal Air Force responded as well as possible under the circumstances.
4. Barbara Tuchman. *The Guns of August,* 122.
5. Charles de Gaulle (1890–1970) organized the Free French Forces and urged the French people to resist both German occupation and the collaborationist French government. The Vichy government sentenced him to death, but eventually he was recognized as the leader of a proud and defiant France.
6. *The Workers* (Labor) *Newspaper.*
7. The evacuation from Dunkirk, code named Operation Dynamo, saved approximately 200,000 British soldiers and more than 100,000 French. While some observers criticized the British for leaving the continent to its fate, a more realistic analysis

suggests that the British commander, General Lord Gort (1886–1946), made the correct decision under difficult circumstances.

8. Marshal Henri Philippe Pétain, a French military hero in World War I, became the head of France's Vichy government.

9. *The Attack* was the newspaper of Minister of Propaganda Goebbels.

10. Marcel Tison of Cherbourg was one of 20,000 soldiers from the Manche region taken prisoner in 1940.

11. Henri Hervieu from Brix spent nearly five years in a German prison camp.

12. Mayenne is in northwestern France about forty-five miles east of Rennes.

13. After the defeat of Poland, Karol Wierzbicki made his way through Hungary and eventually to France to continue the fight against the Germans. He volunteered for action in Finland but was sent to Norway with other Polish volunteers.

14. Many Polish veterans who escaped German-occupied Poland came to fight for the Allies in Western Europe. Jozef Franciszek Nowak, born in 1918 and trained as a pilot in the Polish air force, escaped Poland after the German invasion and made his way first to Hungary and then to France.

15. Tadeuz Wichrowski was born in 1916; like many other Polish army veterans, he was interned in Hungary after the German invasion of his country. He was able to make his way across Yugoslavia and then sailed on a Greek merchant ship to reach France in time for the battle on the western front. Like some other Polish fighters, he was disappointed by the rapid collapse of the French army.

16. Belfort is in eastern France.

17. Emil Reuter was a lawyer and president of the Chamber of Deputies in Luxembourg at the time of the German invasion.

18. German concentration camp located north of Berlin.

19. Caudillo was the title used by Franco.

20. Hermann Göring (1893–1946) was a leading Nazi and head of the air force (*Luftwaffe*). Hitler's plan for the invasion of England, code-named Operation Sealion, envisioned the destruction of the British air force followed by a massive naval assault and landing. For a variety of reasons, including both the continued viability of the Royal Air Force and the lack of sufficient naval ships on the German side, Hitler canceled Operation Sealion in the fall of 1940.

Chapter Four: Invasion of Soviet Union, 1941

1. Hitler Seeks Spanish Participation, February 6, 1941.

2. Franco Answers Hitler on War, February 26, 1941.

3. February 23 was the anniversary of Mussolini's formation of the *Italiani di Combattimento* in 1919.

4. Although the United States was not a belligerent at this time, Roosevelt and Churchill met in August 1941 and issued a statement of principles or war aims that served as a fundamental document for the Allies throughout the war.

5. The German invasion of June 1941 took Soviet forces by surprise and many Soviet planes were destroyed on the ground.

6. Naum Kravets grew up in Moscow. Kravets eventually graduated as an air navigator-radar operator with the rank of master sergeant. In January 1943, he was assigned to the Baltic Navy.

7. With this treaty signed in Moscow, the British and Soviet governments pledged to assist each other in the war against Germany. The U.S.S.R. promised that it would not sign a separate peace with Germany.

8. In this agreement between the Polish government in exile in London and the Soviet government, the U.S.S.R. repudiated the Nazi-Soviet nonaggression pact of 1939. In

exchange, the two governments promised to work together against Germany. Later in the war, the Soviet government would violate some of its promises.

9. Samouil was born in Zhitomir, Ukraine, in 1921. He finished school when he was nineteen years old in 1940, and he was then drafted into the army.

10. Polina was born in Gomel, Belorussia, in 1922. She was seventeen years old when the war started, and she and her eleven-year-old brother were completely alone during the siege of Leningrad.

11. General Tōjō (1884–1948) served as prime minister of Japan from 1941, when he pushed for war against the United States, until 1944, after Japan's defeat in the Battle of Saipan. After the war, he was sentenced to death and hanged at the end of 1948.

12. The official title of this document was "Memorandum Concerning the Participation of Poland in the Planning of the Joint Prosecution of the War."

13. The occupation under the Germans involved various forms of deprivation: food, clothes, soap, shoes, and other everyday items. The Germans required civilian labor battalions to work for them.

14. Todt Organization used forced labor to build German defenses.

15. German officer Otto Ohlendorf described the *Einsatzgruppen* system of mobile killing units deployed on the eastern front. A long-time Nazi, Ohlendorf played a key role overseeing the killing squads active in the Ukraine and responsible for nearly 100,000 deaths. Col. John Harlan Amen, associate trial counsel for the United States, conducted the interview. Ohlendorf was convicted, sentenced to death, and hanged in 1951.

16. Eva Galler was about seventeen years old in 1941; she lived in Oleszyce, Poland.

17. There were thousands of Norwegian prisoners in the German camp system. Cappelen was arrested in November 1941.

18. Born in 1921, Nisim Navon described the insecurity of life under German occupation. Most of the Jewish families in his community did not survive the war.

19. Testimony related to Mauthausen Concentration Camp where Hollriegel, a member of the SS, held an important position. After his testimony, he was sentenced to death.

20. The Jewish population of Lithuania was one of Europe's largest and most vibrant before the war. Abram Suzkever survived the liquidation of the ghetto in Vilna.

21. This notorious decree, known in German as *Nacht und Nebel* (Night and Fog) provided for the disappearance of enemies of the Nazis, who were to face the death penalty or deportation to Germany. Any inquiry into their disappearance would be met with silence as they disappeared into the "night" and "fog."

Chapter Five: Occupation and Terror in Europe, 1942

1. Molotov Note to Roosevelt, June 12, 1942.

2. Soviet Ambassador Speaks in New York, June 22, 1942.

3. Operation Torch was the code name for the Allied invasion of North Africa in 1942.

4. Erwin Rommel (1891–1944) was one of the most important German generals during World War II. He earned the nickname Desert Fox in Africa before taking over the defense of Normandy. He was implicated in the assassination attempt of Hitler in 1944 and forced to commit suicide. The First Battle of El Alamein in the summer of 1942 was a British victory, stopping the Axis advance toward the Suez Canal in northern Egypt.

5. The Second Battle of El Alamein in October-November 1942 saw British forces break through Axis lines in Egypt; Bernard Law Montgomery (1887–1976) was one of the leading British generals (later field marshal) of the war. He became famous for his victory over Rommel in North Africa and went on to play major roles in the invasion of Sicily, Normandy, and Germany. Like Patton, his personality led to difficulties and controversies.

6. Kasserine Pass in Tunisia was a battle in which Axis forces defeated inexperienced American troops in February 1943.
7. Reinhard Heydrich (1904–1942) was a leader of Germany's anti-Jewish policies. He helped plan the so-called final solution at the Wannsee Conference outside Berlin; he was assassinated in 1942 in Prague.
8. Heinrich Himmler (1900–1945) was one of the highest ranking Nazis, in charge of the *Schutzstaffel* (SS) and responsible for running the extermination camps; Adolf Eichmann (1906–1962) oversaw the logistical implementation of the extermination policy. Gestapo section IVA4b dealt with Jewish affairs.
9. Auschwitz and Treblinka were two of the notorious extermination camps in Poland.
10. Dieter Wisliceny (1912–1948) participated in the implementation of the final solution, especially in Hungary, Greece, and Slovakia. After his testimony at Nuremberg, he was hanged in Czechoslovakia.
11. Warren G. Hirt joined the Seabees and achieved the rank of lieutenant senior grade.
12. Bizrete, Oran, Mostaganem, Algiers, and Sidi Bel Abbès were towns in Algeria and Tunisia.
13. A joint declaration by Australia, Belgium, Canada, China, Costa Rica, Cuba, Czechoslovakia, Dominican Republic, El Salvador, Greece, Guatemala, Haiti, Honduras, India, Luxembourg, Netherlands, New Zealand, Nicaragua, Norway, Panama, Poland, South Africa, the United Kingdom, the United States, the U.S.S.R., and Yugoslavia.
14. Gen. George C. Marshall (1880–1959) was army chief of staff and advisor to Roosevelt.
15. *Mein Kampf* (*My Struggle*) was Hitler's official autobiography.
16. This report was sent to Washington by Averell Harriman (1891–1986), Roosevelt's special representative and later ambassador to the U.S.S.R.
17. Fifth Column refers to the fear of internal subversion; when the war started, Stalin questioned the loyalty of some non-Russian nationalities and condemned many of them to labor camps.
18. During the Battle of Stalingrad, this tank driver successfully destroyed some German mortar positions but also suffered severe burns on his face.
19. Despite the agreement between the German government and the Catholic and Protestant churches to allow churches and church schools to remain open in exchange for obedience to state ideology, a small group of clergy expressed their opposition to Nazi techniques. The Confessing Church, a branch of the Lutheran church, produced several well-known resistance leaders such as Martin Niemöller and Dietrich Bonhoeffer.
20. Klaus Reichmuth did not continue his resistance activities. While serving his time in a concentration camp, he noted that prisoners who had been arrested for a second offense were treated very badly. He feared speaking out and being arrested again. After being released in September 1942, Reichmuth served in the German army. He became a pastor after the war. His friend Rendtorff also entered the German army and was killed on the Russian front.
21. Danuta Socha, born in 1927, joined the Polish resistance in 1942 and used the code name "Rad."
22. In southeastern Poland.
23. Reference to Himmler.
24. While in prison, Jan Campert (1902–1943) wrote the poem "The Song of the Eighteen Dead" (*Lid der 18 Toten*) after prisoners had been executed by the Germans. His poem became a symbol of resistance; Campert died in Neuengamme concentration camp near Hamburg in January 1943. The exact cause of his death has become controversial, with reports of death from hunger, tuberculosis, or murder by fellow prisoners after he became an informer in exchange for more food.

25. While Germans targeted Jews for the final solution with the creation of ghettoes and extermination camps, the Nazis also killed many people through direct and personal acts of cruelty.

26. Leo Miechalowski was a priest imprisoned at Dachau concentration camp for five years; Dachau was located near Munich.

27. The final solution was carried out in stages, with the forced transfer of Jews to ghettoes in many parts of Eastern Europe as the first step. Often ghettoes in smaller towns were consolidated into those in larger cities, such as Lodz or Warsaw, before the population was shipped to a concentration camp for annihilation.

28. Oleszyce and Lubaczow are in southeastern Poland in an area that had a large Jewish population.

29. Paul Blobel (1894–1951) was an SS officer and commander of Sonderkommando 4A. His units carried out atrocities in the Ukraine, including the massacre at Babi Yar. He was hanged for these crimes in 1951.

30. Gruppenführer Heinrich Müller helped run the Gestapo and was involved in all aspects of the so-called final solution; *Einsatzgruppen* were the mobile killing units that murdered approximately one million people on the eastern front before the extermination camps were in full operation.

31. The German occupation of every European country included the forced labor of the local citizens, with the greatest burden placed on the Jewish population.

32. On September 23, 1942, Germans killed more than 2,800 citizens of Kortelisy, Ukraine. German atrocities against Ukrainians and other residents of the U.S.S.R. continued throughout the war. John Gregorovich, chairman of the Ukrainian Canadian Civil Liberties Association, provided this testimony.

Chapter Six: Victory at Stalingrad; Italy Invaded, 1943.

1. German Ambassador on Talks with France, December 15, 1943.

2. *Izvestiia*, Moscow, February 3, 1943.

3. The Battle of Kursk took place in the summer of 1943 and was the biggest tank battle of the war. Germany suffered a major loss of armor and, combined with the earlier defeat at Stalingrad, never regained the initiative in the U.S.S.R.

4. Cordell Hull (1871–1955) served as American secretary of state from 1933–1944.

5. A. Gromyko (1909–1989) was Soviet ambassador to the United States (1943–1946) and later foreign minister.

6. Operation Husky was the code name for the invasion of Sicily; the king of Italy was Victor Emmanuel III; Pietro Badoglio (1871–1956) served as premier for one year.

7. Albert Kesselring (1885–1960) commanded the German defense of Italy after 1943.

8. Anthony Eden (1897–1977) was British foreign secretary during the war; Foo Ping-sheung (1895–1965) was Chinese ambassador to the Soviet Union from 1943–1949.

9. Stalin Speech, November 6, 1943.

10. Jürgen Stroop (1895–1951) commanded the Nazi troops that destroyed the Warsaw ghetto. He was hanged in Poland for war crimes.

11. Rudolf Hoess (Höss) (1901–1947) was the commandant of Auschwitz concentration camp. He testified at Nuremberg and was hanged near the Auschwitz crematorium.

12. Vasily Chuikov (1900–1982) was a Soviet general famous for his leadership at the Battle of Stalingrad, the advance through Poland, and the Battle of Berlin.

13. Pierre Laval (1883–1945) was an important French politician in the 1930s who later served in the Vichy government of Pétain. After the war he was tried and executed for collaboration.

14. Joseph Goebbels (1897–1945) was Hitler's minister of propaganda.

15. Semyon Timoshenko (1895–1970) was an important Soviet military commander.

16. Casablanca Conference Protocol, February 12, 1943.
17. Warren G. Hirt joined the Seabees and achieved the rank of lieutenant senior grade.
18. Anzio refers to the Allied landing beach in Italy in January 1944. Allied forces were slow to advance and met stronger-than-expected German resistance. Despite the difficult battles that ensued, the city of Rome was liberated in June, on the eve of the landings in Normandy.
19. Michael John Donoghue served with the First Battalion, London Irish Rifles, Royal Ulster Rifles in North Africa and Italy. He wrote this "personal remembrance" about the difficult fighting across Italy.
20. Raymond Chow was born in China in 1921 and moved to the U.S. when he was ten years old. He entered the American army and served in the 509th Regiment, a parachute battalion that saw action in North Africa, Italy, southern France, and Germany.
21. John Torreano, born in Italy in 1920, moved with his parents to the United States in 1927. He grew up in Michigan and enlisted in the army in 1942. As a private first class in the 82nd Airborne, 505th Regiment, Company A, he saw action in almost every theater in the European war. He left the military in 1945 with a few pieces of shrapnel remaining in his body.
22. Gen. George Patton (1885–1945) was one of the best known American generals in World War II. His aggressive style placed him at the center of military action but also led to controversy.
23. Gen. James Gavin (1907–1990) commanded the 82nd Airborne Division.
24. Keith Campbell was born in 1920 in Hollowtown, Montana, but grew up in Spokane.
25. Katyn Massacre took place near Smolensk after Soviet forces occupied eastern Poland and arrested intellectuals, military officers, and other Polish leaders. More than 20,000 were killed, but when the Germans discovered the graves, the Soviet government denied guilt.
26. Meeting of foreign ministers of Britain, the United States, and the U.S.S.R. (also signed by Chinese ambassador in Moscow).
27. Bomber pilots like Polish air force veteran Nowak made important contributions to the Allied war effort.
28. Benjamin Witten was born in 1918 and served in the U.S. Army Air Force in Europe. He enlisted the day after Pearl Harbor. As a Jewish American, Witten chose the air force because he knew that many pilots were killed during their missions and he preferred death to becoming a German prisoner of war. He attained the rank of first lieutenant.
29. Gen. Curtis LeMay (1906–1990) helped devise American bombing strategy and tactics during the war in Europe and in the Pacific.
30. Roland J. Eggebeen was born in 1923. He served as a staff sergeant in the 8th Air Force in England and in Europe.
31. Oliver Stork was born in 1923 and during the war flew thirty missions in the B-17 Flying Fortress. He participated in fifteen missions over Germany, thirteen over France, and one each over Belgium and the Netherlands. He held the rank of first lieutenant.
32. Charles Joseph Cilfone was born in 1920 and lived in Chicago when drafted in 1941. He served with the 9th Air Force.
33. Willard Reese was born in 1923 and enlisted in 1942. In 1943, he joined the 8th Air Force and served until August 1945.
34. Polish veteran Karol Wierzbicki worked as part of a western underground smuggling operation, moving Allied soldiers and escapees from southern France into Spain for transfer to England. Betrayed by a German agent, Wierzbicki and at least two of his comrades were arrested and placed in concentration camps.

35. Dora-Mittelbau was a subcamp of Buchenwald near Nordhausen in central Germany.
36. Eva Galler saw atrocities but managed to survive. She witnessed the deaths of her younger brother and sister as the three tried to escape deportation to a death camp (Belzec concentration camp was in Poland). She sought the anonymity of a large city—Cracow, but was caught in a police roundup of young people fit enough to work. She survived the war through wits and luck.
37. Marie Vaillant-Couturier, born in Paris in 1912, spent three years in prison for her work with the French resistance. She testified at the Nuremberg Trials about the atrocities she had witnessed at Auschwitz and Ravensbruck concentration camps. Prosecutors, attempting to establish camp procedures for the historical record, allowed her to speak for a considerable length of time.
38. Dr. Josef Mengele (1911–1979) carried out medical experiments on prisoners at Auschwitz. He participated in selecting new inmates for life or death and was known as "the angel of death." His experiments on twins were notorious for their cruelty.
39. Brannik was a pro-Fascist youth organization.
40. While the destruction of the Warsaw Ghetto was under way in Poland, Nazi officials were applying the final solution to the Jews of Greece. Dieter Wisliceny also testified about German atrocities in Slovakia.
41. Alois Brunner (1912–?) worked closely with Eichmann and was responsible for sending thousands of Jews from Greece, France, Slovakia, and elsewhere to death camps.
42. Solomon Radasky was from Poland, and in 1943, he was in Majdanek concentration camp near Lublin, Poland. He was within minutes of death but was saved because he was on a list for transfer to another camp.
43. In many occupied countries, the Germans required forced labor by the local population; some civilians volunteered for work in Germany when threatened with military service or harm to their family.
44. Arrested in 1941 for anti-German resistance activity, this former schoolteacher was sent to Ravensbruck concentration camp. There she was subjected to medical experiments involving "bone regeneration."
45. SiPo or *Sicherheitspolizei* was the security police; SD or *Sicherheitsdienst* was the Security Service; Theresienstadt (Terezín) was a concentration camp in northwest Czechoslovakia.
46. Klaus Barbie (1913–1991) was a member of the SS and Gestapo stationed in France. He is most famous for the torture death of French resistance leader Jean Moulin and the deportation of more than forty Jewish children from an orphanage to Auschwitz in 1944. For these actions he was called the "butcher of Lyon." Put on trial in France in the late 1980s, Barbie was sentenced to life in prison.
47. Ernst Kaltenbrunner (1903–1946), a native Austrian, was one of the highest ranking members of the SS. After Heydrich's assassination, he took over many of his duties and therefore was involved in the implementation of the Holocaust. Convicted of war crimes, he was hanged in 1946.

Chapter Seven: Allies Invade France, 1944

1. Mikhail Kalinin (1875–1946) served as chairman of the Presidium of the Supreme Soviet, a figurehead position called president of the U.S.S.R.
2. Stalin to Roosevelt, February 16, 1944.
3. Albert Kesselring (1885–1960) was a highly decorated German general who is best known for his stubborn defense of Italy in 1943 and 1944; Gustav Line refers to a series of German defensive positions in central Italy.

4. Operation Market Garden was an unsuccessful Allied attempt to seize the bridge in Arnhem (Holland) to facilitate a crossing of the Rhine in the fall of 1944. Eisenhower approved of the plan put forward by Montgomery, but logistical problems and German resistance forced an Allied retreat.

5. Oradour-sur-Glane was a town in central France destroyed by the SS; more than 600 inhabitants were killed.

6. Anne Frank (1929–1945), a young Jewish girl, hid with her family in Amsterdam; they were eventually captured. She died in Bergen Belsen concentration camp; her diary was published after the war.

7. Stalin Order of the Day, November 7, 1944.

8. Western leaders appealed for Soviet aid for the Warsaw uprising; Soviet army claimed that logistical problems prevented military assistance.

9. Note from Soviet ambassador Gromyko.

10. Jesse E. Foster was born in 1923 in New York. He was shot down over Italy. He spent the rest of the war as a prisoner and was liberated in April 1945.

11. Juno Beach, located between Sword and Gold, was the landing beach for Canadian forces on D-Day.

12. Sword Beach was one of the British landing beaches on D-Day. It was located on the eastern end of the five Normandy beaches.

13. Mulberry Harbors were artificial harbors towed across the English Channel to allow the unloading of supplies. The Allies intended to use the harbors until the ports of Le Havre and Cherbourg had been captured, but one of the Mulberries (the American one) was quickly destroyed in a storm. The other harbor (at Arromanches) was used for several months.

14. Dalton Eastus, born in 1920, was drafted in 1942. He served in the U.S. army and participated in the invasion of Normandy in 1944.

15. Warren G. Hirt joined the Seabees and achieved the rank of lieutenant senior grade.

16. Ste.-Mère-Église was one of the first towns assaulted by Allied paratroopers on D-Day. The airborne divisions wanted to secure the area inland to assist the breakout from Utah Beach. Ste.-Mère-Église became famous for its steeple where one paratrooper (John Steele) dangled from his parachute.

17. Eric Strauss was born in Mainz, Germany. In the 1930s, his family moved to a town near Frankfurt, but as Jews, they suffered from growing oppression under the Nazis. The family moved to the United States in 1938, and Strauss served as a private in Company A, 22nd Infantry Regiment, 4th Division.

18. John Misa was born in 1920 and drafted into the U.S. army when he was twenty years old.

19. Arthur Gross grew up in New Jersey.

20. Barfleur and St. Vaast la Hougue are located on the northeast coast of the Cotentin peninsula.

21. Alfred Scott Bates was born in 1923 in Evanston, Illinois. His grandfather and father were lawyers, but Bates broke with family tradition when he developed a love for French literature in college. He was a student at Carleton College when Pearl Harbor occurred, and despite various medical problems, he was drafted in 1942. While rarely seeing combat, Bates traveled with American troops through France and Germany, helping to organize the occupation in parts of Normandy and in Munich.

22. In June 1944, Wolfgang Geritzlehner was a machine-gunner in the 6th Parachutists Regiment and was enjoying a celebration with his comrades when the invasion started.

23. Eighteen-year-old German soldier Heinz Perschke was serving in Denmark when the Allies invaded Normandy. He continued to believe that Germany could win the war or at least defend its own territory against the Allies. He put great faith in the V1 and V2 rocket programs as weapons that would prevent Germany's defeat.

24. Walter Schad was a twenty-eight-year-old German soldier based in Normandy in 1944. He served as an army medical captain in the Third Battalion of the Sixth German Airborne Regiment.

25. Rudolf Schuebl, a seventeen-year-old Austrian who had enlisted in the German army, was transferred from Brittany to Normandy just in time for the Allied invasion.

26. G. Moeller, a nineteen-year-old German soldier, was serving on the eastern front when he heard about the Allied invasion of France. He hoped that the landing would lead to a rapid end to the war.

27. Joachim Hübener was a twenty-two-year-old German soldier serving on the eastern front in the Ukraine when the Allied invasion of France occurred. Hübener volunteered to join the army and expressed strong German nationalistic feelings.

28. Martin Niemöller (1892–1984) was a German theologian whose opposition to Nazi control of Protestant churches landed him in concentration camps during the war.

29. Sabine Leibholz-Bonhoeffer was the twin sister of the noted German theologian Dietrich Bonhoeffer. She was living in England at the time of the Allied invasion and noted that many people in England were celebrating but felt nervous at the same time. "Roll out the Barrel" was also known as Beer Barrel Polka and became popular during World War II.

30. The mayor of Ste.-Mère-Église was Alexandre Reynaud, and his son Henri-Jean, ten years old at the time, remembered the American paratroopers and the fire that broke out in the middle of the town near the church.

31. Raymond Paris was twenty years old in 1944. He witnessed, and barely survived, the American paratroop landing at Sainte-Mère-Église on the night of June 5.

32. Renée Couppey lived in St.-Lô in 1944.

33. Renée Caillemer was thirty-nine years old in 1944.

34. René Lecalier was nineteen years old and involved in the resistance movement. He joined the struggle for the Americans and later in the regular French army.

35. Jeanine Gazengel was twelve years old in 1944. Her parents ran the café-grocery store of La Madeleine in Sainte-Marie-du-Mont. Because of the strategic location of the store only 800 meters from the beach, the Americans were interested in any information her father might have.

36. Geneviève Onfroy, twenty-four years old in 1944, lived on a farm in the village of Hubert in Sainte-Marie-du-Mont.

37. Twenty-two-year-old Charles Gosselin witnessed some of the fighting on the outskirts of Sainte-Marie-du-Mont.

38. Fifteen-year-old Claude Dreno remembered the frightening sound of the bombardment of Valognes.

39. Arrested by the Gestapo for his resistance work, nineteen-year-old Roger Lelaisant was in prison in St.-Lô at the time of the allied invasion. Lelaisant survived an allied bombing raid and then escaped from a hospital to rejoin the resistance.

40. Louis Bihel, nineteen years old in 1944, remembered the constant fighting and the image of piles of dead bodies.

41. Suzanne Duchemin was twenty-two years old in 1944.

42. Georges Dumoncel witnessed a four-day battle between Americans and Germans.

43. Julien Le Bas remembered the horrific noise and the devastation that Allied bombing brought to St.-Lô.

44. Maurice Nordez was a mechanic who worked with his father.

45. Caught between enemy lines for several days, Célestin Pellé and his family tried to assist the Americans as best they could.

46. Jean Taboué, twenty years old in 1944, was a student at the naval dockyard.

47. Sixteen-year-old Claude Haize remembered how his family farm was requisitioned and turned into an air base for the Americans.

48. André Gidon was twelve years old when the Americans created an airfield near his home.
49. The constant sounds of battle left a lasting impression on the fourteen-year-old Paul Bedel.
50. Raymond Bertot lived near a landing beach and, as a result, his father came under suspicion for being in a military zone.
51. Raymond Gardie was a high school student during the war.
52. At the age of thirteen, Emile Bisson witnessed the arrival of the Americans.
53. Raymond Lereculey, a twelve-year-old boy in 1944, had fond memories of the days he spent with American paratroopers.
54. Marie Couespel practiced a few English phrases in anticipation of the Allied arrival in her village. She was extremely happy to be able to use one of them.
55. Yves de la Rüe participated in the burial of American soldiers in a field near the village of Carquebut. After the war, the dead were transferred to the American Cemetery at Colleville.
56. The liberation of France brought freedom and American aid to the local population.
57. Das Reich Division was part of the Waffen SS, an elite unit that had been formed in 1939 and was responsible for this massacre in central France.
58. One of the few survivors of the massacre at Oradour-sur-Glane was Marguerite Rouffanche. She testified at a trial held in 1953 in Bordeaux, France.
59. Germain Voisset was from Clermont-Ferrand in central France. He joined the resistance but was arrested in 1943. Despite the invasion by Allied forces, the machinery that fed the concentration camp system continued to function and Voisset was sent to Dachau.
60. "A Bridge Too Far" refers to Operation Market Garden, an unsuccessful Allied attempt to seize the bridge in Arnhem (Holland) to facilitate a crossing of the Rhine in the fall of 1944. Eisenhower approved of the plan put forward by Montgomery, but logistical problems and German resistance forced an allied retreat.
61. "Liberation of Eindhoven" was written by Mr. J. H. Th. Schipper.
62. The Battle of Hürtgen Forest took place on the Belgian-German border. It was marked by vicious fighting in bitter weather and lasted from September 1944 until February 1945.
63. Chester Mikus was born in 1913 and served as a staff sergeant in the 9th Infantry Division in North Africa, Sicily, Normandy, and finally in the Hürtgen Forest.
64. Leroy D. "Whitey" Schaller was born in 1922 and was drafted in 1942. He served as a private first class in the U.S. army, fought in the Hürtgen Forest, and was a prisoner of war in a German prison camp.
65. Gerd von Rundstedt (1875–1953) was one of Germany's leading generals.
66. Glen Brutus of Indiana was drafted in October 1942. He served in Headquarters Company, First Battalion, 106th Infantry Division.
67. John J. Bertram, Jr. was drafted out of the University of Chicago in 1942. He served in the U.S. army as a corporal in the 924th Field Artillery Group of the 99th Division. Captured during the Battle of the Bulge by the Germans, Bertram spent the last five months of the war in a prisoner of war camp in Germany.
68. David Saltman was a first lieutenant at the time, but he retired from the army with the rank of Lieutenant Colonel.
69. Anthony McAuliffe (1898–1975) led the 101st Airborne in the defense of Bastogne during the Battle of the Bulge. His one-word response to the German demand for surrender made him famous.
70. Fred Litty, whose family emigrated from Austria to the United States, served in the U.S. Army Air Force after enlisting in 1942 at the age of twenty. The 15th Air Force

bombed the Ploesti oil fields in Romania several times, with major raids in May, June, and July 1944 coinciding with the invasion of Normandy.

71. Samuel Pisar was fifteen years old and a prisoner in Auschwitz at the time of the Allied invasion.

72. Stanislav Mikhailovich Severinovsky was born in Odessa in 1925.

73. Women played an important part in the Soviet military, as aviators and as sharpshooters.

74. Karol Wierzbicki survived incarceration in concentration camps, where he witnessed the barbaric treatment that German authorities carried out against prisoners.

75. Maurice Lampe, born in Roubaix, France in 1900, was arrested, spent more than two years interned in France, and was then sent to Mauthausen concentration camp on March 22, 1944. His testimony at the Nuremberg Trial focused on the brutal treatment of prisoners and the arbitrary execution of camp inmates including allied officers.

76. Mauthausen concentration camp was located outside of Linz, Austria.

77. Solomon Radasky survived Majdanek, Birkenau, and Auschwitz.

78. Lodz Ghetto was located in central Poland; approximately a quarter of a million Jews were interned there before being sent to the death camps.

79. Victor Dupont, born in 1909 in France, was sent to Buchenwald concentration camp on January 24, 1944, where he remained until April 20, 1945. He testified at the Nuremberg Trials on the methods of degradation and dehumanization of the camp population.

80. Rudolf Mildner (1902–1951) was head of the Gestapo in southern Poland; Himmler's plan, in violation of international agreements on the treatment of captured enemy combatants, was to interrogate and then execute American prisoners. Himmler's order to the police called for covering the crime by claiming that they had been killed in combat. After testifying at Nuremberg, Mildner spent a couple of years in prison and was released in 1949.

81. Wilhelm Keitel (1882–1946) was chief of staff of the German army. He was convicted and executed after the war.

Chapter Eight: Allied Victory, 1945

1. Edward Stettinius (1900–1949) was the American secretary of state; V. Molotov (1890–1986) was Soviet foreign minister; Anthony Eden (1897–1977) was British foreign secretary.

2. Harry Truman (1884–1972) succeeded Roosevelt as president in April 1945.

3. On May 4, 1945, Stalin sent a similar note to Churchill. In that message, Stalin asserted: "We insist, and shall continue to insist, that only people who have demonstrated by deeds their friendly attitude to the Soviet Union, who are willing honestly and sincerely to cooperate with the Soviet state, should be consulted on the formation of a future Polish Government."

4. Stalin to Truman on Poland, April 24, 1945.

5. Truman Seeks Soviet Cooperation, December 19, 1945.

6. Stalin's Response to Truman on Cooperation, December 23, 1945.

7. Curzon Line was the Russian-Polish border proposed by British Foreign Secretary Lord Curzon in 1920.

8. "Winter 1944–1945 at The Hague" by Tj. Cannegieter written in May 1945.

9. Franklin E. Kameny was born in 1925. He enlisted in 1943 just before his eighteenth birthday and served as a Private First Class in the U.S. army; his testimony discussed his homosexuality as well as his military experiences.

10. DUKW was a six-ton amphibious truck used to bring supplies and troops from ship onto landing beaches.

11. Operation Plunder was the code name for the crossing of the Rhine in a series of separate American and British military actions in March 1945. Field Marshal Montgomery was in overall command.

12. Jesse E. Foster was born in 1923 in New York; he spent the last months of the war as a prisoner, finally liberated in April 1945.

13. Sagan, Poland, was the site of Stalag Luft III, a camp for Allied prisoners, primarily airmen.

14. Alex Haddon was born in 1920 and served in the U.S. Army Air Corps as a tech sergeant.

15. General Patton took command of the 3rd Army in August 1944, and his troops played an important role in France as well as in Germany in 1945.

16. John J. Bertram, Jr. was drafted out of the University of Chicago in 1942. He served in the U.S. army as a corporal in the 924th Field Artillery Group of the 99th Division.

17. German soldier Heinz Perschke was serving in Denmark when the Allies invaded Normandy, but as the Allies approached Germany, he was sent to the front where he saw combat for the first time. After the war he became a pastor.

18. Der Stürmer was a strongly anti-Semitic Nazi publication. Its publisher, Julius Streicher, was tried, convicted, and sentenced to death at Nuremberg.

19. General G. Zhukov (1896–1974) was the most famous Soviet commander of World War II.

20. Tadeusz "Wicher" Wichrowski continued to fight against German and Communist elements in Poland in 1945. As a member of the Holy Cross Brigade, a division of the Polish underground *Narodowe Siły Zbrojne* (NSZ) army, he moved with his unit into Czechoslovakia early in 1945. In May, the Polish fighters liberated a concentration camp (Holysov in Czech, Holiszow in Polish, Holleischen in German) and made contact with American forces.

21. Gen. I. Konev (1897–1973) was one of the most important Soviet military commanders during the war.

22. Majdanek was located near Lublin in Poland and not far from the Ukrainian border. The Russians liberated the camp in the summer of 1944.

23. Gleiwitz was a subcamp of Auschwitz about thirty miles northwest of the main camp.

24. Jack Bowen was born in 1924 and drafted in 1943. He served in the U.S. Army Air Force.

25. Joseph A. Gautsch was born in 1915 in La Crosse, Wisconsin. He served as a medical doctor with the Third Army in Europe and attained the rank of major.

26. Tamara Aronovna Zeveke was born in 1927 in Leningrad, was a university student in Gorky in 1944, and helped load barges on the Volga River in 1945.

Select Bibliography

Adams, Michael C. C. *The Best War Ever: America and World War II*. Baltimore, MD: Johns Hopkins University Press, 1994.

Ambrose, Stephen E. *Citizen Soldiers: the U.S. Army from the Normandy Beaches to the Bulge to the Surrender of Germany, June 7, 1944–May 7, 1945*. New York: Simon & Schuster, 1997.

Ambrose, Stephen E. *D-Day, June 6, 1944: The Climactic Battle of World War II*. New York: Simon & Schuster, 1994.

Association des Familles des Martyrs d'Oradour-sur-Glane. *Oradour-sur-Glane*. 1994.

Balkoski, Joseph. *Utah Beach*. Mechanicsburg, PA: Stackpole Books, 2005.

Beevor, Antony. *Stalingrad*. New York: Viking, 1998.

Beevor, Antony. *The Fall of Berlin 1945*. New York: Viking, 2002.

Black, Robert W. *Rangers in World War II*. New York: Ivy Books, 1992.

Boatner, Mark M. *Biographical Dictionary of World War II*. Novato, CA: Presidio Press, 1999.

Breuer, William B. *Operation Torch: The Allied Gamble to Invade North Africa*. New York: St. Martin's Press, 1986.

Chandler, Alfred D., ed. *The Papers of Dwight David Eisenhower: The War Years*. Baltimore, MD: Johns Hopkins Press, 1970.

Chuikov, V. I. *The Battle for Stalingrad*. New York: Holt, Rinehart & Winston, 1964.

Chuikov, V. I. *The Fall of Berlin*. New York: Holt, Rinehart & Winston, 1968.

Churchill, Winston S. *Their Finest Hour*. Boston: Houghton Mifflin Co., 1949.

Davies, Norman. *Rising '44: "The Battle for Warsaw."* London: Macmillan, 2003.

Dawidowicz, Lucy. *The War against the Jews, 1933–1945*. New York: Holt, Rinehart & Winston, 1975.

De Gaulle, Charles. *The War Memoirs*. New York: Viking, 1955.

Department of State. *The Axis in Defeat: A Collection of Documents on American Policy toward Germany and Japan*. Washington, D.C.: Government Printing Office, 1946.

Department of State. *Bulletin*. Washington, D.C.: Government Printing Office, various years.

Department of State. *A Decade of American Foreign Policy: Basic Documents 1941–1949*. Washington, D.C.: Government Printing Office, 1965.

Department of State (based on German Foreign Ministry). *Documents on German Foreign Policy, 1918–1945*. Washington, D.C.: Government Printing Office, 1950.

Department of State. *Foreign Relations of the United States* (FRUS). Washington, D.C.: Government Printing Office, various years.

Department of State. *Peace and War: United States Foreign Policy 1931–1941*. Washington D.C.: Government Printing Office, 1943.

D'Este, Carlo. *Patton: A Genius for War*. New York: HarperCollins, 1995.

Eisenhower, David. *Eisenhower: At War 1943–1945*. New York: Random House, 1986.

Erickson, John. *The Road to Stalingrad*. New York: Harper and Row, 1975.

Erickson, John. *The Road to Berlin*. Boulder, CO: Westview Press, 1983.

French Ministry of Foreign Affairs. *French Yellow Book: French Diplomatic Papers from September 29, 1938 to September 3, 1939 (Le livre jaune français)*. Paris, 1939.

Gromyko, A. A., ed. *Soviet Peace Efforts on the Eve of World War II: Documents and Records*. Moscow, 1976.

Henderson, Neville. *British War Blue Book*. London: British Foreign Office, 1939.

Holliday, Laurel. *Children in the Holocaust and World War II: Their Secret Diaries*. New York: Washington Square Press, 1995.

Hoyt, Edwin Palmer. *Backwater War: The Allied Campaign in Italy, 1943–1945*. Westport, CT: Praeger, 2002.

International Military Tribunal. *Trial of the Major War Criminals before the International Military Tribunal, 14 November 1945–1 October 1946*. Nuremberg, Germany, 1947.

Keegan, John. *Six Armies in Normandy*. New York: Viking, 1982.

Keegan, John, ed. *Who Was Who in World War II*. London: Routledge, 1995.

Kershaw, Ian. *Hitler, 1936–45: Nemesis*. New York: W.W. Norton, 2000.

La Presse de la Manche. *In the Name of Freedom*. Cherbourg, France, 2004.

La Presse de la Manche. *Notre été 44*. Cherbourg, France, 2004.

Lélion, Agnès. *Sillons de vie Gréville-Hague 1939–1944 et demain*. Association écrire aux éclats: Cherbourg, France, 2006.

Lerski, George J. *Historical Dictionary of Poland, 966–1945*. Westport, CT: Greenwood Press, 1996.

Miller, Edward G. *A Dark and Bloody Ground: The Hürtgen Forest and the Roer River Dams, 1944–1945*. College Station: Texas A&M University Press, 1995.

Ministry of Foreign Affairs of U.S.S.R. *Correspondence between the Chairman of the Council of Ministers of the U.S.S.R. and the Presidents of the USA and the Prime Ministers of Great Britain during the Great Patriotic War of 1941–1945*, 2 Vols. Moscow: Progress Publishers, 1957.

Molotov, V. M. *The Molotov Paper on Nazi Atrocities*. New York, 1942.

Molotov, V. M. *Note Submitted by V. Molotov, People's Commissar of Foreign Affairs of the U.S.S.R. Concerning the Universal Robbery and Despoliation of the Population and the Monstrous Atrocities Perpetrated by the German Authorities on Occupied Soviet Territory*. Moscow, 1942.

Murray, Williamson, and Allan R. Millett. *A War to Be Won: Fighting the Second World War, 1937–1945*. Cambridge, MA: Belknap Press of Harvard University Press, 2000.

Neill, George W. *Infantry Soldier: Holding the Line at the Battle of the Bulge*. Norman: University of Oklahoma Press, 2000.

Niewyk, Donald, and Francis Nicosia. *The Columbia Guide to the Holocaust*. New York: Columbia University Press, 2000.

Office of the Federal Register. *United States Statutes at Large*. Dept. of State: Washington, D.C., various years.

Overy, Richard. *Russia's War*. New York: Penguin Books, 1998.

Overy, Richard. *Why the Allies Won*. New York: W.W. Norton, 1995.

Paxton, Robert O. *Vichy France: Old Guard and New Order, 1940–1944*. New York: Columbia University Press, 1972.

Rhodes, Richard. *Masters of Death: The SS-Einsatzgruppen and the Invention of the Holocaust*. New York: A.A. Knopf, 2002.

Rich, Norman. *Hitler's War Aims*. New York: Norton, 1973–1974.

Roseman, Mark. *The Wannsee Conference and the Final Solution*. New York: Henry Holt and Company, 2002.

Rossino, Alexander B. *Hitler Strikes Poland: Blitzkrieg, Ideology, and Atrocity*. Lawrence: University Press of Kansas, 2003.

Rush, Robert Sterling. *Hell in Hürtgen Forest: the Ordeal and Triumph of an American Infantry Regiment*. Lawrence: University Press of Kansas, 2001.

Sontag, Raymond James, and James Stuart Beddie, eds. *Nazi-Soviet Relations 1939–1941: Documents from the Archives of the German Foreign Office*. GPO: Washington, D.C., 1948.

Stalin, J. V. *War Speeches, Orders of the Day, and Answers to Foreign Press Correspondents During the Great Patriotic War, July 3rd, 1941–June 22nd, 1945*. Hutchinson & Co.: London, 1946.

Stalin, J. *Works*. Foreign Language Publishing House: Moscow, 1953–1955.

Taylor, Telford. *The Anatomy of the Nuremberg Trials: A Personal Memoir*. New York: Alfred A. Knopf, 1992.

Terkel, Studs. *The Good War: An Oral History of World War II*. New York: Pantheon Books, 1984.

Thompson, Julian. *Dunkirk: Retreat to Victory*. London: Sidgwick & Jackson, 2008.

Tuchman, Barbara W. *The Guns of August*. New York: The Macmillan Co., 1962.

Union of Soviet Socialist Republics Embassy. *One Year of Soviet Struggle against German Invasion: June 22, 1941–June 22, 1942*. Embassy of the U.S.S.R.: Washington, D.C., 1942.

Union of Soviet Socialist Republics Embassy. *Soviet Government Statements on Nazi Atrocities*. London: Hutchinson & Co., 1946.

United Nations Information Office. *Punishment for War Crimes*. United Nations Information Office: New York, 1943.

Van der Vat, Dan. *The Atlantic Campaign: World War II's Great Struggle at Sea*. New York: Harper & Row, 1988.

Weinberg, Gerhard L. *A World at Arms: A Global History of World War II*. New York: Cambridge University Press, 1994.

Werth, Alexander. *Russia at War 1941–1945*. New York: Carroll & Graf, 1964.

Whitlock, Flint. *Rock of Anzio: from Sicily to Dachau: A History of the 45th Infantry Division*. Boulder, CO: Westview Press, 1998.

Wright, Gordon. *The Ordeal of Total War, 1939–1945*. New York: Harper & Row, 1968.

Newspapers

Arbeiderbladet, Oslo, Norway
Atlanta Journal, Atlanta, United States
Belgique (later *Bruxelles-Paris*), Paris, France
Boston Daily Globe, Boston, United States
Cassandre, Brussels, Belgium
České Slovo, Prague, Czechoslovakia
Cherbourg-Éclair, Cherbourg, France
Corriere Della Sera, Milan, Italy
Czas, Warsaw, Poland
Daily Mail, London, United Kingdom
Der Angriff, Berlin, Germany
Evening Standard, London, United Kingdom
France Amérique, New York, United States
Gazeta Polska, Warsaw, Poland
Hufvudstadsbladet, Helsinki, Finland
Il Popolo D'Italia, Milan, Italy
Izvestiia, Moscow, U.S.S.R.
Journal de Genève, Geneva, Switzerland
L'Avenir, Brussels, Belgium
L'Espoir: Organe de combat et de libération nationale, Brussels, Belgium
La Croix, Paris, France
La Lettre de la France Libre, London, United Kingdom
La Parole Bulgare, Sofia, Bulgaria
La Presse Cherbourgeoisie, Cherbourg, France
La Presse de la Manche, Cherbourg, France
La Renaissance du Bessin, Bayeux, France
La Voix des Belges, Brussels, Belgium
L'Echo de Belgrade, Belgrade, Yugoslavia

Le Bon Sens, Brussels, Belgium
Le Figaro, Paris, France
Le Monde, Paris, France
Le Nouveau Journal, Brussels, Belgium
Le Petit Parisien, Paris, France
Le Temps, Paris, France
L'Indépendance Belge, Brussels, Belgium
Paris-Soir, Paris, France
Révolution Nationale, Paris, France
Pravda, Moscow, U.S.S.R.
The Times, London, United Kingdom
Tübinger Chronik, Tübingen, Germany
Večerní České Slovo, Prague, Czechoslovakia
Völkischer Beobachter, Berlin, Gemany
Volontés de Ceux de la Resistance, Paris, France
Washington Post, Washington, D.C., United States

Web Sites

Avalon Project, Yale University Law School, www.avalon.law.yale.edu
Central Europe Center for Research and Documentation, www.centropa.org
Crisis over Czechoslovakia, www.st-andrews.ac.uk/~pv/munich/index.html
Dutch Underground, www.msbeliever.tripod.com/Underground.html
Electronic Museum, www.electronicmuseum.ca/Poland-WW2_ww2.html
Historical Resources about the Second World War, www.historicalresources.org
Holocaust Survivors, www.holocaustsurvivors.org.
I Remember, www.iremember.ru
Jewish Virtual Library, www.jewishvirtuallibrary.org
Rutgers Oral History Project, www.oralhistory.rutgers.edu

Libraries and Archives

Bibliothèque de Documentation Internationale Contemporaine, Nanterre
Bibliothèque Nationale, Paris
Bibliothèque Royale, Brussels
Center for the Study of War and Society, University of Tennessee-Knoxville
Holocaust Memorial Museum Archives, Washington, D.C.
Imperial War Museum, London
Library of Congress, Washington, D.C.
National Archives, College Park, Maryland
Nederlands Instituut voor Oorlogsdocumentatie (Netherlands Institute for War
    Documentation), Amsterdam

Index

Stackpole Military History Series

Real battles. Real soldiers. Real stories.

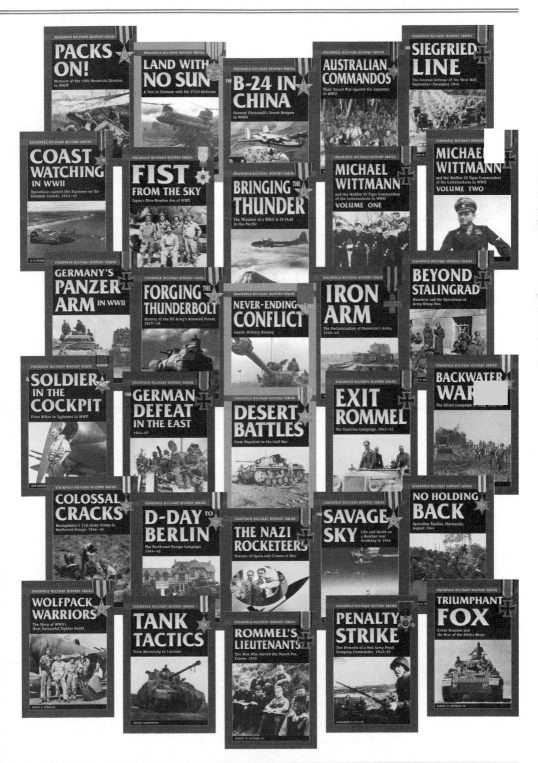

Stackpole Military History Series

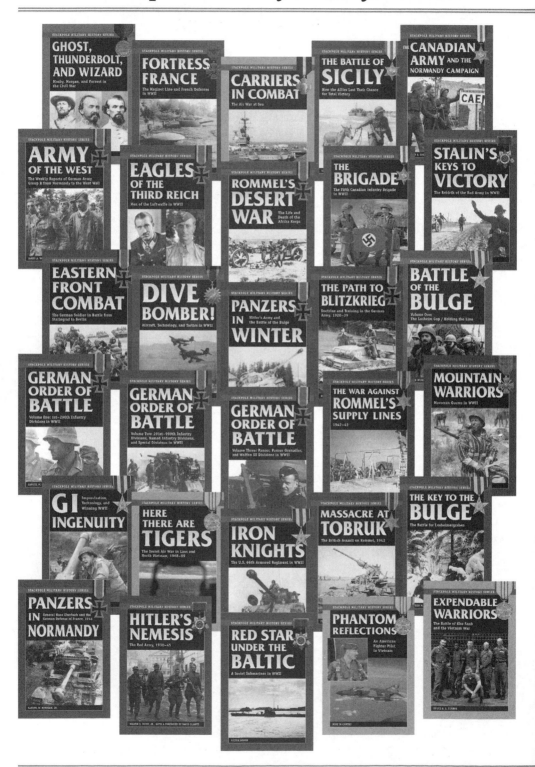

Real battles. Real soldiers. Real stories.

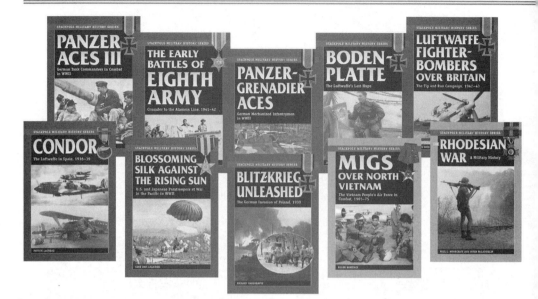

Real battles. Real soldiers. Real stories.

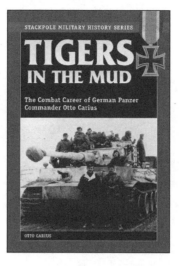

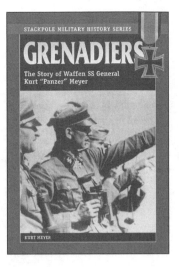

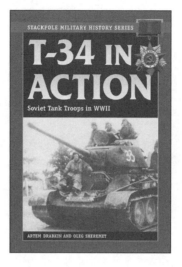

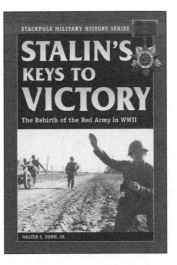

Stackpole Military History Series

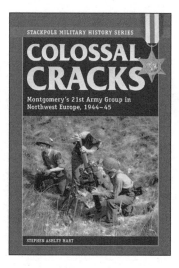

COLOSSAL CRACKS
MONTGOMERY'S 21ST ARMY GROUP
IN NORTHWEST EUROPE, 1944–45
Stephen Ashley Hart

During the Northwest Europe campaign in World War II, British
Field Marshal Bernard Montgomery—seeking to limit casualties,
sustain morale, and secure Britain a high profile in postwar
Europe—developed a cautious, firepower-heavy approach that
concentrated his 21st Army Group at points of German weakness but
may have missed opportunities to achieve a decisive breakthrough.
Stephen Ashley Hart argues that Montgomery's technique was an
appropriate response to the circumstances and that the field
marshal, as well as his two army commanders, British General Miles
Dempsey and Canadian General Harry Crerar, executed the
campaign more effectively than some historians have suggested.

$16.95 • Paperback • 6 x 9 • 256 pages • 12 b/w photos, 3 maps

WWW.STACKPOLEBOOKS.COM
1-800-732-3669